The F Street Mess

CIVIL WAR AMERICA

Peter S. Carmichael, Caroline E. Janney, and Aaron Sheehan-Dean, *editors*

This landmark series interprets broadly the history and culture of the Civil War era through the long nineteenth century and beyond. Drawing on diverse approaches and methods, the series publishes historical works that explore all aspects of the war, biographies of leading commanders, and tactical and campaign studies, along with select editions of primary sources. Together, these books shed new light on an era that remains central to our understanding of American and world history.

THE
F Street Mess

HOW SOUTHERN SENATORS REWROTE THE KANSAS-NEBRASKA ACT

Alice Elizabeth Malavasic

THE UNIVERSITY OF NORTH CAROLINA PRESS
CHAPEL HILL

© 2017 The University of North Carolina Press

All rights reserved. Manufactured in the United States of America.
Designed by Sally Fry Scruggs and set in Utopia by codeMantra.

The University of North Carolina Press has been
a member of the Green Press Initiative since 2003.

Cover illustration: J. Rodgers, *View of the Senate of
the United States in Session*. U.S. Senate Collection, 38.00964.001.

Library of Congress Cataloging-in-Publication Data
Names: Malavasic, Alice Elizabeth, author.
Title: The F Street Mess : how Southern senators rewrote the
Kansas-Nebraska Act / Alice Elizabeth Malavasic.
Other titles: Civil War America (Series)
Description: Chapel Hill : The University of North Carolina
Press, [2017] | Series: Civil War America
Identifiers: LCCN 2017020439 | ISBN 9781469636474 (cloth : alk. paper) |
ISBN 9781469635521 (pbk : alk. paper) | ISBN 9781469635538 (ebook)
Subjects: LCSH: United States. Kansas-Nebraska Act. | Slavery—United States—Extension
to the territories. | Slavery—Political aspects—United States—History—19th century. |
Oligarchy—United States. | United States. Congress—History—19th century. |
Atchison, David Rice, 1807–1886. | Butler, A. P. (Andrew Pickens), 1796–1857. | Hunter,
R. M. T. (Robert Mercer Taliaferro), 1809–1887. | Mason, J. M. (James Murray), 1798–1871.
Classification: LCC E433 .M335 2017 | DDC 320.473/049—dc23
LC record available at https://lccn.loc.gov/2017020439

For my father

MICHAEL JOHN MALAVASIC

1921–2007

CONTENTS

Acknowledgments ix

INTRODUCTION   *Conspiracy* 1

ONE   *Rivalries and Alliances* 19

TWO   *Heirs of Calhoun* 43

THREE   *Nebraska* 60

FOUR   *Senatorial Junta* 81

FIVE   *The Power to Repeal* 111

SIX   *Kansas* 143

SEVEN   *We Must Settle This Question* 171

Epilogue 189

Notes 199

Bibliography 245

Index 261

A section of illustrations begins on page 103.

ACKNOWLEDGMENTS

I am deeply grateful and indebted to the institutions that assisted me with the research for this book. I am and continue to be amazed at the knowledge, skill, and generosity of the congressional, university, and museum staff members who helped me with my questions and obscure searches. These institutions include but are not limited to the National Archives; Library of Congress; Historical Offices of the United States Senate and United States House of Representatives; Office of the Architect of the U.S. Capitol; Alderman Library Special Collections at the University of Virginia; Virginia Historical Society; South Caroliniana Library at the University of South Carolina; Fort Pulaski Historic Site, South Carolina; Western Historical Manuscript Division at the University of Missouri and State Historical Society of Missouri; Omaha Public Library in Omaha, Nebraska; Library Archives at the University of Illinois at Urbana Champaign; and Beinecke Rare Book and Manuscript Library at Yale University.

Success for a novice author such as myself is dependent on an experienced and highly skilled editorial staff, and in that regard I have been truly blessed. The University of North Carolina Press is worthy of its reputation and then some. There are many on its editorial staff whose names I do not know, but I am thankful for all the work they put into the publication of my book. I am especially grateful to executive editor Chuck Grench; Jay Mazzocchi, assistant managing editor; Brian MacDonald, copy editor; and acquisitions assistant Jad Adkins for their wisdom and their patience.

I would also like to thank my Hudson Valley Community College colleagues, Associate Professor of Library Sciences Valarie Lang Waldin, senior clerk Jennifer Acker, and program assistant Kathleen Haynes for their technical support in the preparation of the manuscript's final draft. Their professional skills are second to none. Thank you to my mentors and friends Richard Hamm, Dan White, and Joe Gould for their help on the manuscript and support throughout my academic career. Thank you to my family and friends whose love and support never waivers. And to my parents Michael and Emma Malavasic, both deceased. My mother gave me her southern heritage and love for its flawed but exceptional history. My father gave me his heart and his dreams. Anything good I have ever done or accomplished in this life is because I am their daughter.

Lastly, my profound gratitude to Scott Reynolds Nelson for his unrelenting advocacy of my work, for reading through the entire manuscript more than once, and for his insight and recommendations. I cannot begin to calculate the contributions Scott made except to say I could not have completed my book without him.

The F Street Mess

INTRODUCTION

Conspiracy

The order from Lieutenant General Ulysses S. Grant to Major General Henry W. Halleck[1] was succinct, "Arrest R. M. T. Hunter and John A. Campbell and hold them prisoners in Richmond for further orders."[2] Robert Mercer Taliaferro Hunter of Virginia was a former U.S. senator. John Archibald Campbell of Alabama was a former justice of the U.S. Supreme Court. Both men followed their states into secession and war in 1861. Hunter, who left Washington in March of that year, was expelled from the Senate in April. Campbell resigned from the court the same month. During the war Hunter served briefly as the Confederate secretary of state before resigning in 1862 to join the Confederate Senate. In that same year Campbell was appointed assistant secretary of war by Confederate president Jefferson Davis. Both men, along with Confederate vice president Alexander H. Stephens, were commissioners to the Hampton Roads Peace Conference held on February 3, 1865.[3]

Hunter and Campbell had been picked for the commission in part because of their prewar reputations as leading intellectuals within their respective branches of government. They also shared the kind of noble dispositions that had garnered them the friendship as well as the respect of their political adversaries. Though alike in so many ways, they were startling different physically, Hunter's dark complexion the Ying to Campbell's fair-complexioned Yang. They were both lawyers and strict constructionists. But whereas Hunter's constitutionalism had led him to become a leading defender of slavery and states' rights, Campbell, a Unionist, eschewed both. Nevertheless, in the months leading up to the war, Hunter like Campbell became involved in the Washington negotiations to avoid secession. Then, when secession came anyway, Campbell like Hunter followed his state.

By 1865 both men were among those in the Confederate government calling for a negotiated settlement to end the war. Jefferson Davis opposed settlement but, faced with growing calls for peace in Richmond, appointed Vice President Stephens, Hunter, and Campbell to the peace commission, knowing Lincoln would never agree to an independent southern nation. He was right. After the unsuccessful meeting with Lincoln at Hampton Roads, Stephens, Hunter, and Campbell all returned to Richmond and reported Lincoln's rejection of their proposal for an armistice without the Confederacy's surrender to "the authority of the United States." Davis responded by calling for the continuation of the war as "the only honorable alternative."[4]

On April 3, two months after the Hampton Roads Conference, Richmond fell to Union forces. Abraham Lincoln arrived in the city the following day and requested a meeting with Hunter and Campbell to discuss cessation of hostilities. Hunter did not attend the meeting between Lincoln and Campbell that day, but he and Campbell had been meeting together throughout the previous month.[5] It is likely Hunter was aware of and supported the proposal Campbell presented to Lincoln that day. The proposal requested the president grant the Virginia state legislature permission to convene in order to withdraw Virginia's troops from the Confederacy. Lincoln initially supported the proposal but later withdrew his support after concerns it might imply the legislature's legitimacy, and Lee's surrender four days later made it unnecessary.[6] Grant quickly revoked the convening of the Virginia legislature and put its members on notice that they would be subject to arrest if found in the city twelve hours after the order was made public on April 14. Hunter and Campbell immediately wired Lincoln requesting another meeting and left for their respective homes.[7] Lincoln was shot later that night.[8]

News of Lincoln's assassination had been immediate, and the residents of Washington City, who "lived for four years in constant dread that the Virginia armies would any day come," were gripped by a combustible stew of hysteria, paranoia, sorrow, and anger that grew in intensity as the days passed. Americans living above the Mason Dixon line reacted with similar shock when the news of Lincoln's assassination reached them. Northern anger did not dissipate for months.[9]

Joseph Holt, judge advocate general of the Bureau of Military Justice, was put in charge of the investigation. Within hours five people, believed to have been directly involved in the assassination of Lincoln and the attempted assassination of Secretary of State William Seward, were arrested. Lincoln's assassin, the actor John Wilkes Booth, was located and killed on April 26, at a farm near Port Royal, Virginia.[10]

No one in the North, especially Edwin M. Stanton, the secretary of war, believed Booth and his accomplices had acted independently. Many inside and outside of the government believed Lincoln's assassination had been approved at a much higher level "to avenge the South" and "turn the tide of the war."[11] On April 24 the bureau issued its initial findings that "the President's murder was organized in Canada and approved at Richmond." On May 2, President Johnson ordered the arrest of Confederate president Jefferson Davis and five Confederate officers in Canada.[12] Reflecting the growing anger in the North, the bureau located and arrested several additional high-ranking members of the Confederacy, not named in the president's May 2 order, for disloyalty to the United States, "having committed sundry and divers acts of treason against the same in adhering to their enemies, giving them aid and comfort."[13]

Before his death, Lincoln had ordered that Hunter and Campbell be left alone, but now on the heels of his assassination both men were caught up in Grant's general roundup of the Confederate leadership. Hunter and Campbell were at their homes near Richmond when Union troops arrived at each on May 7. They were arrested and confined to Libby Prison in Richmond. A subsequent search of Hunter's home, Fonthill, uncovered correspondence from Beverly Tucker, a longtime Virginian friend and also one of the Confederates in Canada named in the bureau's initial report and Johnson's May 2nd order.[14]

On May 23 Grant ordered Hunter, Campbell, and former Confederate secretary of war James A. Seddon transferred to Fort Pulaski on Cockspur Island off the coast of Georgia. Its commander, General Q. A. Gillmore, was instructed by Secretary Stanton to hold the men "in safe custody" until "further orders." In July the prisoners were joined by Alexander H. Stephens, Confederate secretary of the treasury George A. Trenholm, Confederate senator David L. Yulee, and an assortment of other Confederate civil and military officers.[15]

Fort Pulaski was a single-story red brick pentagon structure, surrounded by a moat that was thirty to forty feet wide by eight feet deep and inhabited by alligators, turtles, and other marine life. It was built on Cockspur Island, the farthest out in a chain of intercoastal marsh islands at the mouth of the Savannah River. Originally designed to block upriver access, Fort Pulaski was part of a massive coastal defense system begun by the federal government after the war of 1812 and completed at midcentury. Humid in the summer and damp in the winter, the island was frequently submerged at high tide, turning it into a virtual mud "pudding."[16] Confederate troops had occupied the fort after Georgia seceded on January 19, 1861, but it quickly fell to Union bombardment in 1862. The battle for Fort Pulaski on April 10–11 introduced the first significant use of rifled canon, which enabled the Union army to fire from more than a mile away, instantly rendering masonry forts, like Pulaski, obsolete. In 1864 the Union army turned the fort into a prison for 550 Confederate officers, converting the former gun casemates into prison cells measuring fifteen by twenty-six feet. The cells were now home to members of the Confederacy's ruling elite, who, after promising on their "honor... not to attempt... to leave the post," were granted "the liberty of the island" during the day from whence they could contemplate if it would be their Elba or St. Helena.[17]

The belief that Lincoln's assassination had been planned at the highest levels of the Confederacy was the culmination of a conspiratorial style of rhetoric used by northern politicians throughout the war. Before the war, the rhetoric had been used to move abolitionism beyond the religious fringe of reformism into mainstream American politics.[18] Commonly referred to as the Slave Power, such rhetoric ultimately became a critical component in Republican Party ideology.[19] As acceptance of its truth grew among the general public in the North, politicians who used the Slave Power rhetoric rose in political eminence.

Lincoln himself believed in a conspiracy among southern slaveholders, and he frequently used the Slave Power rhetoric during his 1858 Senate race against Stephen Douglas. It figured prominently in his House Divided speech given before the Illinois State Republican Convention on January 16, in which he declared, "I believe this government cannot long endure, permanently, half slave and half free. I do not expect this Union to be dissolved; I do not expect the house to fall; but I do expect it will cease to be divided. It will become all one thing, or all the other."[20]

Similar analogies were being used by Republicans throughout the North, but Lincoln's rhythm and poetry forever linked him with the notion of a house divided. For the delegates listening to Lincoln on that day in Springfield, however, his rhythm and poetry were probably less memorable and less important than his strident attack on the Slave Power.

Belief in a Slave Power had existed in America ever since the inclusion of the three-fifths clause and other slave protections in the 1787 federal constitution. Northern opposition during the Constitution's ratification and after its passage argued that these protections gave the South too much influence in the federal government.[21] Since that time, so the argument went, the Slave Power within the federal government had become an increasingly "commanding power, ever sensitive, jealous, proscriptive, dominating, and aggressive."[22] Slave Power rhetoric resurfaced periodically throughout the early history of the Republic but did not become widely used or accepted in the North until the mid-nineteenth century when the rhetoric shifted from an attack on power to accusations of conspiracy.[23] Most historians agree that this rhetorical shift and the increase in its usage began in 1844 when former president Martin Van Buren failed to secure the Democratic Party's nomination for president. Abolitionists, as well as northern politicians from both sides of the aisle, accused southern Democrats of conspiring to deny Van Buren the nomination because of his opposition to the annexation of Texas.[24]

Northern leaders, playing upon the fears of their constituency, argued that the Slave Power was conspiring to reshape federal law in order to enable slavery to spread beyond its local borders, becoming a national institution to the detriment of a free-labor economy and American civil liberties. It was an "oligarchy of planters in defiance of majority rule . . . a flagrant challenge to the American value that all men, at least all white men, were equal and should have equal voice in government."[25] The ideological use of a Slave Power conspiracy made it possible for the majority of northerners, who had little personal interest in slavery, to become antislavery by making humanitarian concern for the slave distinct from and secondary to the economic and political concerns of white northerners.[26]

Lincoln, in particular, was more concerned with the conspiratorial aspect of the rhetoric than the recitation of statistical evidence of power.[27] In his speech Lincoln summarized the events between 1854 and 1857 that were to him "evidence of design and concert of action." Standing before the assembled delegates at Springfield, he rhetorically asked the audience if it needed to fear that the nation might indeed become all slave. Lincoln responded to the question by pointing to what was seen by a growing number of northerners to be the double-barreled smoking gun of a conspiracy to do exactly that. If anyone doubted the existence of the Slave Power conspiracy, said Lincoln, they had only to "carefully contemplate that now almost complete legal combination . . . the Nebraska doctrine and the Dred Scott decision."

Lincoln asserted the Slave Power not only orchestrated the passage of the Kansas-Nebraska Act, which repealed the Missouri Compromise, but also the Dred Scott decision two years later, which ruled the compromise unconstitutional. To that end, Lincoln did what is rarely done when rhetorically charging conspiracy; he named names, specifically Illinois senator Stephen A. Douglas and the Supreme Court's chief justice Roger B. Taney, accusing both of being in collusion with southern conspirators. "We cannot absolutely know that all these exact adaptations are the result of preconcert," Lincoln stated, but "when we see a lot of framed timbers, different portions of which we know have been gotten out at different times and places by different workmen . . . and when we see these timbers joined together and see they exactly make the frame of a house . . . all the tenons and mortises exactly fitting . . . we find it impossible not to believe that . . . all understood one another from the beginning, and all worked upon a common plan or draft drawn up before the first blow was struck."[28]

It was brilliant rhetoric, what historian Leonard Richards calls "a fighting issue." Lincoln and the Republican Party used the Slave Power rhetoric to unify the disparate elements within the northern electorate, including those who were morally repulsed by the institution of slavery, those who cared little for the slave but coveted the political power that emanated from slavery, and those who simply coveted western lands. "Other than that," continues Richards, "it had no special merit. If they [the Republicans] could have found another fighting issue, one even more popular, they would have jumped on it."[29]

In the twentieth century, academic historians began to question the validity of the Slave Power thesis as material determinism was displaced by more ideological interpretations of the war's causes. Considered the sole cause of the war in the late nineteenth and early twentieth centuries, the Slave Power thesis was dismissed by the mid-twentieth century, the general consensus being that, while no actual conspiracy existed, the Constitution did offer the South advantages that its leadership aggressively pursued. The resulting political power, coveted by many northerners, fueled and played an important part but was not the sole cause in bringing on the war.

In 1952 Richard Hofstadter published *The Paranoid Style in American Politics*, a ground-breaking examination of the psychological and ideological dimensions of conspiratorial rhetoric in American politics. In it he argued that the paranoid style is historically significant in that it is not the style of a lunatic fringe but of a "more or less normal" majority of Americans.[30] The argument that conspiratorial theories are as old as the Republic and central to the culture of American politics was reinforced by the later works of Bernard Bailyn, David Brion Davis, and Gordon S. Wood.[31] These historians agree that the Slave Power thesis was merely a continuation of a paranoid style in American politics that had begun in colonial America. It was "an ideological tradition that had been shaped by English Protestant fears of the Counter-Reformation, by the English Whig interpretations of the Glorious Revolution, by the colonists' alarms over the plots of British ministers, and by Federalists hysteria over the French Revolution."[32] In other words, the paranoid style is the product of liberal republicanism. The belief that the price of liberty is eternal vigilance ultimately becomes the belief that "the very normality of society's surface conceals a gigantic conspiracy that has begun to control the course of history and subvert the values of Christianity and democracy."[33]

Paranoid rhetoric is effective, according to Hofstadter and Davis, because it fixes upon some element of truth. In the case of the Slave Power thesis, it was the historical dominance of the South in the federal government made possible by the original constitutional protections given to slavery in 1787. In post–Civil War histories, written primarily by northern participants who had been "conditioned by their several geographical and cultural backgrounds," the Slave Power was made the singular cause of the war.[34]

Historians Larry Gara and Eric Foner examine the critical role played by the Slave Power rhetoric in the success of the Republican Party in their respective works, "Slavery and the Slave Power: A Crucial Distinction," published in 1969 and *Free Soil, Free Labor, Free Men: The Ideology of the Republican Party before the Civil War*, published in 1970. Gara and Foner both argue that the Republican Party emerged triumphant in the North not because of antislavery sentiment but because of northern jealousy of southern political power. The "often-repeated and highly effective" rhetoric that Foner credits Salmon P. Chase for articulating allowed the Republican Party to unify the various "northern political interests" into a major party that could effectively confront the South's domination of the Democratic Party and the federal government. In turn southerners saw the emergence of a purely northern party as "a serious threat to their political influence" and responded by aggressively pursuing legislation and policies that would protect slavery's constitutional privileges and extend them into the newly acquired western territories.[35] According to Foner, the two "conflicting sectional ideologies" were "in many ways interrelated . . . grew in part as a response to the growth of the other." This development ultimately brought on the Civil War.[36]

Thirty years later Leonard Richards revisited the Slave Power thesis in his 2000 publication *The Slave Power: The Free North and Southern Domination*. Richards's work reiterated Gara's and Foner's earlier findings that constitutional protections gave unfair advantages to slave interests in an otherwise republican government and added that the South's dominance of the federal government was reinforced by the acquiescence of northern conservatives.[37]

To date all the historical work done on the Slave Power thesis has focused almost exclusively on its use as rhetoric by the Republican Party. The works are less about southern power and more about the North's perception of it. No study has examined the differences between the South's perceived power and its actual power in the federal government, or how southerners sworn to uphold the nation's republican institutions were affected by the accusation that they were doing the opposite. The place to begin such an inquiry is the Kansas-Nebraska Act. Was it, as Lincoln accused, the "load bearing timber" in a southern cabin of preconcert or a more loosely jointed shanty of mixed motivations?

For many nineteenth-century northerners, the passage of the Kansas-Nebraska Act in 1854 was the most significant confirmation to date of the

Slave Power conspiracy to undermine their economic opportunities and political freedoms. They believed the act's repeal of the Missouri Compromise's restriction of slavery in the Louisiana territory north of the 36° 30′ parallel was proof positive of a planned design to take over the federal government and nationalize slavery. Shortly after the act's passage, Kansas erupted into armed struggle between pro- and antislavery forces.

The violence in Kansas helped to catapult the Republican Party to victory over the Know-Nothing Party in the 1856 fall elections, thereby securing its position in the third political party system. From that point forward, references to the Kansas-Nebraska Act and the violence in Kansas became central in any discussion of the Slave Power. On December 2, 1856, the Republican senator from New York and presidential hopeful William H. Seward addressed an audience in Detroit, Michigan. In a speech entitled The Dominant Class in the Republic, he gave the Slave Power corporeal form, naming, among others, Senators David Rice Atchison of Missouri, Robert M. T. Hunter and James Murray Mason of Virginia, and Andrew Pickens Butler of South Carolina, known in Washington circles as the F Street Mess, so named for the house they shared together at 361 F Street near the U.S. Patent Office. They were four men, "wonderfully unalike" in upbringing and temperament, but who nevertheless had become the most powerful bloc in the U.S. Senate.

David Rice Atchison was a third-generation Scotch-Irish Kentuckian with a personality and towering physique to match. The firstborn child in a large hardworking family of middling farmers, he disappointed his pious Presbyterian parents by choosing law over the ministry. In 1830 he moved to the western frontier of Missouri, established a law practice, and immersed himself in local politics. By 1843 he was appointed to the U.S. Senate to fill the unexpired term of the late Lewis F. Linn. The farmboy turned lawyer-politician was the first Missouri senator to hail from the state's western border. Atchison had never been further east than Kentucky, and its capital city Lexington was the closest he had ever been to experiencing urban life. But possessed with country charm and a sharp mind, Atchison rose just as quickly atop Capitol Hill in Washington politics as he had on the flatlands of the Missouri Platte. By the time of Seward's speech, Atchison had become the senior senator from his state, president pro tempore of the Senate, and second in line to the presidency.[38]

Robert M. T. Hunter was also a big man though not as tall as Atchison. He was cerebral, contemplative, quiet, and exceedingly well mannered. He never seemed to be aware of or interested in his personal appearance. His friend Mary Chesnut noted in her war diary that Hunter's clothes were always "rather tumbled-up" and his hair unbrushed. Unlike Atchison's frontier upbringing, young Hunter was raised in the traditions of Tidewater privilege, which included private tutors as a child and later enrollment in the first class at Jefferson's University of Virginia. After college Hunter trained for the law under the famed jurist Henry St. George Tucker. But, like many of Virginia's privileged sons, Hunter never took to the practice of law. Instead, he chose a career in politics, and his political star, like Atchison's, rose rapidly. In 1837 he was elected to the U.S. House of Representatives. Two years later at the age of thirty he became the youngest congressman ever elected Speaker of the House.

If Hunter was Tidewater elite, James Murray Mason was royalty. He was the grandson of founding father, George Mason, author of Virginia's first Bill of Rights, signer of the Declaration of Independence, and delegate to the Constitutional Convention. James Murray Mason was raised in his grandfather's republican traditions within the shadow of his grandfather's estate Gunston Hall on the Potomac. It was a life of privilege that far exceeded even Hunter's. And unlike Hunter, who experienced a lonely childhood on a remote plantation, Mason's childhood was filled with an abundance of friends and siblings, outdoor activities, and repeated exposure to the nation's capital. As loquacious as Hunter was quiet, Mason had a natural gift for languages, excelling in French and Spanish. He obtained two degrees, a bachelor's from the University of Pennsylvania and a law degree from William and Mary. While at the University of Pennsylvania in Philadelphia, he met and later married Elizabeth Chew of the equally prominent and even wealthier Chew family. And then he stunned both families by moving himself and young bride to Winchester, a little backwater village at the foot of the Shenandoah Valley, where Mason thrived as a circuit rider on Virginia's frontier. Like his future messmates, Mason immersed himself in local politics and rose just as rapidly. He and Hunter were freshmen congressmen together in 1838, and after a brief hiatus from national politics for both, the two returned to the U.S. Senate in 1847. Each would later be appointed to powerful committee chairs, Mason to Foreign Affairs and Hunter to Finance.

Sixty years old at the time of Seward's iconic speech, Andrew Pickens Butler was the oldest member of the Mess, thirteen years senior to its youngest, forty-seven-year-old Hunter. The Butlers of Edgefield County, South Carolina, were as powerful an Irish clan as has ever existed in America. Large and illustrious, the consequences of its extensive familial ties had shook the halls of Congress and the nation in the spring of 1856 when Butler's cousin, Preston Brooks, to avenge the family's honor, used his cane to savagely beat Senator Charles Sumner of Massachusetts.

Andrew Pickens Butler's early life followed the familiar pattern of southern elites. As a young boy he attended the private academy of Moses Waddell, mentor and brother-in-law of John C. Calhoun. He graduated from South Carolina College in 1817, studied the law, and was admitted to the bar in 1818. After a stint in the state legislature, where he led the fight for nullification in 1832, Butler was appointed to the state circuit court and later the appellate court where he served for thirteen years. Twice widowed, Butler left his sole child, a girl, to be raised by his mother in Edgefield when he was elected to the U.S. Senate in 1846. In Washington, Butler quickly unleashed the sardonic wit he had held in check while on the bench. With a head full of snow white hair and accompanying laughter wherever he went, his presence was readily known in any crowded chamber or room. To everyone in Washington, inside and outside the halls of Congress, friend or foe, he was simply "Judge Butler," chairman of the Senate Judiciary Committee.

Together the F Street Mess held the office of president pro tempore and the chairmanships of Finance, Foreign Affairs, and Judiciary. Seward and other Republicans believed the Mess had used its positions of power in the Senate to shape the Nebraska bill, repeal slavery's restriction above the 36° 30′ parallel, and force the bill's passage. In Seward's words the F Street Mess epitomized the Slave Power's conspiracy to "systematically" pervert the government and "endanger the stability, welfare, and liberty of the Union."

Seward's argument remains part of the ongoing debate regarding the Kansas-Nebraska Act. Historians continue to question whether the act was shaped by ideological or economic concerns. Equally important are the questions regarding Stephen Douglas's motivations as the bill's author of record and whether he or someone else authored the repeal clause. The original interpretation of the act as articulated by Seward was that the Kansas-Nebraska Act was covertly manipulated by the Slave Power and that its author of record, Stephen Douglas, was an amoral traitor, willing to do the Slave Power's bidding in exchange for southern support of his presidential ambitions. Postwar accounts to the contrary, written by either Douglas or southern sympathizers, were largely ignored, the Union victory having produced a "contemptuous dismissal of all things southern."[39]

The earliest divergence from the Slave Power thesis as the motivating force behind the Kansas-Nebraska Act was P. Orman Ray's *The Repeal of the Missouri Compromise* published in 1909. Ray rejected two critical points in the Slave Power thesis: the national debate over slavery was the motivating force behind the Kansas-Nebraska Act, and Stephen Douglas was its author. Instead, he argued that local Missouri politics, not national or constitutional issues, forced the passage of the act; and that Senator David Rice Atchison of Missouri, not Stephen Douglas, authored the repeal of the Missouri Compromise. Ray centered his argument on the personal and political feud between Atchison and Thomas Hart Benton, then congressman and formerly senator from Missouri. Atchison and Benton personified the growing divide between Free-Soil and proslavery interests in the American West. According to Ray, the repeal of the compromise was not the result of an aggressive Slave Power conspiracy but the aggressive campaign activities of Benton, who, having lost reelection to the U.S. Senate in 1851, was using the issue of Nebraska to unseat Atchison in 1854. Ray argued that while Atchison originally opposed Nebraska's organization because he believed it was not possible to repeal slavery's restriction above the 36° 30' parallel, he came to accept its organization, with the restriction intact, as inevitable. Atchison revisited the possibility of repealing the clause only in response to Benton's aggressive campaigning in western Missouri, Atchison's base. Ray concluded that Atchison, not Douglas, authored the repeal clause of the bill in order to assure his reelection.[40]

Ray's thesis was later criticized for being simplistic and "conjectural," resting too much upon on the recorded claims of Atchison.[41] Frank Hodder, in particular, took exception to Ray's thesis. In his studies of the Kansas-Nebraska Act, *The Genesis of the Kansas-Nebraska Act* published in 1913 and *The Railroad Background of the Kansas-Nebraska Act*, published in 1925, Hodder rejected not only Ray's argument but also the earlier contentions that presidential ambition had allowed Douglas to be manipulated by the Slave Power. Instead, Hodder argued Douglas was motivated by a desire to advance the interests of his state and region. He authored the bill with those interests in mind and was the leader of the floor fight in the Senate. More importantly, Hodder was the first historian to advance the central role played by the transcontinental railroad in the passage of the Act.[42] He also found that Douglas had invested in Lake Superior property from which he would profit if a northern rail line was built. For Douglas, organization of the territory advanced regional, state, and personal interests.[43]

As Ray and Hodder fought over whose thesis was more conclusive, the Slave Power thesis was further discredited by the editor of John C. Calhoun's papers, Chauncey S. Boucher. Using Calhoun's correspondence as evidence, Boucher argued in his 1921 article, "In Re That Aggressive Slavocracy," that to present the passage of the Kansas-Nebraska Act "as the product of a united and aggressive Slavocracy is to obscure the truth." According to Boucher, southern leaders were not an organized, proactive cabal of conspirators but rather a reactive, passive, and divided group of individuals.[44] Boucher found no evidence to support the argument that "the repeal feature was the product of a proslavery extension plot among southern leaders at large." Instead, Boucher believed a number of national and local factors combined "in what proportion we do not know" to produce the bill, including the Senate race in Missouri. Boucher agreed with Ray's findings that Atchison supported the repeal of the compromise only when forced "to save his very political life, in spite of the fact that he had said in the preceding March that there was no remedy for the law of 1820, since it could not be repealed."[45]

In general, Boucher found a lack of agreement among southern elected officials on the repeal of the 1820 compromise. While most voted for repeal, many doubted for a variety of reasons the repeal's efficacy or legitimacy. Some shared the northern view that the repeal was a breach of faith, whereas others could find no practical application in the repeal. Others still feared the repeal would only resurrect the sectional hostilities supposedly buried by the earlier Compromise of 1850.[46]

On the centennial anniversary of the act's passage, James C. Malin, a cultural historian and former student of Hodder's, published *The Nebraska Question, 1852–1854*. In his introduction Malin argued the original nineteenth-century Slave Power thesis was experiencing a renewed acceptance in the wake of the modern civil rights movement. Nevertheless, Malin rejected both the thesis and its companion argument that Stephen Douglas, motivated by presidential ambition, was its pawn. He called the attack on Douglas "the most flagrant instances of character assassination in history . . . accepted as true without investigation." He further added that modern historians had "largely been held captives by this formula of liberalism, morality and religion."[47]

Like his mentor, Malin portrayed Douglas as an advocate for the West, arguing that Douglas envisioned a developed trans-Missouri region that would become the nexus of a continental nation. According to Malin, the technological and industrial advancements being made by the nation convinced Douglas and others that a wage, not slave, labor system would be implemented in this new West. The concern of white settlers already in northwestern Missouri was not the extension of slavery but the removal any impediment to white settlement of Nebraska caused by Indian titles to the lands. Malin's thesis is that removal of Indian claims was Douglas's primary motivation.[48]

A half century since its publication, Roy F. Nichols's "The Kansas-Nebraska Act: A Century of Historiography" remains the definitive historiography of the act. Thoroughly reviewing previous interpretations, Malin's included, Nichols rejected them all for being exclusive and inflexible, and for placing Douglas at the center of the act's passage. Nichols argued that these earlier studies failed to "trace adequately the connections between antecedent situations and accomplished fact," what he calls, "the process or becoming" or "the Hamlet which has been left out." Douglas, he argues, was not Hamlet; rather, the political insecurity of Congress was.[49]

Nichols also criticized earlier accounts for focusing too much on the Senate at the exclusion of the House fight, where he believed the answers were to be found as to why "a bill ostensibly to organize a territory had been made an instrument of the fundamental political reorganization." Nichols believed the collapse of the second American political party system caused politicians to be pragmatic, not ideological. A politician during the 1850s, he contended, was motivated not by national or local issues but by personal gain. What was in it for him? How could he use it to secure patronage, reelection, or leadership within new political alignments? According to Nichols, "the Calhoun faction, Southern and Northern Whigs, Free-Soilers, the president's administration, and certain Hard-shell Democrats" had all used the Kansas-Nebraska Act to further their own political ambitions. As a consequence, it was not Stephen Douglas who won the passage of the Kansas-Nebraska bill but a "bipartisan coalition marshaled by the Georgia Whig Alexander H. Stephens."[50]

According to Nichols, the bill's passage was the result of eighteen northern votes in the House that switched. "Here history draws the curtain," writes Nichols, "what they [the congressmen] wanted what they got what they didn't get what motivated them . . . we don't know." For Nichols it was the unknown answers to these questions that would supply the real history of the bill's passage.[51] While Nichols chose to address the unexamined House fight in his essay, he did so only after minimizing Douglas's leadership in the Senate and maximizing the role of the F Street Mess, whose members he labeled the "heirs of Calhoun."[52]

> They were among those who were distressed at Pierce's "weakness" and the seeming disintegration of their party. They liked Pierce personally but they realized that he needed help. They could hardly have been said to approve of his patronage recognition of Barnburners, but they did not want to revolt against him this early by refusing to confirm his "free-soil" appointees. They were the most powerful men in the Senate, but they were burdened by a sense of responsibility and they were looking for a way out . . . . Douglas, as chairman of the committee on territories, must of course be dealt with . . . . The bill of the previous session . . . would not do.[53]

Introduction 13

In Nichols's description of the bill's passage in the Senate, the F Street Mess is motivated less by the desire to extend slavery into the Nebraska Territory than by the desire to maintain southern leadership of the Democratic Party. He depicts Douglas and Pierce as mere puppets, manipulated by a coalition of southern Democratic senators intent on making acceptance of the Missouri Compromise's repeal a litmus test for return of Barnburners and Softshell Democrats to the party.

Both major parties had been struggling internally over slavery since the end of the Mexican-American War in 1848 and Mexico's subsequent cession of territory to the United States. Antislavery Whigs, calling themselves Conscience Whigs, left their party in 1848 rather than support the party's presidential nominee, war hero and slave owner, General Zachary Taylor. Divisions between pro- and antislavery also existed within the Democratic Party and were particularly pronounced in New York State, where three factions existed. Barnburners (named after a fictitious farmer who burned his barn to rid it of rats) were considered the most extreme in their antislavery position, Softshells were the state party's moderates, and the Hardshell Hunkers were the most conservative and least antislavery (though by 1848 Barnburners and Softshells were "rapidly merging"). The New York Barnburners and other antislavery Democrats also left their party in 1848 and, along with Conscience Whigs, fused with the abolitionist third party, the Liberty Party. There was a "nominal reunion" of the Democratic National Party after 1848, but resentments between the factions remained.[54]

Despite Nichols's argument that southern dominance of the party was the primary motivation behind the F Street Mess's support of the bill, he provides little evidence to support his position. His acknowledgment of their influence on the bill and its progress through the Senate is brief, as his focus is instead on the House fight.

Nevertheless, Nichols's and other historians' recognition of the F Street Mess's senatorial power begs for an in-depth study of the group.[55] Some biographies exist on the senators themselves, but these studies fall short because the F Street senators lose significance as individuals. Their power was derived from the group dynamic. It is this group dynamic and its role in the Kansas-Nebraska Act that is historically significant. Understanding the exact nature of the relationship between the four senators and their use of legislative power is the "Hamlet" that has been left out of our understanding of the Slave Power in general and the bill's passage in particular.

The F Street Mess shared leadership in the Senate and fellowship at home, often spending legislative breaks together at Mason's home in nearby

Winchester, Virginia. In short, these men were more than just political allies; they were friends who cared about each other's professional and personal well-being.⁵⁶ In all likelihood Hunter and Mason's friendship began long before they were elected to Congress. Mason was already living and practicing law in Winchester when Hunter moved there in 1829 to study under Henry St. George Tucker. The two men messed together when they were first elected to Congress in 1838 and again when they returned to the Senate a decade later. Butler joined Hunter and Mason in the Senate in 1847 and started messing with them the same year. All three men were protégées of John C. Calhoun and at times messed with him as well. David Rice Atchison was the first of the four men to be elected to the Senate but the last to join their mess. In an age when most members of Congress still rented lodgings, the four men purchased a house at 361 F Street between Ninth and Tenth Streets in 1853 and lived there until 1856.⁵⁷ It was there during the critical months between December 1853 and March 1854 that the four senators not only shared fellowship but also devised the strategy that would repeal the 36° 30′ parallel restricting slavery in the Nebraska Territory.

It was not uncommon for congressmen and senators to live together in the nineteenth century, messing together by state, region, or cross-region.⁵⁸ There had been a critical housing shortage in Washington from the moment the Sixth U.S. Congress arrived to take up residency in November 1800. The first successful business enterprise, in a city otherwise void of economic opportunity, was renting out rooms to members. These early boarding arrangements, called messes, were the subject of James Sterling Young's 1966 study *The Washington Community, 1800–1828*. Young described a partially constructed Washington lacking any physical or political infrastructure. In the absence of streets, lighting, and political party, the boarding mess became a self-contained social and economic entity, and the parlor, a caucus room out of which the member took his "cue."⁵⁹

Young's thesis, that mess affiliation was the primary influence on members' voting behaviors, was reexamined in 1975 by Allan Bogue and Mark Paul Marlaire in their essay, "Of Mess and Men: The Boardinghouse and Congressional Voting, 1821–1842." Bogue and Marlaire found that voting agreement among messmates, while significant (80 percent mean), was not as unanimous as Young had suggested. Nor did it decline, as Young had argued, with the advent of formal political parties. While they acknowledge the continued significance of mess affiliation into the 1840s, Bogue and Marlaire argue voting agreement among the messmates was predetermined before they actually roomed together. Members, according to Bogue and Marlaire, sought out like-minded individuals with whom they could live in harmony.[60]

The political studies by Young and Bogue and Marlaire of nineteenth-century congressional living arrangements reinforce two sociological rules of friendship, the "rule of homogamy," and "spatial proximity." The rule of homogamy states that the more similar adults are in terms of their "social and demographic statuses, attitudes, interests, intelligence, and personality traits," the more likely they are to become friends, and that a "homogeneous" sampling of adults will have a significantly higher number of friendships within it than a randomly selected group of adults.[61] The rule of "spatial proximity" states the more opportunities there are for adults to interact in "close residence and daily rounds" of intersection, the greater chances there are for intimacy to develop.[62]

It was within the "spatial proximity" at 361 F Street that Hunter, Mason, Butler, and Atchison solidified their friendship and created the most powerful senatorial bloc of the 1850s. Of the four members of the F Street Mess, Hunter, Mason, and Butler were the most alike in terms of "social and demographic statuses," and they had messed together for years before Atchison joined them in 1853. He was the lone westerner among the four and from much humbler circumstances. As it will be seen, not until Atchison's "attitudes" and "interests" moved closer to those held by the other three would he join their congressional mess.

The increased availability of housing and longer congressional seasons in Washington has made the nineteenth-century congressional boarding house, including 361 F Street, a thing of the past.[63] Ross K. Baker's 1980 study of the U.S. Senate notes the decline of private and public venues that once dominated senatorial interaction outside the halls of Congress.[64] However, his study found continued existence of certain types of senatorial friendships despite the lack of "spatial proximity." Baker divides political and personal friendships in the Senate into five subtypes: institutional and alliance (both forms of political friendship): and mentor-protégé, social, and pure (all forms of personal friendship). Institutional friendship, the most limited of the five, is simply the pride and collegiality senators' gain from being members of an exclusive group. An alliance friendship is more utilitarian. According to Baker, it is stronger than the institutional kind in that it results from consistent political agreement between members. Baker's mentor-protégé relationship is both political and personal in that it is a combination of friendship based on assistance (utility) and genuine solicitude (goodness). Baker's definition of social friendship is the most superficial of the five in that it does not require political agreement or emotional commitment but merely "leisure time" compatibility.[65]

Baker's analysis of senatorial friendships confirms Aristotle's argument that most friendships last only as long as the usefulness does. He also agrees that "pure" friendship, what he defines as "concern" for the "welfare and problems" of another, is the stablest but rarest form of friendship to be found in the Senate precisely because it is based on affection over political utility. Nevertheless, Baker argues this rare form of senatorial friendship can survive "all but the most serious disagreements over policy."[66]

It is my premise that all five types of friendship defined by Baker, institutional, alliance, mentor-protégé, social, and pure, existed in the Thirty-Third Congress, especially in the microcosmic setting of the house at 361 F Street. The personal and political friendships between Atchison, Butler, Hunter, and Mason influenced their decision making during the debate over the Nebraska Territory and determined the outcome of the bill. While matters of ideology, party, and region were important to the F Street Mess, the Kansas-Nebraska bill had to be made compatible with the group's survival. Friendship became a priority over policy.

The first half of the book juxtaposes the early political careers of Hunter, Mason, Atchison, and Butler and the growing sectional divisions over western expansion between 1837 and 1854. Particular attention is paid to the mentor-protégé relationship that existed between the senators and John C. Calhoun, the coalescing of the Mess's friendship and political power after 1847, and the local and national issues that necessitated the organization of the Nebraska Territory.

The second half of the book examines the ascendancy of the F Street Mess to hegemonic control of the Senate in the Thirty-Third Congress, including its role in the rewriting and passage of the Nebraska bill and its manipulation of President Franklin Pierce and Stephen Douglas, the bill's author of record. It also examines the post-enactment consequences of the Kansas-Nebraska Act on the F Street Mess, the Democratic Party, and the country as a whole—from Atchison's role in "Bleeding Kansas" to the election of Abraham Lincoln in 1860, southern secession, and war. The parallel macro and micro tracks come together with the expulsion of Robert M. T. Hunter, James Murray Mason, and eight other southern senators from the Senate on July 11, 1861.

It took a civil war, 752,000 deaths, and the 13th Amendment to the Constitution before the demise of the Slave Power was acknowledged North or South.[67] No one in 1854, not those in the F Street Mess, their cohorts, or their opponents knew that the passage of the Kansas-Nebraska Act would be the zenith and the nadir of the Slave Power. The Mess's lack of foresight makes its motivation less important historically than how it used its power. The Mess's dexterous blend of fealty, institutional knowledge, and political acumen was the true source of the Slave Power. How the F Street Mess used its power to legalize the expansion of slavery in the face of growing national opposition is not only a lesson in the use of power but also an allegory on the fragility of democracy.

CHAPTER ONE

Rivalries and Alliances

Freshman congressman John C. Calhoun of South Carolina exploded onto the national stage in 1811 earning the moniker "The Young Hercules" for his prowar stance against Great Britain.[1] The name suited him. He was tall, angular, and arrestingly handsome, with thick black hair and "luminous" eyes so hypnotic that those who gazed into them could never quite recall the color.[2] But unlike Dorian Gray, Calhoun's struggles were not locked away in a hidden portrait. Years of chronic poor health would erode the herculean body of his youth. His hair would turn white and brittle, his eyes dark and foreboding. And yet the intellectual vigor and Svengali-like charisma he brought with him in 1811 would never wane. Over the next four decades he would use both to navigate in and out of political alliances, successfully slaying rivals at home, while holding at bay those in Washington. His policy positions would become an ideology, and his ideology would build a following. Two of those followers, Robert M. T. Hunter and James Murray Mason, would join Calhoun's Washington cadre in 1837 and like their leader they would have to learn to swim in the rough political waters of the emerging second political party system.

By the time the Twenty-Fifth Congress convened in special session in Washington on September 4, 1837, the city and the nation had been under a process of physical and political reconstruction for nearly a quarter of a century.[3] The collapse of the first political party system, the rise of universal manhood suffrage, and the election of Andrew Jackson had caused political realignments and personal reinventions that made nineteenth-century America a different world from eighteenth-century America. Even before the Federalist Party was destroyed by its opposition to the War of 1812, the Republican Party had divided internally between "Old Jeffersonians" and "Nationalists" factions. In 1828 the Old Jeffersonians, or "Radicals," aligned themselves with Andrew Jackson, becoming Democratic Republicans or Jacksonian Democrats. The Nationalist Republicans divided between those who stayed with the Jackson party, becoming its conservative wing, and those who left to form the oppositional Whig Party. Unlike the Democrats who were relatively unified behind Jackson, the Whigs of the 1830s were less a cohesive national party than a loose coalition of disparate sectional factions. United initially by mutual opposition to Andrew Jackson and what they believed to be his abuse of executive power, fundamental philosophical and policy differences between nationalists, states' rights conservatives, and nullifiers made each distrustful of the other and unable to agree on a single candidate to run in 1836 against Jackson's hand-picked successor, Martin Van Buren.[4] As a result Van Buren won the presidential election with 170 electoral votes to his closest Whig rival, William H. Harrison's 73 votes. Not even his opponents' combined electoral vote of 124 was close to Van Buren's margin of victory but his percentage of the popular vote, 50.9 percent, suggested a more evenly divided electorate that was also reflected in the congressional results. The Democratic Party's slim control of Congress was susceptible therefore to any issue that affected those interests not yet firmly aligned with either the Democratic or Whig parties, and unfortunately for Van Buren he had inherited two such issues, economic depression and a growing abolitionist movement in the North.[5] The intertwined crises of depression and abolitionism and a growing insurgency against Van Buren's power base of New York and Virginia, led by pro-bank, soft-money Democrats, threatened both the party's control of Congress and Van Buren's control of the party. In order to pass his Independent Treasury bill at the special session in 1837 Van Buren needed an alliance with his old political rival, Senator John C. Calhoun of South Carolina.

In terms of political friendship, those who enter into an alliance do not have to like each other, but often members of alliances have and will "deemphasize personal differences or even deny that they exist" to keep the alliance together. If an alliance holds, it can eventually evolve into personal friendship, but neither political alliances nor personal friendships "stand up well under the strain of repeated and serious divergence of positions."[6] Such was the relationship between John C. Calhoun and Martin Van Buren between 1821 and 1837. Calhoun and Van Buren shifted in and out of political alliances so frequently it was difficult for their loyalists, especially Calhoun's, to follow.

The two men first met in Washington City in November 1821, when Secretary of War Calhoun paid a social call on the newly arrived freshman senator from New York.[7] By some measurements the two could not have been more different. At 6'2" Secretary Calhoun towered over 5'6" freshman Senator Van Buren. Calhoun had been promoting a nationalist agenda since his early days as a War Hawk in the House of Representatives and was not trusted by the "Old" or "Radical" wing of the party, whereas Van Buren, a strict constructionist and states' rights conservative, was. Van Buren supported the congressional caucus system for nominating presidential candidates. Calhoun opposed it and called instead for a national convention. But the two had more in common than their physical and political differences suggested. They were young men, both thirty-nine years old. Both were lawyers. Both had successfully taken on older powerful politicians in their home states and won.[8] Both knew their national ambitions were tied to maintaining political control at home, and both, relentlessly ambitious, needed the other to achieve those ambitions.

Biographers and historians argue that Calhoun never equaled or understood Van Buren's political skills, in part because Calhoun never acclimated himself to the democratic style of politics that emerged in the 1820s. Van Buren not only understood the new democratic politics; he perfected it. The argument is correct to a point. For sixteen years Van Buren the politician bested Calhoun the intellectual. But by the special congressional session in 1837 Calhoun would learn the game.

Van Buren and Calhoun formed their first alliance in 1821, when Van Buren solicited Calhoun's help in defeating the incumbent House Speaker and political opponent from New York, John W. Taylor. Calhoun, who desired Van Buren's support for his first presidential bid in 1824, obliged. With Calhoun's help, Taylor was defeated thereby increasing Van Buren's power in Washington and solidifying his base at home. In return Calhoun got nothing except the election of Virginia Radical Philip Barbour to the speakership. Barbour was a close friend of Calhoun's presidential rival, William Crawford. Three years later, Van Buren became Crawford's campaign manager, and Calhoun withdrew from the race.[9]

After Calhoun's withdrawal, he was placed on both John Quincy Adams and Andrew Jackson's tickets as the vice presidential candidate. Because he was on two tickets, Calhoun won the office of vice president outright with 131 electoral votes.[10] The four-way race for the presidency, between Andrew Jackson, John Quincy Adams, William Crawford, and Henry Clay had to be decided in the House of Representatives. There Andrew Jackson, the leader in both the popular and electoral vote, was defeated by John Quincy Adams. It was known then and today as "the corrupt bargain" because Adams subsequent appointment of Clay was seen by the Jackson people as a deal for Clay's support in the House.[11] For Vice President–elect Calhoun, Adams's election in the House was more than just the overthrow of popular will; it weakened his future presidential chances by positioning his arch rival Clay in an equally strong seat of succession.[12] Calhoun was an oppositional vice president for the next four years.

Rivalries and Alliances

Calhoun and Van Buren reunited again in 1828, this time to elect Andrew Jackson president. Van Buren had just been reelected to a second term in the U.S. Senate by an impressive 105 to 39 victory in the state legislature. Shortly thereafter Vice President Calhoun invited Van Buren to his estate, Oakly, in Georgetown where they devised a strategy.[13] Calhoun, the incumbent vice president under Adams, agreed to be Jackson's running mate in the fall, thereby lending the ticket "respectability" among the establishment still distrustful of Jackson, and Van Buren agreed to bring into Jackson's camp the radical strongholds of New York, Pennsylvania, Virginia, Georgia, and North Carolina.

Van Buren's part of the alliance was more difficult. William Crawford, the titular leader of the Radical faction, distrusted Jackson and hated Calhoun even more. His price for bringing the Radicals into Jackson's camp was the removal of Calhoun from the ticket. But Van Buren feared if Calhoun was dropped from the ticket he would be replaced by Van Buren's rival and early Jackson supporter, Dewitt Clinton. Even if Calhoun was not dropped from the ticket, Jackson leaned toward Clinton for secretary of state, which was the job Van Buren coveted. Calhoun supported Van Buren for State, and Clinton's death on February 11 settled everything else. Calhoun stayed on the ticket, and the Radicals supported Jackson anyway. On March 4, 1829, Andrew Jackson was inaugurated the seventh president of the United States. Vice President Calhoun and Secretary of State Van Buren became the heirs apparent to what many believed was a one-term presidency.[14]

Whether Calhoun's fall from grace was predetermined by Van Buren and the Radicals or the result of unexpected social and political events beyond his control is subject to debate. Calhoun biographer Charles Wiltse argues in his seminal work that Jackson not only accepted Calhoun's elimination as a precondition for the Radicals' support, but he also participated in the plan to politically eliminate him after the election. Jon Meacham's more recent biography on Jackson confirms "the calculating part" of Jackson's character and argues Jackson "tucked away" information on Calhoun "until he needed it." But Irving Bartlett is less conspiratorial in his treatment arguing that most of the events, while beneficial to Van Buren, were unplanned. Added to the serendipity of events was Calhoun's naiveté in believing he could hold himself above the new politics. He left Washington shortly after the inauguration and did not return until Congress reconvened in December.[15]

On the other hand, Van Buren, who had been elected governor of New York upon Clinton's death, resigned the seat immediately after Jackson appointed him secretary of state and moved to Washington. He used the eight months between congressional sessions to establish "a personal rapport with Jackson that Calhoun never enjoyed."[16] Over the next three years Van Buren's friends within the administration engaged in political sabotage against the vice president, while Van Buren went on horseback rides with Jackson. As his relationship with the president evolved from an institutional friendship to a personal one, the relationship between Jackson and Calhoun deteriorated, setting the stage for Calhoun's expulsion from Jackson's ticket in 1831 and the Nullification Crisis in 1833.

The events that led to Calhoun's expulsion began with the social ostracism of Secretary of War John Eaton's wife by Washington's elite in 1829.[17] It culminated in the winter of 1831 after Jackson questioned Calhoun's condemnation of his conduct during the 1819 Seminole Indian War. Fearing that open warfare between Jackson and his vice president would lead to a Whig victory in 1832, some within the Jackson and Calhoun camps endeavored to heal the breach between the two men but to no avail. In February 1831 the correspondence between Jackson and Calhoun regarding the Seminole War was published by Calhoun supporter Duff Green.[18] Jackson, who had announced for a second term, used the scandal to drop Calhoun from the ticket. That March Calhoun left Washington for South Carolina. During his absence Martin Van Buren and John Eaton voluntarily stepped down from the cabinet, allowing Jackson to force the resignations of Secretary of Treasury Samuel Ingham, Secretary of the Navy John Branch, and Attorney General John Berrien, all Calhoun men. Jackson nominated Van Buren for ambassador to England and in August Van Buren left for London.

Van Buren may or may not have been directly involved in the Seminole War controversy, but his supporters, William Crawford, John Eaton, and William Lewis, certainly had been. Whether Calhoun's next move was motivated by personal revenge or professional concerns is also subject to debate, but when Congress reconvened after the New Year, Calhoun's supporters arranged for a tie vote on Van Buren's Senate confirmation, allowing Vice President Calhoun, who had returned from South Carolina, to cast the deciding vote against him. Jackson recalled Van Buren from London, dropped Calhoun from the ticket, and made Van Buren his running mate. The Calhoun–Van Buren alliance was once again over, if it had ever existed at all.

Andrew Jackson often referred to Calhoun as that "Catiline," a reference to the Roman politician who was convicted by the Roman Senate of conspiring to overthrow the Republic. Indeed, the political maneuvering between friend and foe during Jackson's first term resembled something out of ancient Rome. Four years of infighting had created a rift within the party that some Jackson

Democrats feared would lead to a National Republican/Whig victory in 1832. It did not. Jackson, along with his new vice presidential running mate, Martin Van Buren, beat their strongest rival, Henry Clay, with 54.5 percent of the popular vote.[19] The Electoral College margin was even wider, 219 to 49.[20] But looming over Jackson's second term was the pending constitutional struggle over nullification, and the continued presence of his vice president for the remaining four months of his first term, John C. Calhoun.

The 1820s was a time of economic recession in the South. Throughout the decade cotton prices steadily decreased, commodity prices increased, and human resources dwindled. South Carolina alone lost 200,000 people through emigration. The region blamed the protective tariff of 1828, which raised duties on imports 30 percent to 50 percent, for the ongoing depression.[21] Southerners called it the Tariff of Abominations.

In response to the tariff of 1828, the South Carolina legislature published four thousand copies of a pamphlet titled the *South Carolina Exposition and Protest*, which argued the state's right to nullify federal law it determined unconstitutional. The *Exposition and Protest* had been anonymously written by Calhoun, then Adams's vice president. He based his argument on Madison and Jefferson's theory of state interposition espoused in the Virginia and Kentucky Resolutions of 1798 and 1799.

But Calhoun had written the *Exposition and Protest*, "as a warning rather than as a statement of present policy."[22] Like most southerners and westerners in 1828, Calhoun believed the Jackson administration would make tariff reform a top priority. He did not. Instead, Jackson's response was tepid, and his failure to propose a major tariff reduction in his first annual message to Congress convinced Calhoun that northern manufacturing interests were dictating Jackson's tariff policy.[23] A bill was eventually passed in 1832, but it was too little, too late for South Carolina.[24] By the summer of 1832 Calhoun was losing control over the tariff issue in his home state. With state elections looming, extremists had taken Calhoun's warning in the *Exposition and Protest* as justification for secession if the federal government did not lower the tariff. Those opposed to nullification, the "Unionists," called for patience and continued negotiations with the federal government. Their strategy differed little from Calhoun's except that the "Unionists" were in secret communication with Jackson via his secretary of war, Lewis Cass. As the odd man out in the Jackson administration, it was the perfect time for Calhoun to return home and assume control of his state's nullification movement.[25]

Calhoun came out officially on July 26, 1832. In an article published in his local town paper, the *Pendleton Messenger*, known as the Fort Hill Address,

Calhoun acknowledged his authorship of the *Exposition and Protest* and expanded upon its theories. Calhoun rejected state extremists' claims that nullification and secession were synonymous, arguing that secession was a divorce from the Union, whereas nullification, which he preferred to call the "state veto" was the negative power on the federal government reserved by the states within the Union.

Then, just in time to seal the victory for the nullifiers in South Carolina's state elections, news reached the state of a slave rebellion in Virginia. On August 21 Nat Turner led seventy of his fellow slaves in a revolt in Southampton County, Virginia, near the North Carolina border. Seventy-five white people were killed before the rebellion was brutally suppressed. John B. Floyd, the governor of Virginia, told Governor James Hamilton of South Carolina that abolitionists from the north had instigated the revolt. From that point forward abolitionism and northern industrial interests were inextricably linked in the minds of Virginians and South Carolinians, including Calhoun.

Calhoun's leadership during the Nullification Crisis was seen by his critics then and some historians today as a sudden and fundamental shift in his economic and political philosophy done to secure his base at home. This thesis, made famous by Charles Wiltse's three-volume biography on Calhoun has been rejected by the more recent works of Clyde Wilson, Irving H. Bartlett, and H. Lee Cheek.[26] All three argue Wiltse's thesis rests on the false assumption that Calhoun's political philosophy was fully evolved by 1833.[27] It was not. Nor was the country's. Calhoun, as well as Jackson and most politicians of the era, personified the unique yet ambiguous nature of nineteenth-century American political thought. The country was then, as it is today, both local and national because of a bifurcated constitution created by a generation that recognized the need for centralized power, yet nevertheless deeply mistrusted it. The Nullification Crisis of 1833 was the consequence of the nation's founding schizophrenia.

Calhoun never saw any contradiction in his earlier support for the tariff in 1816 and his later opposition to the tariffs in 1832. He believed the general welfare clause of the constitution gave the federal government the power to impose revenue-raising tariffs uniformly "throughout the United States" for improvements of a national and defensive nature. The tariff of 1816 had been passed to raise revenue to improve the defensive infrastructure of the nation, while the tariffs of 1828 and 1832 had been passed to protect the manufacturing interests of the country at the expense of its agricultural "consuming" ones. The tariff of 1816 was constitutional, whereas the tariffs of 1828 and 1832 could not be justified with the same reasoning.

Calhoun rejected nineteenth-century democracy and the growing centralization of power under Jackson. He called for a return to "first" or "pure" principles. For Calhoun this meant a return to "diffused authority," the bedrock of eighteenth-century Jeffersonian republicanism.[28] He believed that Madison's vision of a federated republic in which the various interests of the country acted "in unison" to protect "liberty" and the "rights" of the minority from the "superior force of an interested and overbearing majority" had not worked.[29] Calhoun argued the opposite had happened, that commercial and industrial interests in the north had joined with northern abolitionism to bring "superior force" upon the south. In his Fort Hill Address, Calhoun articulated for the first time the notion of a concurrent majority that would be more fully developed later in his opus *Disquisition and Discourse.* He was just beginning to articulate a dual executive that would protect minority interests in the nation by giving equal and shared authority to both its commercial and manufacturing concerns and its agricultural "consuming" interests.

The Fort Hill Address did not calm the extremists in South Carolina as Calhoun had hoped. Even worse, it alienated many of his supporters in the North. The nullifiers won the state elections, and on October 22 the South Carolina state legislature, led by a newly elected state senator and follower of Calhoun Andrew Pickens Butler, voted to hold a convention to determine the constitutionality of the federal tariffs of 1828 and 1832. The convention met on November 19 and nullified both tariffs. On December 10 President Jackson delivered his proclamation to Congress promising the tariffs would be enforced. Two days later on December 12 the South Carolina legislature elected Calhoun to the U.S. Senate, replacing Calhoun supporter Robert Hayne who had been elected governor of the state. On December 22 Calhoun met with Hayne and the outgoing governor and political extremist James Hamilton in Columbia. Calhoun urged South Carolina to delay implementing the ordinance and give negotiation a chance. He resigned the vice presidency on December 28 and left for Washington. Jackson threatened to have him hanged.[30]

Calhoun was not hanged upon his arrival in Washington. Instead, he met with Henry Clay. Together they hammered out a compromise bill that lowered the tariff rates over a period of ten years until they neared the levels of 1816. Jackson himself inadvertently helped the compromise along by asking Congress for authority to "force" South Carolina's compliance with the federal tariff. Many states' rights conservatives, north and south, including Vice President–elect Van Buren, while doubting the constitutionality of nullification, had misgivings about the constitutionality of Jackson's "force" bill. Calhoun used their concerns to gain support for the compromise, and on March 1 both the tariff compromise and the Force Bill were passed. Jackson signed both bills the following day. On March 3 Calhoun left for South Carolina, arriving in Columbia on March 11, the day the nullification convention reconvened. On March 12 the convention rescinded the nullification ordinance of the tariff and then nullified the Force Bill. Jackson ignored this last face-saving measure. The crisis was over.

By 1833 Calhoun was a man without a party, but not without a following of states' rights conservatives and nullifiers who would grow throughout the South over the next seventeen years. During the final years of Jackson's presidency, Calhoun aligned himself with the Whigs as did many southern states' rights conservatives. Like the Whigs, Calhoun and his followers opposed what they believed to be Jackson's usurpation of power. They pointed as evidence to Jackson's withdrawal of federal funds from the Bank of the United States and deposits in twenty-three state banks, for which he was sanctioned by the Senate, as well as his Specie Circular in which Jackson ordered the federal government to accept only gold and silver in payment for public land. The Specie Circular in particular had profound impact on state economies by draining states of their supply of gold and silver. When Van Buren was elected in the fall of 1836 and economic panic hit later that spring, Calhoun saw an opportunity to renew his alliance with the new president and return the party of Jefferson to its first principles. For sixteen years Van Buren had outwitted Calhoun politically; now it was Calhoun's turn to outwit him.

In April, one month into the Van Buren presidency, major banks in the Northeast closed their doors, refusing to pay gold for their outstanding bank notes.[31] Panic, then depression followed. President Van Buren called for a special session of Congress to convene in September. His proposed economic recovery plan included the establishment of an independent treasury that would separate the federal government from the banking industry.[32] Congress divided three ways. The Whigs were unified in opposition to Van Buren's plan and proposed instead a third national bank. The Democrats split into two camps. The Radicals supported an Independent Treasury but wanted payments in specie (gold or silver). The Conservative soft-money Democrats preferred some sort of deposit bank plan that would include payment in bank notes. Calhoun and his followers held the balance of power.[33] Two of those followers were members of the Twenty-Fifth Congress's freshmen class, Robert M. T. Hunter and James Murray Mason. Like Calhoun, Hunter and Mason had been raised in the political traditions of eighteenth-century republicanism, both were states' rights conservatives and strict constructionists. That Hunter had been elected to the Twenty-Fifth Congress by Virginia

Whigs and Mason by Virginia Democrats was due to Virginia's regional differences and the highly divisive politics of the 1820s in which their political careers had begun.

Virginia's demographics had been changing long before the Panic as Virginians emigrated westward to Kentucky and the southwest. The result was a decline in Virginia's overall population, specifically among the Tidewater planter population, while the non-slave-holding population of Virginia's backcountry increased. The state Republican Party was also declining in influence as its leadership aged and died, Jefferson in 1826, Monroe in 1831, and Madison in 1836. The Federalist Party on the other hand had always been strong in Virginia during the Early Republic, pulling its strength from the large planter-business class. Its interests remained represented in the newly formed Whig Party of the 1830s, experiencing a surge of support from states' rights conservatives opposed to Jackson's tariff and bank policies.

In 1804 Republican Spencer Roane had started the *Richmond Enquirer* to counter Federalist power in the Tidewater region. He put his cousin Thomas Ritchie at the editor's desk. When Roane died in 1822, control of the Republican Party in Virginia passed to Ritchie. His faction became known as the Richmond Junto. By the 1830s it controlled "the judicial, financial, and legislative branches of the state government."[34] In 1816 and 1824 Ritchie and the Junto supported Radical Republican William Crawford for president. But the state party's strength was growing where the state's population was growing, in the Jackson country of Virginia's western counties. Ever pragmatic, Ritchie and the Junto left Crawford in 1828 and joined the Jackson campaign. One year later Virginia's western counties were successful in their push for a state convention to reform the existing constitution. The Tidewater elite felt increasingly under siege from the new democracy.[35]

The elections of Hunter and Mason to Congress in 1837 reflected these regional and political divides in Virginia. Hunter, from the Tidewater county of Essex, was in the state legislature when the Nullification Crisis erupted in 1832. It was his vocal opposition to Jackson's Nullification Proclamation and Force Bill that would get him elected to Congress by the legislature's states' rights Whig faction five years later. James Murray Mason was from the western county of Frederick. His states' rights credentials were as solid as Hunter's, and while he did not hold an elective office in 1832, his vocal support of the president during the Nullification Crisis helped to get him elected in 1837 by the legislature's Jackson Democrats. It would take another ten years before Hunter and Mason could transcend Virginia's regional divisions and become Democratic U.S. senators and devoted followers of Calhoun.

If anyone was born to be Calhoun's heir it was Robert M. T. Hunter. The similarities in temperament and intellect between the two can be traced to the men's very similar childhoods. Both had strong father figures whom they lost early in life. Both had lonely childhoods that they compensated for by developing voracious reading habits. Both went to academies established by the men of the family. Both attended the best colleges and trained for the law under the leading jurists of the day. As adults, both abstained from alcohol. Mutually and relentlessly ambitious in politics, both would strive for and be denied the presidency.

Robert Mercer Taliaferro Hunter, known to his family and closest friends as Bob, was born in 1809 the seventh child of James and Maria Garnett Hunter.[36] While the Hunters and Garnetts had intermarried since the seventeenth century, Maria Garnett's father, Muscoe Garnett, initially opposed the marriage of his daughter to her cousin James Hunter.[37] James's father had squandered his fortune leaving his then fourteen-year-old son without one. Instead of attending school, James Hunter went to work for an uncle in the mercantile business in Portsmouth, Virginia. By twenty-two he owned a small store, but Muscoe Garnett believed it was not yet enough to sustain a family. Maria nevertheless prevailed over her father's concerns, and in 1796 she and James married. Five years later James gave up the mercantile business and moved his family to a farm in Essex County, where he became a successful planter and state legislator.[38]

Unlike his father, James Hunter had an excellent business reputation, and his advice was frequently sought by friends and neighbors. But he was also a nervous and apprehensive man who suffered from insomnia, suggesting a deep-seated insecurity despite his economic and political success. Unable to sleep, James Hunter, who was a voracious reader, would wake his son Robert in the middle of the night to read history to him. Robert Hunter inherited his father's love of reading but not his business acumen. Growing up, he never knew the economic hardship that his father had experienced in his own childhood and, as a consequence, never adopted his father's sense of business caution. The future chairman of the Senate Finance Committee and author of the Tariff of 1857, dabbled in speculative ventures all his life, which resulted in chronic financial difficulties not unlike those of his grandfather.

The family plantation was called Hunter's Mill. Despite the large family, Robert Hunter was a lonely child. His mother died giving birth to his brother, William Garnett, when he was three years old. Two older brothers also died in childhood, William, for whom the younger William was named, and James Jr. Young Robert had no male friends his own age except for a slave named

Austin. The son of a planter, Robert received his early education at home at the hands of his father. James Hunter had a strong library, and his daughters were also well read, particularly Robert's older sister Jane. Robert Hunter was educated at home until the age of eleven when he was sent to Rose Hill Academy, a local private school run by a German named Van Vranken and financed by Hunter's father and uncle, James Mercer Garnett. The school was two and half miles from Hunter's Mill. The slave Austin accompanied Hunter daily to and from school.[39]

James Hunter always lamented his lack of a formal education and placed all his hopes and dreams in his surviving sons. When his eldest son, Muscoe Garnett died while attending William and Mary College, Robert Hunter inherited what was left of his father's unrealized ambitions. James Hunter considered a variety of colleges for Robert including Princeton, William and Mary, and the newly completed University of Virginia. He selected the last of these, but shortly before the commencement of its first session in 1826 James Hunter died. Seventeen-year-old Robert was now the head of a family comprised of three sisters, one younger brother, and a paternal aunt. The family moved to nearby Elmwood, the plantation home of their Uncle James Mercer Garner, where their sister, Maria, the widow of James Mercer Garner Jr., lived. With the family taken care of, Robert Mercer Taliaferro Hunter matriculated in the first session held at the University of Virginia in 1826.

The "bookish" child, "lonesome in his ways," had ended up at a school known in its early days for its dissipated student body. But for the first time in his life, Robert M. T. Hunter was surrounded by a cohort of his own age and gender, including Edgar Allen Poe and Lewis E. Harvie. They gave Hunter the nickname, "Run Mad Tom," after his initials, but perhaps too in the hope he would be inclined toward its suggested behavior. He was not. Nevertheless, the nickname is revealing: Hunter remained throughout his life a well-liked but quiet man.

At the University of Virginia, Hunter was exposed to a structured canon that included mathematics, Greek, Latin, Spanish, moral and natural philosophy, and political economy. He was also exposed to the extracurricular pastimes of gambling, horseracing, and drinking, much to the concern of his sisters and aunt. In a letter home, Hunter denied participating in anything beyond "simple looking," insisting he "did not bet a cent, drink a drop of liquor, swear an oath, or get into any sort of dispute." Nevertheless, he continued, "A certain degree of amusement is as necessary for our existence and the full performance of the task which is set for us in life, as the discharge of almost any other duty we have."[40] Like Calhoun, Hunter never did drink and would gamble only in the business venture of land speculation.

The University of Virginia did not confer degrees in the early nineteenth century, but Hunter was one of its first students to be conferred the title of "Graduate" in July, 1828. He initially stayed on at the University to study law in a class that included future senatorial ally, Robert A. Toombs of Georgia. Neither man stayed long though as a typhoid epidemic closed the school in 1829.[41] Hunter moved to the western hamlet of Winchester in the Shenandoah Valley, where he completed his legal studies under the famed states' rights theorist Judge Henry St. George Tucker. In 1830 Hunter returned to Essex County, passed the bar, and established a small practice near Lloyds, Virginia. He purchased a farm near Lloyds, named it Fonthill, and moved his family there from Elmwood.[42]

Following in his father's and uncles' political footsteps, Hunter was elected to the state legislature in the spring of 1834 by states' rights Whigs. He was twenty-six years old. Hunter had voted for Jackson in 1832 but broke with the administration during the Nullification Crisis, as did most eastern Virginia Democrats, opposing both the president's Nullification Proclamation and the Force Bill. Hunter later supported the president's veto of the Bank Bill but opposed Virginia's Expunging Resolutions in 1835.[43] During his term in the state legislature, Hunter began to court nineteen-year-old Mary Evelina Dandridge, the niece of his former law professor, Judge St. George Tucker.[44] They were married on October 4, 1836.[45] Shortly after his marriage, Hunter was elected to the U.S. Congress by the legislature's states' rights Whigs.

Also elected to Congress from Virginia that year was James Murray Mason.[46] The Masons of Virginia were true cavaliers in a state where such lineage was largely myth. The first George Mason of Virginia had been a member of the House of Commons and supporter of King Charles I during the English Civil War. He moved to Norfolk, Virginia, in 1651 and was quickly elected to the Virginia House of Burgesses. Three generations later his great grandson George Mason IV became a delegate to the Second Continental Congress and author of the Virginia Commonwealth's first Bill of Rights from which Jefferson borrowed heavily in writing the Declaration of Independence. George Mason later attended the Constitutional Convention in Philadelphia in 1787 as a member of the Virginia delegation but did not sign the document because it lacked a bill of rights. He also objected to the Constitution's lack of restriction on the powers of the federal judiciary over the states. Both his concerns were resolved by the adoption of the Bill of Rights in 1791 and the Eleventh

Amendment in 1795. Mason would inherit his grandfather's strict constructionism and states' rights conservatism.

By all accounts James Mason's childhood varied greatly from Robert Hunter's lonely one. He was born November 3, 1798, the second of John and Anna Murray Mason's ten children.[47] The siblings, six boys and four girls, had a lively childhood, spending their summer months at Clermont, the family home on Analostan Island in the Potomac River in view of the Capitol, the White House, and their grandfather's estate, Gunston Hall.[48] Outdoor activities were encouraged. James Mason grew up loving horses and became a skilled horseman. His father especially doted on him, exposing him not only to sport but also his grandfather's world of politics and eighteenth-century republicanism.

Mason's formal education began at an academy in Georgetown. In 1815 he was admitted to the University of Pennsylvania in Philadelphia, where he boarded with a French immigrant family and acquired the first of several languages. After receiving his bachelor's degree in 1818 Mason studied law at the College of William and Mary in Williamsburg, Virginia. In 1820 he moved to Richmond where he completed his legal studies under Benjamin Watkins Leigh and was admitted to the bar in the same year.

While attending the University of Pennsylvania, Mason met the sister of a fellow classmate, Eliza Chew. The Chews, one of the first families of Philadelphia, equaled the Masons' ranking socially. After two years of study and courtship both families assumed the two would marry and James would establish a practice in Philadelphia.

James Mason did not establish his practice in Philadelphia or any other city. Instead, Mason chose Winchester in Frederick County in the Shenandoah Valley. According to his daughter, Virginia, her father was fond of recounting a rather romanticized story of how years before he became a lawyer he stumbled by happenstance upon a tavern in Winchester and never forgot the welcome he had received there from "strangers." Mason moved to Winchester in 1821, set up a legal practice, and began riding the circuit in the western counties. One year later he brought his Philadelphia bride, Eliza, to Winchester. As the wife of a circuit riding lawyer, Eliza spent her first months of married life alone becoming accustomed to rural society. In 1829, the same year Robert M. T. Hunter moved to Winchester, the young couple purchased a stone house a mile outside of the village and named it Selma.[49] It would be the home to their growing family for the next thirty-two years, until war forced them to move.

Mason's early political career was troubled. He was first elected to the state legislature in 1826, where he immediately opposed, for constitutional reasons, federal funding for local internal improvements. The voters in the backwoods of his home county of Frederick, not having the same constitutional qualms, voted Mason out of office in 1827. One year later he was back in the state legislature, having been elected as a Jackson Democrat. Like many in Frederick County, he hoped the election of the man from western Tennessee would benefit western Virginia.

In the fall of 1829 Mason was appointed a delegate to the state constitutional convention, where the western delegates demanded redistricting and other electoral reforms. Mason voted against its final adoption, believing the proposed constitution continued to give too much power to the Tidewater region. The constitution was later ratified by 63 percent of the vote. In 1831 Mason left the state legislature to run for Congress, winning only his home county of Frederick. Mason returned to Selma and spent the next six years expanding his family and law practice.[50]

Late in December 1832, James Mason was appointed by the Frederick County Democrats to a committee of seven to draw up resolutions in support of Andrew Jackson's Nullification Proclamation. The committee drew up seven resolutions that supported Jackson, while at the same time opposing the tariffs of 1828 and 1832. Mason was one of three in the minority whose report offered alternative resolutions that differed little from the majority other than in its use of stronger language in opposing the right of the federal government to implement tariffs for anything other than revenue.

Mason's biographer Robert Young believes that had the crisis been over slavery and not the tariff Mason would have abandoned his support of the president in favor of nullification. But by 1832 Mason, like most Virginians, had already linked the two issues together as evident by his use of the phrase "repugnant to the character of our institutions" in his minority report.[51] Mason did not change his position on nullification in 1832; he just believed it was not necessary to solve the crisis.[52] After expressing his position in the minority report he voted in favor of the majority report, which included the expressed hope that Congress would lower the tariff to revenue-raising levels.

James Murray Mason was elected to Congress as a Democrat in April 1837. Upon arriving in Washington, he joined Hunter in a mess that included fellow Virginia congressman Francis Mallory, Congressman and Mrs. Francis Pickens of South Carolina, and Senator and Mrs. John C. Calhoun.[53] On September 4 the special session of the Twenty-Fifth Congress convened to address the Panic of 1837.

John C. Calhoun was increasingly concerned by what he believed to be two interrelated issues: the growing concentration of political and economic power in the North, and the rise of northern abolitionism. He believed the panic had been caused by Jackson's deposit of federal funds into "pet" state banks that allowed those banks to inflate the value of their own paper, overextend credit, and fuel over speculation in western lands. He liked Van Buren's proposed Treasury bill because it "divorced" the federal government from banking, thereby providing a significant blow to the political and economic power of the northeastern banking establishment. But Calhoun opposed any Treasury plan that included the acceptance of bank notes because he believed it would allow for the continued influence of northeastern banks and the overextension of credit. On September 18 Calhoun introduced an amendment to the administration's bill that required a gradual reduction of note payments until 1841 when the Treasury would accept specie only. He made acceptance of the amendment a condition of his and his followers support. After sixteen long years, Calhoun had Van Buren exactly where he wanted him. Reject Calhoun's amendment and Van Buren alienated hard-money Democrats in both Houses. But if he accepted Calhoun's amendment soft-money Democrats in the House might align with Whigs to defeat the bill. Van Buren accepted Calhoun's amendment hoping concessions made elsewhere would keep soft-money Democrats in the House in line. The bill passed in the Senate on October 3, 1837, and went to the House for consideration.

Virginia's freshmen congressmen Robert M. T. Hunter and James Murray Mason may have been elected from different regions of their state by different parties, but they were both states' rights conservatives, and they revered their messmate John C. Calhoun. For the two to follow their mentor in support of the Independent Treasury bill Mason needed only to stay with the administration and hard-money Democrats, but Hunter would have to break from the Whig Party. Both men made their maiden speeches in the House on October 11 during the Treasury bill debate. Hunter stayed with Calhoun, broke from the Whigs and supported the bill. Mason, despite his allegiance to Calhoun, broke from the administration and hard-money Democrats and opposed the bill.

It was not difficult for Hunter to break with the Whigs and side with the administration. Like Calhoun, he was never particularly attuned to party politics. He had aligned himself with the Whigs only because of his earlier opposition to Jacksonian policies. Equally important, Hunter shared Calhoun's concern that the concentration of political and economic power in the North could create a Whig abolitionist majority. So Hunter threw his support behind the administration openly dismissing party loyalty in his maiden speech, "In taking my course," he proclaimed from the floor, "I form no new connections, I make no alliances; I act as I was sent to act. I legislate not for party, but for the good of our common country. I tread all personal and party considerations into the dust, when they present themselves in competition with the most important interests of the people."[54]

It was not so easy for Mason. He was a states' rights, strict constructionist, soft-money conservative, a true Jacksonian Democrat in every way. Unlike Calhoun and Hunter, Mason had a real affinity with the yeoman farmer of Virginia's backcountry. He had settled in Winchester because he had been drawn to the warmth and hospitality of its people. Unlike Calhoun and Hunter, Mason loved the practice of law and thrived on riding the circuit. And unlike Calhoun and Hunter, Mason knew the common folk, understood the economic hardship the panic had caused them, and felt their pain. He had been loyal to the administration and had supported all its earlier measures, but on the Independent Treasury bill with his mentor's hard-currency amendment attached, he could not go along.

It was clearly painful for Mason to break with Calhoun, South Carolina's "distinguished statesman ... in the other wing of the Capitol." Nor was it easy for him to oppose the administration. It was with the "most reluctance" he stated, "that I am now brought to differ with those with whom I have heretofore acted."[55]

Mason had several problems with the bill. First, he did not believe it would work. "My great objections to the measures proposed in the bill are, they are not at all commensurate with the exigencies of the times," he argued; "the bill simply ordains that the Government, after a limited time, will receive nothing but gold and silver in payment of public dues, and will intrust its keeping to its own officers alone." He also believed the proposed "divorce" of the federal government from the banking system was too immediate and would hamper the recovery by draining specie from the states and limiting the ability of banks to offer notes in smaller denominations to the people. His answer to the economic crisis was classic laissez-faire. "The Government must keep its hands off," he argued, "time must be allowed for the system to re-act, before any new or additional pressure can be borne."

Van Buren's effort to hold the soft-money conservative Democrats in line through concessions elsewhere was not successful. On October 14 the conservative soft-money Democrats, including James Murray Mason, broke with the administration and joined the Whigs to defeat the bill. The House adjourned five days later. Van Buren had been defeated but not Calhoun. The administration's plan to take the bill up again when Congress reconvened presented him with an even greater political opportunity.

When the Congress returned in December, Calhoun made the price for his continued support of the Independent Treasury the administration's support of six resolutions, all designed to protect southern interests through recognition of states' rights principles that included state sovereignty and the protection of domestic institutions. The fifth and sixth resolutions specifically cited any attempt to interfere with slavery in the District of Columbia, territories, or new states as a violation of those principles. The resolutions were introduced on December 27, 1837. All but the sixth resolution, which was tabled, passed. In return Calhoun came out in support of the Independent Treasury bill in a two-hour speech on the Senate floor February 15. Robert M. T. Hunter, followed suit in the House speaking over the course of two days, June 21 through 22. He essentially reiterated Calhoun's position that deposits of federal money in private banks provided the "sinew" by which the banks "control[ed]" the "Government." Hunter further argued that because the Independent Treasury bill would remove this power, it had become in the banks "direct political interest" to use their "tremendous power and mighty machinery" to ensure its defeat.[56]

Despite Hunter's best efforts, opposition to the bill could not be overcome in the House. It was defeated for a second time on June 25. Congress adjourned for the summer two weeks later. The Independent Treasury Act would not pass until July 4, 1840, and only after Calhoun's amendment had been dropped. Calhoun withdrew his support of the bill as a consequence. Less than a year later the act was repealed by a Whig-controlled Congress, only to be restored when the Democrats returned to power in 1846.

Both Hunter and Mason had split with their parties over the Independent Treasury vote, rejecting the idea that party loyalty required "unconsidered sanction" of every party position.[57] Mason continued to proclaim his loyalty to the party. He returned to *Selma* that summer believing his vote against the Independent Treasury had been one of "mere expediency" and did not "in itself ... sever" him from the Democratic Party.[58] His district's Democrats disagreed and refused to renominate him, leaving Mason literally and politically in the wilderness. He would not hold elected office again until 1846 and then would never again go against his mentor Calhoun. Ironically, Hunter, who had never claimed to be a loyal Whig, was returned to Congress that fall by his district's loyal Whig voters.

Just prior to the convening of the Twenty-Sixth Congress, the Democrats caucused to select a candidate for Speaker of the House. As advised by their leader, Calhoun's followers were willing to support the administration's choice if that candidate supported states' rights and if, in exchange for their support, the states' rights Democrats received adequate committee appointments.[59]

The obvious choice was Francis W. Pickens, Calhoun's cousin and closest friend in Congress. Pickens was the only other member of the South Carolina delegation besides Calhoun to support Van Buren's Independent Treasury. But Pickens was not in Washington at the time of the caucus meeting, and infighting forced his name to be withdrawn. The second choice of the Van Buren–Calhoun alliance was Dixon H. Lewis of Alabama. But his candidacy was blocked by Thomas Hart Benton of Missouri, a Calhoun rival with presidential ambitions of his own and an antiadministration Democrat.[60] The caucus finally agreed upon a compromise candidate, John W. Jones of Virginia.

On Tuesday, December 3, 1839, the 242 members of the House of Representatives, 247 if you counted the five Democrats from New Jersey who were challenging their governor's certification of the election of five New Jersey Whigs, convened in a chamber built for 192.[61] Crowded conditions and inadequate ventilation exasperated the political tension between the 125 Democrats, 114 Whigs, 6 Anti-Masons, and 2 Virginia Conservatives, making the chamber politically and physically insufferable. In this atmosphere, the Twenty-Sixth Congress convened. The first order of business, which should have been the election of the Speaker, was put on hold as members debated what to do about the contending New Jersey delegations.[62] The Whig delegation had been certified the duly elected delegation by New Jersey's governor. The state's Democratic Party contested the election and sent its own delegation, certified by the state's secretary of state. The question before the House was whether to allow the governor's certified delegation to vote in the Speaker's election. House Whigs demanded the New Jersey delegation holding the proper state certification be allowed to vote and address the New Jersey Democrats' challenge after. House Democrats wanted both delegations excluded from the vote and the matter sent to the Committee on Elections for settlement. The outcome would create a difference of ten votes and determine which party controlled the House. As the debate continued, the chamber's domed roof, magnified and redirected the member's voices, making the increasingly contentious debate all but inaudible.[63] For nearly two weeks the federal government was paralyzed. President Van Buren could not deliver his annual message to the Congress until there was a Speaker to deliver it to, and the Senate suspended all legislative activity until the House was in order.[64]

Late on the evening of Friday, December 13, House Democrats managed to squeeze through a resolution to proceed with the organization of the House without New Jersey. The next morning Saturday, December 14, House Whigs attempted to introduce one last resolution to have their New Jersey delegation seated before the vote. Rejected, they began a series of appeals and points of order. Confusion prevailed as once again the chamber's acoustical problems and members' rising tempers made it difficult for many to understand which or how many questions were before the House. In the end the Whigs relented, going on the record as having done so only because the "Administration party had disfranchised New Jersey, and Opposition had not the power to prevent it."[65]

On the first ballot, the administration's candidate, Jones, received 113 votes, just 5 shy of the 118 needed to elect, six members of the South Carolina delegation having voted for other Democratic candidates.[66] Whig candidate, John Bell of Tennessee received 102. Without a winner on the first ballot, the Whigs quickly tried to insert another resolution to seat their New Jersey delegation before the second ballot was taken. The chair refused to hear it. On the second ballot, Jones's vote held at 113 and Robert M. T. Hunter, a one-term states' rights Whig from Virginia, received a single vote from Pennsylvania Whig Charles Ogle.

Suddenly the game changed. Jones's support quickly plummeted. By the end of the sixth ballot his votes had dropped to 39. Fellow democrat Dixon Lewis held the lead with 79 votes, and Hunter, who was receiving bipartisan support, was second with 68.[67] Congress adjourned, the vote set to resume on Monday, December 16.

When the House reconvened on Monday morning, George Dromgoole, Democrat from Virginia, announced that Jones requested "his name might be withdrawn from canvass." The administration Democrats now threw their support to Lewis in the hopes of securing the election. But on the first vote of the day, the seventh ballot, Lewis fell short, as Jones had, with 110 votes. Bell followed with 80. With it becoming increasingly clear that neither party's candidate could win, the surprise candidate, Hunter, now became the compromise candidate. Whigs could support him even if grudgingly so because he had supported the effort to seat the Whig delegation from New Jersey. Administration democrats could support him because he had voted for Van Buren's Independent Treasury bill. On the seventh ballot Hunter's support had actually dropped to 12 votes, but states' rights Democrats who had voted for other Democratic candidates on earlier ballots switched their support to Hunter. As the balloting continued Hunter began to pick up strength, 16 votes after the eighth ballot, 59 after the ninth, 85 after the tenth, and on the eleventh ballot, Hunter was elected Speaker of the House of Representatives with 119 votes.

The next day Hunter stood before the collected members of the House. He had barely survived reelection in his own district only weeks earlier. Now at the age of thirty he was the youngest Speaker of the House in U.S. history.[68] Calling the House to order, he thanked the body for the "unexpected" honor and assured it of his commitment to serve:

And although deeply impressed with a painful sense of my inexperience, and of the difficulties of a new and untried station, I am yet cheered by the hope that you will sustain me in my efforts to preserve the order of business and the decorum of debate. I am aware that party fervor is occasionally impatient of the restraint which it is the duty of the Chair to impose upon the asperities of debate, but at the same time I know that the justice of all parties will sustain a Speaker who is honestly endeavoring to preserve the dignity of the House, and the harmony of its members.[69]

Calhoun was somewhat ambivalent about his protégé's election. He had, after all, wanted his cousin Francis Pickens for the speakership. After Pickens withdrew his name from consideration, Calhoun had gone along with the caucus and the administration's compromise candidate, John Lewis, hoping it would give the states' rights block more leverage with the administration on policy matters. But Calhoun and Hunter's relationship led some contemporaries and later historians to mistakenly believe that Calhoun had micromanaged the Speaker's election. He had not. No one, not Calhoun, nor Van Buren, nor the Richmond Junto, had the power to enforce the kind of party discipline necessary to select a Speaker on a first or second ballot. The Democratic majority was too internally divided over how to respond to the economic crisis to be able to respond as a singular disciplined party in the selection process. The Whig Party was still too pubescent to force a candidate of its own upon the House. Hunter, well liked by the majority of House members, had simply fallen through the cracks of a new and unsettled political party system. In a letter written the day after the election to his daughter Anna Marie, Calhoun expressed his surprise at Hunter's "strange run of luck" and, in a not so subtle comment on his own "strange run of luck," added his hope that Hunter would "do much to advance our principles and doctrines."[70] Hunter would become what Calhoun hoped for but not in 1839 and not as a member of the House.

Hunter's rise to power in the House was brief. His agreeable personality had gotten him elected, but it did not translate into a strong political following. As his biographer, David Fisher, notes, Hunter was nominally a Whig but "his states-rights, strict construction, anti-bank, sub-treasury political principles and beliefs" should have made him a Democrat.[71] Then why did Hunter not switch parties? Because Hunter, not yet comfortable with the new-style politics of the second system, feared the appearance of anything overtly political. As Speaker, Hunter refused to reward one party over the other. Instead, he divided committee assignments evenly, appointing majority Democrats to those committees that dealt with executive departments and policies and majority Whigs to those committees that dealt with investigations.[72]

Hunter's bipartisan approach extended to the 1840 presidential election. He refused to endorse either the Whig nominee, William Henry Harrison, or the incumbent Democratic president, Martin Van Buren. It was the final indignity to district Whigs back home, and they refused to renominate him. Hunter was immediately nominated by soft-money Democrats but withdrew his name when the local Democratic Party split over his nomination. Instead, he ran as an independent, winning in a three-way race during an election year that saw the Whigs triumph in the presidential contest and congressional races. Upon his return to Congress, Hunter was not renominated for Speaker. The speakership of the Twenty-Sixth Congress went to the Whig John White of Kentucky instead.

Back home in Virginia, Van Buren Democrats led by Thomas Ritchie and the Richmond Junto exacted its revenge against Hunter and his fellow Calhounites. Under the 1840 census Virginia had lost six congressional seats, dropping from twenty-one to fifteen. The state legislature, controlled by the Junto, gerrymandered the new districts to assure the defeat of its opponents. Not a single Calhounite, including Hunter, was reelected in 1842. It was the zenith of the Richmond Junto's power.

No longer in office, Hunter did not return to his law practice. Unlike Mason, who loved the law and had a flourishing practice in Winchester, Hunter was more like his mentor, Calhoun. Neither liked the law and neither excelled at it financially. Instead of returning to his former practice, Hunter joined Calhoun's 1844 presidential campaign. It would be Calhoun's last attempt at the presidency, and Hunter was selected to head up the central campaign committee charged with organizing each state at the district level. In December Hunter completed writing Calhoun's official campaign biography, *The Life of John C. Calhoun,* published in February 1843. Hunter also bought the Washington newspaper, the *Spectator*, to serve as the campaign's official organ.[73]

Back home in Virginia, Hunter was confronted by opposing strategy of Thomas Ritchie, who was running the Van Buren campaign. Ritchie was working to deny Virginia to Calhoun by holding the party convention early before Calhoun could gain support from other states. Hunter's strategy was to delay the Virginia state convention until Calhoun could gain enough northern delegates to ward off potential Van Buren gains in Virginia. Calhoun hoped for a confrontation with the Van Buren campaign in Virginia, but Hunter refused to engage in open warfare, keeping open the possibility of negotiations with

Ritchie and the Junto if Calhoun's national strategy failed, and it did. Unable to gain enough northern support, Calhoun bowed out of his final race for president just before the Virginia Convention convened in February 1844.[74]

On February 28, Secretary of State Abel Upshur, a close ally of Calhoun, was killed by a freak gun explosion while aboard the battleship Princeton. Upshur had been part of a presidential party that included President Tyler and Calhoun's son Patrick. Tyler and Patrick survived the explosion, but several others did not. In addition to Upshur, the dead included close Calhoun confidant Virgil Maxcy and Secretary of the Navy Thomas Gilmer.[75] Upshur had been in the middle of treaty negotiations with Texas when he was killed. Calhoun, who had been secretly advising Tyler and Upshaw on the negotiations with Texas, was immediately appointed and quickly confirmed to replace Upshur.[76] It had been less than a year since Daniel Webster had resigned the same post in protest against Tyler's pro-Texas annexation position.

By 1844 the evolution of John C. Calhoun from nationalist to sectionalist was complete. Ironically, as secretary of state Calhoun could now use the power of his federal office to promote southern sectional interests, including Texas annexation. Calhoun was not an expansionist per se. In fact, he opposed what he saw as the rapacious expansionism on the part of southwestern planters because he believed it was contributing to the rise of northern abolitionism.[77] Nevertheless, Calhoun supported Texas annexation in order to thwart potential foreign inference in the southwest and to maintain sectional parity in the Senate.[78] On April 18 he signed the annexation treaty that had been negotiated by Upshur. The treaty still faced an uphill confirmation battle in the Senate, where antitreaty forces had formed under the leadership of twenty-one-year incumbent Democrat Thomas Hart Benton of Missouri. Benton was a slave owner, but his opposition to slavery's further expansion had aligned him with the Senate's Free-Soil faction. Despite his antiexpansionism sentiment, Benton's opposition to Texas annexation had less to do with slavery's expansion than with his concerns regarding its impact on financial relations between the United States and Mexico.[79]

While the antitreaty forces were ready for a fight, Calhoun's senatorial faction was not yet the powerhouse it would be by the end of the decade. The Panic of 1837 and Texas had taught many the costs and benefits of moving in Calhoun's wake. That lesson had certainly been learned by Robert M. T. Hunter and James Murray Mason, who, in the spring of 1844, were fighting political battles of their own in the political wilderness of Virginia. But one future Calhounite, David Rice Atchison of Missouri, had been appointed and subsequently elected to the Senate that past December. Atchison was the first Missouri senator to hail from the state's western counties where the majority of Missouri's slave owners resided. Unlike Benton, Atchison did not own a single slave, but he ably represented the interests of Missouri slave owners, which included support for Texas annexation. Initially Benton was "much pleased" with Atchison's appointment, but his "general satisfaction" with Atchison quickly dissipated. In less than a year Missouri's freshman senator would become Thomas Hart Benton's bitter rival and one of Calhoun's ablest allies.

CHAPTER TWO

Heirs of Calhoun

When Roy F. Nichols called the southern leadership of the future Thirty-Third Congress the "heirs of Calhoun," he was referring specifically to their acceptance of Calhoun's constitutional theories, including the argument that the Fifth Amendment protected the expansion of slavery into all the territories. But for the F Street Mess, their inheritance went beyond Calhoun's constitutional thinking to include familial, state, and educational ties. Calhoun and Butler were both from South Carolina and as young men attended the same preparatory school, though not at the same time. Hunter, Mason, and Butler all messed with Calhoun at one time or another during their congressional careers. Hunter shared Calhoun's intellectualism, advised him on his presidential campaigns, and wrote Calhoun's campaign biography in 1843. Calhoun's final speech on the Senate floor in 1850 would be read on his behalf by James Murray Mason. And after Calhoun's death, Mason would lead the congressional delegation that escorted his body back to South Carolina. Clearly the F Street Mess shared a "proximity" to Calhoun that their contemporaries did not. They not only inherited Calhoun's constitutionalism but also inherited his political acumen. But in 1844 only one member of the future Mess, David Rice Atchison, was in the Senate to help with confirmation of the Texas annexation treaty. And he was not yet fully a follower of Calhoun.

Atchison had been appointed to the Senate to fill the unexpired term of Lewis Linn, who had died in October. He hailed from the state's Northwest, where Missouri's heaviest concentration of slaves and slave owners resided. This proslavery constituency placed Atchison immediately at odds with Benton, leader of the state's Free-Soil faction and "undisputed overlord of Missouri politics."[1]

Unlike his future messmates, who could trace their lineage back to landed gentry in England or colonial America, Atchison was third-generation Scotch-Irish.[2] His grandfather Alexander Atchison migrated from Ireland to Lancaster,

Pennsylvania, in the latter half of the eighteenth century, where Atchison's father William was born in 1780. In 1786 Alexander Atchison moved the family to Kentucky, settling in Fayette County near Lexington. In 1806 twenty-six-year-old William married twenty-year-old Catherine Allen from Georgia. The first of their six children, David Rice Atchison, was born August 11, 1807. He was named for the Presbyterian minister and founder of Kentucky's first Presbyterian church, David Rice. Atchison's parents, middle-class farmers, intended for their firstborn to go into the ministry and in 1821 enrolled their fourteen-year-old son in Transylvania University at Lexington, where the Reverend Rice was a professor. The young Atchison's classmates included Jefferson Davis.[3] Atchison graduated in 1825, but rather than going into the ministry, he stayed in Lexington to attend law school and study under Charles Humphreys. He was admitted to the bar in 1827 at the age of twenty. Like his future mentor Calhoun, Atchison would become a lifelong religious skeptic and that skepticism shaped his independent adult life that began in 1830 when he moved to Missouri.

Atchison established a legal practice in the frontier settlement of Liberty in Clay County, Missouri, where he rose quickly in local politics and was elected to the state legislature in 1833. Clay County was one of the western counties that bordered the 2 million fertile acres along the east side of the Missouri River known as the Platte. It was home to the Sacs, Foxes, Iowas, and other Native American tribes, many of which had been forcibly relocated there by the federal government. At the beginning of the decade few whites lived in the area until Mormons from New York and Ohio began to settle the region led by there by their prophet, Joseph Smith, who had envisioned Missouri as the Mormon Zion. These two groups, Native Americans and Mormons, physically and culturally stood in the way of the rest of Missouri's white Christian advance. In 1835 white Missourians by the hundreds began to move into the Platte violating tribal treaty provisions. Two years later the state officially annexed the Platte, known as the Platte Purchase, and forcibly relocated the Native Americans west of the Missouri.

All that was left for the Missourians to have open access to the land were the troublesome Mormons. To remove them, Missourians resorted to a tactic common in the American West of the 1830s, mob violence. For nineteenth-century western Americans popular sovereignty was more than the right to vote; it was a kind of common man's royal prerogative. It allowed Missourians to interpret or create law as they saw fit. It led to an overuse of volunteer militias that often devolved into vigilantism, rendering what little local authority that did exist "powerless in suppressing extralegal violence."[4]

The attack on the Mormons began years before the state successfully annexed the Platte. In 1833 David Rice Atchison was retained by a group of Mormons whose property had been seized in nearby Jackson County by their non-Mormon neighbors. Atchison, his leadership position in Clay County and state legislative office aside, was unable to get the Mormons' property returned. Nor did his local constituents want the Mormons to settle in Clay County. In December 1836, Atchison, along with the only other men in Clay County willing to help the Mormons, representative Alexander Doniphan and Judge Elisha Cameron, got the state legislature to create an exclusive Mormon county out of a portion of Ray County to the north. The newly created county was named Caldwell.[5]

Similar to the treaties negotiated with Native Americans since the first century of European contact, the state agreement with the Mormons did not last because it was not meant to last.[6] For the Mormons, the agreement meant Missourians could not settle in Caldwell County without Mormon permission. It did not mean Mormons could not live anywhere else. For Missourians the agreement meant the opposite: Missourians could settle inside Caldwell County if they chose, but Mormons could not expand beyond Caldwell County. The failure of either side to comply with the agreement as the other interpreted it caused conflict immediately. Both sides raised vigilante armies, and violence ensued. It became known as the Mormon War of 1838.

On September 10, 1838, circuit court judge Austin King, who had been "deluged with reports of disturbances and pleas for military intervention in Daviess County, from both Mormons and Missourians," ordered Atchison, who was a general in the state militia, to call out the militia and restore order. Atchison, who had represented Mormon interests in the past, was literally a man caught in the middle. He hesitated and, in doing so, incurred the wrath of Missouri governor Lilburn Boggs, who solved Atchison's dilemma by relieving him of command.[7]

The Mormon War ended with the surrender of Joseph Smith and his army of eight hundred on November 1, 1838. Thousands of Mormons were expelled from Missouri, most resettling in Illinois. Less than two decades later, Missourians would once again resort to civil warfare in Kansas, and David Rice Atchison would lead them.

After the Mormon War, Atchison was reelected to the state legislature for a second term, and in 1840 he was appointed circuit court judge for the newly created twelfth judicial district for the Platte Purchase. He moved to Platte City shortly thereafter. It was his home for the next twenty-six years.[8] On October 3, 1843 Missouri senator Lewis F. Linn died in Washington. Atchison was appointed to fill his unexpired term, becoming the first U.S. senator from western Missouri. He was thirty-six years old.

At 6′ 2″ and weighing two hundred pounds, David Rice Atchison was an imposing figure when he took his seat in the U.S. Senate on December 4, 1843. He was a strict constructionist, states' rights conservative, western expansionist Democrat who opposed federal funding of internal improvements but supported land-grant legislation to aid in the private construction of railroads. His rank of major general in the Platte County militia got him on the Committee on Militias where he opposed increasing the size of the regular army. As a member of the Committee on Indian Affairs, Atchison had a surprisingly non-western expansionist attitude toward Native Americans, which stemmed from his Marshallesque attitude toward the sanctity of contracts, whether it involved Mormon property titles or Indian treaties.[9] He believed in extinguishing titles and treaties through negotiated settlement. This and his proslavery expansionism would quickly put him at odds with his state's senior senator, Thomas Hart Benton.

Texas had declared its independence from Mexico in 1836, the same year Congress instituted the gag rule, after thousands of antislavery petitions from northern abolitionists, many in opposition to Texas annexation, flooded the Capitol.[10] As historian Michael Holt argues, northerners opposed and southerners supported annexation "for precisely the same reasons . . . more land, more political power and more security for the South in general and for slaveholders in particular."[11] Martin Van Buren and his Whig successor, William Henry Harrison opposed annexation. But Vice President John Tyler, the slave-owning Virginia Whig who became president after Harrison's death in April 1841, was no more philosophically aligned with the Whig Party than his Secretary of State, John C. Calhoun had been in the thirties. Both men wanted Texas annexation in order to protect southern interests.

On June 8 the treaty for Texas annexation was defeated in the Senate. Eight northern Democrats had joined twenty-seven northern Whigs to defeat the treaty by a vote of 35 to 16. Calhoun had anticipated the Senate vote and saw victory in the treaty's defeat. The vote against annexation gave Calhoun what the leadership of both parties feared, a vote along sectional lines.[12]

That summer at the Democratic National Convention in Baltimore, southerners blocked Martin Van Buren's nomination because of his opposition to Texas annexation. The nomination went to Tennessee expansionist James K. Polk instead. The Whig Party saw its chance and nominated party leader Henry Clay of Kentucky, a vocal opponent to annexation. The Whigs mistakenly believed opposition to Texas annexation was a winning issue, not unlike their National Republican ancestors who had mistakenly believed their stance supporting a National Bank was a winning issue against Andrew Jackson.

In his seminal study of the Whig Party, Michael Holt calls Texas the "transcending" issue in the election of 1844. But it was not Texas per se that transcended the election of 1844; it was nineteenth-century Manifest Destiny. In the election, southerners and westerners put aside their differences on the question of slavery to elect an expansionist president. Clay saw the mistake early and tried to modify his position on Texas only to lose the abolitionist wing of the party to the newly created Liberty Party.[13] James K. Polk won the presidency 170 to 105 electoral votes, though the popular vote was much closer, 1,337,000 to 1,299,000. The Democratic Party also made significant gains at the congressional and state level that included the election of Robert M. T. Hunter, who had been gerrymandered out of his House seat two years earlier. It was Hunter's first run as a Democrat, beating incumbent Whig congressman Willoughby Newton.

On January 2 the House of Representatives approved a resolution to immediately annex Texas into the Union bypassing the territorial stage. It passed in the Senate after an amendment, offered by Robert Walker of Mississippi, was added giving the president the option to further negotiate with the Texas Convention. President Tyler did not use the option and signed the resolution to annex Texas on March 1. Three days later James K. Polk was inaugurated. Calhoun, who was not kept on at State, returned home to South Carolina to contend with states' rights politicians who were again agitating against the tariff. On July 4 the Texas Convention approved the annexation treaty and entered the Union on December 29.

Earlier that fall Senator Daniel Huger of South Carolina resigned from the U.S. Senate, and John C. Calhoun was elected to fill his unexpired term. He returned to Washington in December and met with Robert M. T. Hunter and Isaac Holmes to discuss their mutual concerns over the president's aggressive posturing toward Great Britain and Mexico. Great Britain was resisting American overtures toward annexation of the jointly owned Oregon Territory, and Mexico had broken off diplomatic relations after the annexation of Texas. Calhoun, Hunter, and Holmes supported Texas annexation but opposed any additional expansion by conquest. They feared war with Mexico would not be worth the financial and human cost and would adversely affect negotiations with Great Britain over Oregon. Calhoun in particular feared the possibility of European intervention if the United States attempted to take all of Mexico. All three expressed fears typical of nineteenth-century Americans, North and

South, who were uncomfortable about incorporating into the Republic people that were culturally and ethnically different.[14]

On May 13, 1846, the United States of America went to war against the Republic of Mexico on the pretext that American soldiers had been attacked by Mexican soldiers on American soil. The following month the Senate ratified a treaty with Great Britain dividing the Oregon Territory at the forty-ninth parallel. Missouri's two senators, Benton and Atchison, both voted against the treaty, believing it gave up too much territory. As late as 1846 expansion at all costs still trumped either senator's position on slavery.

That same fall George McDuffie, the junior senator from South Carolina to the U.S. Senate, resigned his seat after suffering a stroke. In a tight race between former governor James Henry Hammond and appeals court judge Andrew Pickens Butler, the legislature elected Butler to fill McDuffie's unexpired term.[15] Butler took his seat in the Twenty-Ninth Congress alongside his mentor, John C. Calhoun, on December 5, 1846.

Andrew Pickens Butler was a member of the illustrious Butler family of Edgefield County in western South Carolina on the other side of the Savannah River from Georgia. Like the Garnett and Hunter families of Virginia, the multigenerational intermarriages between the Butlers and other prominent South Carolina families created an Edgefield "elite," a complicated and confusing network of familial alliances that controlled the state socially and politically. Butler's familial ties included contemporaries John C. Calhoun and the future secessionist governor, Francis Pickens.[16]

The Butlers were also a tragic family. Andrew Pickens Butler's grandfather, James Butler Sr., and uncle, James Jr., were killed in the American Revolution.[17] Butler's brother, Pierce Mason Butler, former governor of the state, died in 1847 fighting in the Mexican-American War. His sister Emmala, the wife of Waddy Thompson, died the same year.[18] Butler himself was widowed twice. His first wife, Susan Ann Simkins died in 1830. They had no children. Two years later Butler married Harriet Hayne of Charleston. They had one daughter, Eloise Brevard, called Nancy by the family. Harriet Hayne Butler died in 1834. Nancy was essentially raised by her grandmother Behethland, who kept Butler's home for him in Edgefield until her death at the age of eighty-six in 1851.

Andrew Pickens Butler was born in Edgefield, South Carolina, on November 18, 1796, the fifth son of revolutionary war general William Butler and Behethland Foote Moore.[19] He was named for the illustrious Revolutionary general and guerilla leader Andrew Pickens and called "Pickens" by the family.[20] He received his primary education at what was then the local neighborhood school for sons of upcountry gentlemen, the Moses Waddell Academy in Abbeville.[21]

He later attended South Carolina College in Columbia, graduating in 1817. He studied law for the next two years and was admitted to the bar in December 1818. In 1819 he returned to Edgefield and established both a legal practice and plantation named Stonelands. Butler's practice extended into Lexington, Barnwell, and Newberry districts.

In 1824 Butler was elected to represent Edgefield in the lower house of the South Carolina General Assembly. He was reelected in 1826, 1828, and 1830. As the recognized leader of the Calhoun faction in the General Assembly, Butler was elected to the state Senate in 1832, where he led the fight for nullification. He resigned from the Senate on December 19, 1833, after being appointed first to the state circuit court and advancing the same year to the Court of Appeals, where he served for the next thirteen years.[22]

Despite his longevity on the bench, everyone who knew Butler agreed his temperament was not suited for it. The hours were long, the court schedule packed, and, at least initially, the pay was poor. Butler, who was considered an "honorable and fair judge," nevertheless was known to show his impatience "without knowing it."[23] In 1846, he was rescued from his long years on the bench by his election to the U.S. Senate, just weeks before the election of Robert M. T. Hunter and James Murray Mason to the same body.

Robert Hunter's political star had been on the rise for a second time ever since his reelection to the House as a Democrat in 1844. In 1846 he aggressively pushed for the passage of the Walker tariff bill, written by Polk's secretary of the treasury and former Democratic senator from Mississippi, Robert Walker. The Walker Tariff, which reduced rates only moderately, was nevertheless strongly supported by southerners and westerners.[24] In the same year Hunter introduced a bill to retrocede Alexandria to Virginia. It passed on July 9, followed by passage of the Walker Tariff on July 31. That fall Hunter was elected by the state legislature to succeed the incumbent Whig senator William S. Archer. In January, Virginia's senior senator, Isaac Pennybacker, died in Washington. Pennybacker had been from Harrisonburg in the western part of the state. The legislature voted fellow westerner James Murray Mason to fill his unexpired term.

On March 4, 1847, Hunter and Mason took their seats in the U.S. Senate. For the first time all four members of the future F Street Mess, Robert M. T. Hunter, James Murray Mason, David Rice Atchison, and Andrew Pickens Butler, were together in the Senate, along with their mentor, John C. Calhoun. The newly elected Virginians carried with them resolutions from the Virginia state legislature. The resolutions included instructions to oppose any effort to prohibit slavery in the territories.

Since the early days of the war with Mexico, congressional abolitionists, beginning with Pennsylvania Democrat David Wilmot, had proposed legislation prohibiting slavery in territory ceded by Mexico as a consequence of the war. Calhoun and his followers believed that any federal restriction on slavery in the western territories violated the equal rights of citizens to property guaranteed under the Fifth Amendment. On February 19, 1847, Calhoun introduced six resolutions in the Senate similar to the Virginia resolutions carried by Hunter and Mason. He reiterated the standard arguments of equal protection in the territories, including the District of Columbia, a direct reference to legislative efforts to abolish slavery in the capital city. A year later, on March 10, 1848, the U.S. Senate ratified the Treaty of Guadalupe Hidalgo officially ending the two-year war with Mexico. Under the treaty, Mexico recognized Texas independence and ceded the additional territories of California, New Mexico, and Utah.

Calhoun's focus now turned to Oregon. No one anticipated settlers bringing slaves into Oregon, but after successfully blocking the passage of the Wilmot Proviso and similar efforts to prohibit slavery in the Mexican Cession, Calhoun and his followers feared the House bill prohibiting slavery in Oregon, passed in December 1847, would establish precedent. On July 11, Robert M. T. Hunter made his maiden speech in the Senate in support of Indiana Democrat Jesse Bright's amendment to extend the 36° 30' parallel compromise established for the Louisiana Purchase to the Pacific Coast. Once again, southerners supported and northerners opposed the Bright amendment for the same reason: extension of the 36° 30' to the Pacific would prohibit slavery in Oregon but allow it in the Mexican Cession. On July 12, the day after Hunter's maiden speech, a committee was appointed chaired by Delaware Whig John M. Clayton to study "the related problems of Oregon and the Mexican Cession." Democratic committee members included John C. Calhoun and David Rice Atchison. On July 18 the committee reported out its bill. Known as the "Clayton Compromise," it turned the question of slavery in the territories over to the courts by granting slaves the right "to sue in the federal territorial courts to see if slavery legally existed there and provided that the decision of the territorial court could then be directly appealed to the Supreme Court."[25] Northern and southern senators alike attacked the compromise. Southerners feared without a new federal statute that specifically allowed slavery in the Mexican Cession the federal courts might rule the original Mexican statute that outlawed it "still applied." Northerners feared the courts might prevent California and New Mexico from prohibiting it in their state constitutions.[26]

Despite the senators' misgivings, the chamber passed the Clayton Compromise on July 27. The House tabled it the following day, sending the original Oregon bill with slavery restricted back to the Senate. The Senate responded by passing the bill with the Bright amendment, but the House refused to concur. In the Senate, tempers flared. Andrew Pickens Butler, offended by comments directed at him in a speech by Thomas Hart Benton, challenged Benton to a duel. He and Benton were later calmed down by friends, and the duel was called off.[27] In the early morning hours of August 13, the Senate passed the House version of the Oregon bill after a series of parliamentarian maneuvers, initiated by Benton, stripped the bill of its amendments. Congress adjourned shortly thereafter, with the presidential election looming.

By 1848 John C. Calhoun's lifelong battle with poor health, including chronic heart trouble, tuberculosis, and repeated bouts with pneumonia, was nearing its end. There would be no final run for the presidency as earlier hoped. That summer the Democratic Party split three ways; between those loyal to the party nominee Lewis Cass of Michigan, northerners and westerners who left the party to support former Democratic president and current Free-Soil nominee Martin Van Buren, and southerners who left the party to support the Whig nominee, Virginia slave owner, and war hero Zachary Taylor.[28] Calhoun refused to commit to a candidate. Instead, for the first time he called for a nonpartisan southern party to combat what he saw as the growth of northern abolitionism.[29] The problem for Calhoun's followers, regardless of their state, was they could not afford to remain neutral in the election and win reelection themselves."[30] Nowhere was this truer than in Missouri where David Rice Atchison, facing his first reelection, supported the Democratic nominee, Lewis Cass. Thomas Hart Benton, however, vacillated between Cass and his friend, Free-Soil nominee Martin Van Buren. Unable to come out for either, Benton made himself figuratively absent from the race by making himself literally absent from the state. Missouri Democrats loyal to the party did not forget which of their senators remained loyal to the party nominee and which did not. Similarly, proslavery Missourians did not forget which senator represented their interests and which was increasingly hostile to them.

With just two years left to live, Calhoun had two goals left to achieve, the completion of his political treatises and the establishment of a southern party. Years earlier, in 1844, he had written Robert M. T. Hunter stating that his "treatise on government . . . require[d] thought," and he would "have to progress slowly."[31] Four years later he completed his opus, *The Disquisition on Government*. The *Disquisition*'s sequel, *Discourse on the Constitution and the Government of the United States* would be completed just prior to his death in 1850. Calhoun used material from both works in his final speeches on the Senate floor.[32]

When the Thirtieth Congress convened for its second session on December 4, 1848, Calhoun's final goal of establishing a southern party seemed within reach. On December 11, Stephen Douglas, chairman of the Senate Committee on the Territories, introduced a single bill organizing the Mexican Cession into one territory. President Polk urged two bills, one for the immediate annexation of California as a state, bypassing the territorial stage, and another for the territorial organization of New Mexico. On December 21, the House passed a bill to prohibit the slave trade in Washington, D.C. Two days later Robert Hunter and Senator Henry Foote of Mississippi circulated an invitation to all southern members of Congress to attend a caucus to decide a course of action. It was the first substantive step toward the establishment of a southern party. That evening a bipartisan meeting of southern members was held in the Senate chamber with eighteen senators and fifty-nine congressmen present. Thomas Hart Benton later stated he did not receive an invitation. Kentucky Whig Thomas Metcalfe was appointed chairman. David Rice Atchison and Alabama Whig John Gayle were appointed vice chairs. Metcalfe then appointed a committee of fifteen to draw up a statement of southern grievances not unlike those written by the English House of Commons in the seventeenth century or American Colonial Assemblies in the eighteenth century. For a second time since the Clayton Compromise Committee, Atchison sat on a committee with Calhoun, who was given the task of writing the statement.[33]

The statement, *Address of the Southern Delegates in Congress to Their Constituents*, was presented to the reconvened caucus, on January 22.[34] It listed all the South's grievances from the first federal effort to restrict slavery in Missouri in 1820 to the House bill prohibiting the slave trade in the District of Columbia. The address was adopted only after the most of the Whigs left the room. Those members remaining were asked to sign the address at their convenience. Robert Hunter was the first to sign. Forty-seven Democratic members followed, including Mason, Butler, and Atchison. Southern Whigs, including those who had stayed, refused to sign preferring to wait on the actions of the newly elected Whig president, Zachary Taylor.[35]

On January 24, Andrew Pickens Butler, chairman of the Judiciary Committee, had the Senate bill on California recommitted to a newly appointed select committee. One month later Butler and Hunter joined forces to amend it. The original bill that granted immediate statehood and excluded slavery under existing California law was amended to create a territorial government subject to federal law in which the status of slavery remained unclear. Neither chamber budged. The Thirtieth Congress adjourned on March 3, agreeing only to fund California's operating costs.[36] Just before leaving for South Carolina, Calhoun met with the newly inaugurated president, Zachary Taylor.[37] The meeting was cordial. Calhoun left Washington "convinced Taylor was 'well disposed to settle' the slavery question."[38]

On May 26, 1849, Benton gave a speech in Jefferson City, Missouri's state capital, in which he delivered a blistering attack against Calhoun and his followers accusing them of hypocrisy and treason. He argued that Calhoun had accepted Congress's constitutional right to prohibit slavery in 1820 with the Missouri Compromise only to change his position later, that his *Address to the Southern People* was a call for disunion, and, last but not least, that Calhoun was out to destroy him politically.[39]

Calhoun responded to Benton's attack in the *Pendleton Messenger* on July 20 stating "I never thought of such a thing. We move in different spheres. My course is, and has been, to have nothing to do with him. I never wanted his support, nor dreaded his opposition."[40] Calhoun may not have dreaded Benton's opposition, but he thought Benton a serious enough threat to slavery's expansion to closely monitor his reelection campaign. A review of Calhoun's published letters between August and December 1849 shows twice as many references to Benton's election than those referring to a southern convention. Atchison was Calhoun's lieutenant behind the scenes in Missouri. In no less than five letters, Calhoun mentions Atchison by name, and in one quotes his assurance that Benton had "as good a chance to be made Pope, as to be elected Senator."[41]

John C. Calhoun began his journey back to Washington in late November, spending the night of November 23 in Edgefield, the home of Andrew Pickens Butler. If, as is argued by Clyde Wilson, the purpose of Calhoun's long and about way back to Washington was to give him time to "confer with influential men along the way," it can be assumed Calhoun spent the night in Edgefield to confer with Butler.[42] Calhoun reached Washington on December 1 and took a room at H. V. Hill's boarding house directly across from the Capitol.[43] On December 8, he wrote his son-in-law Thomas Clemson in Brussels, "There is every indication, that we shall have a stormy session."[44]

Congress convened on December 3 far more divided than it had been in 1837 when it took eleven ballots to elect Robert Hunter Speaker of the House. This time the House took sixty-three ballots to elect Howell Cobb, a conservative Democrat from Georgia. Cobb was elected by a Whig majority because he had not signed Calhoun's *Southern Address*. Meanwhile in the Senate, Thomas Hart Benton, who had returned to Washington self-assured of his upcoming reelection back home, was shocked to find he had not been reappointed chairman of the Foreign Relations Committee. The chair was given to James Murray Mason. Benton blamed Calhoun for orchestrating his removal and resigned from the committee. The Democratic Caucus did not give him any other committee assignments.

On January 3, David Rice Atchison presented Missouri resolutions to the Senate, which, like those carried by Hunter and Mason, included instructions to oppose any effort to prohibit slavery in the territories.[45] Benton stated for the record he would not be bound by the resolutions. On January 10, Missouri's state legislature began the balloting for the U.S. Senate seat held by Benton. It continued over the next four days with no one candidate receiving the majority. On January 14, sixteen anti-Benton Democrats cast their votes for proslavery Whig candidate Henry S. Geyer, giving him the victory over Benton on the fortieth ballot, 88 votes to Benton's 55. The Old Bullion's thirty-year term in the U.S. Senate was over.[46] Atchison, who had earlier written the editor of the *Platte Argus*, "Great God, give us a Whig before you give us a doubtful Democrat," could not have been more pleased.[47]

In January, Calhoun was stricken by another bout of pneumonia and confined to his room at Hill's for several weeks. His declining health became national news, second only to Congress's failure to end the stalemate over California and New Mexico and ancillary crises.[48] Calhoun's illness was national news because he was part of the illustrious senatorial trio, including Henry Clay and Daniel Webster, known later in history as the Great Triumvirate. The three men had served together in public office for four decades, becoming the very "personifications of their respective sections: East, West, and South," and the "foremost American statesmen of the age."[49]

The trio's biographer, Merrill Peterson, argues they were "more often political rivals" than "a triumvirate in fact." Nevertheless each was aware of the "interrelationship" and therefore "rarely made a move without calculating its effect on the others."[50] All three men moved effortlessly back and forth between the legislative and executive branches. Calhoun had been secretary of war under James Monroe, vice president under John Quincy Adams and Andrew Jackson, and secretary of state under John Tyler. Clay had been Speaker of the House in multiple Congresses, a commissioner to the peace negotiations with Great Britain in 1814, and secretary of state under John Quincy Adams. Daniel Webster had served as secretary of state under Presidents William Henry Harrison and John Tyler and would again, after Calhoun's death, under President Millard Fillmore. By 1850 each was nearing the end of his life, having achieved everything but their one common ambition, the presidency of the United States.

Henry Clay had just returned to the Senate after an absence of seven years. On January 29, he introduced eight resolutions designed to give concessions to both the North and the South; California would be annexed immediately to the Union as a free state and the remainder of the Mexican Cession would be organized without any restriction on slavery; the boundary dispute between Texas and New Mexico would be settled in favor of New Mexico and the federal government would assume Texas's War of Independence debt; the slave trade would be abolished in the District of Columbia but not slavery itself; Congress would have no power over interstate slave trade, but a new fugitive slave act would be enacted to better enable slave owners to recover property.

Robert M. T. Hunter and Andrew Pickens Butler made frequent visits to the ailing Calhoun's room to keep him abreast of the situation. Fearing the debate on Clay's resolutions would end before he could recover, Calhoun sent Butler a note on February 6. "I must request a favour of you," he wrote "have them postpone to some early day next week, say Tuesday [February 12] by which time my strength, I think, will be sufficiently restored to enable me to speak."[51] Calhoun had little to fear. The debate over Clay's resolutions took over the session. It was still ongoing when Calhoun made a brief appearance on the floor on February 18. On February 28, Butler asked to make a motion, on behalf of the absent Calhoun, that the senior senator from South Carolina be given time to speak before the body on that coming Monday, March 4, at 1:00 P.M. Butler's remarks were cut short by members of both parties. Calhoun was dying. They all knew it, and everyone, Democrat and Whig, northerner and southerner, agreed Butler's motion was not necessary.[52] According to Charles Wiltse, Daniel Webster, who had visited Calhoun on several occasions during the final weeks of Calhoun's life, returned to Hill's on March 2, two days before Calhoun's scheduled appearance in the chamber. By this time Calhoun's speech had been printed, and it was "possible that Webster read the speech in Calhoun's room, or more likely that Calhoun explained generally what he planned to say. In either event, Webster could not have ended his visit in an encouraged frame of mind."[53]

Monday, March 4, was "a bright springlike day."[54] Inside the Capitol the Senate chamber and its galleries were filled with people and expectation. Rules were suspended to allow for "the presence of ladies on the floor of the Senate, by whom the privileged seats were already occupied."[55] Copies of Calhoun's speech had been printed and circulated in advance. Questions as to his health and whether he would address the chamber abounded. Shortly after noon an "emaciated" Calhoun, wrapped in a long coat, entered the chamber on the arm of James Hamilton, former governor of South Carolina during the nullification Crisis and current lobbyist for Texas.[56] Sam Houston, who was in Texas, was the only senator not present.[57] Standing at his desk, Calhoun thanked the Senate for "the very courteous manner in which they afforded" him the "opportunity of being heard." Speaking slowly, he stated the obvious, "apprehending that it might not be in my power to deliver my sentiments before the termination of the debate, I have been reduced to writing what I intended to say." And so his "friend" James Murray Mason would read the speech for him.[58]

The spectral Calhoun "slumped" into his chair.[59] Behind him Mason, who after acknowledging his "great pleasure to comply with the request of the honorable Senator," began to read from Calhoun's prepared remarks, which Mason had asked to be printed to assure he read it accurately. Calhoun had originally asked Butler to read the speech, but Butler, whose eyesight was poor, recommended the younger Mason.[60] As Mason began to read, "Webster leaned forward."[61]

It was Calhoun's last speech, and it was a long one. The South, Calhoun argued, no longer felt safe in the Union. What had caused its fear, he asked? The simple but incomplete answer was "the long-continued agitation of the slave question on the part of the North, and the many aggressions which they have made on the rights of the South during the time." But, Calhoun continued, the greater and "primary" cause was not northern agitation but the loss of "equilibrium between the two sections in the government as it stood when the Constitution was ratified." The North's majority of states and population had given it "a predominance in every department of the government." The northern territories of Oregon and Minnesota had been organized and were likely to become free states within a few years. But no such equivalent progress was happening in the Southwest, where the question of its territorial organization had stalled in the Congress. Unless checked, the consequence Calhoun predicted would be a northern majority of twenty to fourteen states by the end of the decade.

Calhoun also addressed the ongoing issue of protective tariffs, which he argued did not put money in the Treasury but in the "pocket[s] of the [northern] manufacturers." But in the end he returned to the question of slavery. The North felt bound to abolish it. The South felt bound to defend it. Would the South be forced, he asked, to "choose between abolition and secession?" If so it would not be immediate. In words eerily similar to ones that would be used years later by a more optimistic Lincoln, Calhoun addressed the "cords" of Union which held the country together. "The cords which bind these States together in one common Union are far too numerous and powerful," he noted. "Disunion must be the work of time. It is only through a long process, and successively, that the cords can be snapped until the whole fabric falls asunder."

Calhoun's speech concluded with his demands. The South must have equal access to territory. The Constitution's fugitive slave clause must be enforced. Lastly, the Constitution must be amended to "restore to the South, in substance, the power she possessed of protecting herself before the equilibrium between the sections" had been destroyed by the present government.

> I have, Senators, believed from the first that the agitation of the subject of slavery would, if not prevented by some timely and effective measure, end in disunion. Entertaining this opinion, I have, on all occasions, endeavored to call the attention of each of the two great parties which divide the country to adopt some measure to prevent so great a disaster, but without success. The agitation has been permitted to proceed, with almost no attempt to resist it, until it has reached a period when it can no longer be disguised or denied that the Union is in danger. You have thus had forced upon you the greatest and the gravest question that can ever come under your consideration: How can the Union be preserved?

The chamber responded to the conclusion of Mason's reading in silence. Was it shock at the possibility of amending the Constitution in such a way as to change its very nature? Some believed Calhoun's amendment was code for a "dual executive." Or was it simply that Calhoun's pending death was so visible for all to see? No one wanted to rebut a man who was so ill it took two men to help him stand and escort him from the chamber. A decent amount of time would have to pass. It was decided the great orator from Massachusetts, Daniel Webster, would respond on March 7.

Calhoun made three more visits to the Senate chamber, March 6 and 13, to respond to remarks made by the more moderate southern Whig, Henry S. Foote of Mississippi, and March 7 to listen to Webster's speech. Webster visited Calhoun the day before his speech. The two men were alone for six or seven hours.[62] Webster's speech entitled The Constitution and Union or Plea for Union in which he famously spoke "not as a Massachusetts man, nor as a Northern man, but as an American" was a call for conciliation on both sides. Despite his plea for "harmony," Webster received significant criticism from both northern and southern extremists. Nor did it impress Calhoun. Feeling physically better, Calhoun instructed Butler on March 27 to request another delay for Tuesday, April 2 when he would speak again.

At noon Monday, April 1, 1850, the U.S. Senate was called to order. The galleries had filled hours before. Those turned away, nearly one in ten, filled the lobbies and blocked the entrances to the chamber. Inside former members, cabinet secretaries, and other federal officials crowded in with the current members. On a motion by William Rufus King of Alabama, the reading of the journal was dispensed with. The chamber and the galleries grew still as Andrew Pickens Butler of South Carolina rose to make official what all in attendance already knew, that "one of the brightest luminaries [had] been extinguished from the political firmament:"[63] Turning to the dais where his future messmate sat, Butler began his remarks, "Mr. President, I rise to discharge a mournful duty, and one which involves in it considerations well calculated to arrest the attention of this body. It is to announce the death of my late colleague, the Honorable John Caldwell Calhoun. He died at his lodgings in this city, on yesterday morning, at half-past seven o'clock. He was conscious of his approaching end, and met death with fortitude and uncommon serenity."[64]

After reading a brief biography of Calhoun, Butler introduced three resolutions: for the Senate to go into mourning for one month; for the vice president to appoint a committee to supervise the Senate's funeral for Calhoun the following noon; and for the Senate, out of respect, to adjourn immediately.[65] Henry Clay of Kentucky stood to second the resolutions. His career had spanned the same four decades as Calhoun's. Together they had entered the House in 1809 as freshmen Republicans and leaders of the faction known as the War Hawks, whose call for an aggressive foreign policy against Great Britain ultimately led to war in 1812. Clay and Calhoun's political alliance crumbled in the decades following the war, as each joined opposing parties in the second political system that formed in the thirties. Calhoun had spent the last three months of his life opposing Clay's resolutions on the Mexican Cession, which included the admission of California as a free state. By the time of Calhoun's death the increasingly acrimonious debate over whether or not to limit the spread of slavery into the territories ceded by Mexico had brought the country to the brink of civil war.

A murmur rose in the galleries and then silence as the figure of Henry Clay rose to second the resolutions. "Mr. President, prompted by my own feelings of profound regret," Clay stated solemnly, "I wish, in rising to second the resolutions which have been offered . . . to add a few words." Clay did not wish to speak in detail about his differences with Calhoun but preferred instead to focus on the man with whom he had had the "happiness" to agree with in "large part," especially when it came "to the preservation of the peace of the country." He called Calhoun's talents "transcendent" and bemoaned the loss of his "clear, concise, compact logic." He urged those in the chamber, the galleries, and beyond to use the "melancholy occasion" of Calhoun's death to set aside partisan differences and instead learn from the example of his character. He ended by challenging his fellow senators to follow their "consciences, as he [Calhoun] did, according to his honest and best conceptions of those duties, faithfully, and to the last."[66] His remarks finished, Clay sat.

Daniel Webster took the floor next and asked for the body's indulgence. Like Clay, Webster began his remarks acknowledging his political differences with Calhoun but also paying homage to the South Carolinian's intellect and historical impact. Unlike Clay, who had spoken in a solemn tone, the normally stylized Webster struggled to maintain his composure and ended his melancholic remarks by noting "the time shall come that we ourselves shall go, one after another, in succession, to our graves."[67]

"The tripod is broken," wrote the *New York Herald*'s Washington reporter covering the proceedings, "the historical associations of forty years are broken. There were but two of them on the floor of the Senate today, and they stood like the remaining columns of a ruined temple, recalling the reminiscences of an era that is past, and of generations long gathered to the grave. Their voices spoke of the history and experience of the past—their presence blended the living with the dead."[68]

Calhoun was dead, and the two who eulogized him, Clay and Webster, would follow in the next two years.[69] They were the dead addressing a body of the living that included fifty-two senators who had been elected after 1840, nearly one-third of whom after 1847. More than half were under the age of fifty.[70] While many had been state legislators and governors and others U.S. congressmen, they were nevertheless freshmen senators, lacking the institutional experience of a Calhoun, a Clay, a Webster. In the hands of these men, not those of the Great Triumvirate, would be left the crises of the 1850s. Among the fifty-two were eleven followers of Calhoun. Their allegiance to the man and his principles was so absolute it made them, and their associates in the House, a congressional faction to be reckoned with. Four of them, Robert M. T. Hunter, James Murray Mason, Andrew Pickens Butler, and David Rice Atchison (respectively, ages thirty-eight, fifty-one, fifty-four, and forty-two) were poised to become the new institutional power in the Senate. Less romantic than the legendary triumvirate before them, this quadrangle of senators was about to become a "true" power that no individual or group in Washington could ignore. They were glued together by personal friendship and ideological inheritance; they were the heirs of Calhoun.

CHAPTER THREE

Nebraska

John C. Calhoun died on March 31, 1850, at the height of the debate over five separate pieces of legislation relating to the territories ceded by Mexico to the United States two years earlier. Henry Clay, the bills' floor leader in the Senate, hoped they would pass if packaged as an omnibus measure. They did not. Calhoun's followers in Congress, led in the Senate by its president, David Rice Atchison, and fellow senators Robert M. T. Hunter, James Murray Mason, and Andrew Pickens Butler ensured Clay's omnibus package went down in defeat on July 31, four months to the day after the death of their mentor Calhoun. The only one of Clay's bills that passed was the Utah territorial bill which included the clause "when admitted as a State, the said Territory [Utah], or any portion of the same, shall be received into the Union, with or without slavery, as their constitution may prescribe at the time of their admission."[1] It was the first use of congressional nonintervention or "popular sovereignty" in a territorial bill.

Clay left Washington after the defeat of his omnibus package and did not return until the end of the session.[2] It was left to Stephen Douglas, chairman of the Committee on Territories, to revise Clay's strategy to overcome the objections of Calhoun's followers in the Senate. He did so by combining the members' general exhaustion with concessions to the South, specifically the new fugitive slave act authored by Mason of Virginia.[3] This time the measures, though virtually the same as those that had been defeated mere weeks before, passed. The bills were reported out of Douglas's committee on August 5. One by one he shepherded each through the Senate. Texas and California were admitted into the Union as states on August 9 and 13, respectively, thus continuing the informal congressional process begun at the beginning of the Republic of admitting states in pairs, one free and one slave. The New Mexico territorial bill with the same nonintervention language as the Utah bill was passed on August 15. With the statehood and territorial bills out of the way, the Senate, under Douglas's leadership, tackled the more controversial fugitive slave act and abolition of the slave trade in Washington, using an alliance of northern

Democrats and southern Whigs to help carry each bill across sectional lines. Abolition of the slave trade in Washington passed on September 16. Two days later the Fugitive Slave Act passed. The bills followed a similar route in the House of Representatives and on September 20 President Millard Fillmore signed the final act, the abolition of the slave trade in Washington, into law. Congress adjourned ten days later.

Fear of secession and the union's imminent demise had been growing among the public during the crisis of 1850. The country's relief with the passage of what would become known as the Compromise of 1850 was immediate. Public celebrations erupted in Washington spreading throughout the country and into the fall. Congressmen and senators returning to Washington for the second session of the Thirty-First Congress in November were greeted with enthusiastic business advertisements. The painter William Porter, "having full confidence in the patriotism and stability of the American people for self-government, consequently not fearing a dissolution of the Union," ran an ad in the city directory announcing that he "enlarged and improved his Shop," wherein he was "prepared to execute with promptness, in the best manner, all orders in his line of business with which he may be favored."[4]

It had been a singular celebratory sigh of national relief after which most Americans returned to "their daily lives, preoccupied with their personal affairs."[5] Democratic and Whig Party leaders alike saw the country's acceptance of the compromise as key to national victory in 1852. Pro- and antislavery factions within both parties were suppressed, and acceptance of the compromise was made part of each party's platform.[6]

But trouble loomed beyond the Compromise's proclaimed accomplishments of staving off civil war and settling the slavery issue. The Compromise of 1850 had created a bicoastal nation with a hole in its middle. To get from the east side of the United States to the west side of the United States you had to either take a ship around the southern tip of South America, the Cape of Good Hope, up to San Francisco, or travel illegally and unprotected through two thousand miles of Indian Country, the unorganized territory of Nebraska.[7]

None of the issues confronting Congress between 1851 and 1854, including white settlement, Indian land titles, railroad legislation, land speculation, national security, and the Asian trade could be dealt with effectively as long as Nebraska remained unorganized. But Nebraska lay above the 36° 30′ parallel, and under the provisions of the Compromise of 1820 slavery was prohibited. That compromise, which had worked for thirty years, now threatened to undo the very one passed by Congress only four months earlier. Within the next three years the Nebraska question would not only resurrect the slavery issue supposedly settled by the Compromise of 1850 but would also place the needs of the nation in conflict with the private interests of those senators most responsible for solving it: Stephen A. Douglas of Illinois, chairman of the Senate Committee on Territories, and Senate leaders David Rice Atchison, Robert M. T. Hunter, James Murray Mason, and Andrew Pickens Butler. In 1853, with the Nebraska issue looming, Atchison, Hunter, Mason, and Butler would finally find a house, the location of which would give the group its name.

"Judge Butler has returned," Hunter wrote his wife in May 1852, "and we are determined to move out to the suburbs of the town, to Mr. [Havenner's], which is almost in the country."[8] The country for Hunter, Mason, and Butler was Havenner's boarding house on C Street, one mile north of the Capitol. The desire for country living, however, did not last long, and by the second session of the Thirty-Second Congress the trio had moved back closer to the Capitol, to Brown's Hotel on Pennsylvania Avenue, where they were joined by Atchison.[9] By the time the Thirty-Third Congress convened in December 1853 the four men had purchased a house together at 361 F Street between Ninth and Tenth Streets.

Hunter and Mason first messed together as congressmen in 1837 and again when they were elected to the Senate in 1846. Joining them that year was Senator Butler of South Carolina.[10] The mess arrangement of these three men, was typical of the earlier nineteenth century when a member's state, region and philosophical leanings, and not necessarily party affiliation, determined mess arrangements.[11] All three men were from the Southeast, had been born into and later married into old established families, attended distinguished East Coast colleges, and inherited, literally and figuratively, the legacy of slavery. Hunter and Butler owned sizeable plantations dependent upon slave labor, and while Mason did not farm, he maintained a sizable number of house slaves.[12] Who these men were and where they came from made them not just ideological heirs of Calhoun but also natural messmates.

But the fourth member of the Mess, David Rice Atchison, was different. He was a westerner, born in Kentucky, and his family possessed neither lineage nor great wealth. As a young man Atchison moved to Missouri, where he set up a legal practice and rode the circuit. He never married. Atchison's father owned eight slaves, but Atchison never farmed or owned a single slave until his retirement from the U.S. Senate in 1855.[13] Not surprisingly, Atchison's living arrangements during the 1840s were separate from those of his future messmates. Before he became a disciple of Calhoun, Atchison had more in common with fellow midwesterner Stephen A. Douglas. Both chose as young men to move West to make their marks. Atchison was only twenty-two when he moved to Liberty, Missouri, in 1829. Douglas was only twenty when he moved to Winchester, Illinois, in 1833. And both men rose quickly in their respective states' Democratic parties on a platform of aggressive expansionism.

When Atchison voted in favor of Texas annexation in 1844, he had already been advocating Oregon annexation for a year. He introduced his first bill to abrogate the joint treaty with Great Britain and annex all of Oregon up to the fifty-fourth parallel in December 1843. Atchison's position on Oregon put him in direct opposition with then secretary of state John C. Calhoun. His bill was sent to a select committee on Oregon, to which he was named chair. From there Atchison continued to report out bills on Oregon every session until 1846 claiming that such action helped, not hindered, the administration's ongoing negotiations with Great Britain. When at last the Polk administration submitted the Oregon Treaty in April 1846, Atchison voted against it for having given up too much territory. The following month he voted to go to war against Mexico, which Calhoun opposed. The following year he voted against the Treaty of Guadalupe Hidalgo for awarding the United States too little territory. By the end of the decade no one could claim to be more consistently proexpansionist than Atchison. But by the end of the decade this young, nonslaveholding, western expansionist bachelor of modest means had also become a leading proslavery Calhounite, and in 1853 Atchison would find it difficult to reconcile both his expansionist and proslavery leanings.

Why Atchison changed is somewhat elusive. Historically, Atchison is seen as the proslavery counterpart to Missouri's Free-Soil senator Thomas Hart Benton. But this interpretation assumes Missouri's proslavery and Free-Soil constituencies were evenly divided; they were not. Missouri was the second-smallest slave-holding state in the Union next to Delaware. Its slave population was never higher than 15 percent in 1820, and it dropped steadily to 9.7 percent in 1860.[14]

Missouri's slave population was concentrated in a seventeen-county strip through the center of the state from Callaway County just north of St. Louis on the east across to Platte County on the west. The region was called Little Dixie because its seventeen counties' slave percentages, ranging between 20 and 50 percent, were significantly higher than the state average. Little Dixie also contained the state's largest percentage of landowners, 61.4 percent, and contained 43 percent of the state's white population.[15] But Little Dixie's "slave power" did not did not correspond legislatively. In 1837 Little Dixie controlled only 25 percent of general assembly seats and 27 percent in the senate. Atchison lived in Platte City in Platte County, one of six counties in northwest Missouri carved from the 1837 Platte Purchase. Having just been added to the state, Platte County did not even have a senate seat. When the state legislature was reapportioned in 1845, Little Dixie's influence dropped further to 15 percent in the general assembly and 18 percent in the senate. Missouri slave power was decidedly lacking in terms of legislative influence.[16]

When Atchison became the first U.S. senator from northwest Missouri in 1843, the interests of the northwest and the interests of Little Dixie were beginning to overlap. As the slave population declined statewide, it pushed westward through Little Dixie into Platte County. By 1860 Platte's slave population was the tenth largest in the state.[17] The growth of slavery in Atchison's home county may have contributed to his political realignment in the late 1840s as well as his desire to become a planter in the future.

Atchison was born in 1807 on a modest frontier Kentucky farm of less than five hundred acres at the edge of the nation's frontier. By the time he left for college at the age of fourteen, Atchison's social activities comprised little more than hunting and bible reading. At Transylvania University in Lexington, his lack of worldliness was visible to his classmates. Fellow classmate Jefferson Davis described him as "'a tall country boy, true hearted and honest, with many virtues, but without grace or tact.'"[18] When they met again in the U.S. Senate years later, Davis teased Atchison about his boyhood country accent. True to Davis's earlier assessment, Atchison took it with good humor.

In many ways Atchison's background and ambition were strikingly similar to another self-made westerner, Abraham Lincoln. They too were close in age. Both were born on the frontier. Both rejected the lives chosen for them by their fathers. And both chose law as the quickest path to social and political prominence.[19] Biographical descriptions of Atchison's nature, eerily similar to Lincoln's, emphasize his unostentatious, unassuming, and convivial nature. But that's where the similarities end.

Lincoln did not drink. Atchison would develop a reputation for it, as well as a tendency toward profanity and violence. And whereas Lincoln would spend only two years in Congress before returning to provincial Springfield, Atchison would spend twelve consecutive years in the center of national power and society, learning to enjoy the finer things in life and moving in ever-closer concentric circles with Calhoun and his followers.[20] When Atchison first arrived in Washington in 1843, Thomas Hart Benton had assisted him in securing lodging at Masi's boarding house near Benton's home on C Street. Within two years he had moved away from his senior senator, physically and politically.

In 1846 Atchison moved to Coleman's Hotel at the corner of Pennsylvania Avenue and Sixth Street, west. Among the members living at Coleman's that session were Illinois's Senator Sidney Breese and Congressman Edward Baker and Indiana's Senators Jesse Bright and E. A. Hannegan. The high number of westerners suggests Atchison was making a mess choice based on region, but Coleman's hosted members from all over the country including Senators W. H. Haywood of North Carolina and J. W. Huntington of Connecticut. It was one of several hotels on Pennsylvania Avenue that catered to senators and congressmen from across the country.[21] The large number of members living in the hotels along Pennsylvania Avenue suggests more of an informal quorum than a mess, and Atchison may have seen political and social benefits in living there.[22] Intentional or not, it paid off. Just prior to the Twenty-Ninth Congress's adjournment in August 1846, Atchison was elected president pro tempore by unanimous vote. He would be reelected sixteen times between 1846 and 1854, unanimous in all but one.

In December 1847 Atchison presided over a new Senate filled with freshmen senators. Five of them, Robert M. T. Hunter, James Murray Mason, Andrew Pickens Butler, Jefferson Davis, and Stephen Douglas, rose quickly in Senate leadership, becoming committee chairmen of Finance, Foreign Affairs, Judiciary, Military Affairs, and Territories, respectively.[23] All but Douglas were fierce pro-slavery advocates. At the time Atchison remained more aligned with Douglas and other western expansionists whose priority in the Thirtieth Congress was opening up the unorganized territory of Nebraska, also known as "the Platte."[24]

Americans had been using Nebraska's Platte Valley as a route to the Pacific ever since the region was first explored by Lewis and Clarke. In 1834 Congress passed the Indian Intercourse Act permanently designating Nebraska as Indian Country unopened to white settlement.[25] The consequence of the act was evident after the Compromise of 1850 created a bicoastal nation. No two men would be more responsible for fixing the problem than David Rice Atchison and Stephen A. Douglas.

Nebraska was the most northern and last unorganized region of the original 1803 Louisiana Purchase. Approximately 335,882 square miles, it was situated one thousand miles west of the Atlantic coast, "midway between the Gulf of Mexico and the Arctic separated from the east by the Missouri River and the west by the Rockies."[26] Claimed by both the Spanish and the French in the sixteenth century, Nebraska remained largely unexplored and uninhabited by whites. In 1803 it was sold as part of the Louisiana territory to the United States by France, the government of which had granted occupancy, not title, to the tribes living therein.[27]

The Indians' concept of title differed from that of the U.S. government. For the Indians living in Nebraska and beyond, "continuous occupancy and use" determined title, and disputes over hunting rights, "acquired and retained by actual use" or "physical force," were the primary cause of intertribal warfare.[28] It was a loose concept that did not include defined borders. Occupancy by various tribes could and often did overlap. In Nebraska, therefore, the Otoe and Missouri tended to occupy the Southeast. The Omaha were in the Northeast. The Pawnee, the only truly indigenous tribe to Nebraska, were in the central plains and the Republican River Valley.[29] The High Plains was home to the Cheyenne, Apache, and the various bands of the Teton Sioux, including the Dakota, Brule, and Oglala.[30]

The U.S. government definition of title, on the other hand, was based on the English antecedents of discovery and conquest. Under this definition the government retained the "power to grant the soil while yet in the possession of the natives" to anyone it chose.[31] Whether occupancy determined title became the primary factor in the unfolding tragedy of the American West; through a series of "political acts and court decisions," the United States ultimately extinguished the Indians' title to virtually all the land west of the Mississippi."[32]

In 1803 Thomas Jefferson commissioned his secretary Meriwether Lewis and fellow Virginian William Clarke to ascend the Missouri River and find a practical route to the Pacific, mapping the land and making scientific observations along the way. It took Lewis and Clarke four years to reach the Pacific in what became the Corps of Discovery. They reached the southeastern edge of the Nebraska Territory earlier in their explorations, in June 1804, but did not go north of the Platte River. The next American to explore Nebraska was Zebulon Pike. In 1806 Pike escorted a delegation of Osage Indians returning from Washington west along the Missouri into the center of Nebraska to their village in present-day Kansas. But he too did not venture further north than the future border between Kansas and Nebraska. Instead, he traveled southwest along the Republican River to the Arkansas into the Great Plains, the approximate route of the future Santa Fe Trail. By the mid-nineteenth century whites would use either the Santa Fe or the other major trail, the Oregon, to travel westward to California and Oregon.

One of the unique features of Nebraska is that its land mass tilts upward from a low elevation of 700 feet in the southeast to 4,135 feet in the northwest. "The increase in elevation coincides with a decrease in rainfall . . . in steady progression from a generally well-watered country into a country . . . at the land's western end [where] generally semi-arid conditions prevail."[33] Three rivers cut across the territory from west to east, The Niobrara in the north, the Republican in the south, and through the middle the broad, shallow Platte River, named for the French word meaning flat. It was the Platte that tied the territory together, "her broad valley providing one of the finest natural roadways to the world, the great highway to the west."[34]

The climate and topography of the lower eastern portion of Nebraska is similar to the woodlands and fertile flood plain of its eastern neighbor, Missouri. "There the land is undulating, the alluvial lowlands sustaining native stands of oak, walnut, and cottonwood trees."[35] But west of the Platte's limestone hills the topography flattens out into prairie grasslands, and its limestone undergirding is replaced by sandstone. This is the bluegrass prairie of central Nebraska that Pike traveled through. Had he turned north he would have found eighteen thousand miles of "sandy dunes and lake studded valleys . . . covered with native grasses and wildflowers," and the magnificent waterfalls of the Snake and Minnechaduza Rivers.[36]

But Pike did not turn north, instead he continued southwest across the central prairie. As he did, the bluegrass gradually disappeared until only "windswept desolation" remained. Pike and his men had entered the Great or "High" Plains, which he called a barren desert.[37] For the Indians who lived there, it was a place of "austere beauty."[38]

Despite these early nineteenth-century explorations, crossing the Rockies remained a perilous venture. Crossing the Continental Divide was beyond the realm of practicality until 1810 when another group of intrepid explorers, led by Robert Stuart, returning from the Pacific through southwest Wyoming discovered the South Pass, a twenty-mile wide "cavity" at seventy-five hundred feet through the Continental Divide, more than adequate to accommodate wagon trains.[39] Yet little attention was paid to Stuart's discovery or later when, in 1824, the South Pass was rediscovered by Jedediah Smith and James Clyman, the mythologized mountain men of the early American West. The South Pass's potential remained unnoticed for two more decades before it became a nineteenth-century version of a wormhole through the Great American Desert to the Pacific west coast.

White Americans' lack of interest in traveling west across the continent to the Pacific coast was largely due to this perceived "desert" that lay in the center of the continent and the less-than-glowing reviews of the region. The name "Great American Desert" had been given to it by Major Stephen H. Long. In 1819 Long commanded a U.S. Army expedition through the Great Plains. The scientists attached to the expedition found the plain's soil "dry and sand, with gravel," and Long declared it "'wholly unfit for cultivation.'" He labeled the map made from the expedition's survey the "Great American Desert."[40] It was published in 1820, when the western boundary of the United States was the Mississippi River, a quarter of a century before the annexation of Texas and

Oregon, the Mexican Cession, and the discovery of gold in California. It was not long after Long's expedition that federal officials saw in this vast desert the solution to two problems: the remaining Indian tribes east of Mississippi who were increasingly in the way of white settlement, and the presence of foreign powers on the west coast who threatened national security. The idea was to create a permanent Indian Territory in the Great American Desert and relocate the remaining eastern tribes there. It solved the Indian problem at the same time creating a permanent buffer between the United States and foreign powers to the West. White Americans were not interested in the land anyway. The government could not lose. Or so it thought at the time.

Before European contact in the sixteenth century, the indigenous peoples of North America probably numbered 10 million. Over the next three centuries their numbers were decimated by European diseases, warfare, and famine. By the first half of the nineteenth century, less than half a million remained, the majority living west of the Missouri river.[41] Beginning in the 1820s the U.S. government began to negotiate treaties with tribes living in and west of Missouri in preparation of the removal and relocation of the remaining tribes living east of the Mississippi.[42] In 1825 the Osage and Kansa tribes living in Missouri and the Nebraska Territory were systematically forced to cede their "right, title, interest, and claim, to lands lying within the State of Missouri and Territory of Arkansas and to all lands lying West of the said State . . . North and West of the Red River, South of the Kansas River," and moved onto smaller tracts of land further west.[43] It was the beginning of the reservation system.

The Indian Removal Act of 1830 formalized on a national level the seizure of tribal lands. In exchange for title to Indian lands, the United States promised it would "forever secure and guaranty to them [the said tribes], and their heirs or successors, the country so exchanged with them." An interesting caveat followed, "Provided always, that such lands shall revert to the United States, if the Indians become extinct, or abandon the same."[44] Among the first tribes to be removed to Nebraska were the Shawnee, Delaware, Chippewa, Wyandot, Pottawatomie, Miami, Kickapoo, the Ottawa, Fox, Sac, and Iowa.[45]

Four years later, in 1834, Congress passed the Indian Trade and Intercourse Act, which designated the Great American Desert as official "Indian Country." Approximately 60 million acres, it included all U.S. territory west of the Mississippi except for the states of Louisiana and Missouri and the Arkansas Territory, as well as some eastern portions in Florida, Michigan, Wisconsin, and Minnesota.[46] In his annual address to Congress in December 1835, President Jackson guaranteed the land to the Indians forever stating that no one could "doubt the moral duty of the government of the United States to protect, and, if possible, to preserve and perpetuate the scattered remnants of this race, which are left within our borders. In the discharge of this duty, an extensive region in the west has been assigned for their permanent residence."[47] Whites would not be allowed to settle in Indian Country or travel through it. At the time of his promise neither Jackson nor Congress envisioned a bicoastal nation. Their lack of foresight ended up blocking "the natural lines of expansion to the Pacific."[48]

St. Louis and Independence, Missouri, were the two jumping off points for western migration to Texas, Oregon, and California. Missourians themselves composed a significant number of those migrating west and a majority of those who went to Oregon. By midcentury white Americans traveling west from Missouri through the Great American Desert were beginning to doubt the accuracy of its designation. Many saw agricultural potential in the sixty thousand square acres, particularly those whites living in northwest Missouri. But to attempt to settle in or travel through Indian Country was not only illegal; without a federal presence, it was extremely hazardous.

Federal organization of Indian Country was not only desired by white settlers but also necessary for national defense and economic growth. Without a line of military forts and a transcontinental railroad through Indian County, settlers continued to be at risk, the Pacific coast remained vulnerable to external threats, and expanded trade with Asia could not be realized. The question was not whether to build a transcontinental railroad but by what means would it be built and by what route would it run?

Englishman George Stephenson invented the first steam engine train in 1829, but it was American ingenuity and invention that made the train viable. Between 1830 and 1850 Americans invented the swiveling track, which allowed the train to take curves; the equalizing lever, which kept the train on rough tracks; and the switchback, which enabled the train to climb steep inclines.[49] America's technological innovations in rail travel "inspired a revolution" in migration, which until then had always been a slow process done primarily by water travel. The train not only dramatically increased the speed of travel but enlarged the scope of travel by making accessible large landmasses formally inaccessible by traditional means.[50] Knowledge of the fact was particularly evident in northwest Missouri, which did not contain navigable rivers. Some of the nation's earliest rail was laid in this region. But the national benefits of a transcontinental railroad did not immediately translate to the states. In the 1830s and 1840s, states focused on the economic advantages of locally constructed rail. Efforts by western members of Congress to pass Pacific railroad legislation and related bills were consistently defeated by northern and southern members whose states were in a railroad race of their own.[51]

In addition to local and state priorities, federal construction of a transcontinental railroad posed a political problem. By 1850 the majority of U.S. territory west of the Mississippi was located in the North, whereas the majority of states west of the Mississippi were in the South. This forced members of Congress to make constitutional arguments incongruous with their traditional positions. Northern members who had traditionally used loose construction to support an active federal role over the states now used strict construction to argue that federal funds could not be used to construct rail lines inside state borders, arguing instead that the federal government could fund railroad construction only in the territories. The northern position was a well-aimed blow at any southern route, for no road could extend west of New Orleans, or Vicksburg, or even Memphis, without running into the state of Texas.[52] Southerners, traditionally states' rights advocates, now used loose construction to argue for a nationally funded transcontinental railroad west through the states. Additionally, due to slavery's restriction above the 36° 30′ parallel, southerners had become some of the most ardent defenders of the Indians' permanent title to the land. They were "willing to let the Indian Country below the line . . . remain unorganized, if the larger portion above that line also remained unorganized."[53] As early as 1838 southern senators led by John C. Calhoun were calling for the Indian Country to be permanently closed.

By 1852 various routes for the transcontinental railroad had been proposed, and all had drawbacks. Northern routes ran through difficult terrain and had to contend with severe weather conditions. Central routes ran through unorganized territory and Indian land titles. Southern routes ran through the state of Texas and territory still belonging to Mexico. On March 3, 1853, the last day of the Thirty-Second Congress, $150,000 was authorized to survey possible transcontinental routes to the Pacific. The task was given to Secretary of War Jefferson Davis. The most practical route, the central route, starting at Chicago and running west to the Nebraska Territory along the level valley of the Platte to the South Pass through the Rockies to the Pacific, was not among the surveys included.[54] When Stephen Douglas, chairman of the Senate Committee on Territories and longtime proponent of the route, questioned its omission, Secretary Davis replied that the route had already been surveyed by private concerns.

Congress also debated how the construction would be financed. The federal government had more than enough land available to grant what was necessary for construction, but the debate centered on who or what would receive the grants. In January 1845 Asa Whitney, a businessman with trade interests in China, submitted a memorandum to Congress proposing a transcontinental railroad. Believing it would significantly expand the country's commercial interests in Asia, Whitney proposed a line from Milwaukee, Wisconsin, on Lake Michigan, straight through Indian Country to the Pacific coast. The government would sell Whitney the land through which the route would run for sixteen cents an acre, and he would then sell the land to his investors. The Whitney plan also required the government to extinguish Indian titles to the land.[55]

Congress rejected Whitney's plan, which had been opposed in the House by the chairman of the House Committee on Territories, Stephen Douglas, who had been advocating his own plan since his election to Congress in 1842. Douglas's efforts at organizing Nebraska to facilitate construction of a transcontinental railroad became so consuming that biographer Allen Johnson likened it to a "hobby."[56] Douglas continued his advocacy after his election to the Senate in 1847, where he was appointed chairman of the newly created Senate Committee on Territories.[57] Douglas objected to Whitney's proposal first because of the selection of Milwaukee as the main terminus. Douglas argued Chicago's existing eastern rail connections made it the more logical choice. Second, Douglas opposed direct government grants to a private corporation. Instead, he proposed the federal government make direct land grants to individual states and territories through which the railroad would run, allowing the state and locality to determine the means by which the route would be constructed within their borders. In other words, "popular sovereignty" would determine the means by which the transcontinental railroad would be built. Over the next decade, Douglas never wavered in his belief in local autonomy and responsibility.[58] The debate over the means by which the transcontinental railroad would be built preceded and foreshadowed the debate over whether or not slavery would be admitted into the western territories. It reflected a growing divide in the country between its traditional sense of autonomy and the portent of future industrial demands for centralization of government.[59]

Continued technological advancements in train and track construction, the California gold rush, and Douglas's leadership combined to create an explosion of railroad construction after 1850. Within four years, national rail mileage increased from 8,600 to 21,300.[60] In 1850 alone Douglas secured federal grants for Illinois, Alabama, and Mississippi to construct a line from Chicago to Mobile, Alabama. Federal commitment for a rail line from the Great Lakes to the Gulf of Mexico was the fulfillment of Douglas's promise to southern delegates at the 1846 Memphis Convention and part of his southern strategy for his first presidential campaign in 1852.[61] Equally important to Douglas's southern strategy was the selection of Robert M. T. Hunter to be his vice-presidential running mate. While Douglas did not win the Democratic nomination (it went to the dark-horse candidate Franklin Pierce), the ticket established a personal friendship and future business partnership between Douglas and Hunter.

By midcentury everyone—individuals, corporations, and localities—was investing in western lands that the future transcontinental railroad might run through. Historian David Potter called the widespread speculation a giant lottery game, "in which a whole community might win the rich prize of becoming a great metropolitan terminal for all the vast traffic with the Pacific coast," while "secondary and tertiary promoters speculated in local real estate whose value was contingent upon the ultimate route."[62] Douglas had already won at the game. His earlier real-estate investments in and around Chicago made him a small fortune when the federal grants for the Chicago-Mobile line came through in 1850. Douglas's successful speculation in real-estate developments would later lure other senators into his ventures including his former running mate Robert M. T. Hunter. There were enormous profits to be had if Chicago became the main terminus for the transcontinental railroad. But for that to happen the route would have to run through the Nebraska Territory, above the 36° 30′ parallel.

Despite Douglas's leadership role in the Senate and his economic and political efforts at personal advancement, his home state of Illinois was not awarded the first federal land grants for rail lines to the Pacific. In the summer of 1852 Congress awarded land grants to Missouri for two routes westward, named the Hannibal and St. Joseph lines.[63] The growing competition between Chicago and St. Louis to become the terminus for the transcontinental railroad became personified in the developing feud between Douglas and Thomas Hart Benton. The feud began in 1849 when Douglas resigned as president of the national railroad convention held in St. Louis after learning Benton had orchestrated Douglas's election to silence him during the debate over the terminus location. In that same year, Benton introduced his first Senate bill for a transcontinental railroad similar to Whitney's earlier one. It called for a national rail line along a central route through Oregon along the Columbia River to the Pacific to be built by the federal government instead of private investors. It also included an appropriation of $100,000 to be used to extinguish Indian titles. Douglas objected to Benton's idea of a national line as much as he had Whitney's private one. He also objected to the transcontinental terminus being in any city other than Chicago. Benton's bill was tabled.

Stephen Douglas had consistently advocated for a transcontinental railroad since his days in the House. It was part of his overall vision of a trans-Mississippi West expanding in settlement, economic wealth, and political power. Benton had also long advocated for expansion, but whereas Douglas envisioned a trans-Mississippi West dotted with farms and railroad towns Benton saw no feasibility in the settlement of what he still viewed as the Great American Desert. Benton's vision was a trade corridor that would run from St. Louis west to the Columbia River through the Northwest to the Pacific. He called it his Road to India. Benton had earlier submitted land grant bills for road construction and smaller in-state rail lines, but his 1849 bill was his first proposal for a nationally funded transcontinental line. It opened him up to charges of being politically motivated.[64] Benton was up for reelection to the Senate in 1850, and no two men fought more to defeat him than the two whose interests Benton had inadvertently tied together, Stephen Douglas and David Rice Atchison. Their campaign against him worked. Benton lost his reelection to the Senate. In 1852, though, Benton was elected to the House of Representatives, where he continued his fight against Douglas and Atchison.[65]

By 1852 white Missourians were literally dictating their demand for railroad construction and the organization of the Nebraska Territory to their elected officials regardless of party or political prominence. On July 7 Missouri's David Rice Atchison, now senior senator and president pro tempore, presented to the Senate the Platte County Resolution calling for the organization of Nebraska. By the end of the Thirty-Second Congress's first session the Senate, as well as the House, was awash in a sea of rival and interrelated bills on land distribution, white settlement, emigrant protection, railroad and telegraph construction, and mail routes.

Meanwhile in Missouri, the Wyandot tribe, in an effort to get ahead of the inevitable, petitioned Congress in the spring of 1852 to organize Nebraska in hopes of securing a profitable outcome. Originally from Ohio and Michigan, the Wyandot had been relocated during the 1830s and 1840s to the land between the Missouri and Kansas Rivers contiguous to northwest Missouri. They were considered a "civilized" tribe having intermarried with white settlers, converted to the Methodist Church, adopted private ownership, and written a code of law. Nevertheless, their petition was ignored.[66] That summer the white members of the tribe, who controlled tribal affairs, elected Abelard Guthrie, a white man, to travel to Washington and present their case. White Missourians not married into the tribe nominated their own candidate, John E. Barrow, and demanded a new election. Guthrie won the election against Barrow and left for Washington on November 20.[67]

The second session of the Thirty-Second Congress convened on December 6, 1852. One week later, on December 13, Congressman William P. Hall of the Missouri's fourth district introduced a bill to organize the territory of the

Platte.⁶⁸ Despite section 11 of the Indian Intercourse Act of 1834, which prohibited white settlement on Indian land, and section 12, which prohibited the purchase or conveyance of Indian land except by "treaty or convention entered into pursuant to the constitution," Hall rejected the argument that the Treaty of 1834 required extinguishing of Indian title before the land could be settled by whites.⁶⁹ Instead, he argued the territory could be settled immediately without extinguishing the Indian title on the basis that the land had been unassigned for so long the Indian title to it was no longer valid. In defending his bill, Hall also made note that the transcontinental railroad would never be built through Nebraska unless it was opened up to white settlement. The House Committee on Territories, chaired by Douglas's lieutenant, William A. Richardson of Illinois, reported the Hall bill out with two major differences; Richardson renamed the territory "Nebraska" and included the necessity of extinguishing Indian titles to the land. The territory's boundaries were set at the 49° parallel north, 36° 30′ parallel south, the borders of Missouri and Iowa to the east, and Rocky Mountains to the west. The entire territory lay above the 36° 30′ which meant slavery was excluded. The bill passed the House along sectional lines, 107 to 49, on February 10.⁷⁰

Stephen Douglas's first efforts at Nebraska legislation as a member of the House in 1844 had failed. His senatorial efforts thereafter had also failed, blocked by an odd blend of senatorial indifference and intransigence.⁷¹ Following the success of the House bill on February 10, Douglas again tried to bring his bill to the Senate floor on March 2, one day before the last day of the Thirty-Second Congress. Once again the bill was blocked, this time by his friend and former running mate, Robert M. T. Hunter, who demanded the appropriations bill be given preference. Douglas objected, arguing members of the Senate had been using excuses for weeks to prevent the bill from being brought to the floor. The bill to organize the territory of Washington had been introduced in the same session and had passed at once without debate, while Douglas's bill for Nebraska "hung fire."⁷² Despite his pleas, the Senate voted against taking up the bill in favor of the appropriations bill. The next day, March 3, the last day of the session, the Senate appropriations bill passed. Douglas immediately moved for his Nebraska bill to be taken up. Southern opposition to the bill was strong and included Hunter, Mason, and Butler. As the presiding president of the Senate, Atchison could not participate in the debate.

Atchison had been presiding as president of the Senate in the absence of Vice President William Rufus King since the start of the session in December. King had contracted tuberculosis while serving as minister to France under

President Tyler in the 1840s, and his condition had worsened after he was picked to be Pierce's running mate in 1852. He went to Cuba to recuperate after the election but remained too ill to return in March for the inauguration. Congress allowed him to take the oath of office there.[73] King returned to Alabama, his home state, on April 17 and died the following day. Atchison had become second in line to the presidency.

Atchison's situation on March 3 was complicated. As a senator from Missouri he represented both western and southern interests. As a southerner and proslavery leader, he understood and agreed with southern opposition to any territorial organization where slavery was restricted. He was already on the record opposing the organization of Nebraska. But as a westerner and expansionist, Atchison understood that Douglas's bill had little to do with slavery. It was "a western measure ... designed to add to the power and wealth of the west," not weaken the South.[74] As presiding president, Atchison could have stayed out of the debate, but instead he stepped down from the president's chair in order to address the chamber. "It was time," Atchison said, "for the organization of this territory."

While Atchison was ready to support the bill, he told the chamber that the concerns he had with the bill remained. First, the organization of the Nebraska Territory would extend the frontier, and as a result western Missouri would lose exclusive trade with it. "We have now as good a market as any people of the United States, and it grows out of the frontier trade; food for men, food for oxen, food for mules, food for everything, which we produce for California, Oregon and New Mexico. But if we extend this frontier from year to year competition will increase, and we will be compelled to turn our agricultural products down the Missouri and the Mississippi rivers, to the east instead of the west." But "the tide of emigration rolls on," Atchison continued: "You cannot restrain them [Missourians] much longer."[75]

Second, Atchison argued the indigenous Indians and those earlier relocated to the plains still retained title to the territorial lands in question. Before the territory could be organized those titles had to be extinguished. The appropriation bill enabling the president to negotiate new treaties to extinguish Indian titles, supported by Atchison, had passed, but the treaties had not yet been negotiated. Therefore, whites could not yet legally settle the land.

Last but not least, Atchison restated the position he had held at the opening of the session: the Missouri Compromise restricted slavery in the Nebraska Territory unless "specifically rescinded." He admitted he was still not "very clear" on the subject but had come to the conclusion that "there was no prospect, no hope of a repeal." Why then was he now supporting Douglas's bill? It was for the same reason the Wyandot tribe was willing to sell its land: nothing could stop the inevitable. With "no hope" of repeal, Atchison had come to the conclusion it made no difference when the territory was admitted whether it be that year or the "next year, or five or ten years hence."[76]

Atchison and Missouri's freshman Whig senator Henry Geyer were the only southern senators to vote for Douglas's bill. It was tabled anyway 23 to 17, and the session ended.[77] It was now clear to Douglas the bill could not pass in the next Congress without southern support, and he would need Atchison's help to get that support. In the meantime, Atchison had moved in with the very senators leading the opposition to its passage.

At the beginning of the Thirty-Second session Atchison had moved to Brown's Indian Queen Hotel located on the north side of the avenue between Sixth and Seventh Streets. Known simply as Brown's, the hotel was one of the largest on the avenue. Among the senators living at Browns were Stephen Adams of Mississippi, G. E. Badger of North Carolina, Robert M. Charlton of Georgia, W. F. De Saussure of South Carolina, T. J. Rusk of Texas, Isaac Toucey of Connecticut, J. R. Underwood of Kentucky, John B. Weller of California, and last but not least, Atchison's future messmates, Robert M. T. Hunter, James Murray Mason, and Andrew Pickens Butler. Hunter, Mason, and Butler had taken temporary lodging at the hotel after finding country living at Havenner's too difficult during the winter.

Mason, who according to his daughter preferred "domestic life," found living in the hotel "intolerable." Since his one term as a congressman, Mason had always put together a mess where he and a few others could live "together as one family." Adding a fourth to the original trio, Mason, Hunter, Butler, and now Atchison purchased the house at 361 F Street between Ninth and Tenth. Responsibility for the household expenses and staff rotated between the four on a monthly basis. Mason's real family was the closest to Washington, and his home, Selma, in Winchester, Virginia, was often the site of weekend retreats for the Mess. By Martha Mason's account the relationships between the four men developed into "warm and lasting friendship[s]."[78]

The establishment of the Mess on F Street had profound consequences for the future organization of Nebraska. Hunter, Mason, and Butler had all strongly opposed its organization. Atchison, however, was still struggling with his conflicting positions on Nebraska, which remained unresolved at the end of the session. According to the author of cognitive dissonance theory, Leon Festinger, conflict such as Atchison's in which a person holds "contradictory or incompatible beliefs" cannot long last without resolving in favor of one over the other. The internal discomfort created by cognitive dissonance will force the person to seek a way to reduce it or to "avoid situations and information" that might increase it. The level of a person's cognitive dissonance can also be affected by the group dynamic which can either be a "major source" of the dissonance or a "major vehicle" for its elimination.[79] For David Rice Atchison, the F Street Mess would be the latter.

The day after the end of the Thirty-Second Congress, March 4, Thomas Hart Benton, in St. Louis, officially announced his intentions to run against Atchison in 1854 in a written statement called "Letter from Col. Benton to the People of Missouri: Central National Highway from the Mississippi river to the Pacific." It was reprinted in all the major Missouri newspapers.[80] Knowing, as did Atchison, that Missourians' desire for Nebraska organization, immediate white settlement, and railroad construction were "strong enough to make or unmake" elected officials, Benton charged Atchison with inconsistency and obstruction of the issues.[81] Benton himself came out in support of everything Missourians wanted without qualification and spent the month of May stumping around Atchison's power base in the western counties. Atchison's biographer, William Parrish argues that Benton "perceived the opportunity of making much-needed political capital for himself, at the expense of his rival" and, if successful, could "stand an excellent chance of transferring from Atchison to himself the political allegiance of the populous frontier counties."[82] Missouri's major Whig newspaper, the *Republican*, declared "a fiercer war is about to be waged between the Benton and the Democratic factions in this State than has ever been known."[83]

After successfully putting Atchison on the defensive, Benton returned to Washington in June. Atchison, still in Missouri, responded to Benton's accusations in a series of stump speeches between June and November in which he accused Benton of falsifying his record and position on the issues and countering that Benton's sudden advocacy was politically motivated. He claimed Benton had done little during his thirty years in the Senate to promote railroad construction, whereas he, Atchison, had voted for the appropriation for surveys of possible transcontinental routes and introduced several bills since the 1840s that provided public land for construction of lines in Missouri, all of which could be used to continue to the Pacific coast.[84]

Atchison also denounced Benton's argument that Nebraska was ready for immediate white settlement. He stated that much of the Nebraska land was not suitable for agricultural pursuits, and the Indians retained title to the land that was. He rejected as "humbug" Benton's argument that the Indians, by failing to occupy most of Nebraska, had abdicated title to it.[85] As chairman of the Committee on Indian Affairs, Atchison was more familiar than Benton with the treaties of 1830 and 1834 and understood that the treaties had permanently set aside the uninhabited land for Indian, not white, settlement. He explained this to his audiences in Platte City and Weston. "The Nebraska territory could not be settled by whites or organized until Indian title to the land had been extinguished by treaty," and he had voted for legislation in the last session "enabling the President to do so."[86]

In July Benton requested from the Department of the Interior's Bureau of Indian Affairs a map of Nebraska showing the land "held therein" by the Pawnee, Kansas, and Osage tribes. Benton later published the map. Copies were made and sold throughout Missouri showing most of the territory open to white settlement. Benton either willingly misled Missourians or failed to understand the law. Atchison attacked the map and its inferences in stump speeches between August and November. His position was confirmed by the commissioner of Indian Affairs, George W. Manypenny, who, enraged by Benton's deception, publicly refuted the map, stating "no such map was ever drawn in the Indian office . . . for any such purpose," adding that none of the land in Nebraska Territory was "subject at this time to lawful settlement."[87]

Throughout the summer and fall, Atchison struggled to respond to the one charge made by Benton that he could not refute. He had publicly acknowledged the Missouri Compromise restricted slavery in Nebraska and could not be repealed. Nevertheless, he had voted for the Nebraska bill the last day of the session. At every stop Atchison sidestepped his earlier speech and vote of March 3, promising he would oppose in the next Congress any bill to organize Nebraska that restricted slavery. So "that I may not be misunderstood hereafter," Atchison declared, "I now say emphatically that I will not vote for any bill that makes Nebraska free-soil Territory." He had no problem with "the people who may settle there, and who have the deepest interest in this question," deciding "for themselves," but he would "give no advantage to one citizen over another." In rejecting any and all congressional intervention, Atchison had by late summer joined Douglas in advocating popular sovereignty.[88] By fall, newspapers across the South were demanding repeal of the Missouri Compromise. Atchison returned to Washington and his new lodgings at 361 F Street on November 27.[89]

Atchison's messmates, Mason, Butler, and Hunter, spent the recess contending with applicants for federal appointments.[90] Meanwhile President Pierce's efforts to balance his cabinet and share patronage between conservative states' rights and Free-Soil Democrats was not being well received by either side during the recess. In New York State, war had broken out between the party's returning Barnburners and the party's Hunkers, who were not yet ready to welcome the prodigal sons.[91] The infighting in New York was threatening to replicate itself and spread throughout the country. Virginia and New York had long been the bastion of the Democratic majority in the Congress, but the alliance between the two states depended upon Hardshell Democrats maintaining control in New York. Atchison was aware of the necessity to keep New York Hardshells in power and supported Hardshell New Yorker Daniel S. Dickinson for a cabinet position. President Pierce chose his personal friend and Free-Soil New Yorker John A. Dix for the cabinet instead. The president's choice placed him at odds with his own party's leadership before the new Congress even began.

Meanwhile, Stephen A. Douglas was unaware of the growing patronage crisis in Washington or Atchison's policy shift on Nebraska.[92] He had left the country on May 14 for a world tour that took him through all the major cities of Europe and the Middle East, including London, Marseilles, Genoa, Florence, Rome, Athens, Constantinople, Smyrna, Moscow, St. Petersburg, Berlin, Prague, and Paris. He returned to New York City on October 30 and departed immediately for Washington.[93] Douglas could waste no time negotiating a deal for southern support on Nebraska. Without it, Douglas's dream of a bicoastal nation united via rail and dominated politically and economically by the trans-Mississippi West "stood no chance of success."[94]

Douglas's visions for the West and the nation were not his only interests at stake; so too was his latest business venture. Douglas's earlier real-estate investments in and around Chicago in the late 1840s had made him a very wealthy man after the Chicago-Mobile railroad legislation had passed in 1850. In that year, Douglas had partnered with Washington investment banker William Walker Corcoran.[95] Regardless of the War Department surveys of alternative routes, Douglas was confident the first transcontinental railroad would follow his central route. But he hedged his bet by putting together a new investment syndicate to purchase property around Lake Superior, Wisconsin, in case the northern route was selected. The project was largely financed by Corcoran. Everything hinged on gaining southern support for the Nebraska bill, but southern intransigence against Nebraska had deepened since the news of James Gadsden's purchase of territory from Mexico for the southern El Paso route had reached Washington.[96]

Robert M. T. Hunter, who led the opposition against Douglas's bill in the last session, shared his friend and former running mate's love of real-estate speculation but lacked Douglas's success at it. On June 29, during the recess, Hunter had purchased fourteen thousand acres in Nicholas County in the western portion of Virginia. Between July and October, he made improvements on the property. On November 7 he purchased two additional tracts in the same area. Then, on November 21, just before the start of the Thirty-Third Congress, Hunter sold nearly half of the Nicholas Country property to Robert Maury, at no apparent profit, and returned to Washington for the opening session of Congress.[97]

In Washington, the dissatisfaction in Congress over the president's appointments had intensified, not dissipated. In an effort to send a message to the president, states' rights southerners and New York Hard Democrats, led by the F Street Mess, blocked the election of Robert Armstrong, owner of the administration's paper, the *Washington Union*, to the lucrative congressional printing job. The contract was given instead to the editor of the *Washington Sentinel*, Beverly Tucker of Virginia, Hunter's cousin by marriage.[98] Pierce, still wanting to put his friend and Free-Soil Democrat John Dix in the cabinet, hoped to mollify the opposition of the states' rights and Hard Democrats by offering Hunter a cabinet position too. Pierce summoned Hunter to Boston, where on December 27 he offered Hunter the post of secretary of war. Hunter told the president he would consider the offer and returned to Washington to confer with his messmates.

Prior to Hunter's departure to Boston, Senator Augustus C. Dodge of Iowa, on December 14, introduced a bill to organize the territory of Nebraska. It was immediately referred to the Committee on Territories chaired by Douglas, who was now fully aware of the patronage struggle, the Gadsden Purchase, growing southern intransience, and the president pro tempore's change of heart on Nebraska. His bill and his Lake Superior syndicate stood in the balance. The stage was set for rewriting and realignment.

CHAPTER FOUR

Senatorial Junta

On Monday, December 5, 1853, James Murray Mason took his seat in the back-right row along the west wall of the Senate chamber below the curved wrought-iron balcony of the Ladies Gallery.[1] His messmate, Robert M. T. Hunter, sat slightly to the left, two rows ahead. Andrew Pickens Butler, who normally sat two seats to the right of Hunter, had yet to arrive in Washington.[2] The fourth member of the F Street Mess, David Rice Atchison sat at the president's desk on a raised dais in the center of the chamber. The dais was draped in a crimson canopy held aloft by the talons of a gilded eagle suspended overhead.[3] Behind it along the east wall was a second gallery [the East Gallery] supported by eight marble Ionic columns quarried from the river banks of the Potomac and designed after the famed Erechtheion of Athens.[4] Rembrandt Peale's portrait of George Washington hung beneath it.[5]

Seated at the desk on the majestic dais, Atchison was literally and figuratively at the pinnacle of his senatorial career. One of only two senators with ten consecutive years of experience, Atchison had been elected president pro tempore thirteen times and was the acknowledged political slayer of thirty-year Senate incumbent Thomas Hart Benton.[6] The death of Vice President William Rufus King earlier in the spring had not only made Atchison second in line to the presidency; the continued reports of Pierce's declining health had many in the city thinking an Atchison presidency was fast approaching.[7] As physically imposing as the dais on which he stood and the power he held, Atchison rose from his chair and gaveled the Senate into session at noon.

Lost in the grandeur of the chamber and the moment was a small unadorned piece of furniture composed of five shelves supported on "tall spindly legs," the official hopper for the Senate's bills. When a bill was introduced it was placed in the bottom shelf, moving up as it made its way through the legislative process. It was said that the space between the shelves narrowed toward the top because "so few bills survived to become law." It was a certainty even before the Thirty-Third Congress convened that a Nebraska bill would again be introduced and placed on the bottom shelf of the unadorned hopper. What remained uncertain, though, was whether it would be one of the few to make it to the narrow top shelf and what it would look like if it did.

As the Senate waited on the completion of the War Department's surveys of possible Pacific railroad routes, members prepared proposals of their own, primarily in the form of public land grant requests for intrastate railroad construction. Others, like Stephen Douglas, planned to introduce their own Pacific railroad bills. While Douglas's bill called for three possible routes, northern, central, and southern, his personal preference remained the one not being surveyed by the government, the central route from Council Bluffs, Iowa, through Nebraska to the South Pass and on through to the Pacific.[8] This route, already established by earlier wagon train immigration, would guarantee terminals at both St. Louis and Chicago. Douglas had invested heavily in property around the Chicago area but also hedged his bets by investing in the Lake Superior syndicate backed by the pro-southern Washington investment banker William Wilson Corcoran. If the northern route was chosen, Superior City on the lake would be the eastern terminal. Railroad entrepreneur and former Mississippi senator Robert J. Walker, was so enthusiastic about the "northern route from Lake Superior to Puget Sound," he told Douglas he intended to bid on its construction himself.[9]

Corcoran's and Walker's speculation in northwestern properties typified a curious aspect of southern investment interests. As southern demands for protection of the slave labor system became more intransigent, southern capital derived from that system was increasingly invested in northwestern land speculation. Southern interest in northwest properties was so high by the 1850s that northwestern land agents were advertising in southern papers.[10] Southern politicians, including members of the Thirty-Third Congress, were not immune from the speculation in northwest properties. Like Douglas, they too were hedging their bets. Corcoran's Lake Superior investors included several members of the Thirty-Third Congress, many of whom would have leadership roles in the passage of the Kansas-Nebraska Act, including Robert M. T. Hunter, Senator Jesse D. Bright of Indiana, Senator John Slidell of Louisiana, Congressman John C. Breckinridge of Kentucky, Congressman William Waters Boyce of South Carolina, Congressman William Aiken of South Carolina, and Congressman Williamson R. W. Cobb of Alabama.[11]

In the meantime, the Senate waited upon the outcome of Ambassador James Gadsden's negotiations with the Mexican government for the purchase of a small strip of Mexican territory below the Gila River in what is today New Mexico, the success of which was necessary for the proposed southern Pacific route. So, while publicly southern leadership, including the F Street Mess, demanded a southern route, privately many of that same leadership, as well as many of their constituency, stood to gain financially from a northern one. It was a conundrum, but only as long as slavery was restricted above the 36° 30′ parallel.

The first order of Senate business on its opening day was the presentation and swearing in of four new members: Robert W. Johnson, Democrat from Arkansas; Philip Allen, Democrat from Rhode Island; John Bell, Whig from Tennessee; and John Slidell, Democrat from Louisiana. Shortly thereafter the House informed the Senate it had a quorum and was "ready to proceed to business." Seated in the far-left desk in the last row, Augustus C. Dodge, Democrat from Iowa, rose and took the floor to announce his intention to introduce two bills, one for a grant of public land in his home state to aid in construction of a railroad, and a second to organize the territory of Nebraska.[12] Other senators followed Dodge with announcements of their own. In the back of the chamber, James Mason rose to note that actual business could not be conducted until both Houses were organized and had received the president's message. The members agreed with Mason's assessment and adjourned.[13]

The following morning Sidney Webster, Franklin Pierce's secretary, walked from the White House to the Capitol and delivered the president's annual message to a Democratic-controlled yet unhappy Congress. The party's euphoria over winning the White House and majorities in both houses of Congress had been short-lived. Pierce's effort to unite the party by offering seemingly every person of every party or faction therein a cabinet position or patronage appointment had clearly backfired. In the Senate, Atchison received the message, ordered it read and printed, and then adjourned the body.[14]

Confidence stemming from the 1850 Compromise permeated Pierce's message. With the recent domestic crisis over slavery seemingly settled, the president opened by calling for an aggressive foreign policy of commercial and territorial expansion in Central America, Cuba, and Asia and outlined the administration's ongoing negotiations with foreign countries, including Great Britain, Mexico, and Spain.[15] His proposed domestic program was just as aggressive. Harkening to the "amity" and "mutual confidence" that Pierce believed now existed among all sections of the country, he called for meeting the needs of an ever-confident and developing nation by expanding its army, navy, judiciary, and public land system. Then he called for a reduction in the tariff to reduce the treasury surplus brought on by that expansion specifically in international commerce.

Throughout the second half of the message, Pierce repeatedly returned to his belief that the Constitution was a compact between the states and therefore strictly limited the role of the federal government. He would support federal funding of internal improvements in the territories, not the states. He acknowledged the Congress's power to dispose of public land but cautioned the body to be "prudent" in doing so. He supported a transcontinental railroad but called for private investors to take the lead in its construction.

In conclusion, the president returned again to the crisis of 1850, stating it had been brought on by those who had questioned the "domestic institutions of one portion of the Confederacy and . . . the constitutional rights of the States." He reminded the Congress that the compromise had ended the crisis by vindicating those rights and restoring "a sense of repose and security to the public mind." The Compromise of 1850, he declared would "suffer no shock" but would be strictly adhered to.[16]

President Pierce's mixed and somewhat contradictory message of expansionism and states' rights was not unlike the mixed cabinet and patronage appointments that had turned the Democratic majority in the Congress against him. His opponents believed his message was a "dangerous and difficult combination of policies" without the power to safely implement it.[17] Just how little power the president had would become evident in the coming days.

It took another week for the House and Senate to organize, prepare committees, and elect a printer. The congressional printing job was a lucrative contract and traditionally went to the publisher of the administration's newspaper. The Pierce administration had inherited Millard Fillmore's pro-Compromise paper, the *Washington Union*, published by Robert Armstrong. While Armstrong was a Whig, the paper had consistently supported President Pierce's appointments, and Armstrong fully expected to retain his position as House and Senate printer.

Armstrong had been brought to Washington in 1851 to take over the *Union* from publisher Thomas Ritchie, former leader of the Richmond Junto, who had been ousted from state power in Virginia by the Chivalry faction led by Hunter and Mason. Two years later the Virginia Chivalry joined with New York Hard Democrats to force Ritchie out of the *Union*. That same coalition now set up its own opposition paper, the *Washington Sentinel*, and placed Beverly Tucker, the namesake and nephew of the novelist Nathaniel Beverly Tucker, at its helm. Beverly Tucker was the son of Judge Henry St. George Tucker, Robert M. T. Hunter's mentor and Line Hunter's uncle. With such a powerful combination of familial and political connections, Tucker lost no time attacking the president as a Free-Soil Van Burenite Democrat.[18]

On the Wednesday morning of December 7, the House of Representatives voted for House printer. Of the 219 votes cast, 110 votes were needed to win, Armstrong won with 126 votes. The Whigs vote, 64, went to the printer Gates & Seaton. Nine of the remaining 29 votes were single votes for various other candidates, but the remaining 20, a coalition of Virginia states' rights and New York Hard Democrats, had voted as a block for Beverly Tucker.[19] Later in the Senate, the Virginia–New York coalition controlled the majority vote. It overrode the president's and House's choice of Armstrong and elected Tucker outright. It was the first clue of the F Street Mess' control in the Senate. The next clue was committee selections.[20]

Since the early Republic, the Senate had routinely alternated between voting for chairmen and members of committees, a time-consuming process that "produced outcomes that accorded with no one's preferences," and granting the power to appoint to the president pro tempore.[21] By the 1830s committee assignments had become a routine power of the office. But the powers of the president pro tempore began to wane with the rise of organized party structures in the 1840s. In 1845, the year before Atchison's first election as president pro tempore, the process for committee selection changed yet again. In that year, Senate Democrats organized a caucus and, two years later, created the Committee on Committees. The power of the office of president pro tempore declined steadily thereafter.[22] Nevertheless, Atchison as president pro tempore and ranking member remained a leader within the Democratic caucus and wielded immense influence on the committee selection process.[23] Did he have enough power to influence Stephen Douglas, whose Committee on Territories would once again be charged with reporting the Nebraska bill? Later, after the passage of Kansas-Nebraska Act, Atchison would claim he did.

Monday, December 12, was the first full workday in the Senate. Following the recommendations of the Democratic Caucus Committee on Committees, the Senate's fourteen standing committees were enlarged to six members each, and the committee assignments were passed by resolution.[24] Of the fifty-seven senators—thirty-six Democrats, nineteen Whigs, and two Free-Soilers—fifty-five were given two or more assignments.[25] While assignments were evenly divided by region, the South dominated the chairmanships with eleven of the fourteen enlarged standing committee chairs going to southerners or closely aligned westerners. As president pro tempore, Atchison did not sit on any committees, but his messmates chaired the three most powerful ones, Hunter on Finance, Mason on Foreign Affairs, and Butler on Judiciary. All the committees directly or indirectly related to the organization of Nebraska and the Pacific railroad construction were chaired by southerners or westerners and included Stephen Douglas on Territories, Jesse D. Bright of Indiana on Roads and Canals, William K. Sebastian of Arkansas on Indian Affairs, and Augustus C. Dodge of Iowa on Public Lands. Southern and western Democrats composed the majority membership of these committees as well. Edward Everett of Massachusetts was one of only two Whigs and the only northeasterner on Douglas's Committee on Territories. Of the three northeastern members given chairmanships, two, Richard Brodhead of Pennsylvania on Claims and Charles T. James of Rhode Island on Patents and Patent Office, were conservative Democrats aligned with southern interests. Hannibal Hamlin of Massachusetts on Commerce was the only chair openly opposed to the proslavery block of the Democratic Party.

With the Senate and its committees firmly under the control of Atchison, southern Democrats, and their allies, the stage was set for the introduction of yet another bill to organize Nebraska. On Wednesday, December 14, Augustus Dodge introduced his bill to organize the territory of Nebraska. It was an exact copy of Douglas's bill from the previous session.[26] The Dodge bill was read a first and second time and referred to Douglas's Committee on Territories.[27] The *Richmond Enquirer* reported the Free-Soil faction in Congress intended to rush the bill through in order to ensure the exclusion of slavery from the territory.[28]

For the next nine days, the Senate continued to read and refer to committees a variety of bills and resolutions, most dealing with railroad construction through various western states and territories. Committees soon began to report back on other measures, but the Committee on Territories remained silent. In the meantime, its chairman, Stephen Douglas, wrote the Nebraska Delegate Convention in St. Joseph, Missouri, on December 17 assuring it that no cause would "defeat the organization of the Territory this session."[29] In his letter Douglas summarized his ten-year effort to organize the territory but made no reference to slavery or its restriction under the Missouri Compromise. On Friday, December 23, the Senate adjourned for the Christmas holiday. That same day the *Missouri Republican* reported on the continuing "war between Col. Benton . . . and Atchison." Nebraska had become their "field of strife," the outcome of which would determine "the seat in the Senate, and sundry local offices in Missouri."[30]

The Senate reconvened on Tuesday, December 27, and then immediately recessed for the funeral of Congressman Brookins Campbell of Tennessee. The rest of the week was uneventful as members left early for the New Year break. Unable to get a quorum, the Senate recessed until January 3.[31] Throughout the recess southern newspapers continued to report that Atchison was going to oppose any bill that did not explicitly repeal the Missouri Compromise.[32]

Atchison and Douglas had become close friends long before the Thirty-Third Congress, sharing a common love for western expansion and fine cigars and a mutual hatred of Thomas Hart Benton. Given their personal relationship and the leadership roles each had in the Senate, it is logical to assume the two met on occasion, personally and professionally, during the first weeks of the session. In fact, it is illogical to assume they did not. Later, after the conclusion of the historic session, Atchison began to talk publicly about one particular meeting held shortly after December 14, the day the Dodge bill had been referred to Douglas's committee.[33] According to Atchison, he urged Douglas to report a bill out of committee that repealed the Missouri Compromise's restriction of slavery above the 36° 30′ parallel. If Douglas refused to do so, Atchison threatened to resign as president pro tempore and take the chairmanship of the Committee on Territories himself. Atchison claimed that Douglas asked for a day or two to think it over, at the end of which time, if he could not report out the bill Atchison requested, he would step down from the chair "and exert his influence to get Atchison appointed." Opponents of the bill believed Atchison's story and argued that the Nebraska bill had been "concocted by a secret conclave."[34]

Douglas never denied meetings took place between himself and Atchison, only the particulars and timing of the one reported by Atchison. Opponents of the bill accused Douglas of being a puppet of the Slave Power, a charge he had to refute the rest of his life. A year after the bill's passage, Douglas unequivocally proclaimed on the Senate floor that he was the sole author of the substitute bill and accompanying report of the January 4 bill, the writing of which had been deferred to him by his fellow committee members. It "was written by myself," he proclaimed, "at my own house, with no man present."[35]

Douglas also denied meeting with any southern representative before January 4. But what did Douglas mean by the word "southern?" P. Orman Ray called Douglas's use of the word linguistic "quibbling," and an example of his political deftness. He argued that throughout America's relentless expansion westward the territories and later states of the lower Mississippi always straddled both monikers "western" and "southern." Nor are historians immune from mixing the two terms. Robert Johannsen refers to the Committee on Territories as a "western" committee, even though its members, in addition to Douglas, were from slaveholding states, three of which would later secede from the Union: George W. Jones of Missouri, John Bell of Tennessee, Robert W. Johnson of Arkansas, and Samuel Houston of Texas.[36] Of the four senators, only Houston would oppose secession.[37] While at midcentury the lower Mississippi was decidedly "western," on the issue of slavery the region was first and foremost "southern." Furthermore, Douglas is on the record as having met about the bill with Indiana senator Jesse Bright before January 4.[38] Even though Indiana was a free northwestern state, Bright was proslavery and closely aligned with the F Street Mess.[39] By denying any southern involvement in the bill before January 4, Douglas was playing semantics with the act's history.[40]

On Tuesday, January 3, the Senate reconvened. It was the first day back for Andrew Pickens Butler and the first long day of Senate business as members debated a series of measures including the Vermont Senate seat and British actions about Nicaragua.[41] The next day, January 4, Douglas reported out of committee Nebraska bill, S. 22. He had amended three sections of the original Dodge bill. In section 1 the territory was extended north from the forty-third to the forty-ninth parallel. In addition, the first section now included language from the 1850 Utah and New Mexico bills that stated "when admitted as a State or States, the said Territory, or any portion of the same, shall be received into the Union, with or without slavery, as their constitution may prescribe at the time of their admission."[42] Under section 9 of the bill, which dealt with the judicial power of the territorial Supreme Court and the right of appeal, Douglas amended the section to include "all cases involving title to slaves . . . shall also be allowed to the Supreme Court of the United States."[43] Lastly, under section 10, Douglas amended the bill to include a fugitive slave clause, the language of which was also taken from the compromise measures of 1850.[44]

The bill as reported out on January 4 did not address the Missouri Compromise restriction. Instead, the restriction was addressed in the committee report attached to the bill. In the report, Douglas explained that the changes made to the bill had been done to ensure the bill's compliance with the principles of the Compromise of 1850, which both parties had promised to uphold:

> Those measures were intended to have a far more comprehensive and enduring effect than the mere adjustment of the difficulties arising out of the recent acquisition of Mexican territory. They were designed to establish certain great principles which would not only furnish adequate remedies for existing evils, but, in all times to come . . . by withdrawing the question of slavery from the halls of Congress . . . and committing it to the arbitrament of those who were immediately interested in it . . . your committee have deemed it their duty to incorporate and perpetuate, in their territorial bill, the principles and spirit of those measures.[45]

In the committee's accompanying report, Douglas argued that the question of slavery's prohibition in Nebraska was a "disputed" constitutional point, as it had been when Congress debated the Mexican Cession. Mexican law prohibited slavery, and "according to the laws of nations" the United States acquired the Mexican territory "with all its local laws and domestic institutions attached to its soil." However, Douglas added, only on the condition that it "did not conflict with the Constitutions of the United States." Echoing Calhoun's Fifth Amendment doctrine, Douglas argued the Mexican prohibition violated the Constitution because slavery already existed in half the country, and under the Constitution "every citizen had a right to remove to any territory of the Union, and carry his property with him under the protection of law."[46]

Douglas continued that just as Mexico's prohibition had been disputed in 1850, so too was section 8 of the Missouri Compromise that restricted slavery above the 36° 30′ parallel being disputed in 1854. And just as Congress had used the application of popular sovereignty in the Compromise of 1850 to abstain from taking a position on the disputed points in the Mexican Cession, so should Congress abstain on the disputed points in the Missouri Compromise by deferring to popular sovereignty in the Nebraska Territory. "As Congress deemed it wise and prudent to refrain from deciding the matters in controversy then," Douglas argued so the Committee on Territories was "not prepared now to recommend a departure from the course pursued on that memorable occasion."[47] Popular Sovereignty had worked once, Douglas argued. It would work again.

It is not clear if Douglas's changes to the bill were an effort to "accommodate" the wishes of Atchison and the Mess or the result of his "true convictions." P. Orman Ray and William Parrish believe the language used by Douglas in the substitute bill and attached report was an effort on his part to avoid outright repeal of the Missouri Compromise restriction on slavery and still appease Atchison. Douglas biographer Robert Johannsen acknowledges while Douglas wanted to "achieve his ends with a minimum of upset and agitation," the bill and report were nevertheless expressions of Douglas's "true convictions."[48] Accommodation or conviction, it did not matter either way. Not only did Douglas's "equivocal position" fail to appease either the pro- or antislavery factions in the Senate, it failed to stop the ensuing "firestorm" he had hoped to avoid.[49]

On January 7, Beverly Tucker's *Washington Sentinel*, published the text of Nebraska Senate bill, S. 22, without commentary. Three days later the paper republished the bill again without commentary but included a new section, 21, added at the end. It read:

> That in order to avoid all misconstruction, it is hereby declared to be the true intent, and meaning of this act, so far as the question of slavery is concerned, to carry into practical operation the following propositions and principles established by the compromise measures of 1850 to wit;
>
> First, That all questions pertaining to slavery in the territories, and in the new States to be formed therefrom, are to be left to the decision of the people residing therein, through their appropriate representative.
>
> Second, That "all cases involving title to slaves" and "questions of personal freedom," are referred to the adjudication of the local tribunals, with the right of appeal to the Supreme Court of the United States.
>
> Third, That the provisions of the Constitution, and laws of the United States in respect to fugitives from service are to be carried into faithful execution in all "the organized Territories," the same as in the States.

Two questions regarding section 21 were asked then and continue to be asked today. First, was the absence of section 21 from the original January 4 bill the result of a clerical error by the copyist as Douglas claimed or was Douglas forced by the F Street Mess to add the section after the bill had been printed? Second, did section 21 substantively change the bill?

In regard to the first question, physical and circumstantial evidence supports the argument that Douglas was forced by the F Street Mess to add the section. On the original manuscript held in the national archives, section 21 is written on a torn piece of blue stationery in Douglas's handwriting and is pasted onto the very end of the manuscript. The new version of the bill was not printed in the *Washington Union*, the official administration paper, but the *Washington Sentinel*, published by Hunter's cousin, Beverly Tucker.[50] On Monday, January 9, the day before the *Sentinel's* reprint, Atchison announced his appointments to the Committee on the Pacific Railroad, a committee Douglas clearly wanted to be appointed to and was. It is probable that Atchison used Douglas's appointment as a bargaining chip.[51]

Did section 21 substantively change the January 4 bill by adding an implicit repeal of the Missouri Compromise where there had been none? Historians differ. Robert Johannsen and David Potter are inclined to think it did not, but Allen Johnson and William Freehling believe it did. Freehling argues it "explicitly" allowed for the question of slavery to be determined at the territorial stage, and Johnson states the "unavoidable inference" was that residents of the territory would "not to be hampered" by the restrictive feature of the Missouri Act of 1820.[52] The Johnson and Freehling position is exactly the one taken at the time by David Rice Atchison. He was satisfied that the language in section 21 had done the trick, but his satisfaction would be short lived.

On Tuesday, January 10, the same day the *Sentinel* printed the change, Philip Phillips, a freshman Democratic congressman from Mobile, Alabama, approached Robert M. T. Hunter to discuss section 21. That night Hunter repeated their conversation to Atchison. Atchison met with Phillips personally the next day and, on Thursday, January 12, hauled both Phillips and Douglas into the vice president's chambers in the Capitol, where undoubtedly the proverbial "You tell him what you just told me" discussion ensued.[53]

Phillips was a strict constructionist and a bit of a legal phenomenon.[54] In 1832, as a delegate to the South Carolina convention, he had voted against nullification. Now, in Atchison's chambers he rejected the argument that section 21 implicitly repealed the Missouri Compromise. Instead, he argued the Missouri Compromise restriction against slavery remained legally intact. Even with the addition of section 21, the adoption of slavery could occur only at the constitutional stage. The principle of popular sovereignty was mute for slave owners who were still prohibited from residing in Nebraska with their slaves during the territorial stage.[55] "Repeal by implication" had not worked. It could be done only "by express words, or by the passage of an act so inconsistent with the former act that the two could not co-exist." Phillips's argument was persuasive. Subsequent meetings would follow.[56]

As Atchison, Phillips, and Douglas were meeting behind closed doors, activity in the Senate chamber the week of January 9 was uneventful, interrupted midway by adjournment for the funeral of Congressman H. A. Muhlenberg of Pennsylvania. On Thursday, January 12, Salmon P. Chase presented an antislavery petition from New York City signed by some of its leading citizens. It called for the prohibition of slavery in the territories. As with other antislavery memorials, it was ordered "to lie upon the table."[57] Next, William Gwin requested and received funds to hire a clerk for his new committee, and the Senate adjourned for the week.

Over the weekend all of Douglas's efforts to appease Atchison and the F Street Mess began to unravel. On Saturday, the Mess's paper, the *Sentinel*, called for outright repeal of the compromise, "directly and positively . . . so that the principles of the Baltimore platform may apply to Nebraska without let or hindrance." The editorial further suggested that elder statesman, Senator Lewis Cass, be induced to put forth such an amendment, in which case, the editorial continued, Douglas would surely support repeal "and sustain it with all his energy and all his ability."[58] The next evening, Archibald Dixon, the Kentucky Whig senator who had replaced Henry Clay, sat with his wife at their Washington home. Dixon, a personal friend of Atchison's, shared his friend's concerns regarding the bill. Like Phillips, Dixon believed the language in section 21 did not "repeal the restrictive provision in regard to slavery embodied in the Missouri Compromise"; he decided it was "imperiously necessary" for the "deficiency" to be corrected.[59] Dixon's wife recalled "he requested me to get my pen and paper, as he wished me to do some writing for him," and "walking up and down the room with his hands behind him, a favorite attitude, he dictated to me his motion for the repeal."[60]

The next morning, Monday the 16, Dixon showed the amendment to fellow Whig and close friend Senator John Bell of Tennessee. Bell approved. Shortly afterward the Senate convened. Dixon rose and announced his intention to offer an amendment to the Nebraska bill when it came up for consideration. It read:

> That in all territory ceded by France to the United States, under the name of Louisiana, which lies north of 36 degrees 30 minutes north latitude, slavery . . . shall be forever prohibited, shall not be so construed as to apply to the Territory contemplated by this act, or to any other Territory of the United States; but that the citizens of the several States or Territories shall be at liberty to take and hold their slaves within any of the Territories of the United States, or of the States to be formed therefrom, as if the said act, entitled as aforesaid, and approved as aforesaid, had never been passed.[61]

William Seward later claimed he deliberately pushed Dixon to introduce the amendment in order to make the "bill as objectionable as possible to northern antislavery sentiment."[62] Northern Democrats, including Senator Lewis Cass and Secretary of State William Marcy, also believed the Dixon amendment was politically motivated and asked President Pierce to oppose it. The president gave the two men his word that he would oppose the Dixon amendment.[63]

There is no evidence to support either Seward's claim or northern Democrats' fears. Dixon's wife understandably rejected the charges of "intrigues" or "plots," writing that it was "utterly incompatible" with her husband's character. His amendment, she continued, was based on his "keen legal acumen."[64] If anything, the Dixon amendment is evidence of sectional over partisan sentiment in the South regarding slavery. As William Freehling notes, no southern Whig "needed lessons in how to wax more southern than the Democracy."[65] It should also be remembered that the southern press had been talking about possible repeal, and the topic had also been subject to discussion in the halls of Congress. Dixon was easily privy to both.[66] If Dixon was nudged, it more likely came from a southern direction, from a friend perhaps, like Atchison. Because of their personal relationship and shared philosophy, it is probable Dixon was aware of Atchison's concerns with the bill and just as probable Atchison was aware of Dixon's intention that Monday.[67] Lastly, while southern Democrats had little to fear politically from southern Whigs, Democrat Stephen Douglas, with presidential ambitions of his own, had much to fear from his Nebraska bill being hijacked by a Whig. Whether it was planned by the F Street Mess or serendipitous, Dixon's amendment was the perfect gambit to force Douglas's hand.

Dixon believed his amendment took the "Senate by surprise" and that "no one appeared more startled than Judge Douglas himself."[68] Rising from his aisle seat in the last row of the Whig side of the chamber, directly across from Democrat Jesse Bright, Douglas rushed over to Dixon, who was seated in the second row on the Whig side between Samuel Phelps of Vermont and Benjamin Wade of Ohio.[69] Dixon recalled that Douglas's protest was firm but courteous. Douglas argued the repeal of the Missouri Compromise by congressional action was the same as permitting slavery into the territory by congressional action, making Dixon's amendment contrary to the very principles he, Dixon, had voted in favor of in 1850. Dixon replied it was "precisely" because he supported the Compromise of 1850 that he had introduced the amendment. Dixon told Douglas that without repeal the principle of nonintervention was negated. "We talked for some time amicably," Dixon continued, and then "separated."[70]

The Dixon amendment was ordered printed, and the Senate moved on to a long day of business that included the submission of petitions, notices of bills, and committee reports, ending with an executive session after which the Senate adjourned. That evening Dixon took ill and was absent from the chamber the next morning. Members of Congress came to him instead, "Whigs and Democrats," Mrs. Dixon wrote, "our parlor was crowded all day with visitors . . . all congratulatory, all expressing a delighted surprise."[71] Among the visitors, was Democratic congressman from Kentucky John C. Breckinridge, a close associate of the F Street Mess and future investment partner in the Superior properties with Douglas and Hunter. Breckinridge walked up to Dixon and, offering him his hand, said, "Governor, *why did none of us ever think of this before*?"[72]

While the ailing Dixon remained at home enjoying the accolades of his fellow proslavery southerners, the Senate proceeded with the day's business. Following the passage of Salmon P. Chase's bill to divide Ohio into two judicial districts, Douglas rose, acknowledged Atchison, at the president's desk, and spoke, "Mr. President," he said "I wish to give notice that on Monday next [January 23] I shall ask the Senate to take up the bill to organize the Territory of Nebraska. I give this notice for the purpose of calling the attention of Senators to the subject." Douglas took his seat, whereupon Free-Soiler Charles Sumner, dressed in his oratorical finest, rose and announced his counteramendment to Dixon's prohibiting by word or implication the repeal of slavery's restriction in Nebraska "north of thirty-six degrees and thirty minutes north latitude."[73]

The Sumner amendment was received informally and ordered to be printed.[74] It, like the Dixon amendment, was a response to the perceived inefficiencies in section 21 of the Nebraska bill. Ironically each man's concerns were based on opposite interpretations of the section. Dixon believed, as Phillips and the F Street Mess did, that section 21 of the Nebraska bill left the Missouri Compromise restriction intact. Sumner, on the other hand believed section 21 repealed it. Douglas's ten-year effort to organize Nebraska was again unraveling before his eyes. He had to make a choice. The bill could pass without the more extreme antislavery faction. It could not pass without bipartisan southern support.

The next day Douglas called on Dixon at his residence and invited him on a carriage ride "so that they might have the opportunity to talk uninterruptedly." Dixon accepted Douglas's invitation.[75] They rode together in Douglas's closed carriage in a continuous loop around the city. If Douglas hoped to get Dixon to moderate his position, his hope was quickly dashed. According to Dixon's wife, her husband persuaded Douglas to the correctness of his position instead. In Mrs. Dixon's melodramatic retelling, Douglas reportedly said, "By G-d, sir, you are right, and I will incorporate it in my bill, though I know it will raise a hell of a storm."[76] It was more likely that Douglas just wanted to keep control of the bill. He asked Dixon to drop the amendment and allow him to incorporate the repeal into the existing legislation. Dixon accepted the deal.

Thursday morning, January 19, Douglas met with John Breckinridge and Philip Phillips to discuss the repeal language. Douglas wanted the language to ensure two things: first, that the principle of popular sovereignty would remain intact; and, second, that the language would not split the party in two.[77] To that end, Douglas asked Phillips to draft "the least inflammatory language" possible and get it approved by Atchison and the Mess.[78] Phillips promised Douglas the language no later than Saturday.

Friday morning Atchison, Hunter, Mason, and Butler walked from their home at 361 F Street around the corner onto Seventh Street and entered the east wing of the Patent Office, where they met with Phillips in one of the Interior Department's newly completed offices. The decision to meet at the Patent

Office and not their home might have had something to do with the fact that the newly completed east wing "boasted" the latest in modern conveniences, including gas lighting, hot-air heat from furnaces in the basement, hot-and-cold running water piped into marble basins, and even a plant for sterilizing cuspidors.[79] Phillips had an early draft for the F Street Mess's consideration. It read: "That the people of the Territory through their Territorial legislature may legislate upon the subject of slavery in any manner they may think proper not inconsistent with the Constitution of the United States, and all laws or parts of laws inconsistent with this authority or right shall, from and after the passage of this act, become inoperative, void and of no force and effect." Phillips had avoided the more inflammatory use of the word *repeal*, and in doing so left the Missouri Compromise intact in the Minnesota Territory. This could be used to bring along the more reticent northern members of the party. The F Street Mess approved Phillips's draft.

Occupied with foreign policy issues, Franklin Pierce had had little to do with the Nebraska bill.[80] But as Phillips and the Mess were meeting at the Patent Office, the administration's paper, the *Washington Union* published an editorial denouncing both the Dixon and Sumner amendments for not adhering to the principles of the Compromise.[81] Like it or not, Pierce was now in the center of the domestic dispute over Nebraska. He called a cabinet meeting for the following morning to discuss the bill. Saturday morning the cabinet convened in the president's office on the second floor of the White House, overlooking the southeast lawn. The president and his seven secretaries sat at the "long mahogany table" in the center of the room. A portrait of Andrew Jackson hung over the fireplace at the end of the room.[82] Only Jefferson Davis, secretary of war, and James C. Dobbin, secretary of the navy, supported congressional repeal of the Missouri Compromise. The rest of the cabinet, William L. Marcy, secretary of state, James Guthrie, secretary of the treasury, Caleb Cushing, attorney general, James C. Campbell, postmaster general, and Robert McClelland, secretary of the interior, remained vehemently opposed to repeal and urged the president to support the original wording in section 21 of the bill instead. Pierce and Cushing argued that the Missouri Compromise was unconstitutional and drafted their own amendment that called on the Supreme Court to decide the matter. Pierce believed in handing the matter over to the Supreme Court to avoid a protracted struggle in Congress that could ultimately divide the Democratic Party.[83] The meeting lasted all day. In the end, the cabinet agreed to the president's proposed amendment, which read "'the rights of persons and property shall be subject only to the restrictions and limitations imposed by the Constitution of the United States and the acts giving governments, to be adjusted by a decision of the Supreme Court of the United States.'"[84]

After the amendment had been agreed to, the president called John C. Breckinridge in and asked him to deliver the proposed amendment to Douglas and the F Street Mess. Breckinridge did so. Douglas accepted the cabinet's proposal immediately, but the Mess unanimously rejected it.[85] The only language it would accept now was Phillips's. Douglas had no choice but to concede. The new amendment would be taken up on Monday, in both the House and the Senate.

Douglas assessed it was essential to get the president's endorsement of the bill with Phillips's amendment. If Pierce opposed the bill, he argued, it would lead to division within the party and, worse yet, defeat of the bill. If Pierce endorsed the bill, it would become an administration measure that loyal Democrats would be bound to support. But a meeting with Pierce on short notice was complicated by it being Sunday. Pierce and his wife were devout Congregationalists who kept a strict Sabbath. No business was conducted, and no mail was read.[86] Such a devout president would not be inclined to break his Sabbath observance for a group of men who had just rejected his cabinet's proposed amendment. In addition, Pierce and Douglas were not close politically or personally. Pierce had all but ignored Douglas in the doling out of patronage, and Douglas had all but ignored the president in the shaping of the bill. If the president was going to break the Sabbath, the request would have to come from someone Pierce trusted. It would have to come from a friend.

Fortunately, Pierce and Atchison had a mutual friend, Secretary of War Davis. Atchison and Davis had known each other as young men at Transylvania University before Davis transferred to West Point and had rekindled their friendship in Congress. Since joining the administration, Davis and his wife Varina had become extremely close to Pierce and his wife Jane. The young Davis children were of particular comfort to Jane Pierce, who was still mourning the death of her last child, and the bond between the two families only grew over time. Pierce frequently dropped in on the Davis home unannounced and visa-versa.[87] Secretary of State William Marcy may have been closer to Pierce politically, but no one was closer to Pierce personally than Jefferson Davis.

Early Sunday morning just before the church hour, Stephen Douglas, Philip Phillips, and John C. Breckinridge called on Jefferson Davis at his home.[88] Aware of the president's strict adherence to the Sabbath, the men asked Davis to intervene on their behalf. Davis was hesitant at first. They showed Davis the Phillips amendment. Davis not only approved but was convinced that the meeting was "necessary" if the bill was to be taken up the next morning.

Douglas, Davis, Breckinridge, and Phillips then met Atchison, Hunter, and Mason at 361 F Street. Douglas invited Douglas, Atchison, and Davis to ride with him in his carriage to the White House ahead of the rest to gain the president's consent to the meeting. At the White House Davis escorted Douglas and Atchison upstairs to the president's executive offices where he left them in the anteroom while he went to see the president in his private quarters.[89]

In the meantime Hunter, Mason, Breckinridge, and Phillips walked to the White House from F Street, turning right onto Fifteenth Street to the north entrance on Pennsylvania Avenue.[90] The foursome crossed the north lawn of the White House to the main entrance at the north portico, passing along the way the bronze statue of Thomas Jefferson holding a copy of the Declaration of Independence.

At the main entrance they were met by Sergeant Thomas O'Neil, the president's bodyguard. O'Neil had been Pierce's orderly during the Mexican War. He and Sidney Webster were Pierce's two most trusted and devoted assistants, always within sight or sound of the president. O'Neil sat in front of the glass screen at the entrance to the main reception hall. From his seat he sized up each person that came to see the president with a demeanor not unlike the marble busts that surrounded the hall.[91]

Hunter, Mason, Breckinridge, and Phillips entered a White House that was nearing the end of a yearlong renovation. Twelve thousand dollars had been spent on gardens and a greenhouse on the south lawn. An additional twenty-five thousand had been appropriated by Congress for interior repairs. Like the Patent Office, the White House boasted some of the latest in modern conveniences. A new hot-water heating system had been installed that provided central heat throughout the entire mansion, and the plumbing system had been expanded to include a permanent bathroom in the private quarters, the first above the basement level. The carpet and wallpaper in the public state rooms were completely replaced. The ceilings were redesigned and painted to imitate elaborate frescos. Everything was new; window cornices, damask and lace draperies, velvet sofas, gilded mantels and mirrors. Even the tablecloths, napkins, linens, and bath towels were new, and all embroidered with "President's House." Everywhere were vases of fresh cut flowers from the new greenhouse. And the mourning crepe that had earlier draped the state rooms was gone, the Pierces having ended their official mourning. The changes were impressive and could not have failed to escape the attention of the foursome as they were escorted through the west wing of the first floor to the stairwell that led to the president's family quarters.[92] There they joined the president, Davis, Douglas, and Atchison, who were waiting for them in the library.[93] Phillips described the atmosphere as one of "cold formality."

That Pierce agreed to meet with the group alone and on a Sunday was testament to the power of the personal relationship between the president and Davis. But it was not a sound move politically. He was literally, as Robert Johannsen notes, in a "crisis." Pierce's administration had been focused almost exclusively on foreign matters since the Thirty-Third Congress convened. On that particularly Sunday the Senate had yet to confirm Pierce's appointment of Soft Democrat Herman Redfield as collector for the Port of New York. Also pending Senate confirmation were two critical treaties, the Fisheries and Reciprocity treaty with Great Britain and the Gadsden Treaty with Mexico, a copy of which had only arrived the week before. Nevertheless, Pierce had allowed himself to be alone in a room with men who represented the full might of the Congress. It could not have taken long for Pierce to realize his mistake. To refuse these men put his appointments and treaties at stake.[94]

Pierce gave his consent to the repeal, forgetting or ignoring that only two days earlier he had promised Cass and Marcy he would oppose it. Douglas, knowing the president's reputation for making verbal promises he did not keep, demanded written consent. He asked Pierce to draft the language in his own hand. Pierce consented. Borrowing phraseology from Phillips's earlier draft, Pierce wrote that the Missouri Compromise was "superseded by the principles of the legislation of 1850, commonly called the compromise measures, and is hereby declared inoperative and void." Before leaving, the president asked the group to be sure Marcy was apprised of the changes. They agreed. Leaving the White House, Atchison and company called at Marcy's home, found him out, and went home. But at some point, before or after the White House meeting, Caleb Cushing was apprised. The *Washington Union*'s Sunday editorial reversed its earlier position and endorsed the repeal of the Missouri Compromise.

While Douglas and the F Street Mess were meeting with the president, six Free-Soil members of Congress, Senators Salmon P. Chase and Charles Sumner, along with Congressmen Edward Wade and Joshua Giddings of Ohio, Alexander Dewitt of Massachusetts, and Gerrit Smith of New York were also meeting to discuss the Nebraska bill. They were convinced the post–January 4 bill was drifting toward repeal of the Missouri Compromise, hence Sumner's amendment on January 17. The Free-Soilers decided a more organized opposition was needed and together began to draft a statement of opposition.[95]

Monday morning, January 23, Douglas called a meeting of the Committee on Territories to alert the members to the changes in the bill. Few were able to attend on such short notice, and the two that did, Edward Everett and John Bell, were able to give the changes only a brief review.[96] Nevertheless Douglas reported the new bill as the committee's bill. When the Senate convened later that Monday, news of the White House meeting the day before had yet to be leaked to the press. The Reverend William H. Milburn opened the Senate with a prayer. It was followed by the perfunctory reading and approval of the Senate journal, submission of petitions, and other mundane Senate business. After the reports from standing committees and bills signed had been concluded, Stephen Douglas rose and asked the Senate's permission to report the Committee on Territories revised Nebraska bill to be substituted for the bill reported out on January 4. Save for the few that had been at or privy to the White House meeting, the changes to the bill took nearly all by surprise.

First Douglas called attention to two boundary changes in the bill. The southern boundary, 36° 30′, had been moved to the 37° north latitude "in order not to divide" land belonging to "the Cherokee nation by terms of the bill."[97] The remaining Nebraska Territory had been divided into two territories at the fortieth parallel, to be named the Kansas and Nebraska territories. The boundary changes had divided the Nebraska Territory into three parts; the Cherokee nation now completely south of the original territory, Kansas just above the Cherokee nation territory, and Nebraska above the fortieth parallel.[98] Some contemporaries and later historians mistakenly believed the divisions were done to create two territories, one slave, Kansas, and one free, Nebraska. In actuality the divisions were the result of the long competition between Iowa and Missouri, and Chicago and St. Louis, over the future routes and terminus of the Pacific Railroad. Iowans believed Missouri had benefited from Atchison's power in the Senate. Indian title to the land west of Missouri was being quickly extinguished by Indian Commissioner George Manypenny, a proslavery Democrat whom Iowans believed to be Atchison's man, while the titles west of Iowa remained under Indian control.[99] As it stood, Augustus Dodge feared if Nebraska remained a single territory, white settlement would only be able to push westward from Missouri, making it likely that the territorial seat of government and the Pacific railroad would be south of Iowa.[100] The new divisions had been put in place to avoid this and ensure the Pacific railroad would be built along a northern or central route through Nebraska.[101] On a personal level, the divisions also benefited Douglas by protecting his real-estate interests around Chicago and Lake Superior City.[102] It also protected Robert Hunter, who had invested in the Lake Superior properties. In explaining the division, Douglas informed the Senate that the members of the Iowa and Missouri delegations had been informed and concurred. He also recognized the presence in the chamber of Nebraska's two territorial agents, both of whom requested the division.

Douglas was less forthcoming on the changes regarding the Missouri Compromise stating only that changes had also been made to the bill to make certain provisions on "other and more delicate questions more clear." Holding the bill aloft in his hand Douglas ended by requesting it be substituted "for the one reported by the Committee on Territories," on January 4.

Questions from the chamber floor were immediate. Was Douglas asking for a postponement? Had the substitute bill been officially reported out from the committee? If so, were there now two bills before the Senate? Douglas responded to the members' concerns. Consideration of the bill was being postponed for one day, he explained, to give members the "opportunity to look into the [new] bill."[103] He also clarified that there were not two bills before the Senate but two territories with the boundaries for each specified in one bill. The motion to print was then agreed upon, and the Senate moved forward to business from Hunter's Committee on Finance. In the meantime, the *New York Herald* published its story on the rejected Cabinet proposal of the previous Saturday.[104]

Following routine business the next morning, Douglas took the floor and asked the Senate "to proceed to the consideration of the order of the day, the bill to organize the Territories of Kansas and Nebraska." The printed version of the bill had only arrived on the members' desks that morning, and the few who had had the chance to read it began to call for postponement of debate. Most disturbing to those who had read the substitute bill was section 14 that pertained to the "the Constitution, and laws of the United States," having the "same force and effect with the said Territory of Nebraska as elsewhere within the United States." It now read "Except the eighth section of the act preparatory to the admission of Missouri into the Union, approved March sixth, eighteen hundred and twenty, which was superseded by the principles of the legislation of eighteen hundred and fifty, commonly called the compromise measures, and is hereby declared inoperative."[105]

Democrat Morris Norris of New Hampshire rose first. He reminded Douglas that the substitute language had been introduced only the day before and many members "had not yet had time" to read it. On this "matter of great importance," he believed postponement was called for. Douglas responded that the members had had most of the bill for weeks and still not read it. The only way to get them to read it, he believed, was to debate it. Douglas was wary of the strategy of postponement because it had been used against his efforts to organize Nebraska in earlier Congresses. He was not going to allow the subterfuge again, telling the chamber he considered it his "duty" to keep the bill before the members and preventing "other matters for consideration" from overriding the bill at hand.[106]

Salmon Chase responded next, arguing that the bill Douglas referred to, the original Dodge bill, had undergone significant changes since its introduction including those introduced the day before, which he believed had "changed the form of the bill altogether." Chase reminded his fellow senators that any discussion of the bill would be postponed the following day in order to take up the previously scheduled special order regarding the Vermont seat held by Samuel Phelps.[107] "It therefore seems to me," Chase continued, "that the discussion upon that question should precede the discussion on this bill . . . .would it not be better to postpone this bill until some day of next week, and make it the special order, with the understanding that it shall be then proceeded with?"

Douglas relented, "cheerfully," but on the condition that no further interruption or delay be allowed. He then offered the motion "that the bill be postponed to, and made the special order of the day from Monday next, and be the special order from day to day until it is disposed of."

Dixon rose and complimented Douglas on the new bill. Taking the opportunity to speak further, he refuted the charges that his earlier amendment to repeal had been intended to "embarrass the Democratic party." Not true, Dixon declared, "upon the question of slavery I know no Whiggery, and I know no Democracy. I am a proslavery man. I am from a slaveholding State; I represent a slaveholding constituency; and I am here to maintain the rights of that people whenever they are presented before the Senate."[108]

With that Dixon withdrew his amendment and sat down. Douglas thanked the Senator from Kentucky and reminded the others that it had never been the intent of the committee to legislate slavery in the Nebraska Territory but instead to "remove any whatever obstacles Congress had put there, and apply the doctrine of congressional nonintervention, in accordance with the principles of the compromise measures of 1850, and allow the people to do as they pleased upon this, as well as all other matters affecting their interests." After Douglas finished his remarks, Dixon added one final caveat: "I have always believed and maintained, as a sound proposition . . . that the power of Congress never did exist at all over the subject of slavery, either within or without the limits of the Territories." With that the motion to postpone to January 30 was agreed to.[109]

Following the executive session at end of the day, James Mason introduced a motion to postpone Wednesday's session in order for the Senate to attend the funeral of Russian minister Alexander de Bodisco, who had died in residence in Washington. The resolution was agreed to, and the Senate adjourned until Thursday. Later that day the *New York Herald* broke news of the previous Sunday White House meeting. Picking up on its previous cabinet story, the

Herald reported that even though Douglas had accepted the Cabinet amendment, "Atchison, Mason, [and] Hunter" had rejected it and forced the meeting with the president.[110] "The gentlemen," the paper noted, "did not appreciate the difference between the propriety of the President directing them to discuss the matter, Sunday though it was, and his joining in the discussion himself." The paper further reported that Atchison forced the president to meet, telling him that if he declined "they would take it for granted that he favored . . . the amendment abrogating the Missouri Compromise as an Administration measure." The *Herald* story concluded that "the past twenty-four hours [had] witnessed a complete somersault of the President and Cabinet on the Nebraska matter."[111]

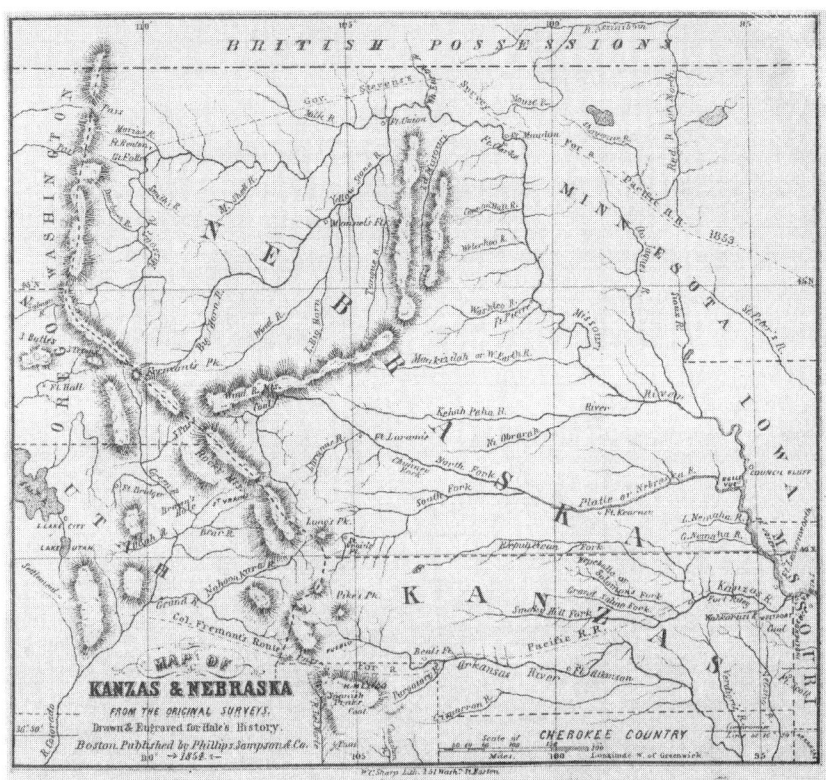

An 1854 territorial map of Kansas and Nebraska, made from the original survey. The 36° 30′ parallel line is marked in the lower right-hand corner. From the collections of the Omaha Public Library.

Franklin Pierce, fourteenth president of the United States (1853–1857). Under pressure from the F Street Mess, Pierce made the repeal of the Missouri Compromise restriction in the Nebraska-Kansas bill an administration measure. Library of Congress.

David Rice Atchison, U.S. senator from Missouri from 1843 to 1857.
Courtesy of the Beinecke Rare Book Collection, Yale University.

Robert Mercer Taliaferro Hunter, U.S. senator from Virginia from 1847 to 1861. Library of Congress.

James Murray Mason, U.S. senator from Virginia from 1847 to 1861. Library of Congress.

Andrew Pickens Butler, U.S. senator from South Carolina from 1846 to 1857. Courtesy of the Beinecke Rare Book Collection, Yale University.

Stephen A. Douglas, U.S. senator from Illinois from 1847 to 1861. Library of Congress.

Philip Phillips, one-term congressman from Alabama during the Thirty-Third Congress, who wrote the repeal language for the Kansas-Nebraska Act. Library of Congress.

CHAPTER FIVE

The Power to Repeal

The F Street Mess had achieved the unthinkable. The restriction against slavery above the 36° 30′ parallel was sacrosanct in the eyes of most northerners as well as quite a few southerners. And yet through the use of institutional power that bordered on arm twisting, the Mess had taken a thirty-four-year-old measure enshrined in principle and magically "superseded" it by the yet untested theory of "popular sovereignty." It was political gamesmanship at its best, above and beyond anything ever achieved by its mentor Calhoun. But the veil of secrecy under which the Mess had maneuvered since December had been lifted. The legislation would now have to pass in the Senate with the country watching. The names Robert M. T. Hunter, James Murray Mason, David Rice Atchison, and Andrew Pickens Butler would become familiar to many as the debate wore on, and amid the backdrop of growing abolitionist protests they would come to personify the Slave Power.

At the same time the *New York Herald* was breaking the story of the Mess's Sunday meeting with the president at the White House, Washington antislavery weekly the *National Era* published a rhetorical diatribe against the Nebraska bill entitled the "Appeal of the Independent Democrats." The article, postdated January 19, was written primarily by Salmon Chase but later modified by those who attended Chase and Sumner's Sunday meeting on January 21. The focus of the Appeal was on section 21 of the January 4 bill. In response to the January 23 substitute bill which had dropped section 21 and replaced it with the more specific language in section 13, which declared the Missouri Compromise "inoperative," Chase and company added a last-minute attack on the Slave Power and Douglas. It accused southern congressmen of "an atrocious plot" to turn the Nebraska Territory "into a dreary region of despotism, inhabited by masters and slaves," and Douglas of complying with the conspiracy in order to further his presidential ambitions.[1] The Appeal called upon Americans to "resist," this "gross violation of a sacred pledge [the Missouri Compromise]," and "criminal betrayal of [their] precious rights," by any means possible. In the weeks to come, state legislators, ministers, and private citizens would answer the Appeal's call, flooding the halls of Congress with letters of protests, petitions, and resolutions.[2]

Historian Michael Holt argues that the publication of the Appeal was the critical moment in the destruction of the Whig Party. He believes that up until January 24 the Nebraska bill had been a partisan issue that could have potentially revived the Whig Party just as the party's united opposition to Texas annexation in 1844 had. Accordingly, "conservative northern Whigs . . . wanted to fight the [Nebraska] bill on grounds of its threat to national tranquility and its violation of the concord reached in 1850, in ways, that is, that could persuade pro-Compromise southern Whigs to oppose it and thus preserve harmony between northern and southern Whigs."[3] But the divisive rhetoric employed by the authors of the Appeal destroyed any chance of southern Whigs joining their northern brethren "by rendering any opposition to the Nebraska bill for whatever reason betrayal of the South."[4]

In the same way the Appeal's divisive and inflammatory rhetoric helped to destroy the organizational structure of the Whig Party, it compensated for the Free-Soil movement's lack thereof. According to David Potter, "the antislavery congressmen were usually politically free lancers who lacked a normal basis of political support through party organization, and they found in this type of propaganda a strategic way to compensate for the weakness of the organizational power."[5] What had been a partisan issue for more than a decade became a sectional issue overnight. And the bill to organize Nebraska, extinguish Indian title to the land therein, and build the Pacific railroad ceased to exist, becoming a bill on slavery instead.[6] But there was a third kind of power in the mix, not organizational or rhetorical, but institutional. This kind of power the F Street Mess had in volumes. It had been instrumental in its control of Douglas and the president. The Mess would use its near lock on it as the bill moved forward to hold the Democratic Party in line and bring southern Whigs along with it.[7]

The simultaneous release of stories on the F Street Mess's backroom power brokering and the Appeal's call to arms took its toll on Douglas. Following Minister Bodisco's funeral on Wednesday, Douglas ran into George Murray McConnel in a Washington hotel. McConnel was the son of a loyal Douglas supporter in Illinois. Reportedly McConnel witnessed a Douglas melt-down. Pacing in front of a fireplace, the "discouraged" Douglas told McConnel, "Never go into politics. . . . If you do so, no matter how sincere and earnest you may be, no matter how ardently you may devote yourself to the welfare of the country, and your whole country . . . your hands are tied and you are bound to do only what you can do . . . rather than what you might prefer to do if free to choose; no matter for all this or more you will be misinterpreted, vilified, traduced, and finally sacrificed to some local interest or unreasoning passion."[8]

When the Senate reconvened the following day, Douglas was silent. But the impact of the previous Sunday's power meeting at the White House was loud and clear. In executive session that day, the long and deliberately delayed confirmation vote was at last held on the president's choice for New York City port collector, Soft Democrat Herman J. Redfield. The Senate voted to confirm by a vote of 35 to 8. Controlled by the F Street Mess, all present for the vote, the Democrats voted unanimously for Redfield. The eight nays, all southern Whigs, included Dixon and Thompson of Kentucky, Toombs and Dawson of Georgia, Bell and Jones of Tennessee, Badger of North Carolina, and Benjamin of Louisiana.[9] In the weeks to come there would be no more division among southern senators, as the F Street Mess made sure to include Dixon, Bell, and the rest of southern Whig leadership in all caucus deliberations on the Nebraska bill. Calhoun's dream of a southern party had been realized within the Capitol walls. The Democratic caucus had become a southern caucus, tying Douglas's hands even tighter.

On Monday January 30, private citizens and public officers rushed to the Senate Chamber to witness the opening debate in the portending historic event. Both the Lady and East galleries were filled to capacity, and congressmen from the other side of the Capitol gathered on the chamber floor behind the senators' desks.[10] Silence came over the chamber as David Rice Atchison gaveled the Senate into session and the Reverend Henry Slicer rose to offer the morning prayer. After its perfunctory duties were completed, the Senate "proceeded to the consideration of the bill to organize the Territory of Nebraska." It had been ten years since Stephen Douglas had introduced his first bill to organize the Nebraska Territory and one week since the publication of the "Appeal of Independent Democrats" opposing his efforts. Douglas believed the Appeal misrepresented the bill's intent, and he took its attack as a personal affront to his integrity. Ironically the Appeal helped Douglas. He was known to be at his best when he was angry, and rising to address the chamber, Douglas did little to hide his anger.[11]

Those who packed the floor and galleries that day took little notice of Douglas's diminutive size and "slovenly" dress. They had come to see the "bantam cock," the "combative" and "frenetic" speaker with an encyclopedic memory from which he could pull at will. Looking at the audiences above and before him, Douglas spoke in "a loud voice . . . shaking his [disproportionately large] head and forefinger" for emphasis.[12] He had not intended to speak for more than "ten or fifteen minutes," just enough time to explain "the provisions relating to the Indians... and... those which might be supposed to bear upon the question of slavery." It had been "all [he] intended to say, if the question had been taken up for consideration on Tuesday." But it had not, and now Douglas felt compelled "to go more fully into the discussion." Looking directly at Chase and Sumner he reminded the audience that the gentlemen from Ohio and Massachusetts had been the ones who requested additional time on January 24 to consider the bill, and Douglas had graciously "yielded" to that request.

> Sir, little did I suppose at the time that I granted that act of courtesy to those two Senators, that they had drafted and published to the world a document, over their own signatures, in which they arraigned me as having been guilty of a criminal betrayal of my trust... of bad faith, and been engaged in an atrocious plot against the cause of free government. Little did I suppose... that on that very morning the *National Era*... contained an address... in which the bill is grossly misrepresented, in which the action of the members of the committee is grossly falsified, in which our motives are arraigned, and our characters calumniated.... And, Sir, what is more I find that there was a postscript added to the address, published the very morning, in which the principal amendment reported by the committee was set out, and then coarse epithets applied to me by name.[13]

Douglas proceeded to read portions of the Appeal and its postscript. He did not need to go any further to suggest duplicity on the part of Chase and Sumner, whom he referred to as "Abolitionist confederates," than noting the date of the postscript, "Sunday, January 22, 1854." But he did. Douglas attacked Chase and Sumner for holding their conspiratorial "conclave" on the "Sabbath," while others were "engaged in attending divine worship," leaving out that he too had failed to respect the Sabbath that day and instead had attended the more exclusive "conclave" at the White House.[14]

Douglas added that the Appeal had been written to facilitate the passage of resolutions against the bill in the Ohio State Legislature and had appeared on January 24 in several New York papers erroneously signed by Ohio Democrats. At this point, traditional Senate decorum disintegrated into a shouting match between Chase and Douglas, with Chase trying to take the floor and Douglas refusing to yield it. Atchison finally ruled Douglas out of order and forced him to return to the provisions of the bill. For the next several hours Douglas refuted the charges made in the Appeal point by point, taking only a handful of questions from the floor.[15]

The remainder of Douglas's speech focused on two points. First he rejected the Appeal's argument that the Founding Fathers had intended to prohibit the spread of slavery in all the territories. Instead, he argued two principles on slavery's extension into the territories, geographic demarcation and popular sovereignty, had coexisted since the Republic's founding, that geographic demarcation written into the 1820 legislation was done so only to "avoid all agitation upon the slavery question by settling that question forever, so far as our territory extended, which was then to the Mississippi River." The same legislation maintained popular sovereignty in Missouri, where the residents were allowed "to exercise their own judgment and do as they pleased upon the subject, without any implication for or against the existence of the institution." He noted the legislation did not apply to the territory west of Missouri, Nebraska, for two reasons. First, slavery existed in the original Louisiana Purchase only under common law, and as such carried only "so far as that usage actually" went and "not further." Second, Nebraska was Indian Country and "local legislation of the state of Missouri did not reach into" it.[16]

Douglas argued further that Congress had intended section 8 in the Missouri Compromise legislation, establishing the 36° 30′ geographic division, to extend beyond "that piece of country . . . by extending that dividing line as far west as our territory went, and running it onward on each new acquisition of territory."[17] It was used until 1848 when his bill to extend the line through the Mexican Cession to the Pacific was defeated in the House by "northern votes, with Free-Soil proclivities."

Douglas's second argument was that the Missouri Compromise had been effectively rendered inoperative ever since the 1848 vote and the resulting measures of the Compromise of 1850. Using Texas as one of many examples, Douglas pointed out that the territory taken from Texas and ceded to New Mexico under the compromise measures was territory above the 36° 30′ parallel, nevertheless under the New Mexico act of 1850, popular sovereignty, and not geographic restriction applied. He also noted that Utah's territorial boundaries contained land from the original Louisiana Purchase and was above the 36° 30′ parallel. Therefore, Douglas concluded the Missouri Compromise had been rendered inoperative by the Compromise of 1850, the principles of which applied "in organization of all new Territories, to all which we now own, or which we may acquire." He warned the Senate to construe otherwise would "reopen the issue every time you make a new territorial government." Toward the end of his remarks Douglas apologized to the Senate for speaking as long as he had. He reminded its members that while it had not been his intention to do so he had nevertheless been compelled to set the record straight and defend his honor against "the Abolition confederates" whose "gross falsification of the laws of the land" had "deliberately mislead the public" and "malign[ed]" his character.[18]

Chase and Sumner were both given a chance to speak after Douglas's remarks. Both denied that the Appeal had been a personal attack against Douglas. The Appeal, they stated, was an attack against the bill, not the author. Chase noted Douglas had not been mentioned by name at all except in the appendix to the Appeal and then only as the bill's author. Sumner followed Chase's remarks, also denying they had intended to attack Douglas. "We did not assail him," Sumner declared, "We did not say a word about him from the beginning to the end of our appeal. He was named only in the postscript, and then merely as the author of the bill. We spoke of the bill. We spoke of its character. We said nothing about the character of the individuals who were its authors; anybody may see that who chooses to read the address."[19]

To prove that the Appeal had not attacked Douglas personally, Sumner concluded by submitting to the Senate the Appeal in its entirety, unlike Douglas who had read excerpts. Nevertheless, Douglas took both the Free-Soil subterfuge on January 24 and the Appeal's attack on the bill's intentions as a personal affront. Following Sumner's concluding remarks, William Seward offered a motion to adjourn. It was carried.

Douglas's strategy was to move quickly through the debate to the vote. The opposition's strategy was to delay debate.[20] When Douglas attempted to move forward on the Nebraska-Kansas bill on Tuesday, Salmon Chase asked for yet another week's postponement. Chase explained his attendance was required in court the next day, and hence he would be unable to complete his response to Douglas's speech of the previous day.[21]

A frustrated Douglas exploded that he had consented to postponement "until yesterday, with the understanding that it should be the special order from day to day until disposed of." Douglas pointed out the contradiction: if Chase had not yet time to study the bill, then why had Chase "published a history of this question to the world without investigating those very facts that he now wishes to examine?" Douglas warned the Senate against further delay: "We all understand the object is to prevent the action of the body upon the question. The enemies of this bill wish to keep it off—to stave it off—to run the discussion into the elections, and get up an excitement and agitation in the country, in order to prevent action."[22]

For a second time in two days the debate disintegrated into a shouting match between Douglas and Chase, each accusing the other of lacking senatorial "courtesy." Atchison ruled both out of order and reminded the chamber that he would not hesitate to do the same to any other Senator "who may be out of order."[23]

The rest of the day was spent in debate on whether to postpone and, if so, for how long. Supporters of the bill put forth a motion to postpone until Thursday. Chase requested postponement until Friday, stating court matters precluded him from attending the Senate on Thursday. The rest of the opposition pushed for a Monday postponement. So many motions were being put forward, including Solomon Foot's attempt to amend the Thursday motion by inserting Monday, that confusion ensued. The Thursday motion carried, but before Atchison could announce the result, Douglas moved to change his vote to nay. The F Street Mess followed in changing its vote as well. In changing his vote to nay, Archibald Dixon spoke for many in the chamber when he said, "I believe none of us understood precisely what we were doing." The Thursday motion was defeated and postponement to Friday was agreed to. Douglas reminded Chase and his followers that he would no longer countenance any further delays, even for "want of preparation."[24]

Debate on the Nebraska-Kansas bill began at long last on Friday, February 3 at 1:00 P.M. Douglas, noting the hour, reminded the Senate it was the time agreed on, and therefore he moved the Senate to "postpone all prior orders of business, for the purpose of proceeding to the consideration of the Nebraska bill." The motion carried, and the Senate "resumed consideration of the bill." Atchison recognized the floor leader for the opposition, Salmon Chase, who offered his amendment to strike "was superseded by the principles of the legislation of 1850, commonly called the compromise measures" from section 14 of the bill and replace it with "That the Constitution, and all laws of the United States which are not locally, inapplicable, shall have the same force and effect within the said Territory of Nebraska as elsewhere within the United States, except the eighth section of the act preparatory to the admission of Missouri into the Union, approved March 6, 1820."[25] Chase's amendment was intended to force debate about Douglas's theory of supersedure. In his speech that followed, Chase countered Douglas's arguments point by point. Regarding Douglas's argument that the compromise measures of 1850 had superseded the Missouri Compromise of 1820, Chase countered that the congressional nonintervention as passed under the New Mexico and Utah legislation was exclusive to those two territories, and no one at the time, not Henry Clay, not Douglas himself, suggested otherwise. "At what time, in what speech," Chase asked, was it "ever suggested" that the Compromise of 1850 superseded the Missouri Compromise? "Did any supporter, or any opponent" suggest it? "No, sir," shouted Chase, "no man, North or South," nor anyone anywhere during the entire debate in 1850 "ever intimated any such opinion."[26]

Chase continued along this line of argument reminding the Senate that the bill's two strongest supporters, Douglas and Atchison, had never prior to the opening of the Thirty-Third Congress suggested "supersedure." Douglas's Nebraska bill in the Thirty-Second Congress had been silent on the matter, and Atchison, "whose authority," Chase stated, "I think, must go for something . . . made a speech upon the bill, in which he distinctly declared that the Missouri prohibition was not repealed, and could not be repealed."

In regard to Douglas's arguments that geographic demarcation and popular sovereignty coexisted in the portions of the Louisiana Purchase that were later incorporated into Texas, New Mexico, and Utah, Chase charged Douglas with "gross ignorance of history and geography of the country." First, the territory ceded to New Mexico by the United States had been acquired from Mexico, not Texas. "Texas had claimed it, but gave up her claim"; therefore, Chase argued, Douglas's assertion, that the measures of the Compromise of 1850 applied to territory outside the Mexican Cession, was not true. As to the portion of the Louisiana Purchase incorporated into the Utah territory, Chase found Douglas's assertion almost laughable. "Here spreads out the vast Territory of Utah, more than one hundred and eighty-seven thousand square miles. Here is the little spot, hardly a pin's point upon the map, which I cover with the tip of my little finger, which according to the boundary fixed by the territorial bill, was cut off from the Louisiana acquisition. The account given of it in the Senator's speech would lead one to suppose that it was an important part of the Louisiana acquisition. It is, in fact, not of the smallest consequence. There are no inhabitants there."

Chase concluded that if Douglas was wrong in his understanding of the territorial boundaries encompassed by the Compromise of 1850, he was "also wrong in his declaration that the compromise act of 1850" did "not preserve and reassert the principle of the Missouri prohibition." Chase spoke for two and half hours, and when he finally finished his remarks, most of the time allotted for debate that day had been consumed. A Saturday session had already been scheduled, but as part of the opposition's general strategy to delay, George Badger, Whig Senator from North Carolina, rose following Chase's conclusion and attempted to make a motion to adjourn until Monday.[27] He was cut off by James Mason who, declaring "I hope not," called for an immediate vote. The motion to adjourn until Monday was defeated. With the exception of four southern Whigs, including Badger, who voted for the motion, the vote had been along sectional lines. Andrew Butler quickly moved to adjourn for the day. The motion was agreed to, debate would continue in the morning.

Douglas and the F Street Mess were determined to push the debate through to a vote before the end of the first session. Chase and the opposition were just as determined to delay it. But Douglas's floor leadership combined with the Mess's institutional control and superior knowledge of the rules effectively blocked all opposition measures designed to delay, including the introduction of petitions and memorials.[28] The Senate debated the Nebraska-Kansas bill straight through the month of February, convening twenty-one of twenty-eight days, including two Saturdays.[29] Atchison and the party leadership met with Douglas in daily caucus meetings before each session to plan strategy. Southern Whigs were invited to the meetings in order to gain their support.[30]

The primary issue for southern Whigs remained whether the wording in section 14 specifically repealed the Missouri Compromise. Southern Whigs wanted to be sure that slaveholders would not be prevented from bringing their slaves into Nebraska during the territorial stage. Ironically while the opposition believed Douglas's January 23 bill repealed section 8 of the Missouri Compromise, southern Whigs believed the phraseology remained ambiguous, and the bill might yet prevent slaveholders from bringing their slaves into the Nebraska-Kansas territories at the territorial stage.[31]

As Atchison worked to solve the problem behind closed doors, the Senate's crowded galleries and packed floor witnessed a debate of historic proportions. Every senator who wanted to speak was allowed to, alternating between those in favor of the bill and those against. The speeches provided valuable information to senators still on the fence, as well as those House members who sat behind the senators listening, and played a significant role in swaying public opinion North and South.[32]

By early February the debate was already having a significant impact on Missouri's fall elections, and Missourians followed it closely in their local newspapers. Atchison knew the outcome of his reelection race against Thomas Hart Benton that fall would be closely tied to the outcome of the bill. Missourians wanted Nebraska organized, and at the start of the Thirty-Third Congress Benton had stated he could support Douglas's bill. The January 23 substitute bill had forced Benton into the opposition camp. Atchison wanted to make sure he stayed there.[33] Douglas's political future (i.e., the presidency) was also tied to the bill. So too were his hopes for advancing his financial interests and those of the trans-Mississippi West. Douglas's multiple motivations for the successful passage of the Nebraska-Kansas bill were colliding in the caucus meetings. Atchison and the southern Whigs' desire for more specific language now added another motivation for him, the well-being of the Democratic Party.

Chase's motion to strike Douglas's "superseded" language from section 14 was defeated easily on Monday, February 6, despite an impassioned speech made by fellow Ohio abolitionist, Benjamin Wade. Early in his speech Wade was interrupted by an ongoing discussion between Senator Dixon, who sat to his immediate right, and Butler, who had come over from the other side of the aisle. The exchange between the three men opened a momentary window into nineteenth-century thinking on race and equality. Wade had been discussing the inherent rights expounded by the Declaration of Independence when he stopped his remarks. "Sir," said Wade, "I hear the gentleman from South Carolina talking to the Senator from Kentucky, and I wish it to go forth that the gentleman from South Carolina say, why should not the free laborer work with the slave? Is he not his equal? Is that the opinion of the chairman of the committee?" Butler did not answer. Instead, Dixon asked Wade if he believed the slave was the equal of a white laborer in the North. If Dixon and Butler intended to embarrass Wade, or trip him up in anyway, he failed to comply. "The slave," Wade said, "is equal to anybody else, but is degraded by the nefarious acts and selfishness of the master, who compels him, by open force and without right, to serve him alone." What of "free negroes," Dixon asked; did Wade consider those who lived in Ohio "equal to the free White people" who lived there? Wade replied if Dixon defined equality in terms of "wealth, riches, and influence," then no, not even in Ohio were free negroes equal to white men, but that did "not prevent that equality of which" he spoke, granted by the Almighty's tenure and imbedded in the Declaration of Independence.[34] Wade's spirited defense opened up a flood of questions from other southern senators, Democrats and Whigs. The day's session had become a forum on the Constitution's recognition of the founding principles of the Declaration. The Nebraska-Kansas bill had never been farther from being a bill about the Pacific Railroad.

It was night by the time Benjamin Wade finished his impassioned defense of Chase's amendment. It failed anyway by a vote of 13 to 30, whereupon Wade moved to strike the entire enabling clause and replace it with a new substitute. Sadly, his command of Enlightenment philosophy was no match for the procedural knowledge of the bill's supporters. Ultimately that was the opposition's greatest weakness. Douglas quickly noted that a substitute amendment could not be replaced but only amended. The presiding chair, Solomon Foot of Vermont, concurred. Douglas, however, feeling the pressure from party leadership, moved to amend his substitute by striking out the phrase "superseded by" and replacing it with "which is inconsistent with." The reason for the change, explained Douglas, was to clarify the clause; he argued that section 8 of the Missouri act "is inconsistent with the principles of the legislation of 1850, commonly called the compromise measure, and is hereby declared inoperative." It did not work. The Senate devolved into a debate over language and the meaning of the words, "supersede" and "inconsistent." Lewis Cass pulled out his dictionary. Andrew Pickens Butler jokingly suggested they secure a copy of *Crabbes's Synonymes*. Douglas gave up and told the assembled body he would go back to the drawing board that evening, "I do not deem it very important to continue the discussion on this point . . . I shall modify the words so as to meet the objection that Senators make as to the meaning of 'superseded by' and 'inconsistent with.'" After that the Senate agreed to postpone "further consideration of the bill until to-morrow."[35]

The Senate resumed its consideration of the Nebraska-Kansas bill the following Tuesday morning, February 7. Douglas spoke first.

> I have drawn an amendment which I believe meets the general approbation of the friends of the measure. I therefore now move to amend the 14th section of the substitute reported, by striking out the words:
> —which [the Missouri compromise act] was superseded by the principles of the legislation of 1850, commonly called the compromise measures, and is hereby declared inoperative,
> And inserting
> —which being inconsistent with the principles of nonintervention by Congress with slavery in the States and Territories, as recognized by the legislation of 1850, commonly called the compromise measures, is hereby declared inoperative and void, it being the true intent and meaning of this act not to legislate slavery into any Territory or State, nor to exclude it therefrom; but to leave the people thereof perfectly free to form and regulate their domestic institutions in their own way, subject only to the Constitution of the United States.[36]

Edward Everett, a member of the Committee on Territories, informed the chamber he was unable to support the bill as reported but was not yet prepared to make remarks. Thomas Rusk of Texas called for postponement to allow Everett time to prepare. Douglas responded there was no reason to postpone as there were plenty of senators prepared to speak on the bill until Everett was ready to do so. William Gwin of California agreed and suggested the Senate "take all the preliminary votes to-day" to perfect the bill allowing the discussion to proceed after that on the bill that would be voted on. In the middle of the discussion William Sebastian, chairman of the Committee on

Indian Affairs, suggested the Senate move forward on the bill by considering his committee's amendments to the clauses of the bill pertaining to Indian land titles. His amendment dealt primarily with the appropriations to do so. Douglas agreed. He withdrew his amendment and submitted it informally to be printed. The Senate moved forward to the Sebastian amendments, and after a brief debate the Senate voted to approve. Douglas renewed his amendment, and on a motion from George Badger of North Carolina, "further consideration of the bill was postponed until to-morrow."[37]

The next morning the Senate galleries were again filled to capacity, with hundreds more clamoring to get in. On the floor Sam Houston rose and asked the presiding chair, Foot of Vermont, to grant the ladies still waiting for seats permission to sit "in the rear of the bar of the Senate." Houston admitted he was normally opposed to allowing women on the Senate floor but noting the inclement weather and the "peculiar circumstances of the occasion," he was willing to make the exception as there were "several hundred of them at the door." The chamber erupted in laughter and shouts of "Oh, no!"[38]

Rising to the occasion, literally and figuratively, Houston called upon his fellow senators' sense of "liberality," "courtesy," and "gallantry." He admitted he might be exaggerating a bit, but even if it was only fifty ladies "it would be exceedingly gratifying to those fifty" to be admitted. Houston's "gallantry" was quickly seconded by Augustus Dodge of Wisconsin, who noted the women had come to hear Edward Everett speak, "a gentleman who is renowned for great eloquence."[39]

John Weller of California spoke next. He did not want to appear "ungracious or ungallant," but he sat "on the frontier," in the last row on the Democratic side to the left of James Mason. When ladies had been admitted in the past, it was difficult for him to hear what was said on the other side of the Chamber. Besides which, Weller admitted, "I am very much more disposed to turn my ear to what is going on behind me than to listen to what is said on the other side of the Chamber." Nevertheless he would agree to their admittance if they would "be as quiet as possible." The chamber again erupted in laughter.[40]

The only objection to the day's lightheartedness was John Pettit of Indiana whose attitude was as inclement as the weather. Pettit stated "in the most solemn form" that he was opposed to admitting ladies to the floor. Solomon Foot reminded him that the rules of the Senate required unanimous consent to adopt Houston's motion.[41] Pettit refused to change his mind, noting he had seen just "the other day a judge of the Supreme Court, seventy years of age, standing here unable to get a seat." And so the ladies were not admitted to the floor. It was arguably the only day that month when an issue other than the Nebraska-Kansas bill took center stage, if only for a moment.

On Monday, February 13, a sore throat prevented Sam Houston from completing his speech in opposition to the bill. Despite Douglas's desire to continue consideration of the bill by allowing other speakers to step in, Andrew Pickens Butler moved for postponement, suggesting it would be a good time to dispose of pending and less controversial bills. The motion was agreed to. A visibly ill Houston labored to continue his speech the following day. Charles Stuart of Michigan interrupted and asked for unanimous consent to postpone the debate. Houston, who opposed the bill because he believed it was yet another violation of the Indians' claim to the territory, refused to relinquish the floor. "I will not act as we have frequently done with the Indians," he said. "I was willing to go and get through, and I will do so." Douglas, relentless in his efforts to push the debate forward, supported Houston in his desire to continue. If "he is willing to go on," Douglas argued, "I think it would be better to have him do, as other persons expected to get the floor to-day to continue the debate." Douglas failed to persuade the chamber. The motion to postpone was agreed to.

Houston finally finished his remarks on Wednesday, February 15. Charles Stuart of Michigan was presiding for Atchison who had stepped down. The vote on Douglas's amendment to the substitute bill was about to be taken when Chase asked for a division of the amendment so that "the reason assigned for the repeal, or for the declaration that the act of 1820 is inoperative and void" could be considered first and on its own merits. Stuart ruled the amendment could not be divided, whereupon William Seward called for the vote. The amendment passed 35 to 10. It was a major victory for Atchison's style of caucus leadership. For the first time in votes related to the Nebraska-Kansas bill, southern Whigs were unanimous in their support. The only southern Whig not voting was George Badger of North Carolina, who though absent favored the substitute language.[42] The only southerner voting with the opposition was Sam Houston. However, it was not purely a sectional vote. Led by Douglas, Atchison, and the Mess, Democrats held the party line. Of the ten votes in opposition, only two were Democrats, Phillip Allen of Rhode Island and Houston.[43]

The affirmative vote on the amendment replaced the original language in section 14, in which "was superseded by" was changed to "is hereby declared inoperative and void." There was no longer any dispute over its meaning. It repealed the Missouri Compromise restriction of slavery above the 36° 30' parallel and replaced it with congressional nonintervention. Still open to debate was whether the bill allowed for the question of slavery to be decided at the territorial or statehood stage. With the amendment adopted, the Senate proceeded to the bill. Chase moved quickly to amend it again by adding immediately after the most recent change the words "Under which the people of the Territory, through their appropriate representatives, may, if they see fit, prohibit the existence of slavery therein." Lewis Cass distilled the debate down to its essential question: did the people of the territory have the power "to legislate upon their internal concerns," or did the Constitution invest "a kind of motive power in slavery that immediately spreads it over any territory, or by virtue of which any slave may be taken into any territory of the United States, as soon as it is annexed to the Union"? Andrew Pickens Butler argued for the latter position, noting that, as the bill prevented congressional intervention on the subject of slavery, "a territorial government has no derivative authority to do so from any act which Congress can pass." The debate went so late into the night of February 15 that Douglas himself called for postponement, noting that other concerns in the bill had to be addressed including the "the veto power of the Governor," and "the revisionary power of Congress."[44] Douglas's motion was agreed to, and the Senate adjourned.

While the Senate had been debating the amendment that repealed the Missouri Compromise, a cryptic message was sent on February 13 from Corcoran employee A. Hyde to J. B. H. Smith stating, "Mr. Corcoran wishes you to bring the case on Douglass to a speedy close." The content of the message is open to interpretation, but its timing, six days after the amendment had been introduced and two days before its passage, strongly suggests a connection to the Lake Superior properties and its syndicate members. The Corcoran collection in the Library of Congress shows that in the months and years following passage of the Nebraska-Kansas Act, Hyde communicated directly with both Douglas and Hunter on matters regarding the Superior properties.[45]

Debate on the final bill began on February 16, following the passage of the repeal amendment on February 15. Much is made of the fact that Douglas gave only two speeches in support of the bill, at the opening of the debate and his summation at the end. Atchison biographer William Parrish also notes Atchison's limited time on the floor, speaking only twice and then in response to a specific part of the bill, not on the bill as a whole. In actuality, so many senators felt so strongly toward the bill, pro and con, that Douglas and the leadership allowed all who wanted to a chance to speak. The result was that no senator gave multiple speeches with the exception of the two floor leaders, Douglas and Chase, and only a few others participated in the floor debate that began on March 2. During the February debate, the speeches tended to alternate between one in support and one in opposition. On Friday, February 24, Douglas informed the Senate that, from his discussions with both "friends" and "opponents" of the bill, he believed the debate could be brought to conclusion by the following Tuesday, February 28. Douglas intended to begin his summation on Wednesday March 1 at 1:00 P.M., with the vote on the bill to follow. Only a few more speeches followed. Robert M. T. Hunter gave his following Douglas's announcement.

At forty-five Hunter had begun to carry some extra weight on his 5′8″ frame. His dark unkempt hair and disheveled dress gave him the appearance of an absent-minded professor. He was soft-spoken, sometimes hard to hear, with a placid manner, "wonderfully unlike" his more vociferous messmates. Friend and foe alike acknowledged his superior intellect.[46]

Hunter's earliest biographer, his daughter Martha, made no comment on her father's Nebraska-Kansas speech other than to state it was one of a handful of "notable" speeches in his political career. Even Hunter's modern biographers give the speech short attention, stating that it was essentially a reiteration of Douglas's argument that the repeal was the "logical consequence of the course of argument and of action which was pursued in 1850 upon what were then called the compromise measures."[47] But the speech goes much farther than merely seconding Douglas on two significant points. First, Hunter argued the Missouri Compromise restriction was unconstitutional, something Douglas had not done. In doing so, Hunter not only foreshadowed the Dred Scott decision but used an 1850 opinion by Chief Justice Roger B. Taney to support it. Second, Hunter went beyond the specifics of the bill to defend both the institution of slavery and white supremacy.

Hunter based his argument that the Missouri Compromise restriction was unconstitutional on the premise that the primary purpose of the Constitution was "to secure . . . the equality of the States," and this resolve, and not the Missouri Compromise, was the "sacred" compact of the Union.

> Here is that sacred instrument—that deed in which the trusts are declared, and by which the General Government is constituted the fiduciary to carry them into execution. Here, too, are the great objects of the trust as declared in the preamble of the Constitution, which they say was ordained "to form a more perfect union." How is a more perfect union to be formed if you have destroyed the existing equality of the States and substituted inequality? To "establish justice." How can you establish justice if you make odious discrimination? To "insure domestic tranquility." How can you do that if you make such inequalities between the States? To "provide for the common defense, promote the general welfare." Remark, the welfare—not of a part, but of all.[48]

In the speech Hunter noted the enumerated powers given to Congress by the Constitution carried with it the caveat of uniformity. For example, Hunter stated, Congress was empowered to regulate commerce but "no preference" could be "given by any regulation of commerce or revenue to the ports of one State over those of another." He noted the Constitution held the states to the same principle of uniformity, prohibiting states from forming "alliances" or anything else "which might enable one State to trench upon the equal rights of another." Ironically to defend the equality of the states, Hunter used the very constitutional clause that Republicans would later use to defend the equality of human beings, Article IV, Section 2, Paragraph 1; *The citizens of each State shall be entitled to all the privileges and immunities of citizens of the several states.* Hunter used this clause because he argued the citizen secured "his equality through that of his State; not in his individual capacity."

Did the constitutional guarantee of equality of the states extend to the territories? Hunter said yes, "the States are as much entitled to share equally in the benefits to be derived from that public property as they are in the benefits of general legislation." The benefits being "twofold: the one is the relief from taxes, which is afforded by devoting the proceeds of the sales of these lands to the public use; and the other, and a far greater benefit, consists in its uses for the occupation and settlement of our fellow-citizens." To support his argument Hunter referenced several Supreme Court decisions, starting with Justice Marshall and singling out in particular Chief Justice Roger B. Taney's 1850 ruling in *Strader v. Graham.*

The case involved three African American slaves owned by Christopher Graham. Two of them, Reubens and Henry, were professional musicians, their lessons and instruments having been paid for by Graham. Since the completion of their training in 1837, Graham had allowed the two men to travel back and forth between Kentucky, Indiana, and Ohio for musical performances. In 1841 Reuben, Henry, and a third slave named George boarded a steamboat in Louisville bound for Cincinnati. The three slaves did not return to Louisville but instead made their way to Canada. Graham sued the owners of the steamboat, Jacob Strader and James Gorman, in the Louisville Chancery Court for the value of the three slaves and the musical instruments they took with them. The steamboat owners were found liable for damages totaling $3,000.[49] Both the plaintiff and the defendants appealed the lower court's ruling. The Kentucky Court of Appeals reversed the lower court's decision in 1847 and "remanded the entire case for further proceedings."[50] Strader and Gorman sued to the U.S. Supreme Court on a writ of error. Lawyers for Strader and Gorman argued the slaves in question were in fact freemen on the basis of their sojourns to and from the free state of Ohio prior to their eventual departure for Canada. The question before the Supreme Court was "whether slaves who had been permitted by their master to pass occasionally from Kentucky into Ohio acquired thereby a right to freedom after their return to Kentucky?" The court's decision rendered by Chief Justice Taney stated the question was not properly before the court because only the "laws of Kentucky alone could decide upon domestic and social condition of the persons domiciled within its territory." Taney continued "there is nothing in the Constitution of the United States that can in any degree control the law of Kentucky upon this subject. And the condition of the negroes, therefore, as to freedom or slavery after their return depended altogether upon the laws of that state, and could not be influenced by the laws of Ohio."

Foreshadowing the Dred Scott decision that would come six years later, Taney went beyond the question that was directly before the court and ruled on the one implied. Did Ohio's law prohibiting slavery have "some peculiar force by virtue of the Ordinance of 1787, for the government of the Northwest territory, Ohio being one of the states carved out of it[?]" Taney ruled that the Northwest Ordinance, including its prohibition against slavery, "ceased to be in force upon the adoption of the Constitution." The only provisions of the Northwest Ordinance that remained in force were those not "inconsistent with the Constitution" and these provisions maintained their "legal validity and force" under the Constitution, not the Ordinance.[51]

Hunter used the Taney decision to tie together his argument that the principle of equality of the States applied to the territories as well, stating: "Congress can do nothing that the Constitution forbids it to do; it can do nothing that interferes with the equal rights of States. . . . Nor could it, under the pretense of exercising its powers in the Territories . . . so use them as to do indirectly with the States what it would not and could not do directly."[52]

Hunter continued, maintaining that "the government of these Territories [Nebraska and Kansas] ought to be administered with the double object of securing the rights of the States as well as those of the people of the Territories, and to these last should be given all the rights of self-government which are consistent with the limitation that they shall not interfere with the equal rights of the States, or violate the provision of the Constitution. With those limitations all the power that could possibly be given to the people of the Territory ought to be given to them." At what stage could the people of the territories decide the question of slavery, at the territorial or statehood stage? Or did it even matter? Could slavery be restricted at either stage? Hunter stated he did "not mean to raise an issue upon that question," or "argue it." He acknowledged,

"There is a difference of opinion amongst the friends of this measure, as to the extent of the limits which the Constitution imposes upon the Territorial Legislatures," but this bill "proposes to leave these differences to the decision of the courts."[53]

Hunter concluded his remarks by making a case for the inevitability of western expansion and the efficacy of white supremacy and slavery as the only just way to "make that expansion consistent with the happiness of the inferior races with which ours may mingle." Such a choice "will be founded upon the just respect to the natural relations between those races." He rejected the right of "the white race of the non-slaveholding States" to "exclusively occupy the territory of the United States" and also rejected their "dogma . . . slavery is wrong, and that, therefore, it must be shut out." Hunter argued that just as the country possessed a "variety of soil and of climate," it allowed for "the people of its different portions" and their corresponding "system[s] of social organization and domestic culture" to coexist.[54]

Hunter argued the alternative that the prevention of slavery's expansion would lead to the "Africanization of the old slave states," as whites emigrated out and the slaves stayed behind. How long would the North allow such a condition to exist before white northerners moved into the "old slave states," and either "again enslave . . . or exterminate" the slaves left behind?

Nor was abolition the answer. Hunter pointed out that even those who supported abolition acknowledged it could not be accomplished in the slave states. "Why pursue this course of annoyance and agitation," asked Hunter, which only harms race relations by sowing "the seeds of jealousy between master and slave, which interrupts the course of ameliorating legislation, and which impedes the progress of both whites and blacks? It is simply mischief, for no good end. No useful purpose, according to your own confession, can be accomplished. You have no power by which you can set them loose; and why then pursue a course which can have no effect except to make them miserable?"

Even if he accepted the premise that slavery was evil, and Hunter did not, "To turn the slaves loose upon the community," by means of abolition, "would be a still greater evil both to blacks and whites." The only solution, Hunter concluded, was the bill before the chamber:

> We have accomplished this great legislative triumph by the simplest of all processes—that of extending the jurisdiction of the Constitution over all the subjects of Federal legislation. We have applied its true and just principles to the question of slavery in common with all others, and thus

removed the great stumbling block in your path to power and fame. Its broad aegis now covers the whole country, in all its parts—slave-holding and non-slaveholding—that all who dwell beneath its shadow may live in the peace of conscious security . . . in so doing we should take the surest means "to form a more perfect union, to establish justice, to insure domestic tranquility, to provide for the common defense, to promote the general welfare, and to secure the blessings of liberty to ourselves and our posterity."[55]

Finished with his remarks, Hunter sat. He had spoken for an hour and half. This time there was no postponement as Douglas pushed the formal speeches to their conclusion. Andrew Pickens Butler was next.

Everything about Butler was a stark contrast to Hunter. At fifty-eight and with a full head of snow-white hair, he was the oldest member of the Mess. Whereas Hunter's personality was "placid," bordering on the "lethargic," Butler's was manic depressive. He could be "cordial and affectionate" but also "impetuous and sour." His wit, for which he was famous, was described as "invective" and "scathing," particularly in response to perceived insults.[56] And on February 24 Butler felt insulted. Unlike Hunter, whose speech had been filled with voting statistics and legal decisions in support of the bill and its repeal of the Missouri Compromise, Butler's speech was filled with racist and sexist jokes. He was not going to spend his time discussing the legal and constitutional issues he felt had been adequately addressed by Hunter and others. He was going to specifically address the "hard things" that had been said by the gentlemen from Massachusetts, Ohio, and New York—namely, Sumner, Chase, Wade, and Seward.[57]

Regarding the Nebraska-Kansas bill, Sumner had earlier declared; *Monstrum horrendum, informe, ingens, cui lumen ademptum,* which translated means "A monster, dreadful, hideous enormous, from whom the light of life is taken away."[58] At first Butler made no comment on Sumner's remarks, choosing instead to address Benjamin Wade's argument that the slave owner did not "stand one whit higher than the meanest slave" before the eyes of God. Butler insisted "Inequality pervades the creation of this universe," and called "sentimental" the Declaration of Independence's suggestion otherwise. Butler wondered out loud whether Wade truly believed in equality between the races. If so, would he enter into a "domestic" relationship with a black woman? Butler would "not ask such a question, because it is a thing that is repulsive." Instead, he told an allegorical story repulsive in racist vitriol. Once there was a young white man, Butler said, who had never seen an African, "and who might therefore be regarded as having no prejudice whatever". And this young man was promised to a "princess whose dowry was islands and provinces, who was possessed of the Archipelago of the South. Now, Sir, just imagine that young gentleman to have such a proposition brought to him." The chamber erupted in laughter as Butler continued:

> The lady is to be introduced to him in a palace, highly decorated. . . . Remember this young man never saw a black woman before, and therefore has no prejudice. She may have observed all the rules of Maria Antoinette . . . she may adopt her dress. She may have her ankles covered with pearls, and her fingers with rings of rubies and diamonds. The young gentleman is standing near the altar of Hymen, of course with a palpitating heart. His betrothed is led out to him. He sees her white teeth; but lo! She has black skin and kinky hair. [Laughter] Now, what do you suppose the youth would say . . . he would instantly exclaim: *"Monstrum horrendum, informe, cui lumin ademptum!"* [Laugher][59]

After speaking for an hour Butler's messmate James Mason called for adjournment. Butler concluded his remarks the following day in a special Saturday session in which he largely followed the constitutional argument laid out earlier by Hunter. Before concluding, however, he returned to his earlier theme of God's social hierarchy. For Butler, the attack on slavery was part of a larger wave of northern reform *isms,* "Abolitionism . . . Maine-liquor-law-ism . . . Strong-minded woman-ism," all designed to breakdown the very foundation of society. "I have a profound respect for woman in all the true relations for which she is fitted," Butler professed. "Man always has a respect for woman. So long as she confines herself within the jurisdiction prescribed to her by the Almighty, she fulfills the ends of her existence . . . But when she unsexes herself, and puts on the habiliments, and claims to exercise the masculine functions of man in society, she has lost the position which she should occupy."

Butler's words were more a defense of the South's slave culture than the bill itself. After he ended his speech, Butler turned the floor over to Albert Brown of Mississippi and Augustus Dodge of Iowa, both of whom spoke in support of the bill, after which the Senate adjourned. On Monday Whig James Cooper of Pennsylvania delivered a speech in opposition to the bill, after which Pennsylvania's other senator, Democrat Richard Brodhead, attacked him for joining "the sectional party which is now getting up in the country." Brodhead asked for time to reply and was given it the next day. Ironically as the time for speeches grew short, the length of those being offered grew longer. Whig James Clayton of Delaware spoke for two and half hours on Wednesday, not concluding until the following day. As the floor speeches grew in length, the citizen petitions against the repeal grew in number. All were ordered to lie on the table.

Final debate began on Thursday, March 2, following the conclusion of Clayton's speech. The question pending before the Committee of the Whole was Chase's amendment to section 14 of the bill, which read, "under which the people of the Territories, through their appropriate representatives, may, if they see fit, prohibit the existence of slavery therein."[60] George Badger of North Carolina cautioned supporters of the bill against any amendment coming from Chase as he was publicly committed to the abolition of slavery. Debate decorum disintegrated. Archibald Dixon tried to question Chase on his lack of support of the fugitive slave act. Chase refused to yield the floor but was forced to address his position: "I stand by the Constitution as it was interpreted by the men who made it at the time they made it; and I deny, standing there, that Congress had any power over the subject of the extradition of servants at all."[61]

Douglas tried to bring the question to a vote, but Dixon would not have it. He demanded Chase to answer whether he understood "the acts of 1850, called the Compromise acts, to be a compact between North and South?" Douglas reluctantly yielded the floor. The debate between Chase and Dixon descended into a bizarre exchange in which each demanded of the other whether he believed the Missouri Compromise and the Compromise of 1850 were compacts or legislation subject to repeal. Chase argued that the Missouri Compromise of 1820 was a compact, but the Compromise of 1850 was a "series of measures, subject to repeal," while Dixon argued the exact opposite. Michigan's Democratic senators Lewis Cass and Charles Stuart brought the debate back to the question at hand. Cass argued the Chase amendment gave the people of the territories the right to prohibit slavery but not "to establish it," thereby throwing "doubts upon the preceding provision," which otherwise had given the people of the territories "both powers, subject to the limitations of the Constitution."

Stuart took issue with the question itself. What exactly was before the Senate? What was being amended, the original bill or the substitute bill? What was "the true condition of the bill"? Douglas tried to summarize:

> I first reported a substitute from the Committee on Territories for the original bill, introduced by the Senator from Iowa. Subsequently, I withdrew that substitute by the unanimous consent of the Senate, and submitted in its place the one which we are now acting upon. There have been one or two amendments made to the substitute for the original bill of the Senator from Iowa, and the question now on the amendment of the Senator of Ohio to that substitute. If that be adopted or rejected the question will recur on the substitute or amendment which I reported, as amended, for the bill of the honorable Senator from Iowa.[62]

In other words the Chase amendment was "an amendment" to the Douglas substitute bill, which was "an amendment" to the original bill, "an amendment to an amendment." Douglas allowed the debate to continue, yielding the floor to several more senators who wished to speak, including Badger, Walker, Butler, Weller, and Dodge of Iowa. At 6:30 P.M. the vote was taken. The Chase amendment was defeated 10 to 36. All votes in favor were cast by northern senators, two Free-Soilers, six Whigs, and two Democrats. Of the thirty-six senators voting against, nine were cast by southern Whigs. The twenty-seven Democrats who voted against were nearly divided, fourteen southerners and thirteen northerners.

The unstoppable coalition of southern Whigs and a unified Democratic Party moved quickly. Badger was first, moving to amend the substitute bill by inserting, "Provided, That nothing herein contained shall be construed to revive or put in force any law or regulation which may have existed prior to the act of the 6th of March, 1820, either protective, establishing, prohibiting, or abolishing slavery." There was no debate. The vote was called. It passed 35 to 6. The amendment was adopted. By unanimous consent the same language was "inserted in the other part of the bill in relation to Kansas, in order to make it consistent." Making the language consistent in relation to the two territories became "a matter of course" as the substitute bill moved forward.

Douglas was next. He "moved to amend the substitute by striking out the provisions that gave the Governor of the proposed Territories an absolute veto power." His amendment inserted in its place language that made the bill consistent with 1839 federal legislation that allowed for legislative override by a two-thirds vote. Douglas's amendment also struck the provision requiring the territories to submit legislation to Congress for approval, inserting instead submission to the territorial governor, which if disapproved, could be overridden by a two-thirds vote of the legislature. The amendment was agreed to.

Delaware's Whig senator, John Clayton, offered his amendment next to strike the provision "And those who shall have declared an oath their intention to become such, and shall have taken an oath to support the Constitution of the United States, and the provisions of this act," to be replaced with "Provided, That the right of suffrage and of holding office shall be exercised only by citizens of the United States." It was a direct assault on the immigrant vote. Southerners feared the German immigrant vote in particular as being antislavery. Isaac P. Walker, Democrat from Wisconsin and supporter of the substitute bill, opposed the Clayton amendment, "as a very large portion of" his "constituency" comprised "good men" and "good patriots" but "not yet citizens." He did not want to see those who wanted to immigrate to the territories be deprived of the "political privileges" they possessed in Wisconsin. Many other supporters of the bill agreed, and the amendment barely passed, 23 to 21.[63]

Salmon Chase "moved to amend the substitute by striking out the second section and inserting" new language that provided for a territorial governor elected by the people not appointed by the president. The Chase amendment was quickly defeated by a vote of 10 to 30. Chase followed up quickly with another amendment, this one designed to exempt the Nebraska Territory from the act altogether. In the short debate that followed, James Mason noted, "I think it is perfectly manifest that the Senator from Ohio does not desire or design to vote for the bill reported from the Committee on Territories, even if his amendments which he is now offering are engrafted on it. I submit, therefore, to the Senate—to the friends of the bill—without any delay to vote his amendment down." And it was, by a vote of 8 to 34.[64]

The last amendment was Augustus Dodge's to ensure that the Nebraska-Kansas boundaries did not "interfere with the present limits of the Utah Territories." After his amendment was agreed to, the time had come to move the substitute bill to engrossment and a third reading. The F Street Mess was on the floor, including Atchison, who had left his chair temporarily to Richard Brodhead. Brodhead gaveled the Senate to attention, announcing "The question now is on concurring in the amendments made as in Committee on the Whole. The question will be taken on them altogether, unless some Senator desires a division." One senator did. Isaac P. Walker asked that the Clayton amendment be separated out, and it was. The rest of the bill was reported to the Senate as amended. Noting it was nearly 8:30 at night, Stephen Adams, Democrat from Mississippi, moved to adjourn. His motion was defeated, and the Senate debated for a second time the Clayton amendment "prohibiting foreigners from voting or holding office."[65]

Signs of fatigue were beginning to show. Given the lateness of the hour, Henry Dodge openly doubted whether the Senate would be able to bring the bill to a vote that evening. With a chorus of "no's" behind him, Douglas confirmed the bill would not be voted on. Dodge then suggested the Senate put off the vote on the Clayton amendment, but Hunter urged the body to push forward on the Clayton vote in order for the bill to "be engrossed before we adjourn." Douglas agreed. The Senate voted to continue and began debate on the Clayton amendment.

The bill as reported allowed noncitizens who had expressed intentions to become citizens to vote in the first Territorial election. "After that," Douglas noted, "the qualifications of voters and of persons to hold office," would be determined by the territorial legislature. The Clayton amendment prevented noncitizens from voting in the first election. It was easy for southern senators, including Atchison's messmates, to support the Clayton amendment because few immigrants lived in their states. Such was not the case for Atchison. Missouri had a sizable immigrant population, primarily German, antislavery, and pro-Benton. If Atchison played it right, and used his support of the Clayton amendment to ensure its adoption, he could use it to hurt his election opponent, Thomas Hart Benton. If Benton supported the Nebraska-Kansas bill when it went to the House, he would alienate his immigrant base. If he voted against it because of the Clayton restriction, he would alienate the rest of Missouri's population.

Atchison had periodically left his chair during the Nebraska-Kansas debate to use his persuasion informally on the floor, but he had never participated in the debate itself until now, and he played it perfectly. It was not that he "fear[ed] the votes of the foreign population." Atchison was all for granting suffrage to those who intended to become citizens, but it was simply a matter of when:

> The objection I have is, that foreigners, men who are not citizens, men who may never become citizens, will mold and form the institutions of the Territories, under the provision of the bill as it stands, unless we concur in the amendment. The first Legislature may decide the question of slavery forever in these Territories, and decide as to the right of the people of one half of the States of this Union to go there or not. It is because they have the right of suffrage, and the right to hold office in these Territories, when their institutions are first formed and first molded, that constitutes my chief and principle objection. If the Senator [Douglas] would alter and amend his proposition so that, in the year 1857 or 1858, persons who have declared their intention to become citizens may exercise the right of suffrage and hold office, I will waive my objection.[66]

The vote on the Clayton amendment was close, 22 in favor to 20 against. Arguably, the Senate gave its concurrence because its president, Atchison, had supported it. It was the last amendment to the substitute bill before it was finally ordered "to be engrossed for a third reading." After that the Senate adjourned. It had been a long session going late into the night. The next day, Friday March 3, would be even longer with Douglas's summation continuing into the early hours of March 4 before the final vote was taken.

Upon convening Friday morning, the Senate suspended consideration of private bills and moved immediately to consideration of the question, "Shall the bill pass?" The session went into the early hours of Saturday morning. Houston would call the session "unusual . . . without precedent in the history of any Congress."[67] The last senator to speak before Douglas's summation was the newly elected antislavery Whig from Maine, William Fessenden.

William Pitt Fessenden was the son of Maine's leading abolitionist Samuel Fessenden. He had been in Washington barely a week. His speech against the Nebraska-Kansas bill was his maiden speech in the Senate, and he came out swinging, attacking specifically the Slave Power's aggressive and undue influence on federal legislation. Toward the end of the speech, Fessenden addressed the South's historic and repeated threat of disunion to force northern compliance with its political and economic interests. Stating he was tired of the South's empty threat, Fessenden got into a brief yet heated exchange with Andrew Pickens Butler, who was himself quickly and unwittingly becoming the personification of the Slave Power.

"We have heard that threat until we are fatigued with the sound," said Fessenden. "We consider it now, let me say, as mere *brutum fulmen*, noise, and nothing else. It produces not the slightest impression upon the thinking portion of the public. You laugh at yourselves." Butler feigned puzzlement. "Who?" he asked. The chamber erupted in laughter.

"You at the South," replied Fessenden. "You do not carry it seriously into private conversation." Butler begged to differ, and he was quite serious: "If your doctrine is carried out, if such sentiments as yours prevail, I want a dissolution right away."

"Do not delay it on my account," replied Fessenden. Butler assured him the South would not. Fessenden shot back, "Sir, if it has come to this, that whenever a question comes up between the free States and the slave States of this Union we are to be threatened with disunion unless we yield, if that is the only alternative to be considered, it ceases to be a very grave question."[68]

Hoping to close the formal debate before things got further out of hand, Stephen Douglas approached the chair. Atchison had stepped down temporarily, perhaps to quiet the temper of his messmate Butler, and Solomon Foot was presiding. Right behind Douglas was John Weller, one of California's two proslavery senators. An angry Weller demanded he be given a chance to respond to Fessenden. "Do it," Fessenden was heard to say. William Gwin, California's other proslavery senator, who still owned property and slaves in Mississippi, interrupted Douglas and demanded Weller be given the chance to speak.[69] Foot ruled Gwin out of order, but Douglas yielded to the Californian's demand anyway cautioning the Senate as he did that the debate was "getting too long" if they hoped to vote on the bill that day.

Weller reminded his audience that he represented a free state and yet had never seen any "evidence of that aggressive spirit" that Fessenden had accused the South of.[70] Instead, Weller argued, the aggression came from the abolitionists. It was they and not the South that threatened the Union. Weller also assailed Fessenden for stating he would vote against any state carved from the Nebraska and Kansas territories that did not restrict slavery. If that was the case, "Why not drive out the State of South Carolina," Weller asked.

> If you are determined, therefore, to prevent the admission of any more slave States into the Union, upon the ground that they are exercising an unjust influence over the institutions of this country, let us expel the State of South Carolina, and get rid of my gallant friend who sits here by my side, [Mr. Butler] and I undertake to say, that God never formed a better man than he is. [Laughter] If I were not well assured that the Senator from Maine does not express the opinions of northern senators generally, I should despair of the Republic. If the North should attempt to exclude a State from the Union because it tolerated slavery, as I said before, a dissolution is inevitable.[71]

As Douglas had feared, Weller's speech in defense of the bill and his southern friends became prolonged. It was approaching midnight when Douglas again approached the chair and asked the Senate if it wished to adjourn. A collective "No" rose from the chamber. Then, Douglas insisted, the debate had to end. "I will state frankly that my object is simply this; we have all agreed to take this vote to-night. The Senator from California, among others, made me pledge to hold on and insist upon taking the vote. The friends of this bill were not to consume all the time. It has been the general impression that I would close the debate, but I [am] willing to waive doing so."[72]

When another collective "No" rose from the chamber, a reluctant Weller yielded the floor. Douglas began his summation shortly before midnight.

First Douglas addressed some general points brought up by earlier speakers, particularly John Bell's and Sam Houston's concerns regarding the potential violation of Indian rights. Douglas stated regulations regarding Indian tribes were not part of the bill because such matters were under the domain of the Committee on Indian Affairs, chaired by William Sebastian of Arkansas. Douglas trusted Sebastian's committee would report the necessary legislation to "do entire justice to the Indians, without contravening the objects of Congress in organizing" the Nebraska and Kansas territories. Douglas added that the territorial boundaries established by the bill had left all tribes with whom the United State had "treaty stipulations" outside the Nebraska and Kansas territories. As to those Indians within the territories with whom the United States had no treaties, it was again "a question for the consideration of the Committee on Indian Affairs."[73]

Douglas reminded both Bell and Houston that the concerns they raised had been present when the Utah and New Mexico territories were organized, and yet neither senator had at that time raised an objection. On the contrary, Douglas noted, Bell and Houston not only voted in favor of those two bills, but most other territorial bills, all of which had included Indian populations.

As to those senators who questioned the necessity of organizing Nebraska at all, Douglas argued they had forgotten the "vast wilderness, filled by hostile savages" that separated the eastern United States from the "immense and valuable possessions on the Pacific." It was through unorganized territory that "nearly a hundred thousand emigrants pass[ed] through ... every year, on their way to California and Oregon." Emigrants that were naturalized "American citizens" were "entitled to the protection of law and government" Not only did the government owe them protection, Douglas argued, the government owed them an infrastructure. How were they to move he asked, without "provision for roads, bridges, or ferries to facilitate travel, or forts or other means of safety to protect life?" As to those senators who question the expense involved, Douglas felt no necessity to reply at all, "for the reason, that if the public interests require the enactment of the law, it follows as a natural consequence that all the expenses necessary to carry it into effect are wise and proper."[74]

Having gotten the ancillary issues out of the way Douglas addressed "the great principle involved in the bill," the repeal of section 8 in the Missouri Compromise. On this Douglas was clear and adamant. When shaping the Nebraska-Kansas bill, the Committee on Territories considered two principles and two principles only. The principle of congressional intervention established in 1820 and the principle of nonintervention established in 1850.[75]

Douglas reminded the body that three decades of abolitionist agitation, from 1820 to 1850, had made it increasingly difficult to organize any territory. It was only by the extraction of congressional intervention from the question of slavery in the territories in 1850 that the agitation had been quelled. The principle of popular sovereignty recognized "the right of the people to decide this question for themselves, subject only to the Constitution." Douglas maintained there was only one question now before the Senate. Would it "adhere to and carry out the principle recognized by the compromise measures of 1850," or go "back to the old exploded doctrine of congressional interference, as established in 1820." It was congressional intervention or popular sovereignty; "there were no other alternatives."[76]

As Douglas continued, he alternated between defending the bill and defending himself. Still smarting from the Appeal, Douglas was outraged over being burned in effigy in northern cities and the accusation that he was motivated by presidential ambitions. Looking directly at Salmon Chase, Douglas unleashed his ire: "I am now to be found in effigy, hanging by the neck, in all the towns where you have the influence."

Chase responded by stating he had "no quarrel with Senators who differ with me." He was deeply regretful for what had occurred in his state but denied personal responsibility, insisting he had always treated Douglas "with entire courtesy." But Douglas would have none of it and instead quoted from the Appeal: "Did he not say . . . that I was engaged with others, in a 'criminal betrayal of precious rights,' in an 'atrocious plot'? Did he not say that I and others were guilty of 'meditated bad faith'? Are these not his exact words . . . Did he not say everything calculated to produce and bring upon my head all the insults to which I have been subjected publicly and privately . . . all these have resulted from that Address." Words became so heated between Douglas and Chase that James Mason, temporarily presiding, had to repeatedly call for order.

Personally wounded, Douglas reminded his audience on the floor and in the galleries that both the Democratic and Whig parties had "solemnly pledged before the world to adhere to the compromise measures of 1850, 'in principle and substance,'" and that the bill as well as "the report of the committee [were] in accordance with this obligation." He believed he had done his best to be "faithful to the trust" given to him, and the vote that night would determine whether the Senate agreed.[77]

Douglas called the opposition's charge that the repeal unjustly revoked a solemn compact "complicated"; nevertheless, he would answer it. First, Douglas stated the "main object and aim of the bill" had not been the repeal as claimed by the opposition. Second, in order to carry "into practical operation" the principle of nonintervention embedded in the new bill it was "necessary to remove whatever legal obstacles might be found in the way of its free exercise."[78]

Douglas denied he ever stated he would "cling with the tenacity of life to the compromise of 1820" and denounced those "Abolition newspapers" that printed as much for participating in "a deliberate act of forgery." As to the charge that neither he nor anyone else considered the Missouri compromise repealed before February 1854, Douglas presented evidence to the contrary, including a speech he made in Chicago in October 23, 1850, and a resolution passed shortly thereafter by the Illinois legislature. He would have liked to present more resolutions "from different States . . . and show what has been the common understanding of the whole country upon this point," but time prevented it. Besides, Douglas felt he had done more than enough to vindicate himself "against the assaults of my calumniators."[79]

Douglas continued to insist that section 8 of the Missouri Compromise had been repealed by the Utah and New Mexico territorial acts of 1850. "It is true," he said "that those acts did not in terms and by name repeal the act of 1820"; nevertheless, "the very act" of granting the people in the territories of New Mexico and Utah the right to decide whether to allow slavery had removed "all obstructions to the exercise of" that right anywhere else.

The fundamental question before the Senate according to Douglas was whether the Missouri Compromise is "a moral obligation in the nature of a compact," and therefore not subject to repeal, or an "ordinary act of legislation" subject to repeal. William Seward argued it was an agreement between two parties, the North and the South, over the division of the Louisiana Territory. The South, he complained, had received all the benefits of the compact and now when the North was about to receive its share, the compact was to be voided.[80]

Douglas answered Seward's charge by noting that no such parties as "North and South" existed under the Constitution, but if the opposition insisted on such distinctions, Douglas read into the record the vote from 1820 which showed the majority of northern senators and congressmen had voted against the compromise. Seward agreed that the majority of northern congressmen in 1820 had voted against the act, but nevertheless the majority of the whole had created "this doctrine of compromises . . . that if so many northern men shall go with so many southern men as to fix the law, then it binds the North and South alike."[81]

Unable to get Seward to rescind his position that the North had been bound to the compact despite its vote against it, Douglas next argued that, if it was a compact, it had been immediately voided when the majority of northern congressmen voted against Missouri's admission as a state. Douglas asked Seward to recall that "after having procured the prohibition in the Territories, the North, by a majority of her votes, refused to admit Missouri as a slaveholding State, and, in violation of the alleged compact, required her to prohibit slavery as further condition of her admission. This repudiation of the alleged compact by the North is recorded by yeas and nays, sixty-one to thirty-three ... With this evidence before us," Douglas asked, "against whom should the charge of perfidy be preferred?"[82]

In response, Seward argued Missouri's statehood bill was initially rejected because its state constitution violated the Privileges and Immunities clause of the Constitution by prohibiting the migration of free blacks into the state.[83] Douglas did not deny Missouri's prohibition but questioned whether it was justification for blocking its admittance to the Union. After all other states had restricted the migration of free blacks, including "Illinois and Indiana." Was Missouri's restriction any different? For Douglas, the agreement of March 2, 1821, abrogated the agreement of March 6, 1820, for this very reason, "Missouri was denied admission by northern votes until she entered into a compact by which she was understood to surrender an important right now exercised by several States of the Union."[84]

The argument descended into a pointless back and forth between Douglas and Seward, neither man moving on his position. Seward insisted both agreements were compacts and the latter did not void the former, while Douglas insisted that the 1820 compromise was never a compact and, if it had been, was voided by the 1821 compromise.

Some historians and Douglas biographers state Douglas's speech was the last before the vote and that he spoke five and a half hours before ending at 5:30 A.M. In actuality, Douglas yielded the floor sometime earlier than that to Sam Houston. It was Houston who spoke last, and his opposition to the bill was the most prophetic of all those given.

Houston took exception to the accusations that he was siding with the Abolitionists and Free-Soilers, declaring himself a defender of the South. He merely opposed the extremes on both sides of the slavery issue. Nevertheless, he had been ostracized, left out of "all consultation," despite his membership on the Committee on Territories. He "never had an intimation that a conference was to take place, a caucus to be held, or stringent measures applied in the passage of the bill.... I have been in the dark in relation to it."[85]

Houston reminded the audience he was one of the few present who had also been present when the compromise measures of 1850 were passed, and he totally rejected Douglas's premise that those measures had repealed the Missouri Compromise. He had been there "and the breeze bore no whisper to our ears that the Missouri compromise had been repealed." He also chastised both sides for quibbling over semantics. It did not matter whether the Missouri Compromise was called a compromise or a compact. Arguing over definitions accomplished little except to waste time and abstract from the real issue at hand; "I do not care what you call it—but as a line, defining certain rights and privileges in the different sections of the Union. The abstractions which you indulge in here can never satisfy the people that there is not something in it." Among those abstractions Houston included the debate over the Missouri Compromise's constitutionality. Personally, he did not know or care if it was "constitutional, technically." What mattered more was its practicality, it had worked for over thirty years. Historically, Houston noted, the country had always been pragmatic, constructing the constitution in the loosest of terms when necessary, from the purchase of the Louisiana Territory to the annexation of Texas. And finally, Houston stated, if the Missouri Compromise was unconstitutional, it was "strange that an unconstitutional law should have remained so long in force."[86]

Houston's opposition to the bill focused on two major points. First, the repeal of the Missouri Compromise would not bring peace but destruction of the northern Democratic Party and the Union itself by creating a newly fused party of Abolitionists, Free-Soilers, and Whigs, which would obtain a "preponderance" of power in Congress. And second, once in power the Abolitionists would impose their will on "every Representative who vote[d] for this measure," and "disastrous consequences" would "ensue to our institutions."[87]

Houston ended his remarks with one last and admittedly futile plea on behalf of the Indians. It mattered not whether the tribes had acquired all the trappings of Western civilization as the Cherokees had or were "wild" and "untutored." The Indians were not "inferior, intellectually, to white men," said Houston; they had a "sense of justice, truth, and honor that should find a responsive chord in every heart." The Senate could pass the Nebraska-Kansas bill and, in doing so, "drive these people away, and give their lands to the white man," but Houston could "not discover the morality of it."[88]

The Nebraska-Kansas bill, he warned, was "an eminently perilous measure." Noting the eagle suspended above the chamber still "enshrouded in black" for those who had recently died, Houston wondered aloud what the great men of America's past would think of their actions that night. Pointing to Washington's portrait he asked the Senate to remember "the contract once made to harmonize and preserve this Union," or, as he had earlier warned, "the sin will lie at your door, and Providence, in His own way, mysterious and incomprehensible to us though it is, will accomplish all His purposes."[89]

Houston sat. Atchison was still on the floor, where he had been for the majority of the seventeen hours of continuous debate between Friday and Saturday morning. Presiding in Atchison's chair was Augustus Dodge of Iowa. He ordered the vote shortly before 5:00 A.M. On the bill to organize the territories of Nebraska and Kansas, the vote was yeas 37, nays 14. The bill passed.[90] The breakdown of the vote was almost a carbon copy of the earlier vote that "voided" section 8 of the original Missouri Compromise. The vote in favor was a coalition of southern Whigs and bisectional Democrats; ten southern Whigs, twelve northern Democrats, and fifteen southern Democrats.[91] The vote against was nearly a solid northern vote; four northern Democrats, six northern Whigs, two Free-Soilers, and two southern votes. The two southerners to vote against the bill were Tennessee Whig John Bell and Texas Democrat Sam Houston. Both would eventually leave their respective parties.[92] The ten members that were absent were a mixture of party and section.

After debating for six weeks, the last session of which was seventeen hours long, the Senate adjourned until Tuesday, March 7. The Slave Power, specifically, the F Street Mess, had won its greatest legislative victory. Their achievement had been a masterful display of institutional knowledge, parliamentarian skill, and personal loyalty. But the impact of victory was uncertain. The bill faced an uphill battle in the House. Even if it passed, Abolitionists were determined to prevent slavery's spread into the newly open territory of Kansas. David Rice Atchison still faced a difficult reelection that fall. Native tribes still held title to lands within and south of the Nebraska and Kansas territories. The transcontinental railroad's route, on which the financial success of the Lake Superior Syndicate rested, had yet to be determined. A presidential election in which Douglas and Hunter were both potential candidates was looming. In the meantime on Sunday morning, March 5, 1854, the Senate chamber at long last sat empty and silent. Outside its door lay the unknown.

CHAPTER SIX

Kansas

The Senate's repeal of the thirty-four-year restriction against slavery above the 36° 30′ parallel was the pinnacle of the F Street Mess's legislative power and a major victory for Calhoun's constitutional argument that the Fifth Amendment protected slavery in the territories. Seventy-nine days after the Senate vote, the bill to organize the territories of Nebraska and Kansas passed the House 113 to 100. Eight days later, on May 30, Franklin Pierce signed into law what would later be known as the Kansas-Nebraska Act. The consequences of the act unfolded quickly thereafter in a series of sensational events—Bleeding Kansas, the Caning of Charles Sumner, Pottawatomie Creek, Dred Scott—until the country stood at the precipice of war. As the decade tumbled toward its climatic end, the F Street Mess attempted to manage events in Kansas and the Senate in an effort to maintain southern power and protect the institution of slavery. But those efforts were increasingly under siege from a growing northern opposition to the Slave Power and its "peculiar" institution.

The F Street Mess had been motivated by a variety of factors during the legislative phase of the Kansas-Nebraska Act that did not necessarily correspond to the ideological cause of slavery. For instance Robert M. T. Hunter's investments in the Superior Properties syndicate, put together by the bill's author of record, Stephen Douglas, had nothing to do with his proslavery ideology. Hunter stood to gain financially whether the bill passed with slavery restricted or not. Unfortunately for the Mess, the successful repeal of the 36° 30′ restriction against slavery did not translate into corresponding political or financial success. As their personal motives became less and less relevant, the Mess turned its attention solely to the ideological issue of slavery's western expansion. Atchison, Hunter, Mason, and Butler led the fight on the ground in Kansas and in the Senate chamber to secure slavery's expansion. Cause and motive became one in the postenactment period but without the same success as when divided during the legislative battle, and the power of the F Street Mess, which initially held after the act's passage, began a precipitous decline soon after.

The Nebraska-Kansas bill's lopsided victory in the Senate was quickly forgotten during the more contested and nearly fratricidal fight in the House.[1] Even though the F Street Mess had forced President Pierce to make the bill an administration measure, the president had assumed its passage in the House of Representatives would not require his active intervention. He was wrong. On March 21 House opponents of the Nebraska-Kansas bill garnered enough support to bypass the Committee on Territories and send it directly to the Committee of the Whole effectively killing the bill by burying it beneath a mountain of pending legislation.

The Pierce administration made support of the bill a test of administration and party loyalty. The president wrote editorials in favor of the bill and, along with Douglas, lobbied former and current members of Congress, using administration and party patronage, privately and not so privately, to win the House vote. Together Pierce and Douglas successfully used the contending wants and desire of individual congressmen to fashion a vote that in the end was based less on party principle and more on parochial interests. On May 8 Douglas protégé and chairman of the Committee on Territories, William Richardson, garnered enough votes to postpone the bills ahead of the Nebraska-Kansas bill and begin debate. Two weeks later the Nebraska-Kansas bill narrowly passed the House 113 to 100. On May 30, 1854, President Franklin Pierce signed the bill into law.

The judgment of Pierce's noted biographer Roy F. Nichols was that the president's efforts in the House were largely ineffective, noting that of the 159 Democratic House members, only 100 voted for the bill.[2] Instead, Nichols credits the bill's passage to the floor leadership of Georgia Whig Alexander Stephens and the thirteen southern Whig votes in the affirmative.[3] But Nichols's assessment ignores the floor leadership of William Richardson. It also ignores that the bill would not have passed without forty-four affirmative votes from free-state Democrats with whom Pierce's pressure was effective.[4] Nichols was correct on one point: Pierce used all the political capital he had left and was unable to effect any other important legislation during his term. In 1856 he would become the first incumbent president in U.S. history to be denied his party's nomination for reelection.

The F Street Mess had little direct influence on the Nebraska-Kansas bill in the House of Representatives, where victory was largely owed to the floor leadership of Alexander Stephens and William Richardson. Nevertheless the F Street Mess was indirectly involved in the House vote because Stephen Douglas and Franklin Pierce were directly involved in the House vote. It should not be forgotten that both men had been placed in the position of supporting the bill's repeal of the Missouri Compromise restriction by the F Street Mess. It forced Douglas to repeal the Missouri Compromise restriction in writing, and it forced the president to make the bill an administration measure. The F Street Mess's intervention in the Senate bill placed it in jeopardy in the House, but it also forced Douglas and Pierce to use every means at their disposal to assure its passage. Directly and indirectly the Kansas-Nebraska Act was the F Street Mess's measure. But no sooner had the act passed than electoral stalemate and death began to decimate the Mess.

Instead of the Kansas-Nebraska Act ensuring Atchison's reelection to the U.S. Senate, his personal motive for its enactment, the repeal of the Missouri Compromise, unexpectedly jeopardized it. Benton's opposition to the act cost him his reelection to the House, and so in defeat Benton turned his eye toward Atchison's seat. Atchison, unconcerned, returned to Missouri in August to campaign. In his view the Kansas-Nebraska Act had two immediate benefits. It had destroyed Benton politically and assured a Democratic victory in the Missouri state elections. A confident Atchison wrote his friend Jefferson Davis that Benton was "no longer in our way." He believed Benton and the Free-Soilers' defeat at the federal level had "relieved a load" from Benton's Democratic supporters in the Missouri legislature, allowing them to "act with the old democratic party" once again. This, according to Atchison, would assure a Democratic sweep in the state elections. Come the New Year there would not be "a grease spot of Whiggery" left in Missouri.

But Atchison was wrong. Benton Democrats did not join the Democracy. Instead, they seriously courted disaffected Free-Soil Whigs. As the state's Whig Party disintegrated, a new third party, the American Party, established a foothold on Missouri soil. The resulting state elections that summer produced a legislature in which no one faction was clearly in control of the U.S. Senate election.[5]

Earlier in June, Atchison had written his constituents from Washington declaring he had kept his promise to organize the Nebraska Territory for slave owner and non-slave-owner alike thereby assuring "the power and wealth of the West."[6] It was his last written campaign statement on the act, and it was also his last statement, written or oral, in which he declared the act "a western measure." When Atchison returned to Missouri in the summer of 1854 to campaign for reelection, he found his political base in western Missouri in crisis. Despite the successful passage of the Kansas-Nebraska Act, New England Abolitionists' widely advertised plan to send men and money into Kansas had literally sent proslavery Missourians into a panic.[7]

For slave owners in the western counties of Missouri in 1854, there was nothing symbolic or pyrrhic in the passage of the Kansas-Nebraska Act. They believed that just as slavery had naturally expanded into the western counties of Missouri, it had to naturally expand into the contiguous territory of Kansas or die. If the looming territorial elections in Kansas went against slavery, Missouri's slave population would not only be unable to expand west, but Missouri slaves could easily run away to a free Kansas. For Atchison and other proslavery Missourians, a free Kansas potentially meant a free Missouri. And a free Missouri potentially meant doom to slavery everywhere. Atchison articulated his domino theory in a letter to Hunter in which he declared that "we are playing for a mighty stake." He continued that an electoral victory in Kansas meant the South "could carry slavery to the Pacific Ocean," but defeat in Kansas would mean the ultimate end of slavery in "Missouri, Arkansas and Texas." Therefore he wrote Hunter that "the game must be played boldly," even if it meant the destruction of the Union.[8]

The "scale" that had once held the Union for Atchison now tipped in slavery's favor. Kansas was his new "holyland."[9] Atchison's letters and speeches that summer and fall show a man becoming less interested in reelection and more focused on the cause of slavery. "All that is required to make Kansas a slave state is for Missouri to do her duty," he declared to a Missouri audience. "I am not here electioneering for your votes. My fate was sealed by your votes last August. I will either be returned to the Senate or be beaten."[10] What had been a "western measure" designed to ensure his reelection to the Senate had instead turned the Kansas Territory into a southern fire wall that Atchison was determined to defend.[11] Along with brothers Benjamin and John Stringfellow, he organized the Platte County Self-Defense Association and spent the remainder of the summer and fall organizing, cajoling, and shaming Missourians to send volunteers into Kansas. If they could not travel a "day's journey" to protect their "peace" and their "property," Atchison declared, they "deserve[d] their fate," and the South and slavery would fall. Too old to fight, asked Atchison, then "send your sons!"[12]

In the fall Atchison wrote the Senate informing the body he would not be in Washington for the opening of the final session of the Thirty-Third Congress and requested the election of a new president pro tempore. When Atchison finally returned to Washington at the end of December he declined to resume the office of president pro tempore, then held by Mess associate Jesse D. Bright.[13] He and the Mess had a contingency plan. "The Judge [Butler] writes me," wrote William DeSaussure of South Carolina to Atchison, "that if the old tumble bug [Benton] defeats you, or causes you to be defeated you will come to the South."[14]

By coming "South," DeSaussure was referring to Atchison's lobbying efforts to secure financing and men for a proslavery grassroots effort in Kansas's spring territorial elections. He may have made some trips into Virginia and Maryland while in Washington, but otherwise Atchison was back in Platte City by February organizing the grassroots effort. He declined speaking offers outside of Missouri and Kansas and chose to solicit additional money and men via correspondence with southern leaders and newspaper editors.[15]

Atchison's absence from the Senate did not go unnoticed. Gideon Welles wrote in his diary that Michigan senator Lewis Cass had told him Atchison stayed for the final session of the Thirty-Third Congress "but a day or two" and then left for "a tour through the Southern States, concocting measures with the Governors and leading men at the South to make Kansas a slave state."[16] By 1855 the northern abolitionist press had made Atchison the "symbolic leader" of the proslavery effort in Kansas and the very "incarnation of the slave power conspiracy."[17]

While Atchison was still east, the Missouri state legislature held its vote for the U.S. Senate seat. Moderate and proslavery Whigs held together and nominated proslavery Whig Alexander W. Doniphan, Atchison's friend and former law partner. Unfortunately for Atchison, the Democrats did not unite under his banner. Instead, they divided, nominating Atchison and Benton. Atchison was further damaged after the Hannibal–St. Joseph rail line, which he had sponsored in the Senate, was taken over by Free-Soil investors from Boston. The capitalist coup took him completely by surprise.[18]

Balloting in the state legislature began on January 4, 1855. Atchison tied with Doniphan or led in every ballot taken, reaching a high of sixty-three votes in the thirtieth ballot, but never enough for election. On the forty-first and final ballot the vote was Atchison fifty-eight, Doniphan, fifty-six, Benton thirty-eight.

Atchison and Benton had taken opposing sides on the Kansas-Nebraska Act, each believing his position on the act would assure his victory in the Senate election. Both had been wrong.[19] In Washington, Atchison took his last recorded roll call vote on February 2, 1855. One week later, on February 10 the Missouri State Senate "adopted by an unrecorded vote on a concurrent resolution postponing the election of a United States senator until the second Monday in November."[20]

The territorial elections in Kansas were slated for March 30, 1855. On March 25, Atchison led eighty-plus men over the border from western Missouri into Kansas. They carried with them twenty-four wagons of arms and supplies.[21] Despite northern abolitionist emigration efforts, territorial proximity and same-day registration gave the proslavery forces in Kansas an overwhelming victory on March 30, winning thirty-six of the thirty-nine legislative seats. The later congressional investigation found 4,908 proslavery voters had crossed over the border on the day of the election.[22] Atchison always maintained that neither he nor any of his men voted in the election but were instead there to maintain order.[23]

Of the eighteen election districts, Governor Reeder threw out the results of seven due to fraud and rescheduled elections in those districts for May 24. The May elections resulted in four Free-Soil victories; the remaining three went to the proslavery candidates elected earlier in March. Atchison reported the proslavery victory to the Mess in Washington. He continued to maintain close contact with it during the ensuing months of conflict in Kansas and the Senate chamber.

Notable in the correspondence between Atchison and his messmates between 1855 and 1857 is the "emotional attachment" that existed between the men. During their years together, the four had formed a bond that went beyond shared political values to include "sharing of personal confidences and personal problems"—what Ross K. Baker refers to as "pure friendship".[24] Their letters provide a glimpse into a group concerned with both slavery's expansion and each other. "My Dear General," Butler wrote Atchison that spring, "I have just returned from my plantation where I have been spending some time talking to practical men on practical affairs—eating well baked cornbread and well cured bacon, and . . . delicious fishing . . . finally shooting ducks." Butler noted that the F Street household properties had been sold at a profit, but he kept the knife box on which he had written all their names. He complemented Atchison on his victory in Kansas and then thanked him for caring for the young relative Butler had sent to join him.[25] The Mess, Hunter and Mason particularly, were also concerned about the reports of election fraud and violence. Atchison reassured them that the reports were abolitionist exaggerations, "You will no doubt see your humble servant held up by the Abolitionist press as a Bandit, a ruffian, an Aaron Burr, don't believe a word of it," Atchison wrote, "I have saved hundreds of their necks, and kept their cabins from being burnt to the ground; there was not the least disturbance where I was present."[26]

On July 2 the Kansas territorial legislature convened in Pawnee City, the settlement established by Governor Andrew Reeder. It refused to seat the four Free-Soil members that had been elected in May and adjourned, reconvening two weeks later on July 16 in Shawnee Mission. Stalemate followed as Reeder vetoed the recent legislation and the legislature overrode his vetoes and then petitioned the president for Reeder's removal. On July 28 President Pierce "terminated" Reeder's appointment on the grounds he had speculated in nonsurveyed Indian lands and, without authority to do so, established settlements on those and other military lands.[27] The president was justified in firing Reeder because his land speculations were illegal and a conflict of interest. Nevertheless, the northern press accused Atchison and Jefferson Davis of orchestrating Reeder's demise and continued to paint the president as a puppet of the Slave Power conspiracy.[28]

By August the proslavery legislature had moved from Shawnee Mission to nearby Lecompton. In September, the newly appointed governor, Wilson Shannon, arrived.[29] In the meantime Free-Soil forces regrouped in Topeka and held their own convention, ratifying a Free-Soil constitution on December 15. It prohibited slavery and the emigration of free blacks.[30] Fearing possible conflict between Lecompton and Topeka supporters, Governor Shannon requested use of federal troops if necessary. His request was denied by the president. Instead, federal troops were ordered to stand by pending orders from the president, which never came.

In January, Free-Soil settlers went to the polls and elected a Free-Soil legislature and their own governor, Charles Robinson, former agent of the New England Emigrant Aid Society and founder of the town of Lawrence. On March 4, the Topeka legislature elected former governor Andrew Reeder and James H. Lane U.S. senators. Reeder was already in Washington, having earlier been elected Topeka's territorial representative.[31] Lane arrived in Washington with a memorial requesting immediate admission into the union under the Topeka Constitution.

Just prior to the start of the Thirty-Fourth Congress, Isaac Holmes, former congressmen from South Carolina, wrote to Butler in Washington praising Atchison's "devotion to the Southern cause," assuring Butler that, while Atchison would be missed in the chamber, "he is well employed at home," fighting the Free-Soil insurgency in Kansas from Missouri.[32] In the meantime, the remaining members of the F Street Mess took up the political fight on the Senate floor.

Atchison's absence was not the only change in the Thirty-Fourth Congress. One of the ironic consequences of the Kansas-Nebraska Act of 1854 was it enabled the new Republican Party to take control of the House of Representatives in the fall elections. As a result, the Democratic-controlled Senate could no longer push legislation through the House as it had with the original Nebraska-Kansas bill. Unlike its predecessor, the Thirty-Fourth Congress would be unable to pass anything regarding Kansas. There would be no pyrrhic victories for either side, only pyrrhic stalemate.

The next stage in the congressional battle over Kansas came on March 12, 1855, when Stephen Douglas submitted the Committee on Territories report on the elections in Kansas. It found the Lecompton government to be the duly elected territorial government.[33] Douglas also announced his intention to submit a bill allowing Kansas to request admission as a state when it had reached a population of 93,420.[34] Until that time administration of the territory remained in the hands of the territorial governor, Wilson Shannon, and the legislature at Lecompton; the constitutional convention was to be held the following year. It took more than three hours for the majority report along with the dissenting opinion to be read into the record, but before the Senate could order the reports printed, Charles Sumner and William Seward announced their intentions to "secure the admission of the State of Kansas," based on the Topeka Constitution.

The Topeka supporters in Congress had two problems. First, the Topeka government was illegitimate and in open rebellion against the federally recognized government in Lecompton. Second, Topeka was asking for immediate admittance into the Union under its constitution, even though Kansas had yet to reach the minimum population required. Congress required a minimum population for admittance into the Union based on the ratio for representation. The principle was enshrined in the 1787 Northwest Ordinance at 60,000, the same ordinance that had enshrined the principle of congressional restriction of slavery in the territories. While the principle of congressional restriction had been abandoned, the principle of a minimum population had held. However, as the nation's population grew, so too did the ratio for representation. In 1856 the minimum population was set at 93,420. Kansas's population at the time of the 1855 census was less than 9,000 but growing.[35]

Topeka's problems meant the remaining members of the F Street Mess could ignore the question of slavery altogether and instead focus on the issues of legitimacy and process. Back in Kansas, Atchison worked with Governor Shannon to secure the peace. He urged his supporters to refrain from violence and instead accused the Topeka insurgency of instigating it. In the meantime, Hunter, Butler, and Mason continued to dominate the debate on the Senate floor by using Senate rules and procedures to obstruct William Seward, Charles Sumner, and the Free-Soil efforts.

Debate immediately ensued between Seward and Butler over whether Congress had the power to bypass a territorial government and admit any territory as a state if it so chose. Butler noted that Congress had always required a minimum population threshold for statehood based on "the ratio of representation in the original formation" of the country, and no territory had ever been admitted below the ratio. Ignoring established precedent, Seward insisted Congress could admit any territory regardless of population. "Even if it only had one hundred inhabitants?" asked Butler. "I do not say that," responded Seward, noting 25,000 settlers were already in Kansas.[36]

Seward and Butler's debate was cut short by Douglas. Both majority and minority reports on Kansas were ordered printed, and the Senate moved on to other concerns. The following week, March 17, Douglas submitted bill, S. No. 172, "to authorize the people of the Territory of Kansas to form a constitution and State government, preparatory to their admission into the Union, when they have the requisite population." Debate began on a motion by Hunter on Thursday, March 20. After Douglas's two-and-a-half-hour opening speech, William Seward took the floor and announced his intention to offer a substitute bill. The substitute "was laid on the table informally" and ordered printed. Debate was postponed to the following week.

Throughout most of April, debate on Kansas was frequently sidelined by other Senate business. Then on April 7 Lewis Cass attempted to submit and have printed a Free-Soil memorial brought by Lane. It was referred to the Committee on Territories while Hunter, Mason, and Butler were absent from the chamber. Two days later Butler offered his strong opposition to the memorial on the grounds that the Topeka government did not constitute the legitimate government of the territory. He argued the Senate should not be the "vehicle for" or bear the "expense of publishing petitions" by a "self-constituted body" openly in opposition to the "legally organized" territorial government.[37]

Douglas, however, supported the printing of the Topeka memorial. No one, he noted, could accuse him or the Committee on Territories of sanctioning "the revolutionary proceedings in Kansas to give validity to this self-styled bogus Legislature," but he was willing to vote for the petition to be printed, "not because they ask it, but because it will give us an opportunity of seeing on what ground they now put their claim" of legitimacy.[38]

Butler and James Mason responded with a clever game of procedural knots. Butler noted that while "resolutions of State Legislatures, or lawful proceedings held within the State," were "entitled to be printed, on the motion of a single member," the memorials of private citizens had to be referred to the Committee on Printing, not the Committee on Territories. Mason agreed and acknowledged the right of a "citizen of the United States alone, or jointly with other citizens," to submit memorials to the Congress, but the Topeka petitioners were not claiming that right as private citizens but as the "senators and representatives in the General Assembly of the State of Kansas." Such a claim, Mason continued, was in "derogation of the laws of the land."[39] Butler even questioned the legitimacy of the signatures, noting they were all written in the same hand. Finally, on April 10 Mason moved to have the memorial returned to the Committee of the Whole. Even members who had been inclined to see the memorial printed now questioned its legitimacy. Mason's resolution passed 32 to 3, the nay votes coming from Harlan, Seward, and Sumner. With the memorial back before the Senate, Cass withdrew it.

Perhaps because of the futility of it all, the Senate did not view the Kansas bill with any particular urgency despite the press coverage and passions of some involved. Douglas was particularly frustrated by the fact that consideration of the bill was given limited time once a week, and any rebuttal to a member's speech had to wait until the following week. Concerned the debate could drag on through the remainder of the session, Douglas pushed for a vote on the bill. On Monday, May 19, he asked the Senate to consider "the Kansas bill from day to day, until it be disposed of."[40] His request was opposed by both sides of the debate. Seward reminded the Senate that it had "a large number" of Commerce bills pending, and Hunter reminded them that his appropriations bill for "consular and diplomatic expenses" was to be taken up the next morning. The Senate continued with its other business, returning to consideration of the Kansas bill later in the day with the scheduled remarks by the senator from Massachusetts, Charles Sumner. He spoke for three hours straight without concluding when the Senate adjourned for the day.

The complacency on the part of the Senate concerning Kansas was not all that surprising, given that up until the spring of 1856 the conflict in Kansas had been relatively peaceful.[41] The violence that would become known as Bleeding Kansas developed slowly. Despite two years of emigration and settlement, federal authorities and settlers were still organizing in the spring of 1856. As late as May most of the territory had yet to be surveyed, and many Indian titles remained intact. Federal authorities and emigrants who came to Kansas after the bill's enactment found a preexisting settlement of squatters. Consequently, the first disputes in Kansas were over land titles, not slavery. Both sides, Free-Soil and proslavery, co-opted these individual disputes into the greater conflict.[42] Three events over four consecutive days, May 21–24, would do exactly that.

On Tuesday, May 20, Charles Sumner concluded his two-day address entitled The Crime against Kansas. The next day the federal marshal arrived in Lawrence, the home of Topeka governor Charles Robinson, with warrants for his and others' arrests and orders to shut down the town's two Free-Soil newspapers and the hotel out of which it operated.[43]

A great deal of myth surrounds the conflict known as Bleeding Kansas, much of which was created by the exaggerated coverage by the abolitionist press and later accepted as fact.[44] Contemporary accounts and later histories depict Atchison as the violent, foul-mouthed, heavy-drinking leader of the proslavery "border ruffians" who had crossed over the border from Missouri into Kansas and terrorized Free-Soil settlements. Atchison's own bellicose words in speeches and letters helped to solidify this image. His public statements also made it easier for Free-Soil sympathizers to circulate copies of speeches supposedly by Atchison that he never made.

Nicole Etcheson's 2004 study on the Kansas civil war did much to strip away the mythology surrounding Atchison and the events known collectively as Bleeding Kansas.[45] Her account shows Atchison as a man whose bellicosity did not match his actions. Despite his public rhetoric, before 1857 Atchison endeavored to keep the peace in Kansas. Simply put, his bark was worse than his bite. Another myth is that Kansas was a free-for-all between two contending forces, the proslavery and the Free-Soil militias. In actuality, there was a functioning territorial government in Kansas that included a territorial governor and a federal court system. Federal marshals, the territorial militia, and federal troops were used by Governor Shannon to maintain order and later by Governor Geary to restore it. Atchison worked with both men.

But Atchison was not willing to accept a free Kansas. Before and after the territorial elections in 1855, he worked tirelessly to raise money and promote proslavery emigration into Kansas. He worked with Shannon to keep the peace, knowing that doing so helped to legitimize the government in Lecompton and delegitimize the insurgency in Topeka. Nevertheless, Atchison's use of violent rhetoric is difficult to reconcile with his willingness to reach a peaceful accord. In one particularly violent speech, he threatened to "mormonize" the abolitionists, telling the "squatters of Kansas and the people of Missouri, to give a horse thief . . . a fair trial, but to hang a Negro thief or abolitionist, without Judge or Jury." Waiting for the applause to die down Atchison continued "we are organizing, to meet their organization. We will be compelled to shoot, burn, & hang, but the thing will soon be over, we intend to Mormonize 'the Abolitionists.'"[46]

Again, Atchison was using violent language publicly, while suggesting a willingness to negotiate privately. With his use of the term "Mormonize," Atchison was referring to his role in the earlier Mormon conflict in Missouri in which the state government extinguished Mormon land titles and later expelled Mormons from the state. As a general in the Missouri state militia during the Mormon War, it was Atchison who ended the bloodshed and negotiated a settlement that removed the Mormons from Missouri. It might not have been an ethical outcome, but it worked. Clearly, Atchison intended to use the same siege-and-negotiate strategy in Kansas that he had used against the Mormons in Missouri.

It is significant that Atchison's letter in which he promises to "mormonize" the abolitionists was written to Jefferson Davis, which again suggests a coordinated strategy between southern leadership in the Senate and Atchison in the field. And while siege-and-negotiation was one strategy, the "sack of Lawrence" suggests that inciting Free-Soilers to violence in order to drive them from the territory was another. The "sack of Lawrence" began over a disputed land claim between two settlers, Franklin Coleman and Jacob Branson, neither of whom were anywhere near Lawrence when the "sack" occurred on May 21. Arbitration had divided the disputed property between the two men, but the boundary remained contested. In November 1855 Charles Dow, a friend of Branson's, was shot dead by Coleman on a road near the property. Coleman, who claimed self-defense, fled to proslavery friends in Missouri. Jacob Branson, now aligned with the Free-Soil movement responded by attacking proslavery settlers and their properties. Samuel C. Jones, sheriff of Douglas County, arrested Branson for disturbing the peace but was later forced at gun point to release Branson by a group of Free-Soil men. Branson made his way to Lawrence, the Free-Soil town established by Charles Robinson, the elected governor of the Topeka government. Territorial, proslavery, and Free-Soil militias all converged on Lawrence where it was presumed Branson was still holed up. By December there was a combined militia force of two thousand territorial and proslavery men outside the town limits and two thousand Free-Soil militiamen inside. Jacob Branson, on the other hand had left town on November 29.

On the night of December 7, Shannon and Atchison ate dinner at Robinson's house. The three hammered out a negotiated agreement in which Robinson agreed that Lawrence would not interfere with the government's actions against criminals, and both sides agreed to disband their militias. Neither side held to the agreement. Instead, proslavery militias remained encamped outside the town limits on the Wakarusa River, maintaining a fairly porous siege of the town for the next six months. The Free-Soil militia remained inside Lawrence, drilling and building up earthworks, turning the town, including its hotel, into an armed fortress.[47] Atchison, however, kept his promise, telling his men "'you cannot now destroy these people without losing more than you would gain.'" He disbanded his militia and went home.[48] During the winter interlude, Atchison maintained contact with the Mess in Washington, campaigned for outside southern support, and on occasion traveled over the border. His activities were increasingly vilified by the northern press. Andrew Pickens Butler promised he would address the attacks against Atchison in his floor speech scheduled for March 5.

On the day of the speech, Butler was visibly ill. Hunter rose, with fellow senators in agreement, and asked the Senate president to postpone the speech, but Butler insisted on going forward. Butler objected to the press attacks on Atchison and even more so those made by Hale and Sumner. "They have attributed to him a ferocity and vulgar indifference and recklessness," none of which, he said, could be "assimilate[d] to his nature." To the accusation that Atchison was the enemy of the Free-Soil emigration efforts, Butler, intent on conquering Kansas for slavery, replied, "I will not say that General Atchison is the enemy of any one. I will not say that he is the enemy of the emigrants of Kansas who have been sent there by the aid societies." Instead, Butler insisted Atchison's mediation in December had saved the Free-Soil town of Lawrence. "But for the gentle advice, and, perhaps, controlling influence of Atchison," he continued, "the houses of the settlement would have been burnt and its highways drenched in blood."[49]

Butler objected to what he and Atchison both called the "squatter sovereignty" of the abolitionist emigrants. Butler argued that if Kansas was left alone, the population of slave owners and slaves would be minimal, and that slave and free labor could coexist:

> He [Atchison] believed that if that competition had been left to itself, and if there had been no hostile demonstration on the part of the northern societies, Kansas would have been settled by neighbors knowing each other, and who would have less objection because they did know each other; and that in the end, perhaps, there might be few negroes . . . perhaps, a population with some masters, but with some servants, and scarcely any slaves . . . Kansas would likely have become a quasi-community, with many white men and few negroes—with labor capable of being usefully and profitably employed—a community of farmers, using labor as they thought proper. In this way, by accretion, Kansas might have become a state.[50]

Butler's March 5 speech is important for several reasons. First, it contradicts Atchison's words and actions, both of which supported large scale slave migration into the territory. Second, it is the first recorded evidence that Butler's health was declining, and his absences from the chamber would increase over the remainder of the session. In May he would go home to South Carolina in an effort to convalesce and, as a result, be absent from the Senate chamber on May 19 and 20, the fateful two days of Sumner's speech, The Crime against Kansas. Third, Sumner later claimed that his speech was in direct response to Butler's speech of March 5. Fourth, in his speech Sumner would ridicule Butler's speech impediment. Butler had a lisp that caused him at times to spit. Historians disagree on whether Butler was born with the lisp or it was caused by a minor stroke. If Butler's slurred speech was caused by a stroke or strokes, it could have occurred just prior to his March speech and may have been the reason why Hunter tried to prevent him from speaking in the first place.

Back in Kansas, the springtime renewal of hostilities was fast approaching.[51] In April, Sheriff Jones returned to Lawrence with federal troops and arrested six men involved in the Branson rescue. Three days later the sheriff was shot in the back just outside the town limits. The chief justice of the Territorial Supreme Court, Samuel D. Lecompte, convened the grand jury. Indictments on nuisance charges were handed down against Robinson, Reeder, Lane, and several other Free-Soil leaders. The judge went one step further and issued an abatement order for the two Free-Soil newspapers in Lawrence and the hotel in which the papers were published.

The details behind the Sack of Lawrence are fuzzy. Historical accounts tell similar stories with subtle differences. Generally, it is agreed that on May 21 Federal Marshal Israel B. (I. B.) Donaldson, accompanied by Atchison, entered the town with warrants, abatement orders, and a proslavery-leaning posse of several hundred. Finding the Free-Soil leaders Reeder, Lane, and Robinson gone, Donaldson and Atchison accepted an invitation to dine at the hotel with the remaining town leaders during which a second negotiated settlement was reached.[52] The town leaders agreed to assist Donaldson in serving his remaining writs, whereupon Donaldson disbanded the posse.

Sheriff Jones was outside the town limits when the now disbanded posse returned to its encampment. Jones, still smarting, literally and figuratively, from being shot in the back, re-deputized the posse and road back into town. The posse confiscated weapons, including a howitzer, set fire to the hotel and several buildings, pillaged others, and finally left town. The residents of Lawrence offered no resistance.[53]

The "Sack of Lawrence" as it became known in the northern press was blamed on Atchison. A speech, supposedly written by Atchison, in which he advocated violence against the people of Lawrence, including women, was circulated among Free-Soil sympathizers and the press. The speech was a forgery.[54] Atchison was present at the destruction and, understanding the potential public relations disaster, tried unsuccessfully to restrain Jones and the posse. Atchison's assessment was correct. The Free-Soil movement could not have bought the kind of press that Jones and the proslavery posse handed them, as northern press reports juxtaposed the violence of Jones's posse to the stoicism of Lawrence's residents, who did not resist the destruction and confiscation of their property.

News of the Sack of Lawrence reached northern papers simultaneously with the news of the assault on Senator Charles Sumner of Massachusetts. On May 20 Sumner concluded his epic two-day speech, The Crime against Kansas, which had been preprinted in pamphlet form and distributed.[55] In the speech, Sumner outlined the history of the Kansas-Nebraska Act and the subsequent territorial elections, but little of that aspect of the speech is remembered. What made the speech particularly memorable and objectionable to the senators who heard it was his use of sexual innuendo and virulent personal attacks on fellow members, including Butler, Mason, Atchison, Cass, and Douglas.

The F Street Mess was, according to Sumner, the embodiment of the Slave Power and Cass and Douglas, their puppets. His attack was particularly pointed and harsh on Butler. The floor debates between the two senators had become increasingly acrimonious since 1854.[56] Butler, who sat directly in front of Sumner, was not in the chamber during Sumner's address. He had spent the previous two weeks at his home in Edgefield recuperating from his earlier illness.[57] Sumner acknowledged "the elder senator['s]" absence from the chamber and then likened him to the befuddled Don Quixote who championed the prostitute Dulcinea. Butler, Sumner declared "has chosen a mistress to whom he has made his vows, and who, though ugly to others, is always lovely to him; though polluted in the sight of the world, is chaste in his sight—I mean the harlot, slavery. . . . Let her be impeached in character, or any proposition made to shut her out from the extension of her wantonness, and no extravagance of manner or hardihood of assertion is then too great for this senator."[58]

After finishing his attack on Butler, Sumner reviewed the history of the Kansas conflict, singling out Atchison as the border ruffian leader known less for his "ability than for the exalted place he has occupied." Even then, Sumner reminded the chamber that Atchison had shirked his final responsibilities as president of the Senate to solicit proslavery emigrants and funds for Kansas. "He stalked into this Chamber, reeking with conspiracy . . . and then like Catiline he skulked away . . . to join and provoke the conspirators, who at a distance awaited their congenial chief. Under the influence of his malign presence the crime ripened to its fatal fruits, while the similitude with Catiline was again renewed in sympathy, not even concealed, which he found in the very Senate itself, where, beyond even the Roman example, a senator [Butler] has not hesitated to appear as his open compurgator."[59]

Sumner ended his two-day address in a spirited defense of the Free-Soil government in Topeka and residents of Lawrence.[60] He concluded with a second attack on Butler, making specific reference to Butler's speech impediment, "incoherent phrases discharged the loose expectoration of his speech . . . nor was there any possible deviation from truth which he did not make . . . the senator touches nothing which he does not disfigure—with error. . . . He shows an incapacity of accuracy. . . . He cannot open his mouth, but out there flies a blunder."[61]

Sumner's diatribe had violated the rules of decorum, long held and adhered to and first established by Thomas Jefferson in his 1801 *Manual of Parliamentary Practice for the Use of the Senate of the United States*. Senate debates were conducted without distractions or interruptions, and a senator in debate could not "by any form of words impute to another Senator or to other Senators any conduct or motive unworthy or unbecoming of a Senator." When William Seward saw the problem in Sumner's prepared remarks and told him to remove the personal references, he did not.[62]

Remarkably there was no response from the floor during Sumner's address. He was not once called to order despite his violation of Senate rules and decorum. Lloyd Benson believes the lack of response was prearranged by southern members whose intent was to "shun" Sumner. He states southern senators made a deliberate effort to ignore Sumner as he spoke by "shuffling papers, whispering to each other, and moving about the chamber."[63] If correct, these behaviors were also prohibited under Jefferson's *Manual*.

Cass, Douglas, and Mason delivered the formal responses to Sumner, immediately following his conclusion. Douglas elicited the first laughter of the day from the tension-filled chamber when he stated he would refrain from responding to Sumner's history of events as "he seems to get up a speech, as in Yankee land they get up a quilt. . . . They cut up these pieces of old dresses and make pretty figures, and boast of what beautiful ornamental work they have made, although there was not a new piece of material in the whole quilt."

Douglas continued Sumner had insulted the Senate as a whole by insulting members in particular. Such behavior, he added was "only pardonable when it is the outburst of a just debate," but Sumner's intemperance was not impulsive, he argued, but was planned. He had written the speech ahead of time for mass circulation, "punctuating the proof-sheets, repeating it before the glass, in order to give refinement to insult." And why, Douglas asked, for what purpose was Sumner's "attacks on individuals by name, and two thirds of the Senate collectively. Is it the object to drive men here to dissolve social relations with political opponents? Is it to turn the Senate into a bear garden, where Senators cannot associate on terms which ought to prevail between gentlemen?"

In other words, Sumner, according to Douglas, was attempting to dissolve the institutional and personal bonds of friendship that were used to bridge sectional and political divides and make the Senate work. It was an argument that not only defended traditional senatorial practices but also the very foundation of the F Street Mess's power within the Senate itself.

James Mason, the last to speak against Sumner, agreed with Douglas's accusation that Sumner's words were disrespectful with the intention to create disharmony between members. In unconcealed anger, he condemned Sumner's attack on Butler and Atchison, noting Sumner's lack of empathy for the ailing Butler and respect for the former Senate president Atchison. Becoming increasingly incensed, Mason declared Sumner so lacking of "manhood" that only the "necessity of political position . . . constrained" him to be in the same room with Sumner and be forced to listen to his "depravity."[64] He concluded by rejecting the existence of a Slave Power, noting that economically the North's power was "three times greater" than the South's, and numerically commanded the majority in both houses of Congress.[65]

Two days later, on Thursday, May 22 Andrew Pickens Butler's cousin, Congressman Preston Brooks of South Carolina entered the Senate chamber shortly after adjournment and approached Sumner who was still seated at his desk.[66] Sumner later testified he was looking down signing copies of his speech to be mailed to supporters. He looked up when he heard Brooks speak. "'You have libeled my state and slandered a relative who is aged and absent,' said Brooks to Sumner, "and I have come to punish you for it."[67]

Brooks commenced beating Sumner over the head with his "gutta percha gold-headed cane."[68] The beating lasted about a minute but was severe. Sumner, unable to get up from behind his desk collapsed. Brooks continued to beat him until restrained by Congressmen Ambrose S. Murray of New York.[69] Brooks turned himself into local authorities immediately because his code of honor required "that the taker of fair vengeance must report his deeds." The Senate and the House immediately formed committees to investigate the affair and make recommendations.

No discussion of nineteenth-century southern honor is possible without the inclusion of the Sumner caning, referred to at the time as the Brooks-Sumner Affair. Brooks was imbued with a southern code of honor that led him to believe it was his "duty to relieve Butler, and avenge the insult" to his State.[70] Dueling, of which Brooks was an ardent practitioner, fulfilled multiple elements of honorable conduct including "revenge against familial and community enemies," and "personal bravery."[71] But southern honor was as exclusive as it was ancient and primal. Only gentlemen could challenge gentlemen, and Charles Sumner was not a gentleman under the southern code of honor.[72] It made the remedy used by Brooks on Sumner the only acceptable option.

Butler later explained Brooks's conundrum in a speech to the Senate.[73] Sumner could have apologized, Butler pointed out, but did not. So, "what was my friend to do," he asked, what "mode" of response was available to him? He could not challenge him to a duel: "That would have been an exhibition of chivalry having no meaning." So, there was no recourse other than to punish him, "according to the old fashion notion, by caning him," as one would spank a child or whip a slave. Butler reiterated Brooks's earlier statements that it had been his intent to shame, not harm Sumner.[74] Sumner's wounds had been caused "by the mere accident of having a foolish stick, which broke . . . that he [Brooks] inflicted blows which he would not have inflicted if he had an ordinary weapon of a kind which would have been a security against breaking."[75]

Before either house could report its findings on the Caning of Sumner, the telegraph wires lit up again. On the evening of Saturday, May 24, John Brown and six men, including four of his sons, took five proslavery men from their homes near Pottawatomie Creek in Kansas and hacked them to death with broadswords. One week after the Pottawatomie Creek Massacre, the Senate and House committees on the Brooks Sumner affair began to release its findings. One week after that, the National Democratic Convention convened in Cincinnati.

The escalating violence of May became the campaign issue heading into the parties' nomination conventions that June. The various antislavery groups used the violence in Kansas to unify under the Republican Party. The Democratic Party, fearing the negative consequences of continued violence in Kansas, also looked to unify under anyone but their incumbent Democratic president, Franklin Pierce, whom they blamed for the party's woes. Among the names being tossed about was Robert M. T. Hunter. Even though he was proslavery, Hunter had as reasonable a chance as any at securing the party's nomination. Unlike his fellow messmates, he had not been labeled an extremist by the northern press. In Congress he worked comfortably with members from across the aisle. And politically he had bisectional support.

On the other hand, Hunter's weakness was twofold. First, though the national party was calling for unity, Virginia's state party remained seriously divided between the followers of Hunter and the followers of Governor Henry Wise, with both sides vying for the state party's favorite-son nomination. Wise, who did not support the repeal of the Missouri Compromise, used Hunter's support of it to paint him as an extremist. Second, many of Hunter's radical supporters feared the opposite, that Hunter was too reserved, too moderate. They wanted him to give up his bid for the presidency and instead become the new sectional leader of the South, the position once held by his mentor John C. Calhoun.

But Hunter wanted to be president and ran an aggressive campaign to secure favored-son status from his state convention, keeping in touch with his Virginia supporters throughout the spring. On May 11, Francis Mallory wrote Hunter an encouraging letter regarding his strength in Virginia but warned him of a new threat from outside the state. "No one is opposed to you," Mallory wrote, "but the idea is afloat that B[uchanan] is the strong candidate."[76] Four days later Mallory wrote again to inform Hunter that Wise's people were trying to get Wise's name entered in place of Hunter's at the county level. Mallory also mentioned the possibility that the state convention might not endorse either candidate, which is exactly what the convention did. Lack of his state's endorsement weakened Hunter's chances at the nomination considerably.[77] His name was not entered at the national convention.

One of the leading candidates going into the convention was Stephen Douglas, and there was growing support among his and Hunter's supporters for a Douglas-Hunter ticket. But the National Democratic Convention was seriously divided over Kansas. Northern delegates blamed the party's loss of the House of Representatives on the passage of the Kansas-Nebraska Act two years earlier and therefore were opposed to both Douglas and Hunter. Many delegates, northern and southern, were also against renominating the president, Franklin Pierce. Balloting began on June 5. Fourteen ballots were cast that day with Pierce's numbers falling to Douglas each time. James Buchanan of Pennsylvania, whom Mallory had warned Hunter about, maintained the lead. The following day, June 6, Pierce and Douglas withdrew from the race, and Buchanan won on the seventeenth ballot. Buchanan was considered the compromise candidate. He had been U.S. minister to Great Britain during the debate over the Kansas-Nebraska Act and had taken no position on the bill either way. Hunter, the quintessential loyal Democrat with an eye on 1860, supported the ticket and threw himself into the campaign.

Though many members of Congress absented themselves from Washington during the political conventions, including Robert Hunter and James Mason, Congress continued to meet throughout the month of June. Erastus T. Montague, a political ally of Hunter's, arrived back in Washington from the Cincinnati convention the day after its conclusion to assess how quickly Hunter needed to return. He wrote Hunter on Monday, June 9, to inform him that Butler had announced his intention to speak on Kansas. Montague added his concern that "the Judge" was "still alone." Mason returned the following day, Hunter on May 23.

Debate on Douglas's Senate bill no. 172, "to enable the people of Kansas territory to form a constitution and state government, preparatory to their admission into the union," became intertwined with the debate on the Brooks-Sumner affair. The five-man committee elected by the Senate on May 23 determined one week later that, while Brooks had breached the privilege of the Senate, it was not within the body's jurisdiction to recommend expulsion. The Senate voted without debate to send the matter to the House. Nevertheless, the debate over whether Brooks had violated the privilege of the Senate continued as the Senate considered state resolutions from Massachusetts that praised Sumner and called for Brooks's expulsion.

Southern members argued that a senator's words were immune from attack or prosecution only when the Senate was in session and made on the Senate floor. Consequently, Sumner's remarks were not protected because he had previously printed and disseminated the speech to his supporters and the press. Also, Brooks had not breached senatorial privilege because he attacked Sumner after the Senate had adjourned. Lastly, southern senators argued that the Massachusetts state resolutions violated procedural rules because they were sent directly to the president of the Senate rather than to the state's congressional delegation, the traditional procedure of submitting resolutions. It was in reference to these resolutions that Butler announced his intention to speak on Thursday, June 12.

Butler began his remarks by noting he had not been present in the Senate when Sumner spoke and was still "worn down" by his return to Washington. He denied Sumner's claim that his speech had been in response to his own of March 5. "I said nothing," Butler told the president, "at any period of my life—much less did I say anything in the course of the debate to which the Senator from Massachusetts purports to have made a reply—that could be called for, much less have justified, the gross personal abuse, traduction, and calumny, to which he had resorted." Butler spoke for two days, his speech being interrupted after two hours on the first day by Clement Clay of Alabama, who, noting Butler's "fatigue," requested the Senate adjourn and allow him to conclude his remarks the next day. The Senate adjourned and went into executive session. Butler continued his remarks the next day, stating that, though his cousin's actions were not justifiable "before a legal tribunal," they certainly were "where honor is concerned, and it is always in the favor of a redress of a wrong." Butler concluded that if he had to pass judgment against Brooks in a civil court, he would have to do so, but "I would say to the man who inflicted the blow . . . 'you are not justified by the law; but it is my privilege to say that, whilst I will enforce the law and maintain its dignity, I shall fine you as small a sum as I possibly can.'"[78]

Robert Hunter spoke on June 24. Unlike many of his fellow southerners, he accepted the right of the Massachusetts state legislature to submit resolutions to the Congress. He just rejected its findings. In his remarks, Hunter went far beyond his messmate's earlier defense of honor to defend the institution of slavery itself. His argument was twofold: first, that the nation's economic system was dependent upon slavery; and, second, that slavery was a benevolent institution that advanced those enslaved.

Hunter blamed England for establishing slavery in the colonies, as Jefferson had argued a century earlier, and northern states for equal participation in the institution since. "If we were the buyers they were the sellers," Hunter argued, "if we sell the product of slave labor they buy it, and contribute their full share to the maintenance of the institution." The only way to end slavery according to Hunter was "to refuse to receive the products of slave labor." And yet trade between the sections continued.[79]

Hunter's position on slavery reflected the white southern mind-set. He believed in a southern society of mutual happiness between "master and slave." He believed slavery provided "progress and improvement" to the African American slave. In fact, Hunter rejected the argument that slaves were kept illiterate and that white southerners who educated slaves were punished for doing so. "I have seen in Virginia thousands of slaves who could read and write," Hunter declared, "and if there ever was any matron, pious or otherwise, who was imprisoned for teaching them, I have yet to hear the history of one." Hunter's belief in the widespread literacy of slaves is based on his own experience as a slave owner in Virginia. And given his own love of reading, Hunter may have been sincere when he declared on the floor, "I believe the progress of light and intelligence in both races is not incompatible with the institution of southern slavery." If that's the case, Hunter's position was in marked contrast with the white southern majority and the laws of most southern states.[80]

Hunter's belief in slavery's benefit and freedom's harm to African Americans provided him with an additional argument for slavery's western expansion. "Pen him [the slave] up in the old States, and the consequence must be either that he must perish under the sufferings of a collision with the stronger race, when population presses too hard upon the means of subsistence, or else the white will abandon the country, and leave it to the negro and his original barbarism."[81]

In defending the Fugitive Slave Act of 1850 Hunter abandoned Calhoun's theory of states' rights and argued for the supremacy of federal law over state law. In doing so, he remained in step with the southern mind-set that now insisted on federal compliance in order to confront the personal liberty laws being passed in the north. "You have no right to enjoy the benefits and protection of the Government, and then refuse to perform the conditions upon which those advantages are extended to you," Hunter argued. "It cannot be right to treat the covenant as binding in all that is beneficial to yourself, and void and invalid so far as you have promised to discharge certain duties toward others." Foreshadowing future events, Hunter told the opposition, "If your obligations to God forbid you to discharge the duties required by the society whose government protects you, nothing is left for you but to abandon that society."[82]

Hunter did not address the Brooks-Sumner affair until the end of his remarks and then only to endorse the arguments already made by Butler and others against censorship or expulsion on the grounds that it was a criminal matter for the courts, "which is independent; the judiciary, which can reach the person or the property of the offender, is sufficient in the case of the citizen." And while he acknowledged the House had discretionary privileges, including expulsion, the Senate could not exercise the same privilege "in regard to the member of another House." Hunter was so opposed to the Senate's involvement that he even opposed the Senate message sent to the House on the matter because it implied a prosecutorial authority he believed the Senate did not have.

The Senate's Democratic majority allowed the message to go to the House because it knew the House could do nothing. The Republican-controlled House lacked the two-thirds majority necessary to expel a member. On July 9 the House voted 121 to 95 in favor of expelling Brooks, 23 votes short of two-thirds.[83] Brooks resigned from the House a week later. He was immediately reelected by his district in South Carolina.

The same day Hunter delivered his speech, Robert Toombs of Georgia, a former Whig turned Democrat, introduced compromise legislation on

Kansas. Toombs's bill called for the creation of a presidential commission to conduct a new population census and voter registration in Kansas. Kansas would elect delegates to a new constitutional convention and the territory would be admitted into the union based on the new constitution, Free-Soil or proslavery. On July 2 Toombs's bill passed the Senate 33 to 12. The House refused to take it up.

Debate on Kansas in the Thirty-Fourth Congress had become an exercise in futility. Every bill, whether it was proposed by Douglas, Seward, or Toombs, was doomed from the start because of the sectional and political divide between the two Houses. As long as southern Democrats controlled the Senate and northern Republicans controlled the House, no bill would pass. Kansas would remain a territory where the chaotic violence of the early summer was escalating into "The August War."[84]

Numerous militias and vigilante groups, Free-Soil and proslavery, roamed the Kansas Territory, but the biggest and best organized were Atchison's militia based out of Missouri and Jim Lane's Free-Soil militia based out of Lawrence, Kansas. Atchison's forces held the Missouri River, blocking any entrance into Kansas by water. Lane's men had organized a land route into Kansas from the north via Iowa and Nebraska. On August 28, Atchison crossed the Missouri into Kansas with one thousand men. They attacked and successfully destroyed John Brown's encampment on the Pottawatomie Creek. Jim Lane responded by sending his men to attack Atchison's main force on Bull Creek. Lane's militia was successful in forcing Atchison's militia back into Missouri. Lane planned to attack Lecompton next, but he and his militia were intercepted by federal troops, dispersed, and driven back to Lawrence. In early September Atchison returned to Kansas with nearly three thousand men and laid siege to Lawrence. It was at the proslavery encampment that the newly arrived governor, John W. Geary, found Atchison on September 15.

Geary was an impartial governor with the willingness and manpower to quell the civil disobedience in Kansas. President Pierce, fearing the effect the continued conflict in Kansas was having on the upcoming elections, had given Geary the authority and necessary troops needed to quell the violence on both sides.[85] Geary quickly disbanded both sides in the conflict and restored order to the territory.

Atchison agreed to disband his militia on September 15. Several reasons factored into his decision, not the least of which was the presence of federal troops and Geary's willingness to use them. Second, Atchison had throughout his own military career deferred to negotiated settlement, as seen in both the Mormon Wars in Missouri and Bleeding Kansas. He urged moderation among the proslavery side because, like Pierce, he was concerned about the detrimental effect the continuing violence was having on the National Democratic Party. Third, by the fall of 1856 Atchison had become increasingly frustrated by the personal attacks in the northern press and what he viewed as a lack of support from other southern states, as evidenced by the shift in Kansas demographics. Proslavery was losing the emigration game. Last but not least, family matters intervened. Atchison's brother died, leaving him the executor of his brother's estate, guardian of his brother's child, and sole owner of his brother's farm. After disbanding his militia, Atchison shut down his lobbying efforts in other states. He went home to his brother's farm in Missouri to live with his brother's widow and child, becoming what he had long championed, a slave master and owner of a large plantation.

A month after Atchison disbanded his militia, Robert M. T. Hunter went to New York as part of an aggressive national Democratic campaign strategy based on public displays of cross-sectional support and identification with the Union against a Republican Party it claimed was dividing the nation. The strategy was created by a Democratic Party dominated by its southern branch. The party's chief fundraiser was Senator John Slidell of Louisiana. The national chairman, who also chaired the party's publicity and speakers' committee, was Representative C. J. Faulkner of Virginia. For Hunter, Slidell, and Faulkner it was important to offset the growing accusations in the northern press of a Slave Power conspiracy by speaking to northern audiences directly.

Hunter had been sent to New York to deliver the keynote address at a carefully timed rally in Poughkeepsie on October 1. In the mid-nineteenth century, state elections were always held a month or two before the national election and, as such, served as a form of exit polling. In September the Democrats had suffered a stunning defeat in Maine. The governor's seat and entire congressional delegation had gone Republican. For the Democratic Party this meant the state elections in Pennsylvania, Indiana, and Ohio, all slated for October 14, were in serious jeopardy.[86] Of the three elections, the Republican paper the *Poughkeepsie Eagle* reported that "Pennsylvania attracts the most attention [where] there are but two tickets, all the friends of freedom supporting one, and the advocates of slavery of all stripes the other, so the result will be a pretty fair test of the strength of the parties."[87]

In the wake of the Maine defeat, Slidell wanted to step up fundraising efforts on Wall Street. He believed a highly successful rally in Poughkeepsie two weeks before the October elections, covered in the national as well as local press, would help raise additional money from those New York merchants who dealt in southern trade and ensure a Democratic victory in Pennsylvania.

And victory in Pennsylvania would also mean less money would have to be spent later in New York. The party leadership also hoped the Poughkeepsie rally would increase Buchanan's margin of victory in New York City and contiguous counties, thereby offsetting the anticipated Republican victory in the upstate districts, and swing New York into the Democratic column come November.

Robert Hunter was selected to deliver the keynote address at the Poughkeepsie rally. On the surface he appears to have been the worst possible choice, especially if the party wished to dispel the image of the Slave Power. He was a states' rights leader in Congress, member of the powerful F Street Mess, chairman of the Finance Committee, and heir to Calhoun. He had helped lead the fight to pass the Kansas-Nebraska Act, supported the Lecompton government, and most recently publicly defended the institution of slavery in his speech opposing the expulsion of Preston Brooks.

But Hunter also possessed widespread bipartisan respect in Congress and had a reputation for fairness and integrity. Republican and longtime resident of Washington, Benjamin Brown French, wrote of Hunter, "He is one of the most upright and amiable men I ever knew."[88] Unlike his more bombastic messmates, Hunter was soft spoken and contemplative. He was thus a good choice to refute the accusations of a Slave Power.

The rally was widely attended by Democrats from the city and contiguous counties. Newspapers reported the attendance from a low of 6,000 to a high of 50,000, depending on the paper's political affiliation. The grounds had a fairlike atmosphere. The alcohol flowed freely, and music played everywhere. Attending clubs sponsored their own booths and speakers. The *New York Herald* reported, "So far as banners and music and stands and hickory poles and big guns and fire crackers could be used to attract an immense crowd, nothing was wanted."[89]

Late in the day, the state party's presiding president David L. Seymour of Troy rose to speak. He applauded those gathered for their Democratic unity and hailed the Democracy as the one true national party that "knew no North no South no East no West," but only "one common country, under the panoply of the Constitution."[90] With the audience whipped up he introduced the keynote speaker.

Hunter prefaced his remarks by stating that he wanted to speak "fully, truly, and frankly," admitting that some of what he was to say might be "unpalatable."[91] But if, as Jean Baker has argued,[92] the northern Democracy was essentially conservative in ideology and committed to a white man's republic, then little of what Hunter said was unpalatable. It was a speech given by a southern conservative to a northern conservative audience augmented by nonparty attendees less interested in Hunter's remarks than the refreshments and entertainment provided elsewhere on the grounds. The Republican press, however, denounced the speech for not only being "unpalatable," but also "confrontational" in its defense of slavery, and accused Hunter of being drunk when he delivered it, despite his known reputation as a teetotaler.[93]

Hunter's address can be broken down into two essential parts. First, he confronted northern furor over the Kansas-Nebraska Act's repeal of the Missouri Compromise by explaining the southern position on slavery's extension into the western territories. Second, he examined the Republican platform and party rhetoric, focusing in particular on the "higher principle" argument of Senator William Seward of New York.

Hunter agreed with the opposition and its press that the crisis of Union was over "the disturbing question of African Slavery" but argued it was less about slavery itself than the Republican Party and the northern press' misrepresentation of the facts regarding slavery's extension into the territories. "I wish to place you in a stand point," he said, "where you may see the Southern view of these questions, upon the other side of which you have already heard so much." The first misrepresentation Hunter argued was the Republican position that the South, in forcing the Kansas-Nebraska Act, had violated its compact with the North made thirty-four years earlier—that the Missouri Compromise had been a compact whereby the North agreed to the removal of slavery's restriction in Missouri in exchange for the South's agreement to its restriction above the 36° 30′ parallel. Hunter stated the Kansas-Nebraska Act could not violate a compact that did not exist, and the Missouri Compromise compact did not exist for two reasons; first, it was two separate pieces of legislation; and, second, the North did not agree to the first piece, voting overwhelmingly against the admission of Missouri as a slave state. Hunter concluded the first part of his remarks by reiterating Douglas's argument that the Compromise of 1850, which adopted the principle of nonintervention, or popular sovereignty, superseded the Missouri Compromise. All the Kansas-Nebraska Act did was repeal in writing what had already been repealed in principle.[94]

Hunter was technically correct in terms of the breakdown of the votes cast in 1820. But had the Compromise of 1850 automatically revoked the Missouri Compromise restriction above the 36° 30′ parallel as Hunter argued? David Potter argues that the facts surrounding the Compromise of 1850 were then, and often today, overshadowed by public perceptions. The Missouri Compromise, which held for three decades before its repeal, had taken on a reverence in the North and West second only to the Northwest Ordinance. But Potter also states that Hunter failed to see that the repeal of the Missouri Compromise did not affect the first piece of legislation: Missouri had been admitted as a slave state and remained so. The repeal affected the second piece of legislation on where the status of slavery had once been restricted but was no longer.[95]

The second major emphasis of Hunter's speech was to refute Seward's higher-law argument. Here Hunter exposes the profound impact of his education and Calhoun's mentorship on his constitutionalism. Hunter pitted Seward's higher-law principle against classical republicanism's emphasis on the impartiality of written law versus the tyranny of the majority.[96] He argued that upon Seward's theory "we hold our institutions and maintain the internal peace only at the pleasure of the majority ... On such a Union, and upon such principles, a Government of law becomes an impossibility; we can have none other than one of force. The law by which we are to be governed, is known only to those who govern us, to whom it is especially revealed, and who will execute it, as they alone understand it."[97]

Hunter was also particularly passionate about the sanctity of property, which he believed was completely undermined by the higher-law principle. He compared the Republican Party's attack on slave property with socialism's attack on property in general, arguing that both believe that ownership was theft and that the unequal distribution of property caused social and political inequality. In true classical republican fashion, Hunter did not deny the existence of social and political inequality. He accepted, as conservatives did, that the Union was an organic community of different groups, and that property, rather than diminishing the lives of the less fortunate, improved them by allowing society and culture to flourish. He furthermore stated that the accusations of a Slave Power oligarchy by the Republican Party and northern press were deliberately intended to create tension between slave owner and non-slave-owner. He cautioned his audience that the notion of class warfare was endemic in socialist principles and therefore would not be contained to the attack on the South's domestic institutions but eventually spread northward.[98]

Hunter ended his speech by harkening back to the important role the New York river counties played in the American Revolution. (Washington had ordered the highlands held which the river counties did.) "What shall I say of it in the Olde Dominion, when they ask me the news from the Empire State," Hunter asked rhetorically. "That I left the Democracy of the State," he answered, "in possession of the Highlands, and that they mean to hold on for the line of the Union."[99]

By 6:00 P.M. the Poughkeepsie rally was over, the grounds empty. The Democratic Party's platform of popular sovereignty coupled with its strategy of sectional unity brought victory in the critical October state elections. One month later James Buchanan was elected president of the United States, sweeping the South as well as winning the crucial states of Pennsylvania and Indiana. It was a stunning victory for the Democratic Party, especially in light of its disastrous congressional loses in 1854 and 1855 when, as a consequence of their support for the Kansas-Nebraska bill, northern Democrats had lost sixty-six seats and the party had lost control of the House of Representatives.[100] In the 1856 election the Democratic Party not only held onto the presidency, but it took back control of the House with a net gain of thirty-five seats. In the Senate, Democrats lost four seats but remained in the majority. But the party's victory was deceptive. Beneath the surface of unity laid the ugly truth. A southern minority controlled the democratic majority. David Potter notes, "One hundred and twelve of his [Buchanan] 174 electoral vote had come from the South. In Congress, 75 out of 128 Democratic representatives and 25 out of 37 Democratic senators were southerners."[101]

In addition to the South's control of the White House and Congress, five of the newly expanded nine-member Supreme Court were southern. On March 6, 1857, two days after Buchanan's inauguration, the Taney Court rendered its Dred Scott decision. In a seven-to-two vote the court declared the Missouri Compromise restriction on slavery unconstitutional. All five southerners plus two northerners, Nelson of New York and Grier of Pennsylvania, voted with the majority, a judicial copy of the Democratic Party's election victory. Republicans, like William Seward, saw the decision as statistical evidence of the Slave Power's control of the federal government. Others, like Abraham Lincoln, saw the combination of the decision with the Kansas-Nebraska Act as evidence of an actual Slave Power conspiracy to constitutionally nationalize slavery. But the Slave Power had always been dependent upon the acquiescence of northern Democrats, whose numbers in Congress were shrinking. That dependence would be the F Street Mess and the Slave Power's Achilles' heel.

CHAPTER SEVEN

We Must Settle This Question

The last great act of bisectional accord came on the last day of the Thirty-Fourth Congress. On March 3, 1857, Congress passed the lowest tariff since 1816. Its author was Robert M. T. Hunter, and but for the looming presence of Kansas it very well could have catapulted him to the party's nomination in 1860. Many of Hunter's supporters wanted him to take a cabinet seat, but his closest friend from childhood, Lewis Harvie, cautioned against it. "You can and will have more power in the Senate."[1]

Hunter was up for reelection in 1858, and his supporters back home feared he might again face "bitter opposition" from Wise.[2] The brief alliance between the Junta and Chivalry in 1855 was over.[3] The Junta planned to run Wise for Hunter's seat and Congressman Charles J. Faulkner for governor. Their friend, former governor John Floyd, was eying a future race against Mason who had just been reelected to another term.[4] Virginia confidant William Old wrote Hunter that he feared the reelection campaign would be "bitter." Another friend, George Booker, worried less about state politics and more about southern rights. He wrote Hunter wanting him to attend the Southern Commercial Convention to be held in late November. Hunter did not attend, but the southern strategy Booker laid out in his letter was the strategy Hunter would adopt in the final years before the war. "If we can succeed in Kansas, keep down the Tariff, shake off commercial dependence upon the North and add a little more territory, we may yet live free men under the stars and stripes."[5]

The tariff of 1857 was not, as would be said later, a sectional bill that primarily benefited the South. As chairman of the Finance Committee, Hunter had fiscal responsibilities. As "heir to Calhoun," he had constitutional concerns. The federal fiscal year was about to end with a $22 million surplus. Hunter opposed any last-minute spending schemes as inherently unsound. He was equally opposed to leaving the money in the Treasury, where it would collect no interest. He also opposed putting the surplus in the banks as it would encourage an increase in paper and dangerous speculation. Politically, Hunter opposed distribution to the states as that would benefit those with a majority in the Congress. Instead, he argued that a reduction in the tariff would reduce the surplus, encourage investment, and lower the per capita tax burden.[6]

Hunter's support included the wool manufacturing interests of the Northeast. The tariff of 1846 had raised duties on raw wool while lowering it on finished cloth and blankets, effectively destroying the domestic wool manufacturing industry. By 1856 wool manufacturers were willing "to try the free-trade method of struggling for life in the open field."[7] The dilemma facing Congress was how to protect both the manufacturer and the farmer.[8]

Hunter's answer was an across-the-board reduction in which both manufacturer and farmer shared. He proposed to lower the "duties on woolens from thirty to twenty-three per cent and on raw wool from thirty to eight per cent." In conference Hunter got the House to agree to his amendment with minor revision. On the last day of the Thirty-Fourth Congress, the Tariff of 1857 passed both houses with bisectional support.[9] After missing much of the session, Andrew Pickens Butler was there to cast his vote for his messmate's bill. It would be his last.

After years of declining health, Butler died at his plantation home Stonelands, outside Edgefield, South Carolina, on May 25, 1857.[10] The oldest member of the Mess, his health had been deteriorating ever since the passage of the Kansas-Nebraska Act. It is likely he suffered a stroke or series of strokes in the late summer or early fall 1855. In September of that year he wrote his nephew Pierce Butler that his hand had gone "lame," and apologized for his correspondence being done "by the hand of another." By 1856 Butler had acquired the lisp and a spitting problem alluded to by Sumner in his Crime against Kansas speech.

Butler's death was announced in the Senate on December 12, 1857, one week after the convening of the Thirty-Fifth Congress. The intimacy that had been a key component to the F Street Mess's power was addressed by James Mason in his eulogy. "It was my good fortune to have known our deceased colleague . . . on terms of more intimate association than most Senators now around me . . . .under a common roof, at a common hearth, and sharing a common board. Our intercourse and association were in every sense fraternal."[11] With only two of the original four left, Hunter and Mason maintained the F Street Mess with new members. Their own relationship grew closer, but time would preclude them from reestablishing a legislative power block as strong as the one they had shared with Atchison and Butler.

Nevertheless, in 1857 both men were celebrating their tenth consecutive year in the Senate together. Mason now ranked eighth and Hunter eleventh in a chamber filled with seasoned veterans. Fifty of the sixty-two Senate members of the Thirty-Fifth Congress had served previously, only eleven, or less than 18 percent, were freshmen. Thirty-three of the returning senators had served in the Thirty-Third Congress that passed the Kansas-Nebraska Act. Inexperience had been replaced by experience, and as long as Democratic unity held, there was hope the Thirty-Fifth Congress would be able to fix that which the Thirty-Third had wrought in Kansas.

The man in the White House had even more experience. By the time James Buchanan was inaugurated the fifteenth president of the United States on March 4, 1857, he had served in elected or appointed office for forty years. David Potter calls Buchanan "one of the best trained men who has ever occupied the presidency," who went into office confident he would be able to bring the slavery issue to an end.[12] To ensure the success of popular sovereignty in Kansas, Buchanan appointed fellow Pennsylvanian, Robert T. Walker its new territorial governor.[13] Walker was also a loyal Democrat and seasoned officeholder, but he was reluctant to accept the appointment, calling Kansas "a grave of governors."[14] Nevertheless, Buchanan, with help from Stephen Douglas, persuaded Walker to accept the appointment. He arrived in Kansas and was inaugurated the fourth territorial governor of Kansas on May 26. Before the end of the year Walker would be gone, and the battle over slavery's expansion would shift from the plains of Kansas to the halls of Congress.

Walker inherited a vastly improved situation in Kansas from John Geary, who had effectively ended most of violence during his term.[15] The spring had brought yet another wave of Free-Soil emigration, and the changing demographics that Atchison had surmised months earlier was complete: the registered vote in Kansas was now overwhelmingly Free-Soil. Even though the Thirty-Fourth Congress had failed to pass enabling legislation, the proslavery Lecompton legislature moved forward and scheduled a June 15 election for delegates to its constitutional convention. Walker met with the Topeka insurgency to urge its participation, promising a fair election free of violence and fraud. But with the proslavery territorial government still in control of the election process, the Free-Soil voters boycotted the election resulting in a proslavery victory.[16]

The constitutional convention convened on September 7 and adjourned four days later, pending the October elections for the new territorial legislature. Walker again promised federal oversight and protection at the polls in the upcoming elections, and with the backing of President Buchanan and Stephen Douglas, he also promised a popular vote on the constitution. It worked. On October 5, 1857, the Free-Soil voters in Kansas went to the polls protected by federal troops. Initial results were close. Walker investigated, threw out two counties' returns, and what would have been a close proslavery win turned into an overwhelming Free-Soil victory.[17]

On October 19 the constitutional convention convened and on November 6 passed a slave constitution. Article VII stated the right of property in a slave "and its increase" was "as inviolable as the right of . . . any property whatever." Under the constitution the legislature could not emancipate slaves without the permission of and compensation to the owner. A partial submission vote was scheduled for December 21. Kansans would only be allowed to vote for a constitution "with Slavery" or "with no Slavery," after which the whole constitution would be submitted to Congress for approval. A negative vote on slavery would not affect slaves already in the territory or their "increase." It would prevent only the further migration of slaves into the state.[18]

Robert Walker had promised many things to the Free-Soil voters in Kansas, not the least of which was his personal pledge to join the Topeka insurgency if his guarantees were not met. By November, Walker had had enough. He left Kansas on November 9 and traveled to Washington, where he met with President Buchanan on November 26. Despite Walker's negative assessment of the situation in Kansas and recommendation against accepting the constitution, Buchanan decided to forward it with his annual message to Congress.

Robert Hunter and other southern members of Congress had openly criticized Walker's activities in Kansas, causing a strain in their relationship with Buchanan.[19] They favored the partial vote on the constitution and its submission to Congress for approval. But Stephen Douglas, for whom the popular vote was sine qua non with popular sovereignty, was furious. On December 3 he met with the president at the White House and informed him of his intention to oppose the passage of the Lecompton Constitution. On December 8 the president's message with accompanying documents that included the Lecompton Constitution was read into the Senate record. Douglas moved that the usual number of copies of the message and accompanying documents be printed along with an additional fifteen thousand copies for the use of the Senate. He ended by formally announcing his opposition to the Lecompton Constitution.

Efforts to dissuade Douglas from opposing the Lecompton Constitution and thereby the administration were not successful. Douglas was up for reelection in 1858, and his constituents back home were increasingly anti-Lecompton. Douglas refused to change his mind. Southern members were stunned. Hunter called the defection "a severe blow."[20] Just two years earlier Atchison had held Douglas in line during the repeal of the Missouri Compromise. Whether Atchison could have held him in line a second time is conjecture.

Douglas began the debate the following day, December 9. His address before packed galleries lasted three hours.[21] In its opening Douglas declared his opposition had nothing to do with the question of slavery. He had no personal interest in whether Kansas entered the Union as a free or slave state. His objections instead related to the manner in which the Lecompton Constitution had come before the Senate. First, the territorial legislature had not been authorized by Congress to convene a convention and pass a constitution. Second, the subsequent constitution had not been submitted in its entirety for ratification by the people of Kansas. Douglas had outlined the two questions behind which both sides on the slavery issue would debate: first, could a territory submit a constitution to Congress without the enabling legislation to do so; and, second, did the partial submission of the constitution to popular vote in the territory violate the principle of popular sovereignty enshrined in the Kansas-Nebraska Act?

For Douglas the two questions were tied together. Douglas argued that the failure of the Thirty-Fourth Congress to pass enabling legislation meant the Lecompton territorial government held the power to legislate for the territory only. It did not have the power to convene a convention to form a state government. However, Douglas argued that the people of Kansas could convene and petition Congress "for the change of government from a territorial to a State government," and this petition could be in the form of a constitution. But Congress could only "accept it as a constitution, and admit them into the Union," if it believed the petition "embodied the will of the people of the Territory, fairly expressed." If the Congress "thought it did not embody the will of the people" it must send the petition back to the people "to have that doubt removed, in order that the popular voice, whatever it might be, should prevail in the constitution." For Douglas the will of the people had not been "fairly expressed" because they had been allowed to vote only on the issue of slavery. On all other matters—the constitution's banking system, the taxation system, "free negroes"—the people of Kansas had been prevented from expressing their will.

Douglas ended his speech by declaring he would "resist to the last" the Lecompton Constitution being "forced down our throats, in violation of the fundamental principle of free government" even if it meant being "severed" from the Democratic Party. "I should regret," he declared, "any social or political estrangement, even temporarily, but if it must be, if I cannot act with you and preserve my faith and my honor, I will stand on the great principle of popular sovereignty, which declares the right of all people to be left perfectly free to form and regulate their domestic institutions in their own way. I will follow that principle wherever its logical consequences may take me."[22]

Douglas's biographer Robert Walter Johannsen calls the speech "the most significant" of Douglas's career. Upon his conclusion, the Senate galleries erupted in cheers and applause, prompting James Mason to move to have the galleries cleared. Mason's motion was met with protest from Seward and other northern members, who argued the real cause for his objection was the visitors' endorsement of the speech, not their behavior. Mason denied his motion had anything to do with any matter other than "decorum," but grudgingly withdrew it on condition "that hereafter, if a like manifestation should be exhibited at any sentiments of any kind which may be promulgated on this floor, the Senate will preserve its dignity and decorum by clearing the Chamber."[23]

Just before Douglas's speech, the acting governor in Kansas, F. P. Stanton, convened the newly elected territorial legislature into session. The Free-Soil majority immediately passed an act to submit the entire constitution to popular vote on January 4. Buchanan promptly removed Stanton and replaced him with James W. Denver. Walker, still in Washington, officially resigned, joining Kansas' "grave of governors."[24]

The partial submission vote in Kansas took place on December 21. Free-Soil voters again refused to participate giving the constitution "with slavery" an overwhelming victory 6,266 to 567.[25] Two weeks later, on January 4, the new territorial election was held. This time Free-Soil Kansans turned out and overwhelmed the proslavery minority. The Lecompton Constitution was voted down in its entirety 10,226 to 162.[26] Despite the election's outcome on February 2, President Buchanan submitted the Lecompton Constitution "with slavery" to Congress with his recommendation for passage.

Congressional debate began in March.[27] The debate in the Senate centered on the two questions posed by Douglas in his December speech.[28] Was federal enabling legislation necessary before submission of a state constitution to Congress? And did the Lecompton Constitution before the Senate represent the popular will of Kansans? Douglas's argument that enabling legislation was necessary unless the constitution reflected the popular will, which it did not, was now repeated by numerous Republican members opposed to the Lecompton Constitution. Likewise, Democratic senators, including the majority of the party's northern members, stood in succession to speak in favor of the Lecompton Constitution.[29]

By March 1858 the Slave Power was under siege. The once powerful F Street Mess was literally half what it had been. Atchison and Butler were gone. James Mason had shifted his attention away from Kansas and was focused on foreign issues.[30] More and more, Hunter found himself working with Jefferson Davis, who was newly returned to the Senate, and political convert Robert Toombs.

All three spoke on the Senate floor in favor of the Lecompton Constitution. It foreshadowed the future composition of Confederate leadership.[31]

Like Douglas, Hunter was facing reelection in 1858. And just as Douglas's reelection was dependent on his strong opposition to the Lecompton Constitution, Hunter's was dependent upon his strong support. Back home in Virginia, Hunter's longtime nemesis Governor Henry Wise was waging a confusing campaign in which he attacked Hunter for breaking with the president by opposing his appointed territorial governor Robert Walker, while at same time Wise himself was opposing Buchanan for his support of the Lecompton Constitution. Wise opposed the measure and called those who supported it "southern extremists."[32] Hunter had vehemently opposed Robert Walker's actions in Kansas but denied any split with Buchanan. On March 12 he delivered a forceful speech on the Senate floor in favor of Lecompton, an administration measure. It was a mixed bag of insightful logic and flagrant errors, typical of the pro-Lecompton responses.

In regard to the question whether the constitution represented the popular will of the people, Hunter acknowledged that a minority of voters had established the territorial government in Kansas, but it had occurred because the majority, Free-Soilers, refused to participate in the earlier elections. Their refusal to participate in the earlier elections, he argued, did not give Free-Soil residents the subsequent right to refuse to abide by the laws established by the territorial government. "A majority have no right to say they will refuse to vote," he argued; "the very existence of free representative government" depended upon participation or government collapses and anarchy prevails.[33]

It was Hunter's strongest argument. He had greater difficulty justifying the lack of enabling legislation. Hunter argued that a territory could be admitted into the Union with or without an enabling act so long as the people of the territory submit an application to Congress with a republican constitution. Technically Hunter was correct. Article IV, section 3, clause 1 of the U.S. Constitution regarding new states makes no reference to enabling legislation. It simply reads that "new States may be admitted by the Congress into this Union." What Hunter did was conveniently ignore the fact that a constitutional clause does not provide the procedure by which a constitutional guarantee is to be carried out. That is for the Congress to legislate, and by 1858 Congress had established the precedent of enabling acts being required for admission into the Union. Hunter was wrong when he noted there had been "numerous instances in which States had been admitted without any enabling act," the only exception to the rule having been Texas, which was admitted by annexation.[34]

After dismissing the necessity for an enabling act, Hunter returned again to the first objection that the people had not voted on the constitution. He argued that the people had voted indirectly for the constitution by voting for representatives to the constitutional convention. "If, then, we say there is not a capacity in a representative assembly to express the opinions and wishes of the people in regard to matters of constitution, is it not obvious that that capacity does not exist in matters of law? And the result would be that a popular form of government is only possible in those communities where there is a small number of people, and where they can meet and deliberate together."[35]

Hunter had explained the principle behind a federated republic but, in doing so, had incorrectly equated the principle of representative government with the principle of constituent convention. He conveniently ignored America's two-tiered level of law, constitutional, which could be created only by the people, and statutory, which could be passed by the people's representative government.[36]

Next Hunter addressed the January 4 election in which the Lecompton Constitution was resubmitted to Kansas voters in its entirety and rejected. He argued that if the Lecompton Convention was legally convened and its constitution legally passed, as he believed it was, the newly elected legislature could not undo "that which belonged to the convention itself to do." But Hunter continued, "If this convention was not an authorized body, that settles the question itself; and it is useless to look further to the votes in relation to it. If it were an unauthorized body, there is no validity in its acts, and it is idle to count the votes that were cast against it." In other words, Free-Soil objectors could not have it both ways.

Hunter also offered an additional argument that would be used by those in favor of the constitution's passage in the Senate and the House. If the majority of Kansans was opposed to slavery, then once Kansas was admitted into the Union there was nothing precluding the state from convening a new constitutional convention and abolishing slavery altogether.[37] Why then, Hunter asked rhetorically, "should any party resist the admission of Kansas under the Lecompton Constitution?" It would occur only if the real objection to Lecompton was something more profound, to block the admission of any new slave state. Those opposed, Hunter observed, desired "to keep the question open for political purposes, or else because they are unwilling to admit, even for a moment, any State which tolerates slavery by its constitution."[38]

Hunter further argued that the right to reject the Lecompton Constitution on the basis of slavery was a violation of the equality of states first established by the admittance of Vermont in 1791.[39] On this point Hunter's intent was to place the principle of state's rights against Seward's "higher law" argument. "You must either claim that general power which is contrary to the equality of the States and to all our notions of their rights," Hunter argued, "or else you must insist that slavery comes under the ban of a law higher than the Constitution, and that all the constitutional guarantees are worthless and good for nothing, so far as that institution is concerned." That was exactly Seward's point, but Hunter argued such a position meant abandonment of constitutional law and a return to mob rule.

Hunter concluded his remarks in defense of white supremacy and empire. He argued that equality and abolition were both abstractions that did not exist in reality. Even the British, he noted, while abolishing slavery in name, had continued to use the indigenous people of its colonial holdings, "subjecting the inferior to the superior race, so as to enable the latter to command a servitude scarcely more voluntary than the older form." Hunter argued the South's approach to western expansion was more pragmatic and humane than the northern exclusionary laws and colonization schemes that reeked of hypocrisy and impracticality. Like the British Empire, Hunter noted, the United States would continue to expand, coming into contact with "the Indian" and other inferior races not capable of caring for themselves. Abolition meant the extermination of these inferior people. Slavery on the other hand, would "develop their resources" and was "the only condition . . . of preserving the proper subordination of the inferior to the superior races—upon which the white man" would rule the continent.[40]

Douglas returned to the Senate chamber on March 22 to deliver his final speech against passage. The following day, on March 23, Missouri Senator James Green gave the final speech in favor. That same day John Crittenden of Kentucky offered a last-minute substitute that would have resubmitted the Lecompton Constitution to Kansas for a popular vote. It was voted down. The Senate passed the Lecompton Constitution 33 to 25. Only three northern Democrats followed Douglas in voting against its passage.

The floor manager for the Lecompton bill in the House was Alexander Stephens, who had managed the Kansas-Nebraska bill two years earlier. Knowing there was little chance of a repeat victory, Stephens worked with William Montgomery of Pennsylvania to reintroduce the Crittenden substitute that had been defeated in the Senate. On April 1 the House rejected the Lecompton Constitution and passed the Montgomery Crittenden substitute by a vote of 120 to 112. Thirteen days later the Senate agreed to a conference with the House. The Senate conferees were Hunter, Seward, and Green of Missouri. The House sent Stephens, William A. Howard of Michigan, and William H.

English of Indiana. Hunter and Green representing southern interests vehemently opposed the Lecompton Constitution being resubmitted to Kansans for a popular vote, but English presented a compromise, proposed earlier by Stephens and backed by the president. The constitution would not technically be resubmitted for a popular vote. Instead, Kansans would vote on an additional federal land grant to the constitution. A vote in favor of the land grant approved the constitution. A vote against the land grant was a vote against the constitution. If Kansans voted against the land grant they would have to wait until their population reached a population level of ninety-three thousand before they could submit another statehood bill. Hunter and Green immediately endorsed the idea. Seward opposed it.

On April 30, over Douglas's continued opposition, the English compromise passed both the Senate and the House. In August Kansans went to the polls and voted down the land grant accepting the continuation of territorial status over a proslavery state. The two-year battle for the soul of Kansas was over. In its wake laid the corpses of the Whig Party, northern Democrats, multiple territorial governors, two presidencies, and a seriously weakened Slave Power. However, some southerners took hope from the vote against the Lecompton Constitution. Kansas was not admitted as a slave state, but neither was it admitted as a free state. And this might have sufficed but for the outcome of the fall elections.

The congressional elections in 1858 were catastrophic for the Democratic Party. Democrats lost 35 seats in the House of Representatives, their number dropping to 98 members in the Thirty-Sixth Congress. Of those, 15 were independent Democrats, 8 of whom were anti-Lecompton. The Republican Party's gain of 26 seats gave it a plurality of 116. The remaining 24 members represented the American and other opposition parties.

The disaster was just as significant in the Senate, where the Democratic Party barely held onto its majority. Democrats had actually gained two seats, but the Republican Party had gained six at the expense of the northern Democracy. Of the five northern Democratic senators whose terms were up in 1859, three had voted for the Lecompton Constitution, two against. Only one of them, Douglas, won reelection that fall. Philip Allen of Rhode Island, who voted yes, did not seek reelection. He was replaced by Republican Henry B. Anthony. William Wright of New Jersey, who voted yes, lost his reelection bid to Republican John C. Ten Eyck. George W. Jones of Iowa, who also voted yes, was not renominated. His seat ultimately went to the Republican James W. Grimes. Charles Edward Stuart of Michigan was one of only three northern Democrats to vote with Douglas against the Lecompton Constitution. He did not run for reelection. His seat was won by Republican Kinsley S. Bingham.

When the Thirty-Sixth Congress opened, there were only ten northern Democratic senators left. The twenty-seven southern Democrats were in a virtual tie with the Senate's twenty-six Republicans. Between the Thirty-Third and Thirty-Sixth Congress, the Slave Power had gone from the zenith to the nadir of its existence. Not only was there a distinct possibility of losing the presidential election to the newly formed Republican Party in 1860, so too was the possibility of losing control of the Senate, which for Hunter, Mason, and the rest of the southern leadership meant loss of their committee chairs. "What are we to look for in the North," wrote a concerned John Randolph Tucker to Hunter shortly after the election, "If Seward has carried New York upon the basis of his *pronounciamentos*, what in 1860?"[41]

Ironically the Republican Party was now beating a dying horse, ramping up its Slave Power conspiracy rhetoric just as southern power was evaporating in Congress. While Hunter campaigned as a moderate southerner in his last effort to secure the Democratic nomination for president in 1860, leading Republican candidates for the presidency, including William Seward and Abraham Lincoln, named him and Mason as the very personification of the Slave Power conspiracy.

With the presidential election barely a year off, Mason was at his plantation home Selma outside Winchester when on the Sunday evening of October 16, 1859, John Brown and twenty-one men seized the federal armory at Harpers Ferry barely twenty miles away. The two towns were connected by rail, and Mason took the train to Harpers Ferry the next morning. By the time he arrived, Brown and his followers had been subdued by federal troops under the command of Robert E. Lee. The troops had been called out by Governor Wise, who was with Mason when he conducted the first interrogation of Brown.

Shortly after the Thirty-Sixth Congress convened in December, the Senate named Mason to chair the select committee investigating Harpers Ferry and those behind its financing. The committee met for six months before submitting its report on June 15, 1860. It made no specific findings but called for legislation to strengthen laws against domestic insurrection. That the committee was unwilling to name names, despite what was publicly known as to who financially backed Brown, is evidence of the Senate's divisions and the F Street Mess's loss of influence.

Mason spent his final two years in the U.S. Senate focused on the international aspects of slavery, in particular the dispute between the United States and Great Britain regarding the sovereignty of U.S. ships on the high seas. While the United States and Great Britain had both outlawed the international slave trade in the nineteenth century, Great Britain maintained the right to stop slave ships suspected of fraudulently flying the U.S. flag. Mason objected to Great Britain's claims and supported putting the U.S. Navy in the Gulf of Mexico to protect America's commercial fleet. His relationship with Britain's ministers remained cordial, however. In February 1859 he hosted a large reception for retiring British minister Sir Francis Napier at the Willard Hotel.[42]

Harpers Ferry briefly intruded into Hunter's otherwise focused pursuit of the presidency. Governor Wise's strong response to the event, calling in federal troops and insisting on the death penalty for Brown, renewed Wise's popularity at home. Once again Hunter found himself in a contest with his longtime nemesis for favorite-son status among Virginia Democrats. "Now in regard to this Harpers Ferry imbroglio, in its political bearing or that which it will be made to assume by designing men, we should like to hear your views," wrote his friend and campaign strategist Lewis Harvie.[43] Hunter's people sought unsuccessfully to postpone the state convention scheduled for February 16, 1860, but were able to get candidate choice turned over to the congressional district conventions, held later, where Hunter's superior organization catapulted him to favorite-son victory.

Nowhere was the demise of the Slave Power more evident than the national convention in Charleston, where the reality of the country's population gave northern delegates a commanding majority.[44] Southern delegates wanted several resolutions protecting slavery in the territories put in the party's platform. Hunter's campaign strategy was to withdraw the South's platform demands in exchange for a southern nominee, preferably himself. Joined by John Slidell, the leader of the administration's forces, Hunter's people attempted to push the nomination ahead of the platform debate, promising to keep the southern demands out of the platform if the convention nominated Hunter. The Douglas campaign, anticipating the potential benefits of a southern walkout, forced consideration of the platform first. The southern resolutions were rejected. Fifty-five delegates from the lower South immediately walked out. That number was more than the Douglas campaign anticipated. Without a necessary two-thirds majority to nominate, the convention was forced to adjourn, to reconvene on June 18 in Baltimore.

A split Democratic Party not only assured the loss of the presidency but also the Senate majority and, with it, the last bastion of southern power, the committee chairs. On May 7 Hunter, Mason, Davis, Toombs, and fifteen other southern Democrats signed "The Address to the National Democracy," written by Davis, in which the signatories openly expressed their anxiety. The letter implored the withdrawn southern delegates to return to the reconvened convention in Baltimore, where all efforts would be made to come to a "satisfactory" agreement. If it could not be achieved, the signatories agreed the remaining southern delegates would "withdraw and unite with the eight States which [had] adjourned to Richmond." From Virginia a less-conciliatory Charles W. Russell asked, "How came Hunter the cautious to be so inconsiderate as to sign that circular? It has unquestionably lost him every vote from our delegation."[45]

The plea had its effect, and several of those who walked out returned to Baltimore. But the Douglas faction, now in complete control of the convention, refused to seat them. Virginia withdrew in protest and joined the southern Democracy in Richmond. Thomas D. Sumter wrote Hunter from South Carolina, "Now [that] the old Boss is dead (Calhoun) we States rights men have to look to you to keep us straight."[46] Hunter opted for unity in the South. He removed his name from consideration and threw his support to sitting vice president John C. Breckinridge, who became the southern Democratic nominee. The northern Democracy at Baltimore nominated Douglas.

Mason's biographer Robert Young, chides Mason, Hunter, and the southern leadership for "merely brac[ing] themselves for the catastrophe instead of doing anything positive" to prevent a Republican victory. But Young's assessment ignores the reality made clear two years earlier in the 1858 congressional elections. There was nothing southern Democrats could do to prevent "catastrophe." The population in the northern states made a Republican victory along strictly sectional lines inevitable. A united Democratic Party would not have prevented Abraham Lincoln's election in 1860. If all the non-Lincoln votes, including those for third-party candidate John Bell, had combined, Lincoln would still have won the Electoral College 173 to 130, losing only California and Oregon. The key to Lincoln's victory was New York, Pennsylvania, and Ohio whose combined electoral vote was 85. The seven states of the lower South had a combined electoral vote of 47. As bad as losing the White House was, Democrats also lost control of the Senate and with it the last bastion of the Slave Power, the committee chairs.

The second session of the Thirty-Sixth Congress convened on December 3. Two days later Senator Lazarus W. Powell of Kentucky introduced a resolution to create a select committee to draft amendments to the constitution and or compromise legislation that would prevent the pending secession of southern states. On December 18 the Senate formed the Committee of Thirteen to report on Powell's proposals. Membership, distributed among the parties and regions included John Crittenden, Democrat from Kentucky, its chair; northern Democrats Stephen Douglas, William Bigler of Pennsylvania, and Henry Mower Rice of Minnesota; southern Democrats Robert M.

T. Hunter, Jefferson Davis, Robert Toombs, and Lazarus Powell; and Republicans William Seward, Benjamin Wade of Ohio, James Grimes of Iowa, and Jacob Collamer of Vermont. Two days after the committee formed, South Carolina seceded from the Union. The lower South prepared to follow. In Virginia, the ever-confusing Henry Wise joined fire-eater Edmund Ruffin in calling for immediate secession.[47]

In an effort to stave off the growing crisis, President Buchanan called "moderate" southerners to Washington for a meeting before the opening of the Thirty-Sixth Congress's final session.[48] The men Buchanan asked to meet with were nearly identical to those who had met with President Pierce on that fateful Sunday evening in 1854. Jefferson Davis, Robert Toombs, and Robert M. T. Hunter formed the nucleus of the new group, "the Southern Triumvirate."

Southern moderates like Hunter opposed secession because they believed a united South within the Union provided greater strength from which to negotiate with the North than to become individual southern republics via secession from the Union. Instead of secession, Hunter called for a "conference of the Southern states," to propose a strategy.[49] Hunter's calls for unity and moderation went unheeded. On December 20 the South Carolina convention voted unanimously for secession. The rest of the lower South stood poised to follow.

Less than a week later, Major Robert Anderson evacuated the U.S. garrison stationed at Fort Moultrie in Charleston Bay one mile across to the better fortified Fort Sumter. Two days later on December 28, Hunter, Toombs, and Davis met with Buchanan to discuss the growing crisis. The self-declared Republic of South Carolina wanted Anderson to evacuate Sumter and return to nearby Fort Moultrie.[50] Hunter suggested to the president that Anderson comply in exchange for an evacuation of southern troops from other seized federal facilities. Hunter also argued that since federal forts were located on land originally ceded by the states, he could introduce a bill that would give the president authority to retrocede federal installations to southern states. Hunter believed the bill would help avoid civil war. Buchanan rejected both proposals.[51] Anderson had become an overnight hero in the North because of his actions. President Buchanan knew to accept South Carolina's demands or any compromise proposal from Hunter would destroy what was left of his and the Democratic Party's credibility in the North.[52] The evaporation of southern influence and control was now evident as Hunter and his fellow southerners could not persuade or dictate policy to a president arguably weaker than Franklin Pierce. Their power, the Slave Power, had simply ceased to exist. All the so-called Southern Triumvirate could control now was the question of remaining in the Union or following the seceding states.

On that question, where did the two remaining members of the former Mess stand? Robert Young, James Mason's biographer, argues Mason was "a spy behind enemy lines," who fought against any effort to preserve the Union.[53] If Mason was a spy he was hardly good at it and certainly not very covert. Like Hunter, he had been called to Washington early by President Buchanan. In his meetings with the president, Mason sought information on the military preparedness of federal forts and arsenals in the South. Buchanan refused to provide it. Undeterred, Mason introduced a resolution in the Senate on January 5 to secure the information, arguing it would assuage the fears of the southern people. The resolution did not pass.

Hunter, on whom more has been written, is depicted by his biographers as a reluctant secessionist, a true moderate interested in reconciliation.[54] They argue his political career up to the secession crisis had been one of bipartisanship and bisectional alliances. He was quiet and studious, qualities more often attributed to moderation than extremism. His membership on the Committee of Thirteen before the war and his attendance at the Hampton Roads Conference at its end contribute to this depiction of Hunter as a reluctant secessionist, not unlike Robert E. Lee. But what Hunter lacked in temperament, he made up for in ideology, in which he was the true heir to Calhoun. For Hunter, "southern determinism," came before Union. On that principle, he was neither "moderate, conciliatory, nor compromising."[55]

As a member of the Committee of Thirteen, Hunter did not initiate proposals but aligned himself with those proposed by Davis and Toombs. All three men wanted the Constitution amended to accord slave property the same federal protections as "real property." In other words, the status of slavery would change from "a state-defined private property tolerated in a federal system to a federally defined form of property."[56] The Republican committee members on the other hand refused to accept any proposal they believed federalized slavery.

The Crittenden Compromise, as the compromise package became known, favored the southern position. Its proposals included a series of amendments to the Constitution that would guarantee slavery in the states where it existed, the District of Columbia, and federal military installations. It also prohibited the federal government from interfering with interstate slave trade and extended the 36° 30′ parallel restriction all the way to the Pacific coast.

It was the last measure that President-elect Abraham Lincoln objected to. Having run on a platform against any further expansion of slavery westward, Lincoln saw the extension of the 36° 30′ as an abrogation of the election itself. From Springfield he instructed the five Republican members of the committee to oppose the compromise stating, "We must settle this question whether in a free government the minority have the right to break up the government whenever they choose."[57]

On December 31 as the lower South continued to secede, the Committee of Thirteen voted the Crittenden proposal down 7 to 6. All five Republican members voted against the proposal. Davis and Toombs, holding true to Davis's promise to support only a bipartisan measure, joined them. Crittenden, Hunter, Douglas, Powell, Bigler, and Rice voted in favor.

Crittenden took his proposals to the Senate floor anyway. During the debate the Senate also took up Hunter's resolution to retrocede federal military facilities to the seceded states. Hunter spoke to both measures on January 11 during which he resurrected Calhoun's theory of concurrent majority and called for the establishment of two presidents. On January 14 the Senate voted against Hunter's retrocession resolution 27 to 24. Two days later the Crittenden Compromise was defeated 25 to 23. In both votes the Republican victory was aided by the absence of fourteen southern senators from seceded states.[58] The final nail in the Slave Power coffin had been driven by the Slave Power itself.

On January 19 the remaining senators from the first five seceded states withdrew from the U.S. Senate.[59] On that same day Robert M. T. Hunter resigned his chairmanship of the Finance Committee to "free himself" to work on reconciliation.[60] Three days later, on January 21, Jefferson Davis formally announced from the Senate floor his withdrawal and left for Mississippi. The provisional Confederate government had convened in Montgomery, Alabama. There had been some talk of Hunter as provisional president, but on February 9 the provisional Confederate government in Montgomery, Alabama, elected Jefferson Davis.[61] Virginia convened its convention on secession four days later. In Washington, Hunter attempted to set up through William Seward a meeting between Confederate commissioners and Lincoln to negotiate a peaceful separation. As he had with the Crittenden proposal, Lincoln again said no. His refusal to compromise on the Republican Party's "previously declared platform of principles" had become for Lincoln a principle unto itself. On March 4 Lincoln began his inaugural address declaring "Upon the plainest grounds of good faith, one so elected is not at liberty to shift his position."

Southern withdrawal from the U.S. Congress did not follow a uniform pattern. After the November elections, many southern congressmen and senators simply did not return to Washington. Others returned only to leave again as the lower South began to secede during the winter of 1860–61. Some senators sent formal letters of resignation to the chamber, while others sent nothing at all. Some followed Davis in making formal resignation speeches from the

Senate floor. Others announced their resignations in their hometown newspapers. Some, like Robert Toombs of Georgia, said nothing and simply left. The variety of ways chosen by southern senators to leave only added to the questions confronting those who remained: what was the difference, if any, between withdrawal and resignation; were the withdrawals permanent; did withdrawal affect committee assignments; and last, but definitely not least, was secession legal?[62] Unable to reach an agreement on these questions, the Thirty-Sixth Congress ended on March 3, 1861.

Abraham Lincoln became the nation's sixteenth president the next day. The Thirty-Seventh Congress convened under Republican control and resumed the debate on withdrawal, resignation, and secession. Not wanting to legitimize the principle of secession, the Senate declared the seats of the absent southern senators vacant and removed their names from the roll.[63] The matters of withdrawal and secession were referred to the Judiciary Committee, which failed to return a report before Congress recessed on March 28. James Mason and Robert Hunter had left Washington ten days earlier.[64] Before leaving they voted to confirm William Seward as secretary of state. It was their final vote as U.S. senators. They considered it an act of concession.[65] Both men were in Virginia when Fort Sumter surrendered and President Lincoln called for seventy-five thousand volunteers to suppress the rebellion. Virginia seceded on April 17 and elected Mason and Hunter to the provisional congress in Montgomery, where Hunter actively lobbied for the relocation of the confederate capital to Richmond.

The Thirty-Seventh Congress reconvened in Washington on July 7. On July 10 Republican senator from Rhode Island Daniel Clark submitted a resolution calling for the expulsion of ten southern senators, including Hunter and Mason, from the U.S. Senate for conspiring "against the peace, union, and liberties of the people and Government of the United States," and whose states "in furtherance of such conspiracy . . . are now in arms against the Government . . . said Senators are engaged in said conspiracy for the destruction of the Union and Government, or, with full knowledge of such conspiracy, have failed to advise the Government of its progress or aid in its suppression." The following day James M. Mason and Robert M. T. Hunter of Virginia, Thomas L. Clingman and Thomas Bragg of North Carolina, James Chesnut Jr. of South Carolina, A. O. P. Nicholson of Tennessee, William K. Sebastian and Charles B. Mitchel of Arkansas, and John Hemphill and Louis T. Wigfall of Texas were expelled from the U.S. Senate for disloyalty to the Union by a vote of 32 to 10. The ten were all that was left of the once mighty Slave Power. Their expulsion from the body they had once controlled was and remains the largest single expulsion case (no. 36) in Senate history.[66]

EPILOGUE

The Slave Power conspiracy was an effective rhetorical device used by abolitionists and Republicans to enlist many Americans in their cause and party. It never existed in reality, but the legislative power of southerners in the federal government did. That power, the Slave Power, was personified by the F Street Mess. The four men that composed the Mess, David Rice Atchison, Robert M. T. Hunter, James Murray Mason, and Andrew Pickens Butler, formed a literal oligarchy in the U.S. Senate around which southern senators and northern Democratic allies coalesced to drive proslavery legislation through the U.S. Congress in the 1850s. Their shared space, personal and professional, created an unbreakable loyalty. Their institutional knowledge and common ideology created an insurmountable block in the Senate. Nothing could defeat the F Street Mess and the Slave Power except its own hubris, which was the Kansas-Nebraska Act and its repeal of the Missouri Compromise restriction of slavery above the 36° 30′ parallel. It was one of the most destructive pieces of legislation in U.S. history. It destroyed the second American political party system, stripped Native Americans of their land in Kansas and Nebraska territories, started internecine warfare in the Kansas Territory, and ultimately led to the American Civil War.

Ironically, Atchison, arguably the single most important person responsible for the act's passage, sat the war out. Having failed to win reelection to the U.S. Senate or a proslavery majority in Kansas, Atchison joined the Missouri secessionist movement and struck out. The Missouri unionists held the day, and the Missouri Convention voted against secession. After some equally unsuccessful skirmishes with federal troops, Atchison left the state with its prosecessionist governor, Clairborne F. Jackson. The two men made their way east to Richmond to plead for financial support for the insurgent secessionist forces in Missouri. While in Richmond, Atchison reunited with Hunter and Mason. It was the first time the former messmates had seen each other since 1855.

Atchison returned to Missouri at the end of the month and participated in some of the early battles in the state. Disapproving of Sterling Price's leadership of the secessionist forces, Atchison left the state in March 1862. He moved to a small farm in Grayson County, Texas, where he watched the war from afar. Union forces held Atchison's home state of Missouri, but it remained a contested battleground between Union troops and prosecessionist insurgents throughout the war.

Like Atchison, Mason also watched the Civil War from afar, but as the "Special Commissioner of the Confederate States to the United Kingdom and Ireland." Jefferson Davis appointed Mason and John Slidell of Louisiana to diplomatic posts in August 1861 on the recommendation of his secretary of state, Robert M. T. Hunter. Slidell was appointed special commissioner to France.

Mason and Slidell were charged with two primary tasks: gain diplomatic recognition for the Confederate States of America and get Great Britain and France to break the commercial blockade of the Confederacy imposed by the United States. Both nations had declared their neutrality in the American Civil War and granted the Confederacy official belligerent status, but neither nation was willing to break the blockade.[1]

Mason and Slidell left Charleston on October 12, 1861, bound for London by way of Cuba, arriving there on October 16. On November 7 they left Havana for Southampton aboard the British mail steamer, the *Trent*. The U.S. Navy had been aware of Mason and Slidell's presence in Cuba as well their departure from the island. The next day, November 8, the USS *San Jacinto* under the command of Captain Charles D. Wilkes fired on and boarded the *Trent*. Mason and Slidell were removed from the ship and taken to Fort Warren in Boston Harbor. Britain filed an official protest, ordered troops to Canada, strengthened her Atlantic fleet, and issued an embargo on all shipments to the United States.[2] The New York stock market plunged. On Christmas Day Lincoln ordered their release.

Mason and Slidell arrived in Southampton on January 29, 1862, where they parted ways. Mason maintained an active social life in London throughout the war and had many allies among the British aristocracy.[3] But Mason was never invited to Parliament or received at court.[4]

While Atchison and Mason viewed the war from afar, Robert Hunter escaped neither the war nor its punishing consequences. Jefferson Davis appointed Hunter secretary of state on July 21, 1861. He resigned not long after to run for the Senate in the Confederacy's first elections. Hunter won his election, was elected the Confederate Senate's first president pro tempore, and assumed the chair of the Finance Committee. He remained in the Senate and Richmond for the duration of the War. He was close to Jefferson Davis and is frequently mentioned by the equally connected Mary Chesnut, who in her diary called Hunter "the sanest, if not the wisest, man" in the Confederacy. Chesnut admired Hunter for a number of reasons, not the least of which being that he afforded her the intellectual respect she deserved but rarely received from men. Once silenced by Barnwell Rhett for questioning war strategy, Chesnut records that Hunter "smiled" and said, "Don't ask awkward questions."

Hunter and Robert E. Lee had also been friends before the war and maintained an open dialogue during it.[5] That along with his elected office made Hunter "vividly" aware of "all that was involved in the collapse of the Confederacy."[6] In February 1863 Lee wrote Hunter asking for help in regard to the army's commissary needs. "We are suffering," Lee wrote. "I have been obliged to deprive myself of artillery and cavalry to a great extent and send them off where they can be subsisted. In case of a sudden attack I do not know what I shall do."[7]

By 1865 Hunter had acquired the reputation in Richmond of being "sick of the war." He later blamed Davis for spreading the rumor to discredit him. But Mary Chesnut writes that Hunter was very frank about his feelings as early as January 1864, when, at a reception being hosted by the president, Hunter told her "we are rattling down hill—and nobody to put on the brakes."

The "brakes" Hunter supported was negotiated settlement with the United States. In January 1865 Jefferson Davis agreed to send Hunter, Alexander Stephens, and former Supreme Court justice John Campbell to meet with President Lincoln and William Seward at Hampton Roads, Virginia. The meeting was held February 3, 1865, aboard the *River Queen* on the James River. For the Confederate delegation it was doomed from the start.

The Hampton Roads Conference, as it became known, had been arranged at the urging of General Grant and William Seward, who had been in communication with the Confederates and assured Lincoln of their sincerity. Privately Jefferson Davis did not believe the United States would accept any negotiated settlement but hoped to use a failed conference to quell the growing peace movement in Richmond. He deliberately tied the hands of Hunter, Stephens, and Campbell with instructions that required negotiations "on the basis of two countries" and then only a negotiated armistice.

Lincoln insisted on no negotiated armistice "until the war ended by 'the re-establishment of the national authority over the United States.'"[8] The South would have to surrender to "one common country."[9]

Despite its futility, the meeting was cordial and lasted four hours. It began with an informal exchange of information regarding mutual friends with whom both sides had been out of touch. Alexander Stephens brought the meeting to its point by asking how to bring the war to an end. Lincoln reiterated his insistence on the South laying down its arms and submitting to the authority of the United States. Stephens asked if there might not be an armistice between the two armies first. When Lincoln said no, Hunter reminded him that even Charles I negotiated with his adversaries without their acceptance of his sovereignty. And Lincoln, while feigning ignorance of British history, reminded Hunter that Charles I had lost his head.[10]

During the meeting the three Southern commissioners were informed the U.S. House of Representatives had passed a bill to abolish slavery on January 31. Seward suggested that, in laying down their arms and returning to the Union, the southern states would be able to vote on the proposed amendment.[11]

Hunter returned the discussion to the terms of surrender, regretting Lincoln offered "the South no peace terms other than 'unconditional submission to the mercy of conquerors.'" Seward assured the southern commissioners that "neither he nor Lincoln ever used the term and that by returning to the Union," the Southern states would fall under the equal protection of the U.S. Constitution.[12] Lincoln sweetened the offer by promising federal compensation of $400,000 to the South if it laid down its arms and voluntarily abolished slavery. At the end of the meeting, Hunter, the onetime powerful U.S. senator and presidential contender, turned to his former colleague and friend William Seward and asked, "Governor, how is the Capitol? Is it finished?" Seward replied yes and told him it was "one of the most magnificent edifices in the world."[13]

The Hampton Roads Conference happened simultaneously with the Confederate Senate debate over the enlistment of slaves. Albert G. Brown of Mississippi introduced a bill to grant freedom to slaves and compensation to the owners in exchange for enlistment and service in the military. Hunter steadfastly opposed the bill because he believed it threatened the very foundation of southern society, namely, slavery, and it was hypocritical of the reason for secession. He stated "mainly on the plea that it was by reason of their fear that the party in power would emancipate the negroes in defiance of the constitution and in violation of their pledge, which we believed, was implied in their adoption of that instrument by which they bound themselves to protect the institution. And now it would be said we had done the very thing which we professed to fear from them."[14]

Hunter's opposition to the bill, which passed anyway, and his refusal to write a report on the Hampton Roads Conference that condemned Lincoln led to a falling-out between Hunter and Davis.[15] Davis attacked Hunter, Stephens, and Campbell publicly as being "conquered" by the enemy. Defiant, Davis wrote his own report condemning Lincoln's demands and submitted it to the Confederate Congress on February 6.

Hunter, Stephens, and Campbell were part of a growing number of southerners who, fully aware of the Confederacy's desperate situation, urged reopening talks with Lincoln and the Union leadership. Judge Campbell, Confederate assistant secretary of war, reported to Hunter and Stephens that "supplies of clothes, food, and arms [were] as nearly, if not entirely exhausted."[16] At the same time Robert E. Lee paid Hunter a late-night visit to discuss possible options for negotiations. Hunter informed Lee that no peace negotiations were possible without Davis's cooperation, but Davis had become completely recalcitrant. Lee told Hunter of his army's desperate condition, his soldiers barefoot and angry. "These and other circumstances betraying," Hunter said "utter destitution," and "a melancholy air and tone which I shall never forget."[17] It was the last time the two men ever saw each other.

On April 2 Jefferson Davis and the Confederate government evacuated Richmond. Union forces entered the city the next day. On April 4 President Lincoln visited the city. While there he expressed a desire to meet with Hunter and Campbell as to the "restoration of Virginia to her relations with the federal Union." The meeting did not occur in part because Hunter had gone home to Fonthill, which was fifty miles away. "I never saw Mr. Lincoln afterwards," Hunter wrote, "I have always regretted that circumstances prevented our meeting."[18]

Robert E. Lee surrendered to Ulysses S. Grant at Appomattox Court House on April 9. Less than a week later on April 14, Abraham Lincoln was assassinated in Washington by southern sympathizer John Wilkes Booth. On May 7 Union troops arrested Robert M. T. Hunter and John Campbell at their homes in Virginia. Jefferson Davis was arrested in Georgia three days later. By the end of May all remaining Confederate forces had surrendered. Eleven years after the passage of the Kansas-Nebraska Act, the war it had wrought was over.

Kansas had entered the Union as a free state less than two months before Fort Sumter on January 29, 1861, becoming the thirty-fourth state. Nebraska became the thirty-seventh state six years later on March 1, 1867. The land titles held by tribes within the borders of the original Nebraska Territory and beyond were systematically extinguished by federal authorities, and Native Americans were forced onto "lands badly situated."[19] Earlier in 1856 Robert Selden Garnett had warned his cousin Robert M. T. Hunter from his remote post at Muckleshoot Prairie, "We cant expect them to change their habits of life, the habits of their race, or to starve to death quietly merely to satisfy the wild schemes of white men."[20] Indian Country nevertheless continued to

Epilogue 193

contract throughout the war and thereafter. In the end, the Army that would free the slaves in the American Civil War would nearly exterminate Native Americans in the postwar era.

David Rice Atchison returned to Missouri from Texas in 1867 and lived out the remainder of his life with his deceased brother's family on a thousand-acre farmstead just outside Plattsburg in Clinton County.[21] He never returned to elected office. He never traveled east or saw Hunter and Mason again.[22] Atchison, who liked to quip that he slept through most of his presidency, died on January 6, 1886, just shy of his seventy-ninth birthday.[23]

James Murray Mason was still in England when the war ended. His final two acts on behalf of the Confederacy were to publicly denounce Edwin Stanton's accusation that the Confederate government had been complicit in Lincoln's assassination and to assist the British Admiralty in confirming to Confederate ships still operating on the high seas that the war was officially over. He joined his family in exile in Canada in late 1865.[24]

The Masons lived in a community of Confederate exiles in the town of Niagara on the Niagara River in Ontario.[25] It included John Breckinridge, numerous other military officers, government officials, and their families. On July 4, 1868, President Johnson proclaimed a general amnesty for all Confederates except those under indictment. The Niagara community began to disband shortly thereafter. The Masons were among the last to leave, returning to the United States in 1869.

The Masons did not return to Winchester. Their home had been burned by Union troops during the war, and the property later sold at auction. But James Mason was far from impoverished as his wife's Chew family fortune remained significant. The family purchased a twenty-six-acre estate, Clarens, just outside of Alexandria and moved there in May. Mason never returned to politics, and though only a few miles from Washington, he never visited the city again. He spent his final years in declining health but maintained an active correspondence with Hunter, W. W. Corcoran, and other prewar associates until his death in 1871. James Murray Mason died in his sleep on April 28, 1871, at the age of seventy-two. He was buried in the Christ Episcopal Church cemetery in Alexandria.

Robert M. T. Hunter outlived all his messmates. More than any other southern leader of the time, Hunter personified the rise and fall of the Slave Power. He began his political career early in life and rose quickly in power and influence. He was and remains the youngest person ever elected Speaker of the House of Representatives. He successfully challenged his own state's party machine and, in doing so, created a political machine of his own. He helped to forge and maintain a political alliance between Virginia and New York that remained at the center of Democratic control of Congress throughout the mid-1800s. Along with Jefferson Davis and the other members of the F Street Mess, he forced the repeal of the Missouri Compromise in 1854. As chairman of the Senate Finance Committee he authored and secured passage of the Tariff of 1857, the last downward revision of the U.S. tariff until the Underwood Tariff of 1913. Presidents sought his counsel and offered him cabinet positions. He was himself a serious candidate for the presidency in 1856 and 1860.

The probable author of John C. Calhoun's autobiography, Hunter was also the closest intellectual heir to Calhoun's ideology. He believed the constitution was a compact between the states and that southern property in slaves was constitutionally protected, equal to any and all real property. In that regard the Slave Power was never a conspiracy because, as articulated by Hunter, there was no hidden agenda. He made no attempt to amend the constitution to protect slavery before 1861 because, prior to Lincoln's election, he and his fellow messmates believed slavery was already constitutionally protected.

Lincoln's election, "by a sectional majority," changed all that. Hunter believed the election and subsequent secession of the lower South had ended the original union of 1787. For Hunter the protection of southern "principles" and "power" required the creation of "a new Union . . . more permanent and efficient than the old" that guaranteed Congress's obligation to "recognize and protect as property whatever is held to be such by the laws or prescriptions of any State." In addition to constitutionally protecting southern property, Hunter resurrected Calhoun's theory of concurrent majority, calling for a "dual executive" and an enlarged Supreme Court comprised of ten justices "five from each section." But by 1861, when Hunter and his fellow southerners began calling for outright changes to the Constitution, which they had been accused of conspiring to do for more than a decade, the very power they needed to achieve such changes had long since evaporated.

The war took a heavy toll on Hunter, financially, politically, and personally. In 1864 Union troops were sent to Fonthill. They burned down his gristmill, the primary source of the farm's income, and took the livestock. Unlike Mason, Hunter had no other source of income to fall back on. At the start of the conflict he owned three thousand acres and properties valued at $44,000. At the end of the war he had two thousand acres and properties valued at $9,400. Hunter's biographers note that these figures do not include the lost capital in slaves.

But the war was not the only cause of Hunter's financial woes. Hunter's personal motivation behind the Kansas-Nebraska Act had been his investment in Douglas's Superior properties syndicate. He had invested both his money and political power to assure its success, but when Superior failed to secure a rail line in 1857 it became a losing proposition. As late as 1858, there were no railroads, no roads, no settlers, and no buyers. The members of the syndicate were asked to make an additional investment to build a road. "The contract is conditioned that a majority of the original share-holders approve," wrote John Dawson to Hunter. "Superior wants relief, and these roads will do much. The town is dull and lots no sale at present."[26] Hunter held onto the property throughout the war.[27] After the war he was unable to sell it or any asset until pardoned by the president.

The personal toll on Hunter was profound. A year into the war his eldest son and namesake died at home after a long battle with tuberculosis. On February 14, 1864, his nephew, former U.S. congressman Muscoe Garnett, with whom Hunter was particularly close, died of typhoid fever. Two more of Hunter's children died while he was imprisoned at Fort Pulaski: daughter Sarah, who died of tuberculosis, and his youngest son, Muscoe, who died in a drowning accident at the age of fifteen. Federal authorities refused to release Hunter to attend the funerals.[28]

In the summer of 1865 Line Hunter traveled to Washington, D.C., to plead her husband's case with William Seward and President Johnson.[29] American women had been using the personal petition since the American Revolution, and by the nineteenth century it was still the only political device available to them in the male-dominated public sphere. As noted by historian Linda Kerber, "This form of appeal... challenged the petitioner's persuasive gifts and placed her directly in contact with people who wielded power."[30] Mrs. Hunter was persuasive. After taking an oath of allegiance to the United States, Robert M. T. Hunter was released from prison on indefinite parole. Because Hunter's properties were valued at more than $20,000 at the start of the war, he had to get a full pardon from the president. Until then, he was unable to sell any assets, his properties could be confiscated, and he remained subject to arrest and indictment. Hunter finally gained his presidential pardon in 1867, which allowed him to settle with creditors by selling off some of his properties.[31] In 1881 Hunter's gristmill, which he had rebuilt, burned down a second time. Hunter never regained a strong financial footing.

Unlike Atchison and Mason, who had no interest in returning to politics, Hunter longed to return to the U.S. Senate but was stymied by the third section of the Fourteenth Amendment, which prohibited former Confederate leaders from holding federal office. In 1872 the Virginia legislature elected Hunter state treasurer. That same year he returned to the national campaign circuit as a spokesman for the Democratic Party, stumping for unsuccessful presidential candidate Horace Greeley. By the 1870s the Democratic Party in Virginia was dividing into factions, the Conservatives and the Readjusters.[32] The Readjusters was a new faction that was supported by biracial wage workers as well as some railroad magnates.[33] On March 3, 1873, Congress dropped the restrictive clause from the Fourteenth Amendment, and Hunter ran for the U.S. Senate on the Conservative ticket. During the campaign Hunter called for federal compensation to former slave owners. He lost the election. The state senate elected the less conservative and wounded war veteran, Robert E. Withers. The Conservatives elected Hunter state treasurer instead.

Hunter's demand for federal compensation to former slave owners eight years after the Civil War and the passage of the Thirteenth Amendment was nothing short of audacious and reflected what his biographer John E. Fisher calls a retreat "from the whole process of change."[34] In 1880 Robert M. T. Hunter lost reelection as state treasurer to a Readjuster candidate. That same year his beloved sister, Jane, who had raised him since childhood, died. The following year his youngest daughter Evelyn died. In 1885 President Grover Cleveland appointed Hunter to the lowly post of collector for the Port of Tappahannock. It paid the bills. On July 18, 1887, Robert Mercer Taliaferro Hunter, the last surviving member of the F Street Mess died at the age of seventy-eight. He remained to his death uncompromising, unsuccessful, and unrepentant, the very epitome of the Slave Power.

NOTES

Introduction

1. Henry Wager Halleck was general-in-chief of the Union armies prior to Grant's appointment in 1864. He served thereafter as the army's chief of staff, commanding the Department of Virginia in the spring of 1865.

2. *The War of Rebellion*, series I, vol. 46, part III, 1106; Cornell University Making of America, accessed June 20, 2008, http://cdl.library.cornell.edu/moa/browse.monographs/waro.html.

3. Lincoln met with the Confederate peace commission on board the Union ship, *River Queen*. His insistence on southern surrender to "one common country," reunion, and emancipation of the slaves brought the meeting to a standstill in four hours. McPherson, *Ordeal by Fire*, 506–7, and *Battle Cry of Freedom*, 822–24, 851; Nevins, *War for the Union*, 302–6; Saunders, *John Archibald Campbell*, 168, 172; *The War of Rebellion*, series I, vol. 46, part III, 735.

4. McPherson, *Ordeal by Fire*, 506–7, and *Battle Cry of Freedom*, 822–24, 851; Nevins, *War for the Union*, 302–6; Saunders, *John Archibald Campbell*, 168, 172; *The War of Rebellion*, series I, vol. 46, part III, 735.

5. Hunter's home, Fonthill, was outside Richmond in Essex County. Traveling between his home and Richmond during March had required safe-conduct passes. If he was home the first three days in April, it would have been impossible for him to return until after the April 4. Nevins, *War for the Union*, 302; Moore, "In Search of a Safe Government," 327–28.

6. On April 6 Lincoln authorized General Godfrey Weitzel, commander of the Union army inside Richmond, to allow the Virginia State legislature to convene. He rescinded his order on April 12. Nevins, *War for the Union*, 303–4; Saunders, *John Archibald Campbell*, 180–82.

7. Nevins, *War for the Union*, 304.

8. Lincoln was shot at Ford's Theatre by John Wilkes Booth on the evening of April 14 (Good Friday) but did not die until the following morning, April 15 at 7:22 AM.

9. Lewis, *Myths after Lincoln*, 49; Hanchett, *The Lincoln Murder Conspiracies*, 59–60; Eidson, "Recent Scholarship on the Lincoln Assassination," 220; Swanson, *Manhunt*, 141–42; Hodes, *Mourning Lincoln*, 130–32.

10. The five arrested included David E. Herold, Lewis Payne, George B. Atzerodt, Michael O'Laughlin, and Samuel Arnold. Three others, Mary E. Surratt, Edman Spangler, and Dr. Samuel A. Mudd, were held in military custody. Despite their civilian status, the eight were charged and put on trial before a military court. The court found

all eight guilty. Herold, Payne, Atzerodt, and Mrs. Surratt were sentenced to death on July 5 and hung two days later on July 7. O'Laughlin, Arnold, and Mudd were given life sentences, and Spangler was sentenced to six years. All four were later pardoned by President Johnson in 1869. John H. Surratt, Mary's son, successfully fled the country through Canada to England. He was captured in Egypt in 1866 and extradited to the United States. He was tried in a civilian court in 1867 and found not guilty. No one else was charged or tried in Lincoln's assassination. See Frank, "The Conspiracy to Implicate the Confederate Leaders"; Linder, "The Trial of the Lincoln Assassination Conspirators."

11. The trial of the eight charged in Lincoln's murder began on May 12, 1865. During the trial evidence was introduced implicating Jefferson Davis and members of the Confederate Secret Service. In general, academic historians have dismissed the validity of the evidence presented. See Frank, "The Conspiracy to Implicate the Confederate Leaders," and Hanchett, *The Lincoln Murder Conspiracies*. Recent scholarship on the subject, however, argues that the Confederate Secret Service was involved in the earlier kidnapping attempt of Lincoln and may have been involved in the assassination, with the knowledge and approval of Davis and his secretary of state Judah Benjamin. See Tidwell, *Come Retribution* and *April '65*; Linder, "The Trial of the Lincoln Assassination Conspirators." James McPherson however argues that "much of the evidence on this matter is circumstantial ... especially for Confederate involvement in Booth's decision to assassinate Lincoln." McPherson, *Ordeal by Fire*, 521.

12. The confederate officials in Canada included Jacob Thompson, George N. Sanders, Beverly Tucker, Clement C. Clay, and William C. Cleary. Their whereabouts were known by the federal authorities, but no effort was made to apprehend or extradite them. Davis was captured by Union troops near Irwinsville, Georgia, on May 10. Clement Clay turned himself over to federal authorities on May 11, the only confederate in Canada to do so. Both Davis and Clay were held at Fort Monroe for two years. They were never charged or brought to trial. Confederate secretary of state Judah Benjamin, also implicated, escaped to England. He never returned to the United States. See Frank, "The Conspiracy to Implicate the Confederate Leaders," 631–32.

13. During the initial hours after the assassination, Grant had ordered the arrest of all paroled Confederate officers but just as quickly withdrew the order. In the end Grant believed Confederate military officers could not be arrested unless they violated their paroles. His position did not extend to Confederate political leaders. Lewis, *Myths after Lincoln*, 62; Swanson. *Manhunt*, 118; *The War of Rebellion*, series II, 8:498.

14. Nevins, *War for the Union*, 305; *The War of Rebellion*, series I, vol. 46, part III, 534, 1152.

15. *The War of Rebellion*, series I, vol. 46, part III, 578, 587, 630, 99; series II, 8:576, 577, 583, 640.

16. Schiller, *Sumter Is Avenged*, 1–4.

17. Ibid., 108–12; Joslyn, *Immortal Captives*, 141; National Park Service, U.S. Department of the Interior; CWSAC Battle Summaries.

18. Slavocracy, the Slave Interest, and the Slave Oligarchy were also terms used synonymously with the Slave Power in northern political speeches and newspapers. The phrase Slave Power will be used exclusively in this study.

19. To understand how the Republican Party used the Slave Power rhetorically, see Gara, "Slavery and the Slave Power"; Foner, *Free Soil*; Leonard Richards, *The Slave Power*; Richardson, *To Make Men Free*.

20. Lincoln, "House Divided, January 16, 1858."

21. Leonard Richards observes that northern political leadership comprised an aristocracy that was "keenly aware of the benefits of power but resentful that others had more power than they did." When the Federalists were voted out of power by the electorate in 1800, they blamed their defeat on the three-fifths clause, calculating "that there were fifteen slave seats in Congress, equal to the combined House vote of six whole states, one more than the combined vote of Connecticut, New Hampshire, and Rhode Island, and two less than the entire vote of Massachusetts." Eric Foner notes that had the three-fifths clause not been in the constitution, John Adams would have defeated Thomas Jefferson outright in the election of 1800. Richards, *The Slave Power*, 28, 45; Foner, *Story of American Freedom*, 44.

22. Henry Wilson and Hunt, *Rise and Fall of the Slave Power in America*, 1:2.

23. In December 1814 New England Federalists, who believed the war with Great Britain was the result of southern dominance in Congress, met in Hartford, Connecticut, and proposed a number of amendments to the Constitution designed to limit southern political power, including the repeal of the three-fifths clause. In 1820 political debate over the Slave Power reached crisis proportions when Missouri's admission into the Union was temporarily blocked by New York congressman James Tallmadge's proviso that linked admission to the gradual elimination of slavery in Missouri. The Nullification Crisis of 1832, the result of South Carolina's repudiation of the federal tariff acts of 1828 and 1832, was seen by many in the North as yet another example of slaveholders' undue influence not only in the federal government but also state governments. In each case, the issue had less to do with a perceived conspiracy than with the actual political power derived from the South's slave-based economy.

24. Prior to his coming out against annexation, Van Buren had the pledged support of a significant number of southern delegates. To get around their commitment to Van Buren, these same delegates voted in favor of the two-thirds majority rule, which had not been used at a party convention since 1832. "This strategy not only blocked the will of the majority, but what was worse, it meant that a number of men pledged to Van Buren were voting for a rule designed to prevent his nomination." Potter, *The Impending Crisis*, 24; Foner, *Free Soil*, 150–51.

25. Holt, *The Political Crisis of the 1850s*, 51.

26. Gara, "Slavery and the Slave Power," 6.

27. While some historians believe that Lincoln used the conspiracy rhetoric for political purposes, Leonard Richards argues that the evidence proves Lincoln sincerely believed in its existence. Richards, *The Slave Power*, 16.

28. Lincoln, "House Divided, January 16, 1858."

29. Leonard Richards, *The Slave Power*, 3.

30. Hofstadter, *The Paranoid Style in American Politics*, 4.

31. Bailyn, *The Origins of American Politics* and *The Ideological Origins of the American Revolution*; David Davis, *The Slave Power Conspiracy*; Wood, *The Creation of The American Republic* and *The Radicalism of the American Revolution*.

32. David Davis, *The Slave Power Conspiracy*, 11.
33. Ibid., 3.
34. Nichols, "The Kansas-Nebraska Act," 187.
35. Gara, "The Slave Power," 12, 16–17; Foner, *Free Soil*, 73–75.
36. Foner, *Free Soil*, 9.
37. Leonard Richards, *The Slave Power*, 1–4, 109–11.
38. William Rufus King, Franklin Pierce's running mate, contracted tuberculosis shortly after the election in November 1852. King traveled to Havana, Cuba, to recuperate where, by special act of Congress, he became the only vice president in U.S. history to take the oath of office outside the United States. He returned to his home near Selma, Alabama, on April 17, 1853, and died the next day. Article II, Section 2 of the U.S. Constitution does not enumerate presidential succession but instead allows for Congress to determine it by law. The first Presidential Succession Act was passed in 1792. It made the Senate president pro tempore and the Speaker of the House third and fourth in line to the office of the presidency. Under this act, David Rice Atchison became second in line to the presidency after King's death. There was no constitutional provision for filling the vice presidential vacancy. In 1886 Congress passed a new Succession Act, removing both the president pro tempore and Speaker from the order of succession and replacing them with the cabinet secretaries in order of the department's creation. Presidential succession was changed for the last time by Congress in 1947. The Speaker of the House was placed third and the president pro tempore fourth, followed by the cabinet secretaries. In 1967 the Twenty-Fifth Amendment to the constitution was ratified. Under Section 2 of the amendment, if there is "a vacancy in the office of the Vice President," the President nominates a new vice president who must be confirmed by a majority of both Houses of Congress. The section was used in 1973 by President Richard M. Nixon after Spiro T. Agnew resigned from the office. Nixon nominated Gerald R. Ford, who was later confirmed by Congress. Ford used the section a year later after he assumed the office of the Presidency upon Nixon's resignation. His nominee Nelson A. Rockefeller was confirmed vice president in 1974. www.senate.gov/artandhistory.
39. Genovese, *The Southern Tradition*, xi.
40. Ray, *The Repeal of the Missouri Compromise*, 22–23.
41. In 1938 Fred Harvey Harrington published an 1855 speech by Nathaniel P. Banks that supported Ray's thesis. Whether Atchison authored the repeal or not, the speech shows that many of his Republican opponents were repeating his claim as truth. Roy Nichols states that Douglas never "categorically or unequivocally denied" Atchison's claim. See Allen Johnson, "The Repeal of the Missouri Compromise: Its Origins and Authorship," 835–36; Mathews, "The Repeal of the Missouri Compromise," 467; Harrington, "A Note on the Ray Explanation of the Origin of the Kansas-Nebraska Act," 79–81; Nichols "The Kansas-Nebraska Act," 204.
42. For more on the role of railroad construction in the territories, see Potter, *The Impending Crisis*; Nelson, *A Nation of Deadbeats*.
43. Roy Nichols later criticized the ongoing debate between Ray and Hodder. "The truth probably would have been more nearly attained," Nichols states, "had each recognized that the other had made a contribution and had they united their points of view." Nevertheless, Hodder's thesis is generally given more credence today than Ray's. Nichols, "The Kansas-Nebraska Act," 193.

44. Boucher, "In Re That Aggressive Slavocracy," 15.
45. Ibid., 60.
46. Ibid., 62.
47. Malin, *The Nebraska Question*, 3.
48. James Malin based his thesis on a then little-known letter written by Douglas to the Nebraska Convention in St. Joseph, Missouri, two weeks before his introduction of the bill in the U.S. Senate on January 4, 1854, and reprinted in *The Nebraska Question*, 16–19.
49. Nichols, "The Kansas-Nebraska Act," 196–97.
50. Ibid., 211.
51. Roy Nichols findings were rejected by Robert R. Russel in his 1963 article, "The Issues in the Congressional Struggle over the Kansas-Nebraska Bill." While he agrees with Nichols that the passage was not "the work of any one man or clique" Russel argues that "not as many as five votes in both houses together turned principally or even largely on the bearing the bill might be expected to have on any issue other than slavery" and that both southern and northern members held strong ideological positions on the role of the federal government in the territories. For Russel the bill was ultimately "a compromise, hammered out with great difficulty in committee, conferences, and caucuses" (187, 192).
52. Nichols, "The Kansas-Nebraska Act," 203.
53. Ibid., 201–2.
54. Nevins, *Ordeal of Union*, 70–71; McPherson, *Battle Cry of Freedom*, 60–62; Nichols, "The Kansas-Nebraska Act," 201–2.
55. Allan Nevins calls the F Street Mess a "cabal" that exercised stern power on the side of slavery. David Potter refers to it as a "senatorial junta." James McPherson writes it was "the most powerful Senate bloc of the 1850s," and to Scott Nelson the Mess was the "mission control for the southern congressional power." Nevins, *Ordeal of Union*; Potter, *The Impending Crisis*, 161; McPherson, *Battle Cry of Freedom*, 122; Nelson, *A Nation of Deadbeats*, 136.
56. The Greek philosopher Aristotle noted that caring for another person's well-being was the only form of true and lasting friendship. "So when people love each other on the ground of utility their affection is motivated by their own good, and when they love on the ground of pleasure it is motivated by their own pleasure; that is, they love the other person not for what he is, but *qua* useful or pleasant. So these friendships are accidental, because the person is not loved on the ground of his actual nature, but merely as providing some benefit or pleasure. Consequently such friendships are easily dissolved if the parties do not continue to show the same kind of qualities, because if they cease to be pleasant or useful to the friendship comes to an end." Aristotle continues, "it is those who desire the good of their friends for the friends' sake that are most truly friend, because each loves the other for what he is, and not for any incidental quality. Accordingly the friendship of such men lasts so long as they remain good; and goodness is an enduring quality." However, sociologist, Beverly Fehr argues friendship is still difficult to define because it does not conform to terms like "colleague" or "cousin" which indicate "the social position of each individual relative to the other." The term "friend" is a relational term that "'signifies something

about the quality and character of the relationship involved.'" Fehr states friendship is something voluntary, personal, and intimate. Some political scientists argue it is the absence of these very components in civic friendship that makes it "disanalogous" to personal friendship. Sibyl Schwarzenbach agrees that intimacy and intrinsic value are lacking in civic friendship but rejects the argument that the instrumentalism of civic friendship makes it "disanalogous" to personal friendship. She maintains that an analogy can be drawn between the intrinsic intimacy of a close personal relationship and the more "general concern" that exists in a civic friendship that expresses itself in an awareness of and concern for the "treatment of persons" within the state and a "knowledge" of constitutional privileges and responsibilities. *The Ethics of Aristotle*, 1156a16-b2-1156b10-12.; Fehr, *Friendship Processes*, 7; Scorza, "Liberal Citizenship and Civic Friendship," 90; Schwarzenbach, "On Civic Friendship," 105.

57. The F Street Mess is first seen at this address in the *Washington and Georgetown Directory, with a Complete Congressional and Department Directory*. Washington Historical Society.

58. For more on congressional living arrangements and social venues in nineteenth-century Washington, see Shelden, *Washington Brotherhood*.

59. James Young, *The Washington Community*, ix, 97–98.

60. Bogue and Marlaire, "Of Mess and Men," 228.

61. The bias toward "like-minded" friends appears in all social categories, and the higher the education and social standing, the greater the bias becomes, as "highest-status people bump against constraints (there are few people higher than themselves) and they compensate by additional choices of same-status friends." Verbrugge, "The Structure of Adult Friendship Choices," 576–77, 588; Fehr, *Friendship Processes*, 57.

62. Verbrugge, "The Structure of Adult Friendship Choices," 578.

63. The modern Patent Office expanded over much of the block of F Street where the house at 361 once stood.

64. The congressional mess is having resurgence in the twenty-first century. Senators Dick Durbin, Chuck Schumer, and Congressman George Miller have been rooming together for three decades and are the inspiration for the online fictional series "Alpha House." Another modern living arrangement include Congresswomen Debbie Wasserman Schultz, Carolyn Maloney, and Terri Sewell. Senate gathering places outside the chamber in which decisions are made are also on the increase. On January 20, 2009, the evening of Barack Obama's first inauguration, Republican leaders, including Eric Cantor, Paul Ryan, Tom Coburn, Jim DeMint, and ten others met at the upscale Georgetown restaurant, The Caucus Room. The dinner, held in the public dining area, lasted for four hours during which time a strategy of obstruction against Obama was planned. It included targeting specific Democratic congressmen in the 2010 elections and "unyielding" opposition to all of President Obama's policies.

65. Ross Baker, *Friend and Foe in the U.S. Senate*, 6–7.

66. Ibid.

67. In 2011 demographic historian David Hacker recalculated the data on civil war casualties. He found the traditional estimate of 620,000 to be under by 20 percent. According to Hacker 752,000 to as high as 851,000 died in the war. See Hacker, "Counting the Civil War Dead"; Gugliotta, "New Estimate Raises Civil War Death Toll."

Chapter One

1. It's not clear who first called Calhoun "young Hercules." Gerald Capers attributes it to Congressman Alexander J. Dallas of Pennsylvania. Merrill Peterson states it was Thomas P. Grosvenor of New York. Capers, *John C. Calhoun*, 34; Peterson, *The Great Triumvirate*, 18.

2. Bartlett, *John C. Calhoun*, 44, 190; Current, *John C. Calhoun*, 5; Capers, *John C. Calhoun*, 7, 28; Peterson, *The Great Triumvirate*, 18, 222.

3. When British troops invaded Washington on August 24, 1814, the Capitol and much of the city were still under construction. The British left private dwellings largely untouched but set fire to all federal buildings except the Patent Office and Post Office, which were located in Blodgett's Hotel. The House chamber located in the south wing of the Capitol and considered "the most beautiful room in America" was totally gutted. All that remained were its exterior walls, colonnade, and entablature. The last two structures, while standing, were so severely damaged that temporary wooden supports were put in place to prevent collapse and destruction to the chamber floor. Outside the chamber the vestibule and east lobby were largely untouched. "Still, the loss was horrific." After the British left, the Fourteenth Congress returned to the burned-out city and reconvened in Blodgett's Hotel, where it authorized the capital city's rebuilding. Construction on the Capitol was begun in 1817, and on December 6, 1819, the Sixteenth Congress convened in the restored south and north wings. Construction on the Capitol continued throughout the following decades, climaxing with the completion of the Rotunda in 1863. The Federalist Party entered the war already weakened by successive Republican victories between 1800 and 1812. In the winter of 1814, what remained of the party self-immolated when it publicly opposed the war at its convention in Hartford, Connecticut. The consequence of the War of 1812 was the complete destruction of the first political party system. What would replace it remained in question for decades thereafter. Allen, *History of the United States Capitol*, 97–99, 102, 140; Remini, *The House*, 97–100, 179.

4. History text books typically list all four of Van Buren's opponents as Whigs but they were not nominees of a national party, rather they were sectional candidates, Daniel Webster of New England, William Henry Harrison of the West, and Hugh L. White of the South. The fourth candidate, Willie P. Mangum was the choice of South Carolina's Nullifiers. Michael Holt objects to even using the term Whig historically before 1836. He argues the "Whigs inability to arrange a national convention or agree on a single presidential candidate revealed that the party was still inchoate," and that the historical use of the term "Whigs" or "'Whig party' in the mid-1830s is more a literary convenience than an accurate description of fact." Holt, *The American Whig Party*, 39; Wiltse, *John C. Calhoun: Nullifier*, 248, 249, 295.

5. Land speculation in the United States exploded between 1834 and 1836, spurred on by easy credit and foreign demand for American cotton. Economic recession hit in the spring of 1837. Whigs argued that the crisis was the consequence of Jackson's fiscal policies, which had destroyed the Bank of the United States and bled eastern banks of specie. The Democrats argued the eastern banks' "excessive credit, speculation, overtrading, and paper money" had caused the depression. Michael Holt argues that both "Whig and Democratic explanations contained elements of truth," but the primary

culprit was the Bank of England, which, "fearing a drain on its own specie reserves, raised its interest rates and curtailed credit to British firms dealing in the American trade." Scott Nelson notes that, as a consequence of the panic, investments shifted from cotton futures to "railroad land in the northern Midwest," thereby launching the railroad boom of the 1850s that would "ultimately lead to bloodshed on the plains of Kansas." As the depression of 1837 continued, so too did the deluge of petitions to Congress from northern states calling for the abolition of slavery in the District of Columbia and a ban on the admittance of new slave states. By May 1838, 415,000 petitions had been forwarded to Washington by the American Antislavery Society despite the fact that a gag rule had been passed in the House, which prevented the petitions from being debated on the floor. A similar rule was being considered in the Senate. The proposed ban on new slave states was a direct reference to the possible annexation of Texas. Holt, *The American Whig Party*, 61–62; Nelson, *A Nation of Deadbeats*, 135; James Stewart, *Holy Warriors*, 83.

 6. Ross Baker, *Friend and Foe*, 27.

 7. In the eighteenth and nineteenth centuries Americans referred to the nation's capital as Washington City. The capital was not referred to as Washington, D.C., until the twentieth century.

 8. Calhoun's control of South Carolina was challenged between 1816 and 1832 by William Smith, an "Old" Republican from the upstate. Smith was appointed to the U.S. Senate in 1816 to fill the vacancy left by the resignation of John Taylor but lost his reelection bid in 1822 due to Calhoun's interference. Smith returned to South Carolina and led the Radical opposition to Calhoun inside the state. He was appointed to the U.S. Senate again in 1826 to fill the vacancy left by the death of John Gaillard and became a Jackson Democrat. Smith was defeated for a second time by Calhoun in 1830. He left South Carolina for good in 1832 moving first to Louisiana and then Alabama, settling on a plantation ironically called Calhoun's Place, where he died in 1840. The Calhoun-Smith rivalry is overshadowed historically by the infamous feud between Governor Dewitt Clinton of New York and the young Martin Van Buren of Kinderhook. Van Buren rose quickly in an organization known as the Albany Regency, which opposed Clinton's "New" Republican policies. Highly organized, the Regency was a forerunner of modern campaign structures. In 1821 Van Buren was elected to the U.S. Senate. Two years later, his machine, the Regency, succeeded in amending the state constitution despite Clinton's opposition to its democratic changes. Clinton stepped down as governor but ran and won again in 1825. He was being considered for an appointment in the Jackson administration when he died of a heart attack in 1828. Niven, *Martin Van Buren*, 65, 101, 191; Bartlett, *John C. Calhoun*, 140–42.

 9. William H. Crawford was a senator from Georgia between 1807 and 1813 and served as President Monroe's secretary of the treasury. He was considered a radical by nationalists because of his states' rights and strict constructionist positions.

 10. The electors meet in their respective states on the first Monday after the second Wednesday in December and vote separately for president and vice president.

 11. Only the top three vote getters were considered in the House. Clay, who finished last, convinced the Kentucky delegation to vote for Adams even though they had been instructed by Kentucky's electors to vote for Jackson.

12. Of the first six presidents, four had been secretaries of state, Thomas Jefferson, James Madison, James Monroe, and John Quincy Adams.

13. John and Floride Calhoun had a home on E Street where they resided during the winter months. Oakly in Georgetown was purchased for them by Floride's mother, Floride Bonneau Colhoun. Calhoun moved his family back to South Carolina in 1826 after the death of their baby daughter Elizabeth, believing the climate better for the family's health. They sold the Oakly three years later. The estate is now part of Dumbarton Oaks, Harvard University's institute for Pre-Columbian and Byzantine Studies and Garden and Landscape studies located in Georgetown. Bartlett, *John C. Calhoun*, 123; James N. Carder, Archivist and House Collection Manager, Dumbarton Oaks Research Library and Collection, e-mail message to author, July 29, 2016.

14. It was publicly and privately speculated that Jackson's age (he was sixty-two), and poor health would make him a one-term president. Jackson implied as much before the election. Capers, "Calhoun's Transition from Nationalism to Nullification," 81; Bartlett, *John C. Calhoun*, 159–60; Meacham, *American Lion*, 49.

15. All three historians agree the Radicals planned Calhoun's demise before Jackson's first term began. Charles Wiltse believes Jackson was fully informed by 1830. Wiltse, *John C. Calhoun: Nullifier*, 15–17; Bartlett, *John C. Calhoun*, 138; Meacham, *American Lion*, 36, 170.

16. Van Buren ran for governor of New York to keep the state in the Regency hands. Niven, *John C. Calhoun*, 30–31; Bartlett, *John C. Calhoun*, 162.

17. John Eaton was the former senator from Tennessee and one of Jackson's closest personal friends. In January 1829, after he had been appointed secretary of war, he married a young widow, Peggy O'Neal Timberlake. Peggy was the daughter of a boardinghouse and tavern owner, John O'Neal, and had a notorious reputation about town. The Eatons were immediately shunned by Washington society. Jackson believed the ostracism was started by his vice president's wife, Floride Calhoun and that Peggy was being victimized in the same way his deceased wife Rachel had been during the campaign. John and Floride Calhoun left Washington shortly after the inauguration. In the meantime, the Eatons played upon the president's feelings and what started as a social crisis turned into the administration's first political crisis because of President Jackson's insistence that his cabinet accept the Eatons socially. Even Jackson's niece and White House hostess, Emily Donelson, refused to cooperate and left Washington with her husband Andrew Jackson Donelson rather than be forced to socialize with the Eatons. Cultural historians have made much of the fact that Peggy was the daughter of a tavern owner and typically portray her as a victim of social classism, the result of Washington elites' angst over losing their political power in the new American democracy. But Irving Bartlett argues that to see Peggy as a victim of an unjust social order "is to ignore the real cultural issues involved," and "that at the same time Peggy Eaton was striving for acceptability in the highest social circles in Washington middle-class Americans everywhere were embracing a set of values which would consign to American wives and mothers the role of preserving moral standards in a rapidly changing, acquisitive, industrializing democracy. Peggy Eaton was challenging those values." Bartlett, *John C. Calhoun*, 165. For more on Washington culture and the Eaton affair, see Allgor, *Parlor Politics*; Jacob, *Capitol Elites*; Marszalek, *The Petticoat Affair*; Meacham, *American Lion*.

18. According to Calhoun biographer Irving Bartlett, Green's strategy in publishing the correspondence was to show "the President was being manipulated by unscrupulous political adventurers into impeaching the character of his loyal Vice President." Bartlett, *John C. Calhoun*, 173.

19. Henry Clay did not run as a Whig in 1832 but as a National Republican.

20. Anti-Mason candidate William Wirt won seven electoral votes. South Carolina gave its eleven electoral votes to John Floyd in protest over the tariff.

21. Calhoun hailed from South Carolina's upcountry where, as noted by the historian, John McCardell, the price of cotton dropped 72 percent, during the 1820s, while the cost of living fell only 50 percent. "Faced with such a crushing discrepancy, selling their cotton in a contracting free market while buying clothing and other supplies in an uncertain market regulated by import duties . . . the tariff seemed to be a barrier designed to impede his [the upcountry planter] economic freedom." McCardell, *The Idea of a Southern Nation*, 30.

22. Ibid., 35.

23. Niven, *John C. Calhoun*, 169.

24. Ironically the tariff of 1832 passed in the House due to the leadership of Congressman John Quincy Adams. It was during his term as president that the Tariff of Abomination had been passed. While the Tariff of 1832 lowered some duties, the tax on imported finished cotton, wool, and iron remained high.

25. Niven, *John C. Calhoun*, 180.

26. Charles Wiltse's three volumes on Calhoun include *John C. Calhoun: Nationalist, 1782–1828*, published in 1944; *John C. Calhoun: Nullifier, 1829–1839*, published in 1949; and *John C. Calhoun: Sectionalist, 1840–1850*, published in 1951.

27. See Clyde Wilson, introduction to *The Essential Calhoun*; Cheek, *Calhoun and Popular Rule*; Bartlett, *John C. Calhoun*.

28. Cheek, *Calhoun and Popular Rule*, 38.

29. Madison, *Federalist #10*.

30. Wiltse, *John C. Calhoun: Nullifier*, 174; Bartlett, *John C. Calhoun*, 193; Niven, *John C. Calhoun*, 193.

31. Correctly referred to as the suspension of specie payments.

32. Bartlett, *John C. Calhoun*, 236; Holt, *The American Whig Party*, 65–66.

33. Bartlett, *John C. Calhoun*, 236; Holt, *The American Whig Party*, 65–66.

34. Beach, "Spencer Roane and the Richmond Junto," 1–2, 16.

35. Virginia's state constitution used the federal constitution's three-fifths formula in determining state representation. It gave the state's eastern counties, where the bulk of the state slave population resided, a disproportionate share of the seats in the state legislature, not unlike what had happened at the federal level. The state convention of 1829 appropriated additional seats to the western counties in the lower house, but the Tidewater region maintained a slight majority overall. McCardell, *The Idea of a Southern Nation*, 26–27.

36. The biography on Hunter is based on Charles Henry Ambler's preface to *The Correspondence of Robert M. T. Hunter, 1826–1876* and Martha T. Hunter's *A Memoir of Robert M. T. Hunter*.

37. The Hunters were merchants originally from Scotland. The Garners, successful planters, were the older of the two Virginia families and politically more prominent.

After James and Maria Hunter's marriage in 1796, their younger siblings, Muscoe Garnett Hunter and Grace Fenton Garnett, also married. James and Maria's oldest daughter, Maria, married her cousin James Mercer Garnett Jr., the son of her mother's brother, James Mercer. Robert Hunter's daughter, Maria, described the two families as "very closely allied."

38. James and Maria Hunter had eight children, five sons and three daughters—Maria, Muscoe Garnett, Martha Fenton, James, Jane Swann, William, Robert Mercer Taliaferro, and William Garnett. Maria died in 1819 from complications in childbirth. James Hunter remarried in 1819. His second marriage produced one daughter, Sally.

39. James Hunter gave his son the choice of a horse to ride to school or the slave Austin. Robert Hunter chose his childhood companion. It is not known if Hunter shared any of what he learned with his slave, but it is not out of the realm of reason to suppose they would have talked about something during a daily five-mile round trip.

40. "Letter to sister, October 29, 1827," in Hunter, *A Memoir of Robert M. T. Hunter*, 39.

41. Robert Hunter's youngest brother, William Garnett, also a student at the university, died in the epidemic. Robert Toombs returned to Georgia and was admitted to the state bar the following year.

42. Like Calhoun, Hunter would rarely be in residence at his plantation. The day-to-day operations fell to the women.

43. After Congress censured Jackson for his removal of the federal deposits, the Democrats launched a campaign in the state houses throughout the country to pass resolutions demanding the expunging of the censure from the record.

44. Mary Evelina Dandridge was called "Line" by those closest to her.

45. The Hunters had nine children, only four survived their parents.

46. The biography of James Murray Mason is based on Virginia Mason's *The Public Life of James M. Mason*.

47. The Masons were a large family. James Mason's father John was the fourth of eight children born to George Mason.

48. Gunston Hall was a six-thousand-acre plantation twenty miles from Alexandria on a peninsula that jutted out into the Potomac.

49. While there is no written record that Hunter and Mason knew each other at this time, it is reasonable to assume their paths would have crossed at some point professionally or socially.

50. Mason's fifth child and future biographer, Virginia, was born December 12, 1833.

51. *Richmond Enquirer* 29, no. 74 (January 8, 1833).

52. Robert Young, *James Murray Mason*, 12–13.

53. Francis Mallory was a freshman Whig congressman representing Norfolk. He was a former U.S. Navy midshipman and held a medical degree from the University of Pennsylvania, Mason's alma mater. He served three terms in Congress before stepping down. He died in 1860. Francis W. Pickens was the grandson of Revolutionary War general Andrew Pickens and John C. Calhoun's cousin. He was first elected as a Nullifier to the Twenty-Third Congress in 1833. He served five terms before stepping down. In 1860 he was elected governor of South Carolina just prior to the outbreak of the Civil War. *Biographical Directory of the United States Congress*.

54. Hunter, "Speech of Mr. Hunter of Virginia, October 11, 1837."

55. Mason, "Speech of Mr. Mason, October 11, 1837."

56. Hunter, "Speech of Mr. Hunter of Virginia, June 22, 1838."

57. Mason, "Speech of Mr. Mason, October 11, 1837."

58. Robert Young, *James Murray Mason*, 19–20.

59. Wiltse, *John C. Calhoun: Nullifier*, 405.

60. Thomas Hart Benton would later align himself with Van Buren and Free-Soil Democrats in the 1840s.

61. Remini, *The House*, 107.

62. The Whig delegation comprised John B. Aycrigg, John B. Maxwell, William Halsted, Thomas C. Stratton, and Thomas Jones Yorke. The Democratic delegation comprised Philemon Dickerson, Peter D. Vroom, Daniel B. Ryall, William R. Cooper, and John Kille. Benton. *Thirty Years View*, 159.

63. According to Robert Remini, the chamber was "an accoustal horror," and a "sound committee" was appointed to investigate possible solutions, including drapes across the front of the gallery, dipped in "arsenic to protect it from moths." The source of the acoustical problem was as it had been in the original chamber, the domed ceiling, but no one was willing to alter it. Complaints continued throughout the increasingly turbulent decades. In 1850 the Senate proposed a competition for the enlargement of the Capitol. Architects and plans swarmed the halls of Washington. In 1857 the House of Representatives moved to the new House wing of the Capitol to its new chamber where it remains to this day. Remini, *The House*, 86; Architect of the Capitol, National Statuary Hall.

64. Beginning with Thomas Jefferson, presidents delivered their annual message in writing to the Speaker of the House. The practice was not changed until the election of Woodrow Wilson, who became the first modern president to deliver a State of the Union address before Congress. Early precedent also had the Senate suspend legislative activity until the House was in order and had elected a speaker. Hinds Precedents, chap. IV, sec. 122–25; Deschler's Precedents, vol. 1, chap. 1, sec. 12.

65. Ultimately the House Committee ruled in favor of the secretary of state's certified returns and on March 10, 1839, nearly one hundred days after the dispute had begun, Congress sat the five Democratic members from New Jersey.

66. The members were Isaac E. Holmes, James Rogers, and Thomas D. Sumter, who cast their votes for the administration's first choice, Francis Pickens; John Campbell and John Griffin, who cast their votes for the administration's second choice, Dixon Lewis; and Waddy Thompson Jr., who voted for W. C. Dawson of Georgia. *Congressional Globe*, 26th Cong., 1st sess.

67. Hunter voted for Democrat Francis Pickens on the first through the fifth ballot. He did not vote on the sixth ballot. *Congressional Globe*, 26th Cong., 1st sess.

68. To date, Hunter remains the youngest person elected Speaker of the House.

69. *Congressional Globe*, 26th Cong., 1st sess.

70. John C. Calhoun to Anna Maria Calhoun Clemson, December 18, 1839, *The Papers of John C. Calhoun*, 15:19.

71. Fisher, "Statesman of the Lost Cause," 70.

72. Simms, *The Life of Robert M. T. Hunter*, 46.

73. Ever since Robert Barnwell Rhett first claimed in 1854 that Robert M. T. Hunter was not the author of the Calhoun biography, historians have debated whether or not

Calhoun wrote it himself. Charles Wiltse dismisses the "autobiography" argument, concluding instead that it was a compilation of various authors, including Calhoun's daughter Anna, with the final editing done by Hunter. Using undiscovered Hunter letters in the University of Virginia, James L. Anderson and W. Edwin Hemphill concluded in 1972 that Hunter was the sole author. See James Anderson and Hemphill, "The 1843 Biography of John C. Calhoun."

74. Hunter led Calhoun's delegation at the state convention and negotiated a deal with Ritchie not to block the state's nomination of Van Buren in exchange for a pro-states' rights, anti-abolition platform. Hunter did not attend the national convention in Baltimore where southern delegations denied Van Buren the nomination anyway. The party nominated dark-horse candidate James K. Polk of Tennessee. Eric Foner marks the beginning of the Slave Power conspiracy thesis with the South's rejection of Van Buren at Baltimore.

75. Bartlett, *John C. Calhoun*, 307.

76. Peterson, *The Great Triumvirate*, 345.

77. McCardell, *The Idea of a Southern Nation*, 230, 236.

78. Bartlett, *John C. Calhoun*, 308; McCardell, *The Idea of a Southern Nation*, 230; Clyde Wilson, *The Essential Calhoun*, 143, 411.

79. According to Tom Chaffin, Benton was a "conservative" expansionist who supported the expansion of "trade and currency" more than "territorial acquisitions." Chaffin, *Pathfinder*, 85.

Chapter Two

1. Atchison, "David R. Atchison: A Study in American Politics," 503.

2. Biographical information on David Rice Atchison is limited. His papers were destroyed in a fire at the family home in 1881. The biography that appears here is based on Theodore Atchison, "David R. Atchison"; Stevens, "A Day and Night with 'Old Davy': David R. Atchison"; and Parrish, *David Rice Atchison of Missouri: Border Politician*.

3. Jefferson Davis left Transylvania College in his junior year to attend West Point. Townsend, "David Rice Atchison," 39.

4. LeSueur, *The 1838 Mormon War in Missouri*, 2–3. For more on the simultaneous rise of Jacksonian democracy and group violence in the nineteenth century, see Gilje, *The Road to Mobocracy: Popular Disorder in New York City, 1763–1834*.

5. The Mormons' description of their "suffering and poverty . . . moved Atchison to tears." LeSueur, *The 1838 Mormon War*, 78.

6. Regarding U.S. government treaties with Native Americans, Stephen Ambrose notes in Ric Burns's 1995 documentary *The Way West*: "The treaties didn't hold because one party of the treaties never meant it to hold. It was simply a temporary expedient."

7. Stephen LeSueur argues that "a degree of enmity" previously existed between Boggs and Atchison. This added to Boggs's belief that Atchison's indecision contributed to the conflict's escalation and led Boggs to relieve Atchison of command. Ibid., 88, 157.

8. David Rice Atchison never married.

9. Chief Justice John Marshall defended the sanctity of contract in his famous ruling in *Dartmouth College v. Woodward*, 17 U.S. 518 (1819). In it he argued the U.S. Constitution,

Article 1, Section 10, prohibited state law from violating the sanctity of contracts. However, contracts can be extinguished through legal means such as bilateral termination, which is in itself a contract between two parties. Atchison believed in extinguishing Indian treaties through bilateral termination.

10. The gag rule was the term applied to the procedural measures enacted by Congress in 1836 that effectively tabled antislavery petitions. Between 1836 and 1844 thousands of antislavery petitions from northern states flooded Congress. The gag rule prevented the petitions from being read on the chamber floors or referred to committees. James Stewart, *Holy Warriors*, 83–85; Holt, *The American Whig Party*, 155–56.

11. Michael Holt does not make a distinction between southwest and southeast attitudes toward expansionism and political security. John McCardell however argues for such a distinction to be made. He states southern expansionists were primarily from the southwest along the Alabama and Mississippi frontier. Southeasterners, including Calhoun, were opposed to expansionism for purely economic gain. They believed it would only embolden the growing abolitionist movement in the North. Calhoun and southeasterners did support measured expansion to maintain political security, and that is how they viewed the annexation of Texas. Holt, *The American Whig Party*, 169; McCardell, *The Idea of a Southern Nation*, 234–36.

12. Holt, *The American Whig Party*, 170–71.

13. Liberty Party membership rose from 7,000 in 1840 to 62,000 in 1844. The rise in membership came primarily from Whigs in New York, costing Clay the state and the election. Tindal and Shi, *America*, 1:607.

14. Niven, *John C. Calhoun*, 304.

15. Hammond's brother-in-law, Wade Hampton, the father of future Confederate general Wade Hampton III, threatened to expose the ugly family secret that Hammond had been sexually involved with his four nieces, ages thirteen to seventeen. Hammond had privately admitted to the charges. Hammond would succeed Butler in the Senate after Butler's death in 1857. Bleser, *The Hammonds of Redcliffe*, 10.

16. According to Orville Vernon Burton, "The elite's leadership of the community and the state made the family linkings of this group significant. Marriages were important factors in political alliances and allegiances, as well as in individual success." Burton, *In My Father's House Are Many Mansions*, 66.

17. The Butlers were members of a thirty-man militia unit under the command of Captain Stirling Turner. On November 17, 1781, the unit was surrounded at a location on Clouds Creek, near Lexington, South Carolina, by three hundred Loyalist troops under the command of Major William "Bloody Bill" Cunningham. Except for two members of the unit, all , including both Butlers, were massacred after surrendering, hacked to death by broadswords. It was said James Sr.'s body was so brutally dismembered that his wife picked it up in pieces and carried it away in a basket. Cunningham's command was chased throughout the remainder of the war by Andrew Pickens Butler's father, William, who met his future wife Behethland Foote Moore, when she, then seventeen, road on horseback in the middle of the night to warn Butler and his men of advancing British and Loyalist troops. Andrew Pickens Butler later stated "his father spoke rarely of the Revolutionary difficulties," not wishing his sons "to know the causes of hatred which were then engendered." "Andrew Pickens Butler," *Dictionary of American Biography*, vol. 2; O'Neall,

Biographical Sketches of the Bench and Bar of South Carolina; "Clouds Creek," http://gaz.jrshelby.com; "Bloody Bill Cunningham and the Cloud's Creek Massacre."

18. Pierce Mason Butler was an Indian agent and colonel in the state militia. He fought in the Seminole Indian War and served as governor of the state from 1836 to 1838 before becoming a captain and then colonel in the U.S. Army. He was killed leading a charge in the Battle of Churubusco on December 22, 1847. Emily Butler Thompson, wife of Waddy Thompson, died shortly after her brother Pierce Mason. Waddy Thompson was a member of the House of Representatives from South Carolina from 1835 to 1841. He was U.S. minister to Mexico from 1842 to 1844. Death continued to follow the extended Butler family, most notably the sudden death of Andrew Pickens Butler's nephew, Preston Brooks in January 1857, just eight months after his infamous caning of Charles Sumner. "Pierce Mason Butler, 1798–1847," Manuscript Division, Library of Congress; *Directory of American Biography*; Aldrich, *A Memoir of A. P. Butler*.

19. Biographical information on Andrew Pickens Butler is extremely limited. Despite membership in an illustrious family and sitting on the bench for thirteen years, Butler left almost no papers. His biography here is based on Aldrich, *A Memoir of A. P. Butler*; "Andrew Pickens Butler," *Dictionary of American Biography*; O'Neall, *Biographical Sketches*.

20. William and Behethland Butler had eight children. Andrew Pickens Butler was the only child to outlive both his parents.

21. Moses Waddell was John C. Calhoun's childhood tutor and brother-in-law. Prior to establishing his academy in South Carolina, Waddell taught in Georgia, where his students included William H. Crawford, Howell Cobb, and Augustus Baldwin Longstreet. His South Carolina graduates included John C. Calhoun, James Louis Petigru, George McDuffie, Hugh Swinton Legare, and Andrew Pickens Butler.

22. Even after his election to the U.S. Senate in 1846, associates continued to refer to him to as Judge Butler.

23. Perry, "Andrew Pickens Butler," 112–13; O'Neall, *Biographical Sketches*, 203.

24. The Walker Tariff was an ad valorem tax on a percentage of the import's value. It's successful passage in 1846 removed the tariff as a sectional issue for the next decade. In 1857 Robert M. T. Hunter would author a more significant reduction of the tariff. It would be the last downward revision of the tariff before the Civil War. The tariff would not be lowered again until the passage of the Underwood Tariff in 1913.

25. Holt, *The American Whig Party*, 335.

26. Ibid., 336.

27. Niven, *John C. Calhoun*, 318.

28. According to Charles Wiltse, "Van Buren did not carry a single state, but he rolled up more than 10 percent of the aggregate popular vote, and by defeating Cass in New York he gave the election to the Whigs. As in 1844, the abolitionists elected a southern slaveholder to the presidency. This time, however, he was a Whig, and the Whig doctrine of central power would mean in time the triumph of their cause. None knew it better than John C. Calhoun." Wiltse, *John C. Calhoun*, 373.

29. Ibid., 369.

30. Ibid.

31. *The Papers of John C. Calhoun*, 27:529.

32. Bartlett, *John C. Calhoun*, 351, 360.

33. The remaining members of the committee of fifteen were, Alexander Stephens of Georgia, chair; Edward C. Cabell of Florida; William R. King of Alabama; Henry S. Foote of Mississippi, Solomon W. Downs of Louisiana,; Thomas J. Rusk of Texas; William K. Sebastian of Arkansas; John M. Clayton of Delaware; John G. Chapman of Maryland; Thomas H. Bayly of Virginia; Meredith P. Gentry of Tennessee; and Abraham W. Venable of North Carolina. Wiltse, *John C. Calhoun: Sectionalist*, 381.

34. Also known as *Address to the Southern People*.

35. Atchison was the only border-state representative to sign the address. Marc Egnal attributes the border states' moderation to the region's "strengthening ties with the North and lessening dependence on slavery." Egnal, *Clash of Extremes*, 188.

36. Wiltse, *John C. Calhoun: Sectionalist*, 393.

37. Because the constitutionally designated inauguration date, March 4, fell on a Sunday in 1849, Taylor asked for a postponement until Monday, March 5. It was later argued by some that since President Polk and his vice president George M. Dallas's terms expired at noon on March 4, Atchison, as president pro tempore of the Senate and third in line for succession, had become president for the day. However, the terms of the Thirtieth Congress also expired at noon on March 4. Atchison was not sworn in a president pro tempore of the Thirty-First Congress until Monday, March 5. No one was president between the expiration of Polk's presidency and Taylor's inauguration. "The office was vacant." Richard Davis, Office of the Senate Historian, emails to author, March 23, 1998 and March 5, 1999.

38. Wiltse, *John C. Calhoun: Sectionalist*, 396.

39. Ray, *The Repeal of the Missouri Compromise*, 30–31, nn. 21, 23.

40. Ibid., 30, n. 21.

41. *The Papers of John C. Calhoun*, vol. 27, August 1–December 2, 1849.

42. Ibid., 3.

43. Hill's boarding house was the site of Old Capitol, which housed Congress after Washington was burned in 1814. Rachel Shelden states that congressmen preferred boarding houses to hotels because of their "proximity to the workplace . . . on Capitol Hill or near the departments where politicians might have business. By contrast, most of the hotels were located on Pennsylvania Avenue close to the White House and nearly a mile from the halls of Congress." Shelden, *Washington Brotherhood*, 103.

44. *The Papers of John C. Calhoun*, 27:127.

45. The Missouri Resolutions were named for their author, Clairborne Jackson.

46. Thomas Hart Benton's nickname.

47. Henry Geyer served only one term in the Senate and, as Atchison hoped, voted with the Democrats more than the Whigs. Parrish, *David Rice Atchison*, 95, 113–14.

48. Ibid., 128.

49. Peterson, *The Great Triumvirate*, 5.

50. Ibid.

51. Parrish, *David Rice Atchison*, 168.

52. Wiltse, *John C. Calhoun: Sectionalist*, 459.

53. Bartlett, *John C. Calhoun*, 371, n. 28.

54. Wiltse, *John C. Calhoun: Sectionalist*, 460.

55. *Congressional Globe*, 31st Cong., 1st sess.

56. Hamilton went on to lobby for passage of the Compromise of 1850, shocking many former South Carolina nullifiers and extremists.

57. Wiltse, *John C. Calhoun: Sectionalist*, 461.

58. *Congressional Globe*, 31st Cong., 1st sess.

59. Peterson, *The Great Triumvirate*, 460; Bartlett, *John C. Calhoun*, 371; Wiltse, *John C. Calhoun: Sectionalist*, 461.

60. Peterson, *The Great Triumvirate*, 460.

61. Wiltse, *John C. Calhoun: Sectionalist*, 465.

62. Ibid., 469.

63. *Congressional Globe*, 31st Cong., 1st sess.

64. Ibid.

65. John C. Calhoun's body remained in Washington for three weeks before being escorted to Charleston by a congressional delegation led by James Mason. Calhoun was buried in St. Phillips Episcopal church in Charleston, despite a committee of friends who wanted to take the body back to Calhoun's home, Fort Hill, in upstate Anderson County. The state legislature denied the request, stating that Calhoun's resting place belonged in the state's largest city, Charleston. Ford, *Origins of Southern Radicalism*, 190.

66. *Congressional Globe*, 31st Cong., 1st sess.

67. Ibid.

68. *New York Herald*, April 1, 1850.

69. Henry Clay continued to serve in the U.S. Senate until his death on June 29, 1852. Daniel Webster left the Senate in July to become Millard Fillmore's secretary of state, which he held until his death on October 24, 1852.

70. Fisher, "Statesman of the Lost Cause," 120.

Chapter Three

1. *Congressional Globe*, 31st Cong., 1st sess., appendix.

2. Johannsen, *Stephen A. Douglas*, 294; "Western Expansion and the Compromise of 1850," 26. Senate Historian Office.

3. Robert M. T. Hunter wrote home at the end of the debate, "We have been kept here week after week, and we are worn out"; in Johannsen, *Stephen A. Douglas*, 294.

4. William Porter, House and Sign painter, *Business Department of the Washington City Directory*, 204.

5. Potter, *The Impending Crisis*, 145.

6. Nichols, *The Stakes of Power*, 45; Potter, *The Impending Crisis*, 121–23; Gienapp, *Origins of the Republican Party: 1852–1856*, 14–17; Wilentz, *The Rise of American Democracy*, 3:171–72, 198–200.

7. The Indian Territory created by treaty prohibited whites from entering without consent of the said tribal group.

8. Martha T. Hunter, *A Memoir of Robert M. T. Hunter*, 105.

9. Atchison's biographer, William E. Parrish, places the foursome at "Birth's on the east side of Third Street West between Pennsylvania Avenue and C Street North." But the Washington directory shows all four at Browns Hotel by 1853. Parrish., *David Rice*

Atchison of Missouri, 116; *Washington and Georgetown Directory and Congressional and Clerks' Register* (Kirkwood and McGill, 1853), 48.

10. John C. Calhoun had also messed with the men during several congressional sessions.

11. James Young, *The Washington Community*, and Bogue and Marlaire, "Of Mess and Men." Rachel Shelden disagrees with earlier studies that find congressmen housed together by region and "like mindedness." She argues the F Street Mess's living arrangement was "atypical" of the time and that most congressmen at midcentury lived in cross-sectional housing. Shelden bases her argument on an 1854 Congressional Directory that shows 148 members in cross-sectional housing versus only 76 in sectional housing. Shelden, *Washington Brotherhood*, 103. However, Shelden's figures combine the members residing in hotels with those residing in boarding houses, thereby skewing the results. Hotels accommodated significantly higher numbers than boarding houses resulting in a higher frequency of cross-sectional occupancy. The length of residency in a hotel was also shorter than in boarding houses. The F Street Mess's living arrangement was typical, not atypical, of members who took rooms at hotels for a short period before moving to permanent lodgings in a boarding house by state or region.

12. Plantation was a seventeenth-century term meaning farm. Historians generally use it only for farms with 20 or more African American slaves. The 1850 Census Slave Schedules show Hunter owned 98 slaves: 53 working adults, 41 children under the age of 15, and 4 seniors 60 and over. Butler owned 73 slaves: 61 working adults, 11 children under the age of 15, and one senior. Mason owned 10 slaves: 3 working adults, 5 children under the age of 15, and 2 seniors 60 and over. Slave Schedules, 1850 U.S. Federal Census.

13. The Missouri State Archives Reference Staff searched census records and was "unable to locate David Rice Atchison with any slaves in Missouri prior to 1860." See Slave Schedules, 1860 U.S. Census Records, "Schedule 2-Slave Inhabitants."

14. "Missouri History: Geographical Distribution of Slavery," http://missouri-history.itgo.com/slave.html.

15. Fuenfhausen, "Slave Housing in Missouri's Dixie."

16. "Laws of the State of Missouri and the Journal of the Senate, 1837–1845," document 2011-06-22-143440.pdf, Missouri State Archives, Jefferson City.

17. Slavery's westward expansion through Missouri did not go north of Platte County. The other counties carved from the Platte Purchase—Buchanan, Andrew, Holt, Nodaway, and Atchison—were all northwest of Little Dixie and contained much smaller slave populations.

18. Townsend, "History of David Rice Atchison of Kentucky," 40.

19. As Lincoln biographer Joshua Shenk, notes in his work, "In the early nineteenth century, attorneys commanded a kind of awe, embodying the stately Anglo-Saxon tradition of common law and domestic order." Shenk, *Lincoln's Melancholy*, 17. For more on the legal profession as a vehicle for economic and social mobility in the nineteenth century, see Dirck, *Lincoln the Lawyer*, and Lawrence M. Friedman, *A History of American Law*.

20. "I had the pleasure of sending 500 cigars which I hope will reach you in good order," wrote New Orleans congressman and businessman Emile LaSere to Atchison in December, 1852. "They are of the same quality as those I sent you last year." Emile LaSere

to David Rice Atchison, December 12, 1852, Western Historical Manuscript Collection, Atchison Papers, 1837–1953, roll #1, folder, #1.

21. *The Washington Directory: Part I, 1846*, Washington Historical Society, Washington, D.C.

22. Washington's social life and the importance it played in public policy in the lead-up to the Civil War is the topic of Rachel A. Shelden's study, *Washington Brotherhood*.

23. Davis, Douglas, and Butler became chairmen of their committees in the Thirtieth Congress. The Committee on Territories was created specifically for Douglas who had chaired the same in the House. Prior to the Thirtieth Congress, the Senate did not have a Committee on Territories. Hunter and Mason chaired lesser committees in the Thirtieth Congress. Hunter became chairman of Finance in the Thirty-First Congress. Mason was appointed chairman of Foreign Affairs in the Thirty-Second Congress after it was taken from Thomas Hart Benton for his failure to support the Democratic nominee for president, Franklin Pierce in 1852.

24. The Platte was the name given to the "sandy bottom river" northwest of the Missouri River that ran through the center of Nebraska.

25. While the language used in the Intercourse Act of 1834 did not specifically prohibit white transit through Indian Country, it is implied in several sections. For instance, in section 6 of the act "foreigner[s]" were prohibited from going into Indian Country without first securing from the U.S. government a "passport . . . and such passport shall express the object of such person, the time he is allowed to remain, and the route he is to travel." Section 9 of the act prohibits whites from feeding, ranging, or driving cattle in or through Indian Country "without the consent of such tribe." See Act of June 30, 1834, 4 Stat 729. Chapter CLXI—*An Act to regulate trade and intercourse with the Indian tribes, and to preserve peace on the frontiers*. https://lawfare.s3-us-west-2.amazonaws.com/stagin/s3fs-public/uploads/2013/01/Act-of-June-30-1834-4-Stat-729.pdf, accessed June 12, 2014. Wiki Document Library.

26. The geographic dimensions of the territory were "the parallel of 49 north latitude; on the east by the White Earth and Missouri Rivers; on the south by the parallel of 40 north latitude, and on the west by the Rocky Mountains," *Journal of the American Geographical and Statistical Society*, 1:257; Creigh, *Nebraska*, 20–21.

27. Europeans defined title to New World lands by discovery and exploration. Spain and France both claimed the Nebraska territory, but neither had undertaken any kind of significant exploration of the region. Under the terms of the Treaty of Paris of 1763, France ceded her North American holdings to the victorious British. Britain retained the lands east of the Mississippi and ceded the lands west of the Mississippi and east of the Rockies to Spain. After the American Revolution, the lands east of Mississippi, which the crown had claimed title to by way of discovery and cession, "passed to the United States" under the terms of the Paris Peace Treaty of 1783. Spain still held the land west of the Mississippi but ceded it back to France thirty-seven years later. In 1823 the Supreme Court ruled in *Lewis v. McIntosh* that while the Indians occupied territorial land, the government held "ultimate domain," thereby establishing the precedent that "conquest" determined title. Sheldon, "Land Systems and Land Policies in Nebraska," 14–15.

28. Ibid., 5.

29. Most of the Nebraska tribes entered the territory in the seventeenth century, having moved from the east over a period of centuries. Creigh, *Nebraska*, 17.

30. Sheldon, "Land Systems and Land Policies in Nebraska, 7; Creigh, *Nebraska*, 18.

31. Sheldon, "Land Systems and Land Policies in Nebraska," 15.

32. Ibid.

33. Kenneth Davis, *Kansas*, 8–9.

34. Creigh, *Nebraska*, 3-4.

35. Ibid.

36. Ibid.

37. Ibid.

38. Kenneth Davis, *Kansas*, 12.

39. Stuart's expedition was privately funded by John Jacob Astor. East of the continental divide, the Rio Grande and Mississippi Rivers flow eastward. West of the divide the Columbia and Colorado Rivers flow westward. "Its geographic oddity was that from points so close together streams should flow in opposite directions to destinations so far apart." Ted Morgan, *A Shovel of Stars*, 137.

40. The Great American Desert included the Nebraska and Oklahoma territories and portions of Wyoming, Montana, and northern Mexico. By the end of American westward expansion only Utah and Nevada would be so designated. www.digitalhistory.uh.edu.

41. McCullough et al., *The Way West* (DVD).

42. Tribes known as the "civilized nations"—85,000 Cherokee, Choctaw, Creek, Chickasaw, and Seminole—were relocated west of the Mississippi. McPherson, *Battle Cry of Freedom*, 45.

43. Kappler, *Indian Affairs: Laws and Treaties*, 2:217.

44. *Congressional Globe*, 21st Cong., 1st sess., chap. CXLVIII.

45. Kenneth Davis, *Kansas*, 30.

46. Map of the Indian Territory created by the Indian Trade and Intercourse Act of 1834, www.rootsweb.ancestry.com; McCullough et al., *The Way West* DVD.

47. "The Intercourse Act of 1834 and Progress of the Indian Tribes."

48. Malin, "Indian Policy and Westward Expansion," 11–12.

49. Ambrose, *Nothing Like It in the World*, 25.

50. Malin, *The Nebraska Question*, 91.

51. Up until 1840 the South had 44 percent of the track in the nation. By the end of the decade, northern had so outpaced southern construction that the South's percentage dropped to 26 percent. The lack of railroads in the South contributed to the South's growing sense of economic subordination to the North and became one of the major topics of discussion at the Memphis Convention in 1845. See McPherson, *Battle Cry of Freedom*, 91; Malin, *The Nebraska Question*, 96.

52. Potter, *The Impending Crisis*, 150–51.

53. Gittinger, "The Separation of Nebraska and Kansas from the Indian Territory," 454.

54. Historians differ on the number of routes commissioned. David Potter states three. Stephen Ambrose states four. Roy Gittinger states five.

55. Whitney continued to resubmit his proposal to Congress each session until 1852.

56. Allen Johnson, *Stephen A. Douglas*, 221.

57. The committee was created specifically for Douglas. Prior to its creation, the Senate Judiciary and Interior Committees handled territorial bills.

58. Johannsen, *Stephen A. Douglas*, 164.

59. Malin, *The Nebraska Question*, 100.

60. Gittinger, "The Separation of Nebraska and Kansas from the Indian Territory," 447; Ambrose, *Nothing Like It in the World*, 28.

61. Johannsen, *Stephen A. Douglas*, 171.

62. Potter, *The Impending Crisis*, 146–47.

63. Atchison co-sponsored the federal land grant of 600,000 to make the Hannibal–St. Joseph line possible. Nelson, *A Nation of Deadbeats*, 137. The grants were made in July 1851. Gittinger, "The Separation of Nebraska and Kansas from the Indian Territory," 447.

64. Benton's son-in-law John Charles Fremont tried unsuccessfully to convince Benton of the feasibility behind a line through the South Pass as well as the economic potential of the plains. Benton was not convinced of either. Chambers, *Old Bullion Benton*, 340; Chaffin, *Pathfinder*, 246, 389–90.

65. The Benton-Atchison feud is the central component of P. Orman Ray's thesis on the Kansas-Nebraska Act. Roy Gittinger agrees with Ray's argument that Benton's interest in the proposed transcontinental railroad was for political purposes only. Ray, *The Repeal of the Missouri Compromise*, 72–74; Gittinger, "The Separation of Nebraska and Kansas from the Indian Territory," 447.

66. Ray, *The Repeal of the Missouri Compromise*, 84; Malin, *The Nebraska Question*, 81–82.

67. Malin, *The Nebraska Question*, 81–82.

68. Missouri's fourth district was traditionally a Whig stronghold, but Hall was a Democrat. He served two terms, from 1849 to 1853, and retired. The district went back to the Whigs. Ibid., 89.

69. Act of June 30, 1834, 4 Stat 729, sections 11 & 12.

70. David Potter recorded the vote 107 to 49. Roy Gittinger recorded it as 98 to 43, with 88 members not voting. Potter did not do a breakdown of the vote. Gittinger did, stating the 80 of the 98 affirmative votes were northern, while 30 of the 43 negative votes were southern.

71. Johannsen, *Stephen A. Douglas*, 391.

72. Allen Johnson, *Stephen A. Douglas*, 224.

73. William Rufus King is the only elected federal executive in the nation's history to take his oath of office outside the country's borders. King took the oath in the small village of Matanzas, Cuba, just outside Havana on March 4, 1853. Hatfield, "Vice Presidents of the United States, 1789–1993."

74. David Rice Atchison, *Missouri Republican*, June 21, 1854, in Robert W. Johannsen's notes, University of Illinois at Urbana-Champaign Archives.

75. Community meetings of white Missourians demanding immediate settlement of Nebraska had been going on since 1852 and were growing in number. Ray, *The Repeal of the Missouri Compromise*, 104, 164.

76. Atchison was not alone. No one in Congress before the spring of 1853 saw any possibility in repealing the Missouri Compromise. Ibid., 104, n. 147; 105.

77. Potter, *The Impending Crisis*, 151–52; Gittinger, "The Separation of Nebraska and Kansas from the Indian Territory," 449–50; Malin, *The Nebraska Question*, 102–4.

78. Atchison's biographer, William Parrish uses Virginia Mason's description of the technical aspects of the mess arrangement and its personal relationships to describe Atchison's relationship with his new messmates. In actuality, Martha Mason's descriptions refer to the earlier messes before the addition of Atchison. She makes no mention of the Mess in 1853 or after and never mentions Atchison by name. However, it is unlikely the arrangement changed after Atchison's addition, and his letters to Butler after his retirement suggest the personal friendship was real and lasting. Mason, *The Public Life of James M. Mason*, 52.

79. Festinger, *A Theory of Cognitive Dissonance*, 3–5.

80. Benton had made his intentions known as early as February. But the earlier statement lacked the March 4 letter's specifics. Malin, *The Nebraska Question*, 124; The major newspapers in Missouri included the *Daily Missouri Democrat* (St. Louis), the *Inquirer* (Jefferson City), and the *St. Joseph Gazette*, all of which supported Benton; and the *Examiner* (Jefferson City), the *Lexington Chronicle*, the *Northeastern Reporter* (Canton), the *Banner* (Glasgow), the *Chronicle* (Bloomington), and the *Courier* (Hannibal), all of which supported Atchison. Ray, *The Repeal of the Missouri Compromise*, 109, 111.

81. The Hannibal *Union* insisted that James S. Green of Canton had lost his seat in 1850 because of apathy, and that Willard P. Hall saved himself belatedly: "Accordingly we find that after the organization of the House, the very first notice of a bill to be introduced, was given by Mr. Hall." Malin, *The Nebraska Question*, 59, 128; Parrish, *David Rice Atchison*, 125.

82. Parrish, *David Rice Atchison*, 115.

83. According to P. Orman Ray, "The *Republican* . . . maintained a neutral position . . . but as the campaign waxed hotter, it became more antagonistic toward Benton." Ray, *The Repeal of the Missouri Compromise*, 111, n. 156.

84. Parrish, *David Rice Atchison*, 127; *St. Joseph Gazette*, June 29, 1853, State Historical Society of Missouri.

85. *St. Joseph Gazette*, June 29, 1853.

86. Ibid.

87. Manypenny traveled to the Nebraska territory in September to begin negotiations with the tribes on behalf of the president. When he returned to Washington without any treaties extinguishing Indian titles, Benton accused him of being Atchison's puppet and deliberately delaying white settlement. Manypenny responded that his visit was preliminary and fact finding only. Ray, *The Repeal of the Missouri Compromise*, 125–27, 158–61; Parrish, *David Rice Atchison*, 129–31; Allen Johnson, *Stephen A. Douglas*, 225.

88. Atchison gave speeches in Parkville on August 6 and Fayette in November. He began his speech in Parkville praising Douglas and calling him "a statesman and devoted friend of the west," *St. Joseph Gazette*, August 31, 1853; Ray, *The Repeal of the Missouri Compromise*, 135–37; Malin, *The Nebraska Question*, 137, 140–41.

89. Allen Johnson, *Stephen A. Douglas*, 226.

90. No records exist for Mason and Butler for the time between March 4 and December 4, 1853, when Congress was in recess. However, on the basis of Hunter's correspondence during the period, which dealt primarily with job applicants, it can be assumed Mason and Butler were dealing with similar issues.

91. In New York the Democratic Party split into three factions, Free-Soil Democrats known as Barnburners who had returned to the party after Van Buren's failed Free-Soil campaign, Hardshell Democrats known as Hunkers who refused to share patronage with the returning Barnburners, and Softshell Democrats who wanted to share patronage for the sake of party unity. Robert W. Johannsen called it the "never-to-be-ended . . . quarrel" that threatened to "split the party throughout the nation." Johannsen, *Stephen A. Douglas*, 387.

92. Ibid., 385–86.

93. The tour masked Douglas's real purpose, which was to solicit investors for the transcontinental railroad.

94. Johannsen, *Stephen A. Douglas*, 398.

95. "I think the time has arrived for purchasing those Illinois Bonds," Douglas wrote to investors and copied to Corcoran on September 10, 1850. Corcoran Papers, 7:7694. Manuscript Division, Library of Congress.

96. James Gadsden was a railroad promoter and U.S. minister to Mexico. In 1853 he negotiated a treaty with Santa Anna for 55,000 square miles of Mexican territory, now southern New Mexico and Arizona, for $15 million. McPherson, *Battle Cry of Freedom*, 108.

97. "The Papers of R. M. T. Hunter," 1817–1887, Alderman Library Manuscript Division, University of Virginia.

98. Parrish, *David Rice Atchison*, 135, 139–40; Martha T. Hunter, *A Memoir of Robert M. T. Hunter*, 46.

Chapter Four

1. The solid mahogany senate desks, arranged in four semicircular rows, were built by New York cabinetmaker Thomas Constantine. Originally commissioned in 1812 the desks were not completed until 1819, five years after the 1814 fire. Architect of the Capitol, "The Old Senate Chamber."

2. Butler's mother was ailing and would die later that month. He would not arrive in Washington until January 3, 1854. Andrew Pickens Butler Papers, South Caroliniana Library, Manuscript Collection.

3. The desk was also draped in a crimson "modesty" curtain. Architect of the Capitol, "The Old Senate Chamber."

4. The Erechtheion, built on the hill of the Acropolis in Athens, was the temple to both Athena and Poseidon.

5. The Peale portrait was purchased by the United States in 1832 on the centennial of Washington's birth. It was framed in "a painted stone porthole surrounded by an oak wreath and topped by a keystone bearing the head of Jupiter." Architect of the Capitol, "The Old Senate Chamber."

6. The ranking member was Whig senator James Alfred Pearce of Maryland. His term began March 4, 1843. Atchison was first appointed to fill the expired term of the late Lewis F. Linn October 14, 1843. Pearce was last elected in 1861 as a Democrat. *Biographical Directory of the United States Congress*; Byrd, *The Senate: 1789–1989*.

7. Franklin Pierce suffered from depression, alcoholism, and malaria. News of his declining health began to circulate shortly after his inauguration. By June he was forced

to cancel a series of engagements, further fueling the speculation surrounding his health. Nichols, *Franklin Pierce*, 243.

8. Douglas's three-in-one bill did not make it out of the Committee on Railroads. Capers, *Stephen A. Douglas*, 90.

9. Johannsen, *Stephen A. Douglas*, 394–95.

10. Gates, "Southern Investments," 156, 177.

11. The general assumption that southern planters and businessmen invested surplus capital into more slaves and land in the South is discredited by Gates's obscure 1939 study. Gates's research shows considerable southern investments in northern territories beginning in 1816 and continuing up to the Panic of 1857. These investments accelerated after the passage of the Kansas-Nebraska Act. When war broke out, most of the properties were confiscated by local and state authorities in the North. Amazingly some southerners, including former vice president of the United States and Confederate general James C. Breckinridge, were able to hold onto their northern investments. Gates, "Southern Investments."

12. Augustus Dodge served in the Senate with his father, Senator Henry Dodge of Wisconsin. They would be on opposing sides on the final Nebraska bill. Augustus would support it, his father would oppose it.

13. *Congressional Globe*, 33rd Cong., 1st sess.

14. Nichols, *Franklin Pierce*, 328; *Congressional Globe*, 33rd Cong., 1st sess.

15. Negotiations were ongoing with Great Britain over several items, including competing transisthmian canal companies in Central America and fishing rights off the coast of Canada. The United States was also expanding its commercial interests in China and attempting to open up trade with its more recalcitrant neighbor Japan. Pierce's expansionist objectives also went in a southward direction. Many northerners believed his administration's later $10 million purchase of land from Mexico, the Gadsden Purchase, and his failed attempt to purchase Cuba from Spain as evidence of his being a pawn of the Slave Power. When it became public in 1854 that three U.S. diplomats, James Buchanan, minister to Great Britain, John Y. Mason, minister to France, and Pierre Soule, minister to Spain, had signed a document calling for the acquisition of Cuba by force, known as the Ostend Manifesto, Pierce was forced to disavow their actions in an attempt to quell the growing northern criticism of his administration's expansionism. See Nichols, *Franklin Pierce*. For more on the South's expansionist plans for Cuba, Nicaragua, and the Caribbean, see Walter Johnson, *River of Dark Dreams*.

16. Pierce, "First Annual Message, December 5, 1853."

17. Nichols, *Franklin Pierce*, 220.

18. Gara, *The Presidency of Franklin Pierce*, 52.

19. *Congressional Globe*, 33rd Cong., 1st sess.

20. In the Senate the vote was delayed by the observance of Vice President King's passing. Eulogies were read by Robert Hunter and Edward Everett of Massachusetts. The Senate adjourned on December 8 and did not reconvene until December 12.

21. Gamm and Smith, "Last among Equals," 9.

22. The Senate Democratic Caucus did not keep records of leadership and the Committee on Committees assignments until the twentieth century after the Caucus was formally adopted on March 6, 1910. See Gamm and Smith, "Last among Equals"; Byrd, *The Senate:1789–1989*.

23. P. Orman Ray and Atchison biographers, William E. Parrish and Eda Roberts, accord Atchison total power over the committee assignment process. None of the historians note the rise of the caucus or the subsequent changes in the assignment process.

24. There were thirteen additional committees with two to five members each. *Congressional Globe*, 33rd Cong., 1st sess.

25. Four additional senate seats were vacant and would not be filled until later in the session. Freshman Whig from Missouri, Henry S. Geyer, was one of only two senators with one assignment. Nevertheless, as a proslavery Whig, he was given a seat on the powerful Judiciary Committee. The other senator, the once powerful Democrat from Michigan, Lewis Cass, requested a reduced workload. He was given a seat on the committee on the Library. Ibid.

26. Potter, *The Impending Crisis*, 158, n. 27.

27. The House version of the bill was introduced the same day by Representative J. G. Miller of Missouri and referred to the House Committee on Territories chaired by W. A. Richardson of Illinois. *Congressional Globe*, 33rd Cong., 1st sess.; Ray, *The Repeal of the Missouri Compromise*, 196.

28. According to Robert Johannsen, the national press supported the position that the Compromise of 1850 had superseded the Missouri Compromise of 1820 as the basis for organization of Nebraska, but "there was little apprehension in the North that the area of slavery would actually be enlarged" but "excluded from Nebraska by natural forces." P. Orman Ray argued however that the southern press remained fearful of Free-Soil efforts to exclude slavery from the territory and continued to insist on outright repeal of the Missouri Compromise. Johannsen, *Stephen A. Douglas*, 403–4; Ray, *The Repeal of the Missouri Compromise*, 197–98, 200; Parrish, *David Rice Atchison*, 142.

29. The Nebraska Delegate Convention met in St. Joseph on January 9, 1854. Iowa held a Nebraska convention at the start of the year as well. The two competing Nebraska delegations supported the eventual division of the territory into two, Kansas and Nebraska. Malin, *The Nebraska Question*, 18–19.

30. Ray, *The Repeal of the Missouri Compromise*, 199, n. 278.

31. *Congressional Globe*, 33rd Cong., 1st sess.

32. Ray, *The Repeal of the Missouri Compromise*, 197–98, 200; Parrish, *David Rice Atchison*, 142.

33. The specific date of the meeting is not known. William Parrish states the meeting was held shortly after the bill was referred to the Committee on Territories. Parrish, *David Rice Atchison*, 143.

34. Learned, "The Relation of Philip Phillips to the Repeal of the Missouri Compromise in 1854," 304.

35. Ibid.

36. Massachusetts Whig Edward Everett was the only northerner on the Committee on Territories.

37. Houston's opposition to the Kansas-Nebraska Act and later to southern secession cost him his political career. In 1861 he was deposed as governor of Texas for refusing to swear an oath of allegiance to the Confederacy. John Bell ran for president in 1860 on the Unionist ticket but later embraced the Confederacy in 1861 after Lincoln's call for troops to suppress the rebellion.

38. Capers, *Stephen A. Douglas*, 93.

39. Bright was expelled from the U.S. Senate on February 5, 1862, for disloyalty to the Union. Butler and Wolff, "Case 40," in *United States Senate*, 106.

40. Ray, *The Repeal of the Missouri Compromise*, 286.

41. Samuel S. Phelps had been appointed in 1853 by the governor of Vermont to fill the vacancy caused by the death of William Upham while the Vermont state legislature was in recess. The problem arose when the Vermont state legislature reconvened and later adjourned without filling the vacancy. The question before the U.S. Senate was whether Phelps continued to hold the seat or whether it was vacated by the Vermont state legislature's failure to fill it. It continued to be debated throughout the session. Phelps left Washington and did not participate in the debate or vote on the Nebraska bill. On March 16, 1854, the Senate decided Phelps was not entitled to the seat and declared it vacant. Democrats were upset over the Clayton Bulwer treaty during the Zachary Taylor's administration in which the United States had agreed to British involvement in a possible isthmus canal. They believed the treaty was a violation of the Monroe Doctrine and overtures by the British in Nicaragua plagued the Pierce administration.

42. Bills and Resolutions, Senate, 33rd Cong., 1st sess., S. 22, sec. 1; Johannsen, *Stephen A. Douglas*, 405.

43. Bills and Resolutions, Senate, 33rd Cong., 1st sess., S. 22, sec. 1.

44. Ibid.

45. Douglas Report, January 4, 1854.

46. Ibid.

47. Ibid.

48. Ray, *The Repeal of the Missouri Compromise*, 209–10; Parrish, *David Rice Atchison*, 143; Johannsen, *Stephen A. Douglas*, 407–10.

49. David Potter argued the substitute language not only confused Douglas's contemporaries but has also confused historians ever since, noting Nichols's argument that Douglas was "gulling his northern associates by scuttling the Missouri Compromise while seeming not to," and Harry V. Jaffa's argument that "Douglas was gulling his southern associates by maintaining the Missouri Compromise while seeming not to." Potter doesn't find either argument correct. Potter, *The Impending Crisis*, 160, n. 30; Nichols, *Franklin Pierce*, 230.

50. James Malin and David Potter both cite the *Union* (Washington) as the paper that reprinted the change on January 10. They are incorrect. Malin never cites from the *Union* directly. His references to it are based on the two Missouri papers he used in his study, the *St. Joseph Gazette* and the *Liberty Tribune*, both of which incorrectly cited the *Union*. Potter's citation of the *Union* is also based on secondary sources. All other historical sources cite the *Washington Sentinel*. A review by the Library of Congress of both papers found the *Sentinel* and not the *Union* printed the bill on January 10.

51. The Committee on the Pacific Railroad was dominated by proslavery southerners. Its chairman, Democratic senator from California William W. Gwin was born in Mississippi and still owned slaves there. He served in the U.S. Senate until 1861. His southern sympathies caused him to be arrested twice during the war for disloyalty to the United States. In 1863 he traveled to France in an effort to get Napoleon III's support for a settlement program in Mexico for American slave-owners. He did not get the emperor's

support. The rest of the committee included Henry Geyer, Democrat from Missouri; Thomas J. Rusk, Democrat from Texas; John Bell, Whig from Tennessee; Josiah J. Evans, Democrat from South Carolina; Jesse D. Bright, Democrat from Indiana; Edward Everett, Whig from Massachusetts; and William Seward, Whig from New York. *Biographical Directory of the United States Senate.*

52. Neither P. Orman Ray nor James C. Malin addressed the change that occurred in the bill between January 4 and 10. It is a significant oversight on the part of Ray since his thesis centers on the role Atchison played in the bill. Johannsen, *Stephen A. Douglas,* 408; Potter, *The Impending Crisis,* 159; Allen Johnson, *Stephen A. Douglas,* 232–33; Freehling, *The Road to Disunion,* 552.

53. There is some discrepancy on the dates of the actual meetings. William Parrish states that Phillips first approached Hunter on January 4 thereby placing all of the meetings before the addition of section 21 on January 10. However, Philip Phillips stated in 1860 the meetings occurred shortly before the introduction of the Dixon amendment on January 16, placing the meetings during the week of January 10. Parrish, *David Rice Atchison,* 144; Learned, "The Relationship of Philip Phillips to the Repeal of the Missouri Compromise," 310.

54. Philip Phillips was born in 1807 in Charleston, South Carolina. His parents, Aaron and Martha Lazarus Phillips, were members of Charleston's vibrant Jewish community. Young Phillips was educated at the New England Academy of Captain Alden Partridge and was a classmate of Gideon Welles. He was admitted to the South Carolina bar in 1828, and four years later, as a member of the South Carolina convention, he courageously voted against nullification. In 1835 Phillips moved to Mobile, Alabama, bringing his bride, Eugenia Levy, also of Charleston, there a year later. He was elected to Congress in 1853 moving his family to Washington the same year. He served only one term in Congress during which time he played a critical role in formation of the Kansas-Nebraska Act. Phillips voluntarily resigned in 1855 but remained in Washington where he became a renowned attorney for the bar of the U.S. Supreme Court. He served in that capacity until his death in 1884. Learned, "The Relationship of Philip Phillips to the Repeal of the Missouri Compromise"; Ted Morgan, "Philip Phillips and Internal Improvements in Mid-Nineteenth Century Alabama."

55. Johannsen, *Stephen A. Douglas,* 413; Learned, "The Relationship of Philip Phillips to the Repeal of the Missouri Compromise," 311; Parrish, *David Rice Atchison,* 144, n. 14; Potter, *The Impending Crisis,* 159.

56. Johannsen, *Stephen A. Douglas,* 413; Learned, "The Relationship of Philip Phillips to the Repeal of the Missouri Compromise," 311; Parrish, *David Rice Atchison,* 144, n. 14; Potter, *The Impending Crisis,* 159.

57. Tabling was used to postpone consideration or debate of an issue. *Congressional Globe,* 33rd Cong., 1st sess.

58. *Washington Sentinel,* January 14, 1854; Parrish, *David Rice Atchison,* 145.

59. Parrish, *David Rice Atchison,* 145.

60. Dixon, *History of the Missouri Compromise and Slavery in American Politics,* 442–43.

61. *Congressional Globe,* 33rd Cong., 1st sess.

62. Johannsen, *Stephen A. Douglas,* 412.

63. Nichols, *Franklin Pierce*, 321.

64. Dixon, *History of Missouri Compromise and Slavery in American Politics*, 437.

65. Freehling, *The Road to Disunion*, 555; Holt, *The American Whig Party*, 808-9; Johannsen, *Stephen A. Douglas*, 412.

66. Weeks before the bill was reported out of committee on January 4 Senator William Dawson stated someone in the House planned to introduce an amendment to repeal the Missouri Compromise. Holt, *The American Whig Party*, 808.

67. Ray, *The Repeal of the Missouri Compromise*, 211; Allen Johnson, *Stephen A. Douglas*, 236.

68. Dixon, *The History of the Missouri Compromise and Slavery in American Politics*, 446.

69. In the Old Senate Chamber the desks were divided evenly on each side of the aisle forcing the majority party to place some of its members on the minority side. The Whigs were seated to presiding officer David Rice Atchison's right, the Democrats to his left. "Senate Chamber Desks," http://www.senate.gov/artandhistory.

70. Dixon, *The History of the Missouri Compromise and Slavery in American Politics*, 447.

71. Ibid., 444; Parrish, *David Rice Atchison*, 146.

72. The emphasis is Mrs. Dixon's.

73. When Sumner planned to speak he always dressed in lavender or patterned colors. David Stewart, *Impeached*, 37; *Congressional Globe*, 33rd Cong., 1st sess.

74. Sumner was not a successful legislator. According to David Stewart only one of his bills passed the Senate during his entire career. See David Stewart, *Impeached*, 37.

75. Traditionally Congress did not convene until noon as to allow for morning social calls. It is likely Douglas and Dixon's ride occurred in the morning before the start of the session.

76. Dixon, *The History of the Missouri Compromise and Slavery in American Politics*, 445.

77. Allen Johnson, *Stephen A. Douglas*, 237.

78. Freehling, *The Road to Disunion*, 556; Johannsen, *Stephen A. Douglas*, 413; Learned, "The Relationship of Philip Phillips to the Repeal of the Missouri Compromise," 308; Parrish, *David Rice Atchison*, 146.

79. Reflecting the growth of the country itself, the Patent Office remained under constant expansion from 1838 until 1868. In 1854 the house at 361 F Street was only three doors down from the then existing Patent Office and in all likelihood was later demolished to make room for expansion of the building that in the end took up two and a half blocks of F Street. The east wing facing Seventh Street was completed in 1853 except for its portico, which was completed two years later. The first and second floor of the wing was reserved for the Department of Interior, which the Patent Office had been transferred to in 1849. Robertson, *Temple of Invention*, 43-45.

80. Numerous foreign policy crises were plaguing Pierce during the first weeks of the congressional session including a less than hoped for treaty brought back from Mexico by James Gadsden, the likelihood of Great Britain and France's entrance into the Crimean War between Russia and Turkey, and Great Britain's and France's perceived interference in American expansionism in the Caribbean and Pacific. See Nichols, *Franklin Pierce*, 333; Potter, *The Impending Crisis*, 161.

81. Caleb Cushing, Pierce's Attorney General, wrote most of the Union's editorials. Parrish, *David Rice Atchison*, 147.

82. Nichols, *Franklin Pierce*, 237.

83. Freehling, *Road to Disunion*, 555-56; Johannsen, *Stephen A. Douglas*, 414; Parrish, *David Rice Atchison*, 147; Potter, *The Impending Crisis*, 161; Ray, *The Repel of the Missouri Compromise*, 213.

84. Quoted in Johannsen, *Stephen A. Douglas*, 414.

85. Ray, *The Repeal of the Missouri Compromise*, 213.

86. Anthony, *America's First Families*, 228.

87. In the winter of 1857 Pierce risked his own health during a blizzard that had shut the capital city down to reach the Davis home, where Varina Davis lay seriously ill. Nichols, *Franklin Pierce*, 313, 497; Cooper, *Jefferson Davis, American*, 248; Seale, *The President's House: A History*, 309.

88. The scenario of the Sunday meeting in regards to time, people in attendance, etc. varies slightly from text to text. For the purpose of this study, the Davis memoir is used. Davis states that "gentlemen of each committee" and Douglas called on him that morning. Phillips was a member of the House Committee on Territories. Breckinridge was on the House Ways and Means. Given that Breckinridge, Phillips, and Douglas were inseparable that weekend, Davis has to be referring to Breckinridge and Phillips. Jefferson Davis, *The Rise and Fall of the Confederate Government*, 1:28; Allen Johnson, *Stephen A. Douglas*, 237.

89. Jefferson Davis, *The Rise and Fall of the Confederate Government*, 28; Johannsen, *Stephen A. Douglas*, 414; Nichols, *Franklin Pierce*, 322.

90. Jefferson Davis, *The Rise and Fall of the Confederate Government*, 28; Johannsen *Stephen A. Douglas*, 414; Parrish, *David Rice Atchison*, 148; Potter, *The Impending Crisis*, 161; Freehling, *The Road to Disunion*, 556.

91. Seale, *The President's House*, 310.

92. The public stairwell that led to the president's executive offices was on the east end of the reception room. These rooms were shut off from the family's private quarters. Seale, *The President's House*; Anthony, *America's First Families*.

93. Pierce had one of the bedrooms converted into the library. Seale, *The President's House*; Anthony, *America's First Families*.

94. Nichols, *Franklin Pierce*, 323; Johannsen, *Stephen A. Douglas*, 389.

95. Potter, *The Impending Crisis*, 162.

96. Johannsen, *Stephen A. Douglas*, 416.

97. The thirty-seventh parallel divided the lands belonging to the Cherokee and the Osages. *Congressional Globe*, 33rd Cong., 1st sess.

98. Malin, *The Nebraska Question*, 317.

99. Allen Johnson, *Stephen A. Douglas*, 239.

100. Johannsen, *Stephen A. Douglas*, 416-17.

101. James Malin notes that none of the western newspaper editorials at the time discussed the issue of slavery; rather, the concerns centered on extinguishment of Indian title and the Pacific railroad route. Malin, *The Nebraska Question*, 317-19.

102. Robert Johannsen, *Stephen A. Douglas*, 417.

103. *Congressional Globe*, 33rd Cong., 1st sess.

104. Ray, *The Repeal of the Missouri Compromise*, 213.

105. Bills and Resolutions, 33rd Cong., 1st sess.

106. *Congressional Globe*, 33rd Cong., 1st sess.

107. Former Whig senator Samuel Phelps was called out of retirement when he was appointed by the governor of Vermont on January 17, 1853, to fill the Senate seat left vacant by the death of Senator William Upham. When the Thirty-Third Congress convened in December 1853, the Vermont state legislature had yet to confirm Phelps's appointment. William Seward questioned whether Phelps's executive appointment had expired by virtue of the Vermont legislature having met in two consecutive sessions without confirmation. The matter was sent to the Judiciary Committee chaired by Andrew Pickens Butler. The committee ruled in favor of Phelps agreeing with his position that "the executive nomination continued in force until superseded by the action of the legislature." Butler wrote the minority opinion that "once a legislature met . . . a gubernatorial appointment would automatically terminate, even if the body did not use its power to elect a successor." The majority of the Senate agreed with the minority of the committee and voted Phelps not to be entitled to the senate seat on March 16, 1854. He was given "mileage and per diem to the date of the vote." Butler and Wolff, *United States Senate*, Case #26, 67–68.

108. *Congressional Globe*, 33rd Cong., 1st sess.

109. Ibid.

110. Each story was written the day before its publication. Ray, *The Repeal of the Missouri Compromise*, 212–13.

111. Ibid., 214.

Chapter Five

1. Johannsen, *Stephen A. Douglas*, 418.
2. Ibid., 422; Gara, *Franklin Pierce*, 92–93.
3. Holt, *The American Whig Party*, 816.
4. Ibid., 817.
5. Potter, *The Impending Crisis*, 164.
6. Ibid., 163; Holt, *The American Whig Party*, 815.
7. Potter, *The Impending Crisis*, 165; Freehling, *The Road to Disunion*, 550.
8. Capers, *Stephen A. Douglas*, 98; Johannsen, *Stephen A. Douglas*, 419.
9. *Journal of the Executive Proceedings of the Senate of the United States of America*, Thursday, January 26, 1854; Nichols, *Franklin Pierce*, 324.
10. So many congressmen left the House chamber to watch the action on the Senate floor the House could not get a quorum. Johannsen, *Stephen A. Douglas*, 419.
11. Goodwin, *Team of Rivals*, 162–64.
12. Roy Morris, *The Long Pursuit*, 2, 23, 81; Johannsen, *Stephen A. Douglas*, 57, 79, 132.
13. *Congressional Globe*, 33rd Cong., 1st sess.
14. Ibid.
15. Ibid.
16. Douglas's argument that slavery existed in the original Louisiana Purchase under common law contradicts British jurist Lord Mansfield's 1776 Somerset decision that slavery was antithetical to common law.

17. As evidence of the continuation of the Missouri Compromise in later acquisitions, Douglas read from the 1845 joint resolution of Texas that stated, "And as such states as may be formed out of that portion of said territory lying south of the 36° 30′ latitude, commonly known as the Missouri Compromise line, shall be admitted into the Union with or without slavery, as the people of each State asking admission may desire. And in such State or States as shall be formed out of said territory north of said Missouri compromise line, slavery or involuntary servitude . . . shall be prohibited." *Congressional Globe*, 33rd Cong., 1st sess.

18. Ibid.

19. Ibid.

20. After January 23, the record referred to the bill as the Nebraska-Kansas bill. For the purpose of this study the same title will be used.

21. *Congressional Globe*, 33rd Cong., 1st sess.

22. Ibid.

23. Ibid.

24. Ibid.

25. Ibid.

26. Ibid.

27. According to Michael Holt, George Badger and John Clayton of Delaware wanted to make the "bill more palatable to southern Whigs" without alienating northern Whigs, "for, it must be emphasized, southern Whigs by no means intended their support to disrupt the national Whig party." Holt, *The American Whig Party*, 818.

28. Public petitions against the bill were ordered to lie on the table. Requests to read memorials into the record were voted down.

29. The Senate met Monday through Friday. It did not meet on Wednesday, February 22, in observance of George Washington's birthday.

30. Ray, *The Repeal of the Missouri Compromise*, 217; Allen Johnson, *Stephen A. Douglas*, 243–44; Johannsen, *Stephen A. Douglas*, 424; Holt, *The American Whig Party*, 819.

31. Johannsen, *Stephen A. Douglas*, 423.

32. Some historians dispute the floor debate's importance, arguing the outcome in the Senate was never in doubt. Michael Holt states even if the nine southern Whigs who voted for the bill had not, the bill would have still passed 28–24. Holt, *The American Whig Party*, 819. Holt's position ignores the fact that while southern Whig senators may not have been needed to win in the Senate, southern Whigs were needed to win in the House and southern Whigs in the House might not have supported the bill if southern Whigs in the Senate had not. Gerald Capers, on the other hand, argues forcibly for the role the floor debate played in swaying senators and the public's opinion on the bill. See Capers, *Stephen A. Douglas*; Ray, *The Repeal of the Missouri Compromise*; Allen Johnson, *Stephen A. Douglas*; Johannsen, *Stephen A. Douglas*.

33. Ray, *The Repeal of the Missouri Compromise*, 222–25.

34. *Congressional Globe*, 33rd Cong., 1st sess.

35. Ibid.

36. Ibid.

37. Ibid.

38. Ibid.

39. Edward Everett was the keynote speaker at the dedication of the national cemetery at Gettysburg in 1863 where he was outshone by Abraham Lincoln. Augustus Dodge was the son of Senator Henry Dodge of Wisconsin. Augustus was born in Missouri before his father moved to Illinois. Henry Dodge would later move to Wisconsin, and Augustus would move to Iowa. They would serve together in the Senate representing their respective states from 1848 to 1855. Henry Dodge's half-brother was Lewis Fields Linn, senator from Missouri from 1833 to his death in 1843. His seat was filled by David Rice Atchison. *Biographical Directory of the United States Congress.*

40. *Congressional Globe*, 33rd Cong., 1st sess.

41. Admitting women to the floor was the "equivalent to a motion to suspend the rules, and that require[d] one day's notice, unless by unanimous consent." *Congressional Globe*, 33rd Cong., 1st sess.

42. Badger gave a speech in favor of the bill on February 16.

43. *Congressional Globe*, 33rd Cong., 1st sess.

44. Revisionary power had been given to Congress in earlier territorial bills in which territorial legislatures had not been provided for but later territorial bills provided for legislative bodies. Douglas stated the Committee on Territories was still considering the question of whether "such a revision" was necessary in the Nebraska-Kansas bill. *Congressional Globe*, 33rd Cong., 1st sess.

45. The February 13 message caught the attention of Robert Johannsen while he was researching his seminal biography on Douglas, enough to write next to his copy of it the question, "Is this Stephen?" Nevertheless, Johannsen did not use the Hyde letter in his biography on Douglas. Little is known about Hyde or Smith. The Corcoran Papers do not provide information on either. Both men's names appear in Washington City directories from 1843 and 1846 but not after that. In 1843 Hyde had been an employee of the Treasury Department, a natural stepping-stone to employment in private investment banking such as Corcoran's. Smith was a lawyer who lived on F Street between Fourteenth and Fifteenth Streets West. See A. Hyde to J. B. H. Smith, February 13, 1854, Washington, Corcoran Papers, Library of Congress; Robert Johannsen note cards, University of Illinois at Urbana-Champaign Library Archives; Kiplinger Research Library of the Historical Society of Washington, D.C., library@historydc.org.

46. Woodward, *Mary Chesnut's Civil War*, 61, 63, 87, 171; Fisher, "Statesman of the Lost Cause," 6–7; French, *Witness to the Young Republic*, 111, 269; William Gibson Guerrant, "Letter 1858 Feb. 28," Virginia Historical Society.

47. *Congressional Globe*, 33rd Cong., 1st sess., appendix, The Nebraska and Kansas Bill, Robert M. T. Hunter February 24, 1854.

48. Ibid.

49. Graham also sued for expenses incurred in his attempt to recover damages. *Strader v. Graham*; Finkelman, *An Imperfect Union*, 196–200, and *Slavery in the Courtroom*, 35–37.

50. Finkelman, *An Imperfect Union*, 197.

51. Paul Finkelman states Taney "used or perhaps misused" the *Strader v. Graham* case as a precedent for the court's decision in *Dred Scott v. Sanford*. Ibid., 196.

52. *Congressional Globe*, 33rd Cong., 1st sess., appendix, Hunter, February 24, 1854.

53. Ibid.

54. Ibid.

55. Ibid.

56. Aldrich, *A Memoir of A. P. Butler*, 4; Herriott, "James Grimes versus the Southrons," 333–34; Perry, *Reminiscences of Public Men*, 112–13.

57. *Congressional Globe*, 33rd Cong., 1st sess., appendix, The Nebraska and Kansas Bill, Andrew Pickens Butler.

58. Josiah Gould, email to author, July 23, 2012.

59. *Congressional Globe*, 33rd Cong., 1st sess., appendix, The Nebraska and Kansas Bill, Andrew Pickens Butler.

60. Submitted to the Senate on February 15, 1854.

61. *Congressional Globe*, 33rd Cong., 1st sess.

62. Ibid.

63. Ibid.

64. Ibid.

65. Ibid.

66. Ibid.

67. 33rd Congress, 1st sess., March 3.

68. Ibid. Fessenden became an antislavery leader in Congress. He replaced Salmon P. Chase as Lincoln's treasury secretary in 1864. Fessenden had three sons in the Union army, including Samuel Fessenden, named for his grandfather, who was killed at the Second Battle of Bull Run. *Biographical Directory of the United States*; The Latin Library, http://www.thelatinlibrary.com/chron/civlwarnotes.

69. Despite California's free-state status, the proslavery faction in the state was strong. John Weller eventually moved to New Orleans in 1867. William Gwin was arrested twice during the Civil War for activities disloyal to the Union that included his unsuccessful effort to relocate American slave owners and slaves in Mexico. *Biographical Directory of the United States Congress*.

70. Weller's declaration that there was no "evidence" of an "aggressive spirit" on the part of southerners in California is startling given that slave owners had been migrating to California before and after the passage of its antislavery constitution. Historian Stacey Smith suggests that California was a free state in name only. She estimates between 500 to 600 slaves were brought in during the 1848 Gold Rush alone. She further notes that by 1852 census records showed 2,200 African Americans in California though it did not delineate between slave and free blacks. Proslavery Californians were strong in both the state legislature and courts. Their efforts culminated in the passage of the California Fugitive Slave Act of 1852 that protected slave owners' rights and "severely constricted the scope of the antislavery constitution," so much so "that one antislavery Californian lamented that 'this State now is, and forever hereafter must remain, a slave State.'" Smith, "Remaking Slavery in a Free State," 29, 31, 49.

71. *Congressional Globe*, 33rd Cong., 1st sess.

72. Ibid.

73. Ibid.

74. Ibid.

75. Ibid.

76. Ibid.

77. Ibid.
78. Ibid.
79. Ibid.
80. Ibid.
81. Ibid.
82. Ibid.

83. The Missouri state constitution prohibited the emigration of free blacks into the state. Article IV, Section 2, paragraph one of the constitution states "The Citizens of each State shall be entitled to all Privileges and immunities of Citizens in the several States." However, when the bill reached the House, it was amended and passed to read "that neither slavery nor involuntary servitude shall ever be allowed in said State of Missouri." A compromise was negotiated by Henry Clay in which Missouri was admitted as a slave state on condition it agreed not to construe the state constitution in such a way as to violate the privileges and immunities clause. Missouri was admitted into the Union on March 2, 1821.

84. *Congressional Globe*, 33rd Cong., 1st sess.
85. Ibid.
86. Ibid.
87. Ibid.
88. Ibid.
89. Ibid.

90. The title to the bill was amended to read as such after the vote was taken.

91. For the purpose of this study, California's two proslavery senators are counted as southern Democrats because both men were southerners and California's proslavery proclivities included state legislation that restricted the state's antislavery constitution. For more on California being a free state in name only, see Stacy Smith, "Remaking Slavery in a Free State."

92. John Bell ran for president on the Constitutional Union ticket in 1860. Sam Houston became a member of the American Know-Nothing Party and was elected governor of Texas in 1859. He was deposed in 1861 for refusing to take the Oath of Allegiance to the Confederacy. *Biographical Directory of the United States Congress.*

Chapter Six

1. On Monday, March 27, a verbal war of words erupted between Democrat Francis B. Cutting of New York and Democrat John C. Breckinridge of Kentucky on the House floor stemming from Cutting's successful motion to bury the Nebraska-Kansas bill in the Committee of the Whole the previous week. Decorum broke down between the two men as each accused the other of ulterior motives. That night Cutting challenged Breckinridge to a duel. Breckinridge being the challenged member chose rifles. Thomas Hart Benton's last-minute intervention stopped the duel from actually being carried out but not before news of it had been spread across the front pages of the country's major newspapers. *Congressional Globe*, 33rd Cong., Special sess., March 4, 1853–April 11, 1853 (March 27, 1854); "The Duel Yesterday," *New York Daily Times*, March 30, 1854, Stony Brook University Libraries, Stony Brook, N.Y.; Potter, *The Impending Crisis*, 171; Neely,

"The Kansas-Nebraska Act in American Political Culture," in Wunder and Ross, *The Nebraska-Kansas Act of 1854*, 14–15; Powers, "'If Men Should Fight': Dueling as Sectional Politics, 1850–1856," 1–2.

2. Roy Nichols argues that Pierce's efforts on the Nebraska-Kansas bill also squandered any political capital he had left for other pressing measures, including tariff reform, land grants and railroads, and other internal improvements. Nichols, *Franklin Pierce*, 335–37.

3. While Michael Holt agrees with Nichols's argument that the president's pressure on members was "unrelenting," he disagrees with the assessment that party alignment was breaking down and notes even with Stephens's efforts southern Whigs largely voted against the bill. Holt, *The American Whig Party*, 820–21.

4. Historians generally agree that the floor leadership of Alexander Stephens was essential to the bill's victory. But recent scholarship also acknowledges the floor leadership of William Richardson in the House and Douglas's party leadership. Credit is also given to Pierce for securing the necessary democratic votes. Roy Morris, *The Long Pursuit*, 71; Potter, *The Impending Crisis*, 167; Holt, *The American Whig Party*, 820; Gara, "Slavery and the Slave Power," 94; Foner, *Free Soil*, 158; Allen Johnson, *Stephen A. Douglas*, 254–55.

5. Parrish, *David Rice Atchison*, 154.

6. Ibid., 150.

7. Abolitionist Eli Thayer's Immigrant Aid Society in Massachusetts was incorporated by the state legislature before the Nebraska-Kansas bill even passed. Northern press coverage of Thayer and other Abolitionists efforts made the Free-Soil emigration to Kansas appear more successful and threatening to southerners than it actually was. Potter, *The Impending Crisis*, 199; Holt, *Crisis of 1850s*, 193. For more on Missourian agitation, see Malin, *The Nebraska Question*, 367–74, 396.

8. Ambler, *The Correspondence of Robert M. T. Hunter*, 161.

9. Ibid.

10. *New York Tribune*, December 31, 1854, in Eda Isabel Roberts, "The Life of David Rice Atchison."

11. William Parrish, Atchison's biographer, notes that by the spring of 1855 Atchison was declining local convention efforts to have his name put forward as a senatorial candidate, noting "Atchison's refusal to use this opportunity for self-advancement indicates the extent to which he had become imbued with the proslavery cause in Kansas; it took precedence over all other matters including his own re-election." Parrish, *David Rice Atchison*, 176.

12. Platte City speech, December 1854, in Roberts, "The Life of David Rice Atchison."

13. Parrish, *David Rice Atchison*, 168.

14. DeSassure to Atchison, January 21, 1855, David Rice Atchison Papers, Western Historical Manuscript Collection, University of Missouri.

15. Atchison's recruitment efforts paid off to a degree as young southern men, like their New England counterparts, began to immigrate to Kansas and join Atchison's force. The recruits included an unusual number of men from South Carolina, including a relative of Andrew Pickens Butler whom Atchison took personal charge of. Parrish, *David Rice Atchison*, 188–92.

16. June 29, 1855, diary entry. Gideon Welles Papers, Manuscript Division, Library of Congress; Parrish, *David Rice Atchison*, 168, n. 18.

17. Parrish, *David Rice Atchison*, 164.

18. According to Scott Nelson, the takeover of the railroad occurred while Congress was debating the "territorial status of Kansas." The surveyor of the Hannibal–St. Joseph route, Mr. Duff, had not been paid for his services. Boston investors John Murray Forbes and Nathaniel Thayer "used the surveyor's claim to put a lien on the railroad, used the lien to buy a majority stake in the company at a deep discount, quickly voted to change the directors, then created a 'fiscal agency' of the company that would meet in New York to settle Duff's claim. The New York agency became the actual board of directors that then demanded payments from all Missouri stockholders who had stock but had only paid the 10 percent down payment." The Missouri stockholders were required to make the remaining payments or turn over the stock. Forbes and Thayer "effectively voided most of the stock held in Missouri." Nelson, *A Nation of Deadbeats*, 139, 143.

19. Benton would later run for governor of Missouri and lose. He died shortly thereafter.

20. The election stalemate continued for the next two years during which time Missouri was without a second senator in the U.S. Senate. Parrish, *David Rice Atchison*, 184.

21. Ibid., 170.

22. The proslavery vote on March 30 was 6,307. Governor Reeder's earlier census had reported 2,905 eligible voters in a territorial population of 8,501. However the law did not provide a clear definition of residency, and same-day registration was rampant on both sides. Nevertheless historians agree the proslavery vote was fraudulent and unnecessary. They would have won without the additional over the border votes. Potter, *The Impending Crisis*, 201; Holt, *Crisis of the 1850s*, 193; McPherson, *Battle Cry of Freedom*, 146.

23. James McPherson argues Atchison and his men were responsible for seventeen hundred votes cast in the earlier November 1854 election for a delegate to Congress that elected proslavery candidate John Whitfield. McPherson, *Battle Cry of Freedom*, 146.

24. Ross K. Baker argues that pure friendship remains the rarest form of friendship in the U.S. Senate. Baker, *Friend and Foe*, 22.

25. A. P. Butler to David Rice Atchison, April 15, 1855, David Rice Atchison Papers, Western Historical Manuscript Collection, University of Missouri.

26. David R. Atchison to R. M. T. Hunter, March 4, 1855, in Ambler, *The Correspondence of Robert M. T. Hunter*, 161.

27. Report, the Committee on Territories No. 34, 34th Cong., 1st sess.

28. Reeder, who had traveled to Washington in the spring of 1855 to meet with the president, later testified before the House select committee investigating Kansas that Atchison had demanded his termination to the president through Secretary of War Davis. James A. Rawley argues that "Pierce was fully justified in dismissing Reeder for his land deals," but that Atchison was "determined to have Reeder's head." Rawley, *Race and Politics*, 90, 92. James McPherson ignores the issue of Reeder's land deals and places the blame for his firing on Atchison and Douglas. McPherson, *Battle Cry of Freedom*, 147.

29. Shannon, a Democrat, had twice been governor of Ohio after which he moved to California, where he gained attention for bringing civil order to San Francisco.

30. The Free-Soil constitution also denied the franchise to free blacks already in Kansas. Potter, *The Impending Crisis*, 203.

31. The proslavery government had already sent John Whitfield to Washington as its territorial representative. This meant the House had two contending delegates from Kansas, Whitfield and Reeder.

32. Isaac Holmes to A. P. Butler, March 17, 1856, in Ambler, *The Correspondence of Robert M. T. Hunter*.

33. The dissenting minority report written by Judge Collamer was also submitted and read into the record.

34. The figure 93,420 was the population ratio required for a representative to Congress in 1856.

35. *Congressional Globe*, 34th Cong., 1st sess., March 12, 1856.

36. Ibid. James McPherson states that by the fall of 1856 Free-Soil settlement had overtaken proslavery settlement. McPherson, *Battle Cry of Freedom*, 148.

37. *Congressional Globe*, 34th Cong., 1st sess.

38. Ibid.

39. Ibid.

40. Ibid.

41. Michael Morrison argues the violence in Kansas was always less than what was reported in the northern press. Morrison, *Slavery and the American West*, 161.

42. Potter, *The Impending Crisis*, 202–4; Etcheson, *Bleeding Kansas*.

43. The newspapers were the *Herald of Freedom* and the *Kansas Free State*.

44. The abolitionist spin on events in Kansas benefited from having more reporters on the ground. McPherson, *Battle Cry of Freedom*, 149.

45. Etcheson, *Bleeding Kansas*.

46. Letter to Jefferson Davis, September 24, 1856, David Rice Atchison Papers, Western Historical Manuscript Division, University of Missouri.

47. The hotel was built out of stone and had parapets and port holes for canon. Potter, *The Impending Crisis*, 208–9; Rawley, *Race and Politics*, 131.

48. McPherson, *Battle Cry of Freedom*, 148.

49. *Congressional Globe*, 24th Cong., 1st sess.

50. Ibid.

51. The winter of 1855–56 was particularly harsh in Kansas and contributed to a lull in the conflict.

52. Robinson was caught in Missouri and incarcerated for four months.

53. The posse's first attempt to destroy the stone-walled hotel with canon was unsuccessful, and it set fire to the interior instead.

54. Three different versions of the speech appeared in northern papers. Atchison always denied he had written the speech. Contemporaries of Atchison stated Atchison's rhetoric was always exaggerated. Parrish, *David Rice Atchison*, 200–201; Etcheson, *Bleeding Kansas*, 105.

55. Sumner always prepared written copies of his intended speeches, practiced beforehand, and delivered each from memory.

56. For a closer examination of the two years of exchanges between Sumner and Butler, see Benson, *The Caning of Senator Sumner*, and Hoffer, *The Caning of Charles Sumner*.

57. Butler returned to Washington in late May.

58. *Congressional Globe*, 34th Cong., 1st sess.

59. Ibid.

60. Lloyd Benson notes an early defense of Second Amendment rights in Sumner's speech when he attacked Butler's call to disarm the Free-Soil settlers. Benson, *The Caning of Senator Sumner*.

61. Williamjames Hoffer states Sumner had already ridiculed Butler's speech impediment in an earlier June floor speech. Hoffer, *The Caning of Charles Sumner*, 58.

62. Harlan Joel Gradin states that from Sumner's earliest days as a young reformer in Boston he was never able to "control the manner in which he disagreed with others," and that he always insisted "on using personal abuses in his speeches." Gradin, "Losing Control," 102; Van Deusen, *William Henry Seward*, 170.

63. Benson, *The Caning of Senator Sumner*.

64. Benson argues Mason's "insults against Sumner were as strong as any in Sumner's speech." Mason's questioning of Sumner's manhood might also have been a veiled reference to Sumner's rumored homosexuality. Harlan Joel Gradin does not directly address Sumner's possible homosexuality but does acknowledge Sumner's obsessive dependence on his male friends, especially Henry Wadsworth Longfellow and Samuel Gridley Howe. He was "devastated" when Howe married, and when Longfellow married, he joined the couple on their honeymoon. Benson, *The Caning of Senator Sumner*, 127; Gradin, "Losing Control," 119–20.

65. *Congressional Globe*, 34th Cong., 1st sess.

66. Brooks's father, Whitfield Brooks, and Andrew Pickens Butler were first cousins. Benson, *The Caning of Senator Sumner*, 24.

67. Gradin, "Losing Control," 35.

68. Gutta percha is made from the sap of trees indigenous to Malaysia. It is a hard rubber-latex type of material that was used in the nineteenth century to make affordable walking sticks. The canes were made to look like the far more expensive black ebony type by dipping them in sulfuric acid to turn them black. The lack of value in the cane itself is evident by the fact that Brooks told his friend, Congressman Laurence Keitt, just to retrieve the gold head. Zasky, "The Rise and Fall of Gutta Percha."

69. The chamber was nearly empty. Sumner said Douglas and Toombes were there and did not help. Historians say they were outside.

70. Williamjames Hoffer argues much of it was tied to his desire to emulate his older brother who had died in the Mexican-American War. Hoffer, *The Caning of Charles Sumner*, 70.

71. Brooks used a walking cane because of a hip injury sustained from a duel that had left him with a limp. Ibid.

72. Wyatt-Brown, *Southern Honor*.

73. Butler returned to Washington immediately upon hearing the news of the caning, arriving there four days later. He delivered his speech in defense of his cousin's actions on June 12 during the Senate debate on whether to censure Butler for "breach of privilege."

74. Harlan Joel Gradin states Sumner's effort to defend himself against Brooks by trying to grab him made Brooks "strike the Senator 'harder' than he intended." Gradin, "Losing Control," 36.

75. Butler was clearly referring to the inferior quality of the gutta percha canes against the stronger and more expensive ebony ones.

76. Ambler, *The Correspondence of Robert M. T. Hunter*, 190.

77. Ibid., 192–93.

78. *Congressional Globe*, 34th Cong., 1st sess.

79. Ibid.

80. Ibid.

81. Ibid.

82. Ibid.

83. Benson, *The Caning of Senator Sumner*, 149.

84. President Pierce had at long last given Colonel E. V. Sumner, commander of U.S. troops in the territory, the authority to assist the territorial governor. On July 4 Sumner dispersed the Topeka legislature, and Governor Shannon began negotiations with the Free-Soil leaders in Lawrence, reaching a truce on August 16. Shortly thereafter, Shannon learned he had been fired by the president and replaced by John Geary of Pennsylvania.

85. The federal troop presence under Shannon had been too few to effectively control the decentralized nature of the conflict.

86. Nevins, *Ordeal of Union*, 470–71.

87. *Poughkeepsie Eagle*, October 4, 1856.

88. French, *Witness to the Young Republic*, 111.

89. *New York Herald*, October 2, 1856.

90. *New York Daily Times*, October 2, 1856.

91. Hunter, *Speech before the Democratic Mass Meeting in Poughkeepsie, October 1, 1856*.

92. Baker, *Affairs of Party*.

93. *New York Tribune*, October 2, 1856; *New York Herald*, October 2, 1856.

94. Ibid.

95. Potter, *The Impending Crisis*.

96. Jean Baker calls it the republicanism of the conservative Democratic Party. Baker, *Affairs of the Party*, 147–48, 153, 177.

97. *Speech of Robert M. T. Hunter of Virginia before the Democratic Mass Meeting in Poughkeepsie, October 1, 1856*.

98. Ibid.

99. Ibid. For more on southern nationalists' rhetorical use of the American Revolution, see Quigley, *Shifting Grounds*.

100. The Kansas-Nebraska Act not only cost northern Democrats sixty-six congressional seats in 1854 and 1855, many Democrats, including Salmon P. Chase, left the party outright. Jean Baker, *Affairs of Party*, 133; Potter, *The Impending Crisis*, 175–76; McPherson, *Battle Cry of Freedom*, 125–26.

101. Potter, *The Impending Crisis*, 313–14.

Chapter Seven

1. Lewis E. Harvie to R. M. T. Hunter November 23, 1856, in Ambler, *The Correspondence of Robert M. T. Hunter*.

2. Moore, "In Search of a Safe Government," 214, n. 2.

3. The Junta and Chivalry joined forces in the 1855 state elections to prevent the American Know Nothing Party from establishing a foothold in Virginia. It was a success. Wise was elected governor but continued to challenge Hunter despite his promises not to. Ibid., 225.

4. Ibid.

5. George Booker to R. M. T. Hunter November 16, 1856, in Ambler, *The Correspondence of Robert M. T. Hunter.*

6. Simms, *The Life of Robert M. T. Hunter*, 105; Nancy Howe, professor of Economics, interview by author, Troy, N.Y., August 6, 2013.

7. David M. Stone to R. M. T. Hunter, March 25, 1856, in Ambler, *The Correspondence of Robert M. T. Hunter.*

8. According to Richard Hofstadter "the wool growers would be crushed if raw wools were admitted free of duty, it was held, and seriously harmed as consumers if manufacturers were protected and increased their prices. On the other hand, if woolen goods were not protected, domestic manufactures would be ruined and the growers deprived of their only market." Hofstadter, "The Tariff Issue on the Eve of the Civil War," 52.

9. The tariff passed in the Senate 33 to 12, in the House 118 to 72. Simms, *The Life of Robert M. T. Hunter*, 106.

10. Butler's estate included fifty-five slaves. *South Carolina Slave Schedules, Edgefield County*, South Carolina Department of Archives and History, Columbia, South Carolina.

11. Mason, *The Public Life of James Murray Mason*, 120.

12. Potter, *The Impending Crisis*, 297.

13. John Geary resigned the governorship the day Buchanan was inaugurated.

14. Rawley, *Race and Politics*, 204.

15. The last major incident was the Marais des Cynges massacre on May 19, 1858. Five Free-Soil men were killed by proslavery vigilantes. Between 1855 and 1858 an estimated fifty-five people died in Bleeding Kansas.

16. The election for delegates to the constitutional convention had been held in June. The Lecompton government's control of the electoral process combined with the refusal of Free-Soil residents to participate assured a proslavery victory. Rawley, *Race and Politics*, 209–10.

17. The Free-Soil movement had won not only the majority of seats in the territorial legislature but also the county office seats and the delegate to Congress. James Rawley called the October elections the "turning point in the history of territorial Kansas." Ibid., 213; David Potter, *The Impending Crisis*, 306.

18. David Potter argues that the proslavery majority backed away from the promise of a full submission to the voters because it was angry at Walker for throwing out the contested returns. Potter, *The Impending Crisis*, 309–10.

19. Ibid., 302–3; Rawley, *Race and Politics*, 215.

20. Johannsen, *Stephen A. Douglas*, 592.

21. James Rawley compares the attendance to that of Daniel Webster's March 7 speech during the crisis of 1850. Rawley, *Race and Politics*, 229.

22. Dec. 9, 1857, 35th Cong., 1st sess.

23. Ibid.

24. Robert Johannsen argues Walker would never have been confirmed by the Senate. Johannsen, *Stephen A. Douglas*, 594.

25. According to James Rawley, a later investigating committee found 2,720 fraudulent votes. Rawley, *Race and Politics*, 233.

26. The 162 votes were cast for the partial submission, 138 for the constitution "with slavery" and 24 "without slavery." Ibid.

27. Robert Johannsen argues the Lecompton debates were anticlimactic, stating "the arguments had all been expressed before, and little that was new was advanced." Johannsen, *Stephen A. Douglas*, 606.

28. Douglas fell ill in March and was absent for most of the debate. He did not return until the last day of debate, March 22. Ibid., 607.

29. Only three northern Democrats followed Douglas in opposing Lecompton: Broderick of California, Pugh of Ohio, and Stuart of Michigan. Allen Johnson, *Stephen A. Douglas*, 335.

30. Mason did not deliver a speech on the Lecompton Constitution, but his biographer Robert Young is incorrect when he states Mason was largely absent from the debate. Mason regularly attended sessions during March and interjected himself into the debates on March 8, 14, and 24.

31. Democrat Jefferson Davis was first elected to the U.S. Senate in 1847. He resigned in 1851 for what was to be an unsuccessful bid for governor of Mississippi. He next served as Pierce's secretary of war from 1853 to 1857, after which he was reelected to the Senate. Former Whig Robert Toombs was first elected to Congress in 1845. He switched parties in 1852 and was elected the same year to the U.S. Senate.

32. Hunter later won reelection in the state legislature 185 to 10. Simms, *The Life of Robert M. T. Hunter*, 137–39.

33. *Congressional Globe*, 35th Cong., 1st sess.

34. Ibid.

35. Ibid.

36. Palmer, *The Age of Democratic Revolution: A Political History of Europe and America, 1760–1800*.

37. Robert Johannsen argues that many southerners and many Democrats worried about the wisdom of admitting a slave state into the Union that had just elected a Republican governor and Republican legislature, fearing that neither slavery nor the state Democratic Party would last long. Johannsen, *Stephen A. Douglas*, 603.

38. *Congressional Globe*, 35th Cong., 1st sess.

39. The new state clause in the constitution had originally read "new States shall be admitted on the same terms with the original States." The line was removed on a motion by Gouverneur Morris over the objections of James Madison. However the first Congresses, "utilizing the discretion allowed by the Framers, adopted the policy of equal status for newly admitted states." Forte, "New States Clause."

40. *Congressional Globe*, 35th Cong., 1st sess. For more on the inherent racism in both the pro- and antislavery positions, see James A. Rawley's *Race and Politics*.

41. John Randolph Tucker to R. M. T. Hunter, November 6, 1858, in Ambler, *The Correspondence of Robert M. T. Hunter*.

42. Ball Invitation, February 17, 1859, Willard Family Papers, Manuscript Division, Library of Congress.

43. Lewis Harvie to R. M. T. Hunter October 18, 1859, in Ambler, *The Correspondence of Robert M. T. Hunter*.

44. The convention met from April 23 to May 3.

45. "Charles W. Russell to R. M. T. Hunter, May 24, 1860," in Ambler, *The Correspondence of Robert M. T. Hunter*, 329.

46. Ambler, *The Correspondence of Robert M. T. Hunter*.

47. Henry Wise's ideological stands are only logical in the context of his competition with Hunter. He opposed the proslavery Lecompton Constitution which Hunter supported and called for immediate secession when Hunter called for negotiations.

48. The term "moderate" has been used historically to describe those southern politicians who advocated "union, conciliation, and moderation in the face of Republican intransigence and southern extremism." Hitchcock, "Southern Moderates and Secession," 872.

49. Crow, "R. M. T. Hunter and the Secession Crisis, 1860-1861," 277.

50. James McPherson states South Carolina had been demanding the cession of all federal property within the state since before the state's actual secession on December 20. He describes Fort Moultrie as "an obsolete work a mile across the bay from Sumter on an island easily accessible from the mainland and exposed to capture from the rear." McPherson, *Battle Cry of Freedom*, 264-65; Crow, "R. M. T. Hunter and the Secession Crisis," 279.

51. Simms, *The Life of Robert M. T. Hunter*, 180; Crow, "R. M. T. Hunter and the Secession Crisis," 279.

52. McPherson, *Battle Cry of Freedom*, 265-66.

53. Robert Young, *James Murray Mason*, 100.

54. Moore, "Robert M. T. Hunter and the Crisis of Union, 1860-1861," 25; D. R. Anderson "R. M. T. Hunter"; Martha Hunter, *Robert M. T. Hunter*; Crow, "R. M. T Hunter and the Secession Crisis," 276-77.

55. Hitchcock, "Southern Moderates and Secession."

56. Ibid., 878.

57. Shenk, *Lincoln's Melancholy*, 171; Foner, *The Fiery Trial*, 153.

58. McPherson, *Battle Cry of Freedom*, 254.

59. The order of secession was South Carolina, December 20; Mississippi, January 9; Florida, January 10; Alabama, January 11; and Georgia, January 19. The two remaining lower south states, Louisiana and Texas would secede January 26 and February 1, respectively.

60. Hitchcock, "Southern Moderates and Secession," 881.

61. Hunter and Mason opposed the possible election of radical fire-eater William Yancy to the Confederate presidency and warned that Virginia would not secede if it occurred. Robert Young, *James Murray Mason*, 101; Simms, *The Life of Robert M. T. Hunter*, 180; D. R. Anderson, "R. M. T. Hunter," 63; Crow, "R. M. T. Hunter and the Secession Crisis," 283.

62. Butler and Wolff, *United States Senate Election*, 90.

63. The action also allowed for a new senator with credentials to be seated. Ibid., 91.

64. The Thirty-Seventh Congress immediately convened in a special session from March 4 to March 28. There is some debate over exactly when Hunter and Mason left Washington. William Hitchcock has Hunter leaving the week before adjournment. Randall Moore states they left on the last day, March 28. Hitchcock, "Southern Moderates and Secession," 881; Moore, "In Search of a Safe Government," 33.

65. Hunter supported Seward for secretary of state because Seward had promised Fort Sumter would be abandoned.

66. Case no. 36 in Butler and Wolff, *United States Senate*, 97.

Epilogue

1. Lincoln and the war congress did not recognize the constitutionality of secession. As "domestic insurrectionists," the Confederates were denied belligerent status under international law. Foreign nations could not conduct business with the Confederacy. But when the United States blockaded the east coast, which under international law is an act of war, this granted belligerent status to the Confederacy under international law, thereby allowing Great Britain and other nations to declare neutrality and conduct international relations with the Confederacy. Great Britain declared her neutrality on May 13, 1861. An incensed Secretary of State William Seward sent a message to Great Britain threatening the severing of diplomatic relations. President Lincoln stepped in. The message was not delivered in writing. Instead newly arrived American minister Charles Francis Adams met personally with England's foreign minister, Lord Russell. The situation between the United States and Great Britain remained tense when Mason and Slidell left for Europe. For a detailed analysis of the intricacies and nuances regarding neutrality and belligerent status under international law, see McPherson, *Battle Cry of Freedom*, 387–88.

2. James McPherson argues it was the U.S. purchase of British saltpeter, needed for the production of gun powder and blocked by the embargo, that was the primary factor in the release of Mason and Slidell. Ibid., 390.

3. As a child during the War of 1812, Mason often accompanied his father, the commissioner general of prisoners, on his camp inspections. Mason would bring the British prisoners gifts of food and books. Half century later in London at a private reception in his honor, Mason was reintroduced to one of the former prisoners he had befriended as a boy. Robert Young, *James Murray Mason*, 3.

4. Mason's biographers state he met unofficially with Lord Russell, but James McPherson states that the unofficial meetings between Russell and Confederate envoys occurred before Mason's arrival. One of the consequences of Mason and Slidell's release was the improved relations between the United States and Great Britain. Russell had a good working relationship with Charles Francis Adams and never again held unofficial meetings with any Confederate, including Mason. McPherson, *Battle Cry of Freedom*, 389.

5. Fisher, "Statesman of the Lost Cause," 251; Martha T. Hunter, *A Memoir of Robert M. T. Hunter*, 118, 159.

6. Martha T. Hunter, *A Memoir of Robert M. T. Hunter*, 120.

7. Simms, *The Life of Robert M. T. Hunter*, 200.

8. Stahr, *Seward: Lincoln's Indispensable Man*, 422.

9. Hunter blamed both Davis and Lincoln for prolonging the war. See "The Peace Commission—Hon. R. M. T. Hunter's Reply to President Davis' Letter," 306-8.

10. Stahr, *Seward: Lincoln's Indispensable Man*, 423.

11. Stahr argues that Seward "was prepared to delay ratification of the antislavery amendment in order to hasten the reunification of the nation. But that did not mean he or Lincoln was willing to go back on the amendment. Seward wanted the South to be a part of the abolition of slavery and believed in the end it would be. Ibid., 425.

12. Ibid., 426.

13. Walter Stahr bases his account of and quotations from the meeting on the personal recollections left by Alexander Stephens and John Campbell. Ibid.; Van Deusen, *William Henry Seward*, 385.

14. R. M. T. Hunter, "R. M. T. Hunter's Reply to President Davis' Letter," 313; R. M. T. Hunter to James R. Micou et al., December 10, 1860, in Ambler, *The Correspondence of Robert M. T. Hunter*; Simms, *The Life of Robert M. T. Hunter*, 196-97; Fisher, "Statesman of the Lost Cause," 239.

15. The bill's passage owed much to Robert E. Lee's support of the measure.

16. R. M. T. Hunter, "R. M. T. Hunter's Reply to President Davis' Letter," 306.

17. Ibid., 309.

18. Martha T. Hunter, *A Memoir of Robert M. T. Hunter*, 116.

19. Robert Selden Garnett to R. M. T. Hunter April 20, 1856, in Ambler, *The Correspondence of Robert M. T. Hunter*.

20. Ibid.

21. The house caught fire in 1870, destroying most of Atchison's papers. Parrish, *David Rice Atchison*, 223.

22. Ibid., 217.

23. Atchison was referring to the twenty-four-hour period between Polk's presidency that ended on a Sunday and Taylor's presidency that began on a Monday.

24. Robert Young, *James Murray Mason*, 187-89.

25. Canada's southern border towns had been home to runaway slaves from the American South for years.

26. John Dawson to R. M. T. Hunter, August 17, 1858, in Ambler, *The Correspondence of Robert M. T. Hunter*.

27. Moore, "In Search of a Safe Government," 335.

28. Ibid., 330; Simms, *The Life of Robert M. T. Hunter*, 206.

29. Simms, *The Life of Robert M. T. Hunter*, 207.

30. Kerber, *Women of the Republic*, 93-94.

31. Moore, "In Search of a Safe Government," 346.

32. The postwar "Lost Cause" was and remains a swirling vortex of mythology that includes the ancillary myth of continuity between "Old South" and "New South." This myth was given credence by W. J. Cash in his seminal study on southern identity, *The Mind of the South*. Cash argued that southern leadership at the state and federal level remained the same before and after the war. If we accept his argument, the Slave Power simply was resurrected in another guise. Indeed, through the use of white primaries, poll taxes, literacy tests, and other voter suppression measures, white southern Democrats regained control of their state legislatures, seniority in Congress, and with it

their former committee chairs. But Cash's argument was challenged in the 1960s by C. Vann Woodward. Beginning with his 1951 study of the postwar South, *Origins of the New South*, and numerous works after, Woodward argued that a "change of guard" had occurred after the war, from a white aristocracy based in ownership of land and slaves to a new entrepreneur class whose power was based in capitalism and industry. Woodward further argues that those planters who managed to make the change did so not just economically but philosophically as well, accepting fully the new ethos of market capitalism.

33. The Readjusters lost power with the rise of white violence in the 1880s. By 1886 the state was back in control of the white Democratic Party. Levin, "Who Were the Readjusters?"

34. Fisher, "Statesman of the Lost Cause," 279.

BIBLIOGRAPHY

Archival Sources

Charlottesville, Va.
  Alderman Library Special Collections, University of Virginia
    A. P. Aldrich, *A Memoir of A. P. Butler* (Charleston: Evans & Cogswell printers)
    Papers of R. M. T. Hunter, 1817–1887, microfilm
Columbia, Mo.
  Western Historical Manuscript Collection, University of Missouri and State Historical Society
    David Rice Atchison Papers, 1837–1953, Roll no. 1, Folder no. 1
Columbia, S.C.
  South Caroliniana Library, Manuscript Collection
    Preston Smith Brooks Papers (1819–57)
    Andrew Pickens Butler, Pierce Mason Butler, and Butler Family Papers, 1767–1970
Richmond, Va.
  Virginia Historical Society
    William Gibson Guerrant, "Letter to His Father 1858, Feb. 28"
Savannah, Ga.
  National Park Service, Fort Pulaski National Monument
    The War of the Rebellion: A Compilation of the Official Records of the Union and Confederate Armies, series 1, vols. 46, 47, and 49; series 2, vol. 8
Urbana, Ill.
  University of Illinois at Urbana-Champaign Archives
    Robert W. Johannsen, Notes
Washington, D.C.
  Manuscript Division, Library of Congress
    W. W. Corcoran Papers
    Gideon Welles Papers
    Willard Family Papers

Published Primary Sources

Ambler, Charles Henry, ed. *The Correspondence of Robert M. T. Hunter, 1826–1876*. New York: DaCapo Press, 1971.

"Appeal of the Independent Democrats, January 19, 1854." Accessed July 2, 2012. http://teachingamericanhistory.org.

Aristotle. *The Ethics of Aristotle: The Nicomachean Ethics*. Translated by J. A. K. Thomson. 1952. Reprint, Penguin Books, 1986.

Baker, George E., ed. *The Works of William H. Seward*, vol. 4. Boston: Houghton, Mifflin, 1889.

Benton, Thomas Hart. "Jefferson City Speech, 26 May 1849." Internet Archive. Accessed Mar. 2, 2011. http://www.archive.org.

———. *Thirty Years' View; or, A History of the Working of the American Government for Thirty Years from 1820 to 1850*, vol. 2. New York: D. Appleton, 1866.

Bleser, Carol, ed. *The Hammonds of Redcliffe*. New York: Oxford University Press, 1981.

———. *Secret and Sacred: The Diaries of James Henry Hammond, a Southern Slave Owner*. New York: Oxford University Press, 1988.

Business Department of the Washington City Directory for 1850. Washington, D.C.: C. Alexander Printer, 1850.

Calhoun, John C. *The Papers of John C. Calhoun*, vol. 14, *1837–1839*. Edited by Clyde N. Wilson. Columbia: University of South Carolina Press, 1981.

———. *The Papers of John C. Calhoun*, vol. 15, *1839–1841*. Edited by Clyde N. Wilson. Columbia: University of South Carolina Press, 1983.

———. *The Papers of John C. Calhoun*, vol. 27, *1849–1850*. Edited by Clyde N. Wilson. Columbia: University of South Carolina Press, 2003.

———. *The Papers of John C. Calhoun*, vol. 27, *1849–1850*, with Supplement. Edited by Clyde N. Wilson and Shirley Bright Cook. Columbia: University of South Carolina Press, 2003.

———. "The Southern Address, 1850." Accessed Jan. 24, 2011. http://eweb.furman.edu.

"Census of 1860 Population Effect on the Representation of the Free and Slave States." *New York Times*, Apr. 5, 1860. Accessed Apr. 27, 2011. http://www.nytimes.com.

Chislett, John. "Journal Entry, October 1856." *The Pioneer Story*. Accessed Mar. 30, 2011. http://lds.org/library/pio_sto/Pioneer_Trail/31_South_Pass.html.

Congressional Directory for the Thirty-First Congress of the United States of America: Index to the Diagram of the Senate. Washington, D.C.: G. S. Gideon, 1850.

Congressional Directory for the Thirty-Third Congress of the United States of America: Index to the Diagram of the Senate. Washington, D.C.: G. S. Gideon, 1854.

Davis, Jefferson. "Address to the National Democracy, May 7, 1860." Rice University. *The Papers of Jefferson Davis*. Accessed Sept. 23, 2013. http://jeffersondavis.rice.edu.

———. *The Papers of Jefferson Davis*, vol. 4, *1849–1852*. Edited by Lynda Lasswell Crist. Baton Rouge: Louisiana State University Press, 1983.

———. *The Rise and Fall of the Confederate Government*, vol. 1. New York: Thomas Yoseloff, 1958.

Davis, Varina. *Jefferson Davis, Ex-President of the Confederate States of America: A Memoir*, vol. 1. New York: Belford, 1890.

Dixon, Mrs. Archibald. *History of the Missouri Compromise and Slavery in American Politics: A True History of the Missouri Compromise and Its Repeal, and of African Slavery as a Factor in American Politics*. 1903. Reprint, New York: Johnson Reprint, 1970.

Douglas, Stephen A. "Douglas Report, January 4, 1884." http:www.historycentral.com/documents/Douglas.html. Accessed May 31, 2012.

French, Benjamin Brown. *Witness to the Young Republic: A Yankee's Journal, 1828–1870.* Edited by Donald B. Cole and John J. McDonough. Hanover: University Press of New England, 1989.

Hart, Albert Bushnell, and Edward Channing. *Documents Relating to the Kansas-Nebraska Act, 1854.* New York: A. Lovell, 1894.

Hunter, Martha T. *A Memoir of Robert M. T. Hunter.* Washington, D.C.: Neale Publishing, 1903.

Hunter, R. M. T. "The Peace Commission—Hon. R. M. T. Hunter's Reply to President Davis' Letter." *Southern Historical Society Papers* 4, no. 6 (Dec. 1872): 303–18.

———. *Speech before the Democratic Meeting at Poughkeepsie, October 1, 1856.* New York: J. W. Bell, Daily News Job Office, 1856.

———. "Speech of Mr. Hunter of Virginia, October 11, 1837."

———. "Speech of Mr. Hunter of Virginia, June 22, 1838."

Johannsen, Robert W. *The Letters of Stephen A. Douglas.* Urbana: University of Illinois Press, 1961.

Journal of the American Geographical and Statistical Society, vol. 1. New York: John H. Schultz, 1859.

Journal of the Executive Proceedings of the Senate of the United States of America, Thursday, January 26, 1854.

Journal of the Senate of the State of Missouri, Eleventh General Assembly, 1840, and Thirteenth General Assembly, 1844. Missouri State Archives, Jefferson City.

"July 18, 1847, Presidential Succession Act." Accessed Aug. 20, 2009. http://senate.gove/artandhistory.

Kappler, Charles J., ed. *Indian Affairs: Laws and Treaties*, vol. 2. Washington, D.C.: Government Printing House, 1904.

Laws of a Public and General Nature, of the District of Louisiana, of the Territory of Missouri and the State of Missouri, up to the Year 1824, vol. 1. Jefferson City: W. Lusk & Son, 1842. Missouri State Archives, Jefferson City.

"Lecompton Constitution, November 7 1857." Kansas Memory. www.kansasmemory.org.

Lincoln, Abraham. "A House Divided, June 16, 1858." In *The Collected Works of Abraham Lincoln II, 1848–1858*, edited by Roy P. Basler, 461–68. New Brunswick: Rutgers University Press, 1953.

Madison, James. *Federalist No. 10.* http://www.constitution.org/fed/federal10.htm. Accessed November 17, 2005.

"Map Showing the Distribution of the Slave Population of the Southern States of the United States." 1850 U.S. Federal Census. Accessed Apr. 27, 2011. http://www.vizworld.com.

Mason, James Murray. "Speech of Mr. Mason, October 11, 1837." 25th Cong., 1st sess.

Mason, Virginia. *The Public Life of James M. Mason: With Some Personal History by Virginia Mason (His Daughter).* New York: Neale Publishing, 1906.

Niven, John, ed. *The Salmon P. Chase Papers*, vols. 1 and 2. Kent, Ohio: Kent State University Press, 1993–98.

O'Neall, John Belton. *Biographical Sketches of the Bench and Bar of South Carolina.* Charleston: S. G. Courtenay, 1859.

Pierce, Franklin. "First Annual Message, December 5, 1853." American Presidency Project. Accessed Jan. 9, 2012. http://www/presidency.ucsb.edu.

Slave Schedules. 1850 U.S. Federal Census. Accessed May 13, 2011. http://search.ancestry.com.

Slave Schedules. 1860 U.S. Federal Census. Missouri State Archives, Jefferson City. archref@sos.mo.gov/archives.

South Carolina Slave Schedules, Edgefield County, 1850. South Carolina Department of Archives and History, Columbia, South Carolina.

Stephens, Alexander H. *A Constitutional View of the Late War between the States: Its Causes, Character, Conduct and Results*, vol. 1. Philadelphia: National Publishing, 1868.

Strader v. Graham-51 U.S. 82 (1850). Accessed July 18, 2012. http://supreme.justice.com/cases/federal/us/51/82/case.html.

Ten Eyck's Washington and Georgetown Directory, 1855. Washington Historical Society, Washington, D.C.

U.S. Congress. *Congressional Globe*. 21st Cong., 1st sess., 1830-31; 25th Cong., 1st sess., 1837; 25th Cong., 2nd sess., 1837-38; 26th Cong., 1st sess., 1839-40; 31st Cong., 1st sess., 1849-50; 33rd Cong., 1st sess., 1853-54; 35th Cong., 1st sess., 1857-58; 36th Cong., 2nd sess., 1860-61.

U.S. Congress. Senate. *A Bill to Organize the Territory of Nebraska*. 33rd Cong., 1st sess. *Congressional Globe*, Jan. 4, 1854, 522; *Congressional Globe*, Jan. 16, 1854, Amendment by Mr. Dixon to 522.

U.S. War Department. *The War of the Rebellion: A Compilation of the Official Records of the Union and Confederate Armies* 46, no. 1, part III. Accessed June 30, 2008. http://cdl.library.cornell.edu.

———. Series 1, XLVII, part III; Series II, VIII.

Warren, G. K. "Geography and Resources of Nebraska." *Journal of the American Geographical and Statistical Society* 1 (1859): 257-68. http://www.jstor.org/stable/196262. Accessed Mar. 4, 2011.

Washington and Georgetown Directory and Congressional and Clerks' Register. Washington, D.C.: Kirkwood & McGill, 1853.

Washington and Georgetown Directory, with a Complete Congressional and Department Directory. Washington, D.C.: I. Ten Eyck, 1855.

The Washington Directory and Congressional and Executive Register for 1850. Washington, D.C.: Ed Waite, 1850.

The Washington Directory: Part 1, 1846. Washington Historical Society, Washington D.C.

Whipple, Nelson W. "Journal Entry, August 1850." *The Pioneer Story*. Accessed Mar. 30, 2011. http://lds.org/library/pio_sto/Pioneer_Trail/31_South_Pass.html.

Wilson, Henry, and Samuel Hunt. *The Rise and Fall of the Slave Power in America*. Boston: James R. Osgood, 1872.

Unpublished Secondary Sources

Buggs, James Luckin, Jr. "The Political Career of James Murray Mason: The Legislative Phase." Ph.D. diss., University of Virginia, 1950.

Fisher, John E. "Statesman of the Lost Cause: R. M. T. Hunter and the Sectional Controversy, 1847-1887." Ph.D. diss., University of Virginia, 1968.

Gradin, Harlan Joel. "Losing Control: The Caning of Charles Sumner and the Breakdown of Antebellum Political Culture." Ph.D. diss., University of North Carolina, 1991.

Martin, David L. "David Rice Atchison: The President That Wasn't—or Was He?" David Rice Atchison file. U.S. Senate, Senate Historical Office, Washington, D.C.

Moore, Richard Randal. "In Search of a Safe Government: A Biography of R. M. T. Hunter of Virginia." Ph.D. diss., University of Virginia, 1993.

Powers, Annie. "'If Men Should Fight': Dueling as Sectional Politics, 1850–1856." Charles H. Perry Undergraduate Grant for Public Affairs Research Papers, Institute of Government Studies, UC Berkeley. eScholarship, 2011.

Roberts, Eda Isabel. "The Life of David Rice Atchison as Told by Himself and Contemporaries." Master's thesis. University of Chicago, 1920.

Taylor, Michael C. J. "The Tinge of the Tempest: The Kansas-Nebraska Act and the Destruction of the Franklin Pierce Presidency, 1853–1857." Master's thesis, University of Missouri, 1997.

"Western Expansion and the Compromise of 1850." In *Congress and the Shaping of American History*, vol. 1, *1789–1865*. National Archives, Center for Legislative Archives, Washington, D.C. Proof #4.3, Aug. 2, 2001. U.S. Senate, Senate Historical Office, Washington, D.C.

Published Secondary Sources

Agresto, John. "John C. Calhoun and the Reexamination of American Democracy." In *History of American Political Thought*, edited by Bryan-Paul Frost and Jeffrey Sikkenga, 316–24. New York: Lexington Books, 2003.

Allen, William C. *History of the United States Capitol: A Chronicle of Design, Construction, and Politics*. Washington, D.C.: U.S. Government Printing Office, 2001.

Allgor, Catherine. *Parlor Politics: In Which the Ladies of Washington Help Build a City and a Government*. Charlottesville: University of Virginia Press, 2000.

Ambrose, Stephen E. *Nothing Like It in the World: The Men Who Built the Transcontinental Railroad, 1863–1869*. New York: Simon and Schuster, 2000.

Ammon, Harry. "The Richmond Junto, 1800–1824." *Virginia Magazine of History and Biography* 61, no. 4 (Oct. 1953): 395–418. Accessed Jan. 10, 2012. http://www.jstor.org.

"Ancient Athens-Erechtheion." Accessed Aug. 31, 2011. http://www.athens-greece.us/acropolis/erechtheion.

Anderson, D. R. "R. M. T. Hunter." *The John P. Branch Historical Society Papers* 2, no. 2 (June 1906): 4–77.

Anderson, James LaVerne. "Robert Mercer Taliaferro Hunter." *Virginia Cavalcade* 18, no. 2 (Aug. 1968): 9–13.

Anderson, James LaVerne, and W. Edwin Hemphill. "The 1843 Biography of John C. Calhoun: Was R. M. T. Hunter It's Author?" *Journal of Southern History* 48, no. 3 (Aug. 1972): 469–74. Accessed July 10, 2010. http://www.jstor.org.

Anthony, Carl Sferrazza. *America's First Families: An Inside View of 200 Years of Private Life in the White House*. New York: Simon & Schuster, 2000.

Atchison, Theodore C. "David R. Atchison: A Study in American Politics." *Missouri Historical Review* 24, no. 4 (July 1930): 502–15.

Bailyn, Bernard. *The Ideological Origins of the American Revolution*. Cambridge, Mass.: Belknap Press, 1967.

———. *The Origins of American Politics*. New York: Vintage Books, 1967.

Baker, Jean. *Affairs of Party: The Political Culture of Northern Democrats in the Mid-Nineteenth Century*. Ithaca: Cornell University Press, 1983.

Baker, Richard A. *Traditions of the United States Senate*. Senate Publication 110-11.

Baker, Ross K. *Friend and Foe in the U.S. Senate*. Acton, Mass.: Copley Publishing Group, 1999.

Barrington, Linda. "Native Americans and U.S. Economic History." In *The Other Side of the Frontier: Economic Explorations into Native American History*, edited by Linda Barrington, 1–52. Boulder: Westview Press, 1999.

Bartlett, Irving H. *John C. Calhoun: A Biography*. New York: W. W. Norton, 1993.

Battle Summary: Fort Pulaski, GA. American Battlefield Protection Program. Accessed May 6, 2008. http://www.nps.gov.

Beach, Rex. "Spencer Roane and the Richmond Junto." *William and Mary Quarterly*, 2nd ser., 22, no. 1 (Jan. 1942): 1–17. Accessed Feb. 16, 2011. http://www.jstor.org.

Becker, Carl. "The Unit Rule in National Nominating Conventions." *American Historical Review* 5, no. 1 (Oct. 1899): 64–82. Accessed July 23, 2013. http://www.jstor.org.

Benson, T. Lloyd. *The Caning of Senator Sumner*. Belmont, Calif.: Wadsworth/Thomson Learning, 2004.

Biographical Directory of the South Carolina Senate, 1776-1985, vol. 1. Columbia: University of South Carolina Press, 1986.

Biographical Directory of the United States Congress, 1774-Present. Accessed Feb.–May, 2011. http://bioguide.congress.gov.

"Bloody Bill Cunningham and the Cloud's Creek Massacre." Accessed Feb. 15, 2011. http://sciway2.net/2003/revwar-sc-midlands.

Bogue, Allan G., and Mark Paul Marlaire. "Of Mess and Men: The Boarding House and Congressional Voting: 1821-1842." *American Journal of Political Science* 19, no. 2 (May 1975): 207–30. Accessed June 3, 2014. http://www.jstor.org.

Boucher, Chauncey S. "In Re That Aggressive Slavocracy." *Mississippi Valley Historical Review* 8, nos. 1–2 (June–Sept. 1921): 13–79. Accessed July 1, 2002. http://www.jstor.org.

Brainard, Rick. "The Zebulon Pike Expedition of 1806/07." 18th Century History. Accessed Mar. 28, 2011. http://history1700s.com/articles.

Brown, Guy Stone. *Calhoun's Philosophy of Politics: A Study of a Disquisition on Government*. Macon, Ga.: Mercer University Press, 2000.

Burton, Orville Vernon. *In My Father's House Are Many Mansions: Family and Community in Edgefield, South Carolina*. Chapel Hill: University of North Carolina Press, 1985.

Butler, Anne M., and Wendy Wolff. *United States Senate: Election, Expulsion and Censure Cases, 1793-1990*. Washington, D.C.: Government Printing Office, 1995.

Byrd, Robert C. *The Senate: 1789-1989, Historical Statistics: 1789-1992*. Washington, D.C.: U.S. Government Printing Office, 1993.

Capers, Gerald M. "A Reconsideration of John Calhouns Transition from Nationalism to Nullification." In *John C. Calhoun: A Profile*, edited by John L. Thomas, 74–88. New York: Hill and Wang, 1981.

---. *John C. Calhoun-Opportunist: A Reappraisal*. 1960. Reprint, Chicago: Quadrangle Books, 1969.

---. *Stephen A. Douglas: Defender of the Union*. Boston: Little, Brown, 1959.

Cash, W. J. *The Mind of the South*. New York: Vintage Books, 1941.

Chaffin, Tom. *Pathfinder: John Charles Fremont and the Course of American Empire*. New York: Hill and Wang, 2002.

Chambers, William Nisbit. *Old Bullion Benton – Senator from the New West: Thomas Hart Benton, 1782–1858*. Boston: Little, Brown, 1956.

Cheek, H. Lee, Jr. *Calhoun and Popular Rule: The Political Theory of the Disquisition and Discourse*. Columbia: University of Missouri Press, 2001.

"Clouds Creek." Accessed Feb. 15, 2011. http://gaz.jrselby.com.

Cloutier, Philip R. "John C. Breckinridge Superior City Land Speculator." Reprinted in the *Register of the Kentucky Historical Society*, January 1959. Kentucky Department for Libraries and Archives, Frankfort, Ky.

Coit, Margaret L. *John C. Calhoun: American Portrait*. Boston: Houghton Mifflin, 1950.

Combs, H. Jason. "Early Settlement of a Frontier Community: The Platte Purchase, 1836–1850." ETD Collection for the University of Nebraska. Accessed Mar. 30, 2011. http://digitalcommons.unl.edu/dissertations/AA19967413.

Cooper, William J., Jr. *Jefferson Davis: American*. New York: Alfred A. Knopf, 2000.

Cooper, William J., Jr., and Thomas E. Terrill. *The American South: A History*, vol. 1. Boston: McGraw Hill, 2002.

Creigh, Dorothy Weyer. *Nebraska: A Bicentennial History*. New York: W. W. Norton, 1977.

Crofts, Daniel W. *Old Southampton: Politics and Society in a Virginia County, 1834–1869*. Charlottesville: University Press of Virginia, 1992.

Crow, Jeffrey J. "R. M. T. Hunter and the Secession Crisis, 1860–1861: A Southern Plan for Reconstruction." *West Virginia History* 34, no. 3 (Apr. 1973): 273–90.

Cunningham, Noble E., Jr. "Who Were the Quids?" *Mississippi Valley Historical Review* 50, no. 2 (Sept. 1963): 252–63. Accessed Aug. 8, 2010. http://www.jstor.org.

Current, Richard N. *John C. Calhoun*. Great American Thinkers Series. New York: Washington Square Press, 1966.

Davis, David Byron. *The Slave Power Conspiracy and the Paranoid Style*. Baton Rouge: Louisiana State University Press, 1969.

Davis, Kenneth Sydney. *Kansas: A Bicentennial History*. New York: W. W. Norton, 1976.

Davis, William C. *The Union That Shaped the Confederacy: Robert Toombs and Alexander H. Stephens*. Lawrence: University Press of Kansas, 2001.

Deschler's Precedents. Chap. 1, section 2. Washington, D.C.: Government Printing Office, 1973. https://www.gpo.gov/fdsys/pkg/GPO-HPREC-DESCHLERS-V1/html/GPO-HPREC-DESCHLERS-V1-1-2-6.htm.

Diket, A. L. "Slidell's Right Hand: Emile La Sere." *Louisiana History: The Journal of the Louisiana Historical Association* 1, no. 3 (Summer 1963): 177–205. Accessed June 28, 2011. http://www.jstor.org.

Dirck, Brian R. *Lincoln the Lawyer*. Urbana: University of Illinois Press, 2009.

Donald, David Herbert. *Charles Sumner and the Coming of the Civil War*. New York: Alfred A. Knopf, 1961.

Eaton, Clemont. *Freedom of Thought in the Old South*. New York: Peter Smith, 1951.

———. *Jefferson Davis*. New York: Free Press, 1977.
Egnal, Marc. *Clash of Extremes: The Economic Origins of the Civil War*. New York: Hill and Wang, 2009.
Eidson, William G. "Recent Scholarship on the Lincoln Assassination." *Filson Club History Quarterly* 62 (Apr. 1988): 220–50.
Etcheson, Nicole. *Bleeding Kansas: Contested Liberty in the Civil War Era*. Lawrence: University Press of Kansas.
Fehr, Beverly. *Friendship Processes*. Thousand Oaks: Sage, 1996.
Festinger, Leon. *A Theory of Cognitive Dissonance*. Stanford, Calif.: Stanford University Press, 1957.
Finkelman, Paul. *An Imperfect Union: Slavery, Federalism, and Comity*. Chapel Hill: University of North Carolina Press, 1981.
———. *Slavery in the Courtroom: An Annotated Bibliography of American Cases*. Washington, D.C.: Library of Congress, 1985.
Fisher, John E. "The Dilemma of a States' Rights Whig: The Congressional Career of R. M. T. Hunter, 1837–1841." *Virginia Magazine of History and Biography* 81, no. 4 (Oct. 1973): 387–404.
Foner, Eric. *The Fiery Trial: Abraham Lincoln and American Slavery*. New York: W. W. Norton, 2010.
———. *Free Soil, Free Labor, Free Men: The Ideology of the Republican Party before the Civil War*. New York: Oxford University Press, 1970.
———. *The Story of American Freedom*. New York: W. W. Norton, 1998.
Ford, Lacy K., Jr. *Origins of Southern Radicalism: The South Carolina Upcountry, 1800–1860*. New York: Oxford University Press, 1988.
Forte, David F. "New States Clause." *The Heritage Guide to the Constitution*. Accessed June 3, 2014. http://www.heritage.org.
Frank, Seymour J. "The Conspiracy to Implicate the Confederate Leaders in Lincoln's Assassination." *Mississippi Valley Historical Review* 40, no. 4 (Mar. 1954): 629–56. Accessed May 6, 2008. http://wwwmjstor.org.
Freehling, William W. *The Road to Disunion: Secessionists at Bay, 1776–1854*. New York: Oxford University Press, 1990.
Friedman, Lawrence M. *A History of American Law*. New York: Simon and Schuster, 1973.
Fuenfhausen, Gary Gene. "Slave Housing in Missouri's Little Dixie: A Partial List of Little Dixie Plantations and/or Houses with Slave Quarters." Missouri's Little Dixie. Accessed Apr. 27, 2011. http://littledixie.net/slave%Housing.t=ht.
Gamm, Gerald, and Steven S. Smith. "Last among Equals: The Senate's Presiding Officer." Paper presented at the annual meeting of the American Political Science Association, Boston, Sept. 3–6, 1998.
Gara, Larry. *The Presidency of Franklin Pierce*. Lawrence: University Press of Kansas, 1991.
———. "Slavery and the Slave Power: A Crucial Distinction." *Civil War History: A Journal of the Middle Period* 15, no. 1 (Mar. 1969): 5–18.
Gates, Paul Wallace. "Southern Investments in Northern Lands before the Civil War." *Journal of Southern History* 5, no. 2, (May 1953): 155–85. Accessed June 6, 2012. http://www.jstor.org.

Genovese, Eugene D. *The Southern Tradition: The Achievement and Limitations of an American Conservatism*. Cambridge, Mass.: Harvard University Press, 1994.

"Geographical Distribution of Slavery." Missouri History. Accessed Apr. 27, 2011. http://Missouri-history.itgo.com/slave.html.

Gienapp, William E. *The Origins of the Republican Party, 1852–1856*. New York: Oxford University Press, 1987.

Gilje, Paul A. *The Road to Mobocracy: Popular Disorder in New York City, 1763–1834*. Chapel Hill: University of North Carolina Press, 1987.

Gittinger, Roy. "The Separation of Nebraska and Kansas from the Indian Territory." *Mississippi Valley Historical Review* 3, no. 4 (Mar. 1917): 442–61. Accessed Mar. 14, 2011. http://www.jstor.org.

Goldstein, Mark L. "Washington and the Networks of W. W. Corcoran." Business and Economic History On-Line. Business History Conference, 2007. http://www.thebhc.org.

Goodwin, Doris Kearns. *Team of Rivals: The Political Genius of Abraham Lincoln*. New York: Simon and Schuster, 2005.

Gugliotta, Guy. "New Estimate Raises Civil War Death Toll." *New York Times*, Apr. 2, 2012. Accessed June 11, 2014. http://www.nytimes.com.

Hacker, J. David. "Counting the Civil War Dead." *Civil War History* 57, no. 4 (Dec. 2011). Accessed June 10, 2014. http://muse.jhu.edu.

Hanchett, William. *The Lincoln Murder Conspiracies*. Urbana: University of Illinois Press, 1983.

Harrington, Fred Harvey. "A Note on the Ray Explanation of the Origin of the Kansas-Nebraska Act." *Mississippi Valley Historical Review* 25, no. 1 (June 1938): 79–81. Accessed Feb.2, 2010. http://www.jstor.org.

Harrison, Joseph H., Jr. "Oligarchs and Democrats: The Richmond Junto." *Virginia Magazine of History and Biography* 78, no. 2 (Apr. 1970): 184–98. Accessed Jan. 1, 2012. http://www.jstor.org.

Hatfield, Mark O. "Vice Presidents of the United States, 1789–1993." Reprint, 1997. U.S. Senate, the Senate Historical Office. Accessed July 19, 2011. www.senate.gov.

Hayes, Benjamin. Office of the Historian. U.S. House of Representatives, email to author, Aug. 10, 2009.

Haynes, George H. "President of the United States for a Single Day." *American Historical Review* 30, no. 2 (Jan. 1925): 308–10.

———. *The Senate of the United States: Its History and Practice*. Boston: Houghton Mifflin, 1938.

Hendrick, Burton J. *Statesmen of the Lost Cause: Jefferson Davis and His Cabinet*. New York: Literary Guild of America, 1939.

Herriott, F. I. "James Grimes versus the Southrons." *Annals of Iowa* 15, no. 5 (July 1926): 323–432.

Hinds, Asher C. *Precedents of the House of Representatives of the United States: Including References to the Provisions of the Constitution, the Laws, and Decisions of the United States Senate*. Washington, D.C.: Government Printing Office, 1907-8.

Hitchcock, William S. "Southern Moderates and Secession: Senator Robert M. T. Hunter's Call for Union." *Journal of American History* 59, no. 4 (Mar. 1973). http://www.jstor.org/stable/1918366. Accessed July 1, 2002.

Hodder, Frank Heywood. "The Railroad Background of the Kansas Nebraska Act." *Mississippi Valley Historical Review* 12, no. 1 (June 1925): 3-22. Accessed Aug. 8, 2005. http://www.jstor.org.

Hodes, Martha. *Mourning Lincoln*. New Haven: Yale University Press, 2015.

Hoffer, Williamjames Hull. *The Caning of Charles Sumner: Honor, Idealism, and the Origins of the Civil War*. Baltimore: John Hopkins University Press, 2010.

Hofstader, Richard. *The Paranoid Style in American Politics and Other Essays*. New York: Vintage Books, 1967.

———. "The Tariff Issue on the Eve of the Civil War." *American Historical Review* 44, no. 1 (Oct. 1938): 50-55.

Holt, Michael F. *The Fate of Their Country: Politicians, Slavery Extension, and the Coming of the Civil War*. New York: Hill and Wang, 2004.

———. *The Political Crisis of the 1850s*. New York: John C. Wiley and Sons, 1978.

———. *The Rise and Fall of the American Whig Party: Jacksonian Politics and the Onset of the Civil War*. New York: Oxford University Press, 1999.

Husband, Michael B. "Senator Lewis F. Linn and the Oregon Question." *Missouri Historical Review* 66, no. 1 (Oct. 1971): 1-19.

Huston, James L. *Stephen A. Douglas and the Dilemmas of Democratic Equality*. Lanham: Rowman and Littlefield, 2007.

"The Intercourse Act of 1834 and Progress of the Indian Tribes." A History of the State of Oklahoma: 1908. Accessed Mar. 14, 2011. www.usgennet.org.

Jacob, Kathryn Allamong. *Capitol Elites: High Society in Washington, D.C. after the Civil War*. Washington, D.C.: Smithsonian Institutional Press, 1995.

Johannsen, Robert W. *Stephen A. Douglas*. New York: Oxford University Press, 1973.

Johnson, Allen. "The Repeal of the Missouri Compromise: Its Origins and Authorship." *American Historical Review* 14, no. 4 (July 1909): 835-36.

———. *Stephen A. Douglas: A Study in American Politics*. New York: DaCapo Press, 1970.

Johnson, Walter. *River of Dark Dreams: Slavery and Empire in the Cotton Kingdom*. Cambridge, Mass.: Belknap Press of Harvard University Press, 2013.

Jordan, H. Donaldson. "A Politician of Expansion: Robert J. Walker." *Mississippi Valley Historical Review* 19, no. 3 (Dec. 1932): 362-81. Accessed June 4, 2012. http://www.jstor.org.

Joslyn, Mauriel P. *Immortal Captives: The Story of 600 Confederate Officers and the United States Prisoner of War Policy*. Shippensburg, Pa.: White Mane Publishing, 1996.

Kerber, Linda. *Women of the Republic: Intellect and Ideology in Revolutionary America*. New York: W. W. Norton, 1980.

Klein, Philip Shriver. *President James Buchanan: A Biography*. University Park: Pennsylvania State University Press, 1962.

Klunder, William Carl. *Lewis Cass and the Politics of Moderation*. Kent, Ohio: Kent State University Press, 1996.

Lattimore, Ralston B. "Fort Pulaski: National Monument, Georgia." *National Park Service Historical Handbook Series*, no. 18. Washington, D.C., 1954. Reprint, 1961.

Learned, Henry Barrett. "The Relation of Philip Phillips to the Repeal of the Missouri Compromise in 1854." *Mississippi Valley Historical Review* 8, no. 4 (Mar. 1922): 303-17. Accessed July 5, 2006. http://www.jstor.org.

LeSueur, Stephen C. *The 1838 Mormon War in Missouri*. Columbia: University of Missouri Press, 1987.
Levin, Kevin. "Who Were the Readjusters." Civil War Memory. Accessed Jan. 17, 2014. http://cwmemory.com.
Levy, Naphtaly. Editor's Note to *A Disquisition Government*, by John C. Calhoun, iii–xi. New York: PoliSci Classics, 1947.
Lewis, Lloyd. *Myths after Lincoln*. Peter Smith, 1973.
Linder, Doug. "The Trial of the Assassination Conspirators." Famous American Trials (2002). http://www.law.umkc.edu/faculty/projects/ftrials/lincolnconspiracy/lincolnaccount.html.
Link, William A. *Roots of Secession: Slavery and Politics in Antebellum Virginia*. Chapel Hill: University of North Carolina Press, 2003.
Malin, James C. "Indian Policy and Westward Expansion." *Bulletin of the University of Kansas Humanistic Studies* 2, no. 3 (1921): 34–104. Lawrence: The University Press.
———. *The Nebraska Question, 1852–1854*. Lawrence, Kans.: James C. Malin, 1953.
"March 6, 1903, Senate Democratic Caucus Organized." Accessed Mar. 19, 2012. http://www.senate.gov/artandhistory.
Marszalek, John F. *The Petticoat Affair: Manners, Mutiny, and Sex in Andrew Jackson's White House*. New York: Free Press, 1997.
Mathews, J. M. "The Repeal of the Missouri Compromise." *American Political Science Review* 4, no. 3 (Aug. 1910): 467. http://www.jstor.org. Accessed August 8, 2005.
McCardell, John. *The Idea of a Southern Nation: Southern Nationalists and Southern Nationalism, 1830–1860*. New York: W. W. Norton, 1979.
McPherson, James M. *Battle Cry of Freedom: The Civil War Era*. Oxford: Oxford University Press, 1988.
———. *Ordeal by Fire: The Civil War and Reconstruction*. 3rd ed. New York: McGraw Hill, 2001.
Meacham, Jon. *American Lion: Andrew Jackson in the White House*. New York: Random House, 2008.
Meaney, Peter J. "The Prison Ministry of Father Peter Whelan, Georgia Priest and the Confederate Chaplain." *Georgia Historical Quarterly* 71, no. 1 (Spring 1987): 4–13.
Milton, George Fort. *The Eve of Conflict: Stephen A. Douglas and the Needless War*. 1934. Reprint, New York: Octagon Books, 1963.
Mitchell, Robert D., and Paul A. Groves, eds. *North America: The Historical Geography of a Changing Continent*. Lanham: Roman and Littlefield, 1987.
Moore, Richard Randall. "R. M. T. Hunter and the Crisis of Union, 1860–1861." *Southern Historian* 13 (Spring 1992): 25–35.
Morgan, David T. "Philip Phillips and International Improvement in Mid-Nineteenth Century Alabama." *Alabama Review* 34 (Apr. 1981): 83–93.
Morgan, Ted. *A Shovel of Stars: The Making of the American West, 1800 to Present*. New York: Simon and Schuster, 1995.
Morris, Roy, Jr. *The Long Pursuit: Abraham Lincoln's Thirty-Year Struggle with Stephen Douglas for the Heart and Soul of America*. New York: Harper Collins, 2008.
Morrison, Michael A. *Slavery and the American West: The Eclipse of Manifest Destiny and the Coming of the Civil War*. Chapel Hill: University of North Carolina Press, 1997.

Murphy, Charles Beckman. *The Political Career of Jesse D. Bright*. Indianapolis: Indiana Historical Publications 10, no. 3, 1931.

"National Statuary Hall" and "The Old Senate Chamber." Architect of the Capitol. Accessed 2009-11. http://www.aoc.gov.

Neely, Mark E., Jr. "The Kansas-Nebraska Act in American Political Culture: The Road to Bladensburg and the *Appeal of the Independent Democrats* . . ." In *The Nebraska-Kansas Act of 1854*, edited by John R. Wunder and Joanne M. Ross, 13-46. Lincoln: University of Nebraska Press, 2008.

Nelson, Scott Reynolds. *A Nation of Deadbeats: An Uncommon History of America's Financial Disasters*. New York: Alfred A. Knopf, 2012.

Nevins, Allan. *Ordeal of Union: A House Dividing, 1852-1857*, vol. 2. New York: Charles Scribner's Sons, 1947.

———. *War for the Union: The Organized War to Victory, 1864-1865*. New York: Konecky and Konecky, 1971.

Nichols, Roy F. *Franklin Pierce: Young Hickory of the Granite Hills*. Philadelphia: University of Pennsylvania Press, 1958.

———. "Kansas Historiography: The Technique of Cultural Analysis." *American Quarterly* 9, no. 1 (Spring, 1957): 85-91. Accessed July 5, 2006. http://www.jstor.org.

———. "The Kansas-Nebraska Act: A Century of Historiography." *Mississippi Historical Review* 43, no. 2 (Sept. 1956): 187-212. Accessed July 5, 2006. http://www.jstor.org.

———. *The Stakes of Power: 1845-1877*. New York: Hill and Wang, 1961.

Niven, John. *John C. Calhoun and the Price of Union*. Baton Rouge: Louisiana State University Press, 1988.

———. *Martin Van Buren: The Romantic Age of American Politics*. New York: Oxford University Press, 1983.

———. *Salmon P. Chase: A Biography*. New York: Oxford University Press, 1995.

Nye, Russel B. "The Slave Power Conspiracy: 1830-1860." In *Conspiracy: The Fear of Subversion in American History*, edited by Richard O. Curry and Thomas M. Brown, 78-99. New York: Holt, Rinehart and Winston, 1972.

Palmer, R. R. *The Age of Democratic Revolution: A Political History of Europe and America, 1760-1800*. Vol. 1, *The Challenge*. Princeton, N.J.: Princeton University Press, 1974.

Parrish, William Earle. *David Rice Atchison of Missouri: Border Politician*. Columbia: University of Missouri Press, 1961.

"Party Division in the Senate, 1789-Present." United States Senate. Accessed Sept. 9, 2013. http://www.senate.gov.

Perry, B. F. *Reminiscences of Public Men*. Philadelphia: John D. Avil, 1883.

Peterson, Merrill D. *The Great Triumvirate: Webster, Clay, and Calhoun*. New York: Oxford University Press, 1987.

"Platt Purchase." Kansas Cyclopedia-1912. Accessed Feb. 14, 2011. http://skyways.libks.us/genweb/archives.

Potter, David M. *The Impending Crisis: 1848-1861*. New York: Harper and Row, 1976.

Quigley, Paul. *Shifting Grounds: Nationalism and the American South, 1848-1865*. New York: Oxford University Press, 2012.

Rawley, James A. *Race and Politics: "Bleeding Kansas" and the Coming of the Civil War*. Lincoln: University of Nebraska Press. 1969.

Ray, P. Orman. *The Repeal of the Missouri Compromise*. 1909. Reprint, Boston: J. S. Canner and Company, 1965.
Remini, Robert V. *The House: The History of the House of Representatives*. New York: Smithsonian Books in Association with Harper Collins, 2006.
Richards, Leonard. *The Slave Power: The Free North and Southern Domination, 1780–1860*. Baton Rouge: Louisiana State University Press, 2000.
Richardson, Heather Cox. *To Make Men Free: A History of the Republican Party*. New York: Basic Books, 2014.
Robertson, Charles J. *Temple of Invention: History of a National Landmark*. Washington, D.C.: Smithsonian American Art Museum National Portrait Gallery in association with Scala, 2006.
Rogers, George C., Jr. *Generations of Lawyers: A History of the South Carolina Bar*. Columbia: South Carolina Bar Foundation.
Russel, Robert R. "The Issues in the Congressional Struggle over the Kansas-Nebraska Bill." *Journal of Southern History* 29, no. 2 (May, 1963): 187–210. Accessed July 15, 2005. http://www.jstor.org.
Saunders, Robert, Jr. *John Archibald Campbell, Southern Moderate, 1811–1889*. Tuscaloosa: University of Alabama Press, 1997.
Schiller, Herbert M. *"Sumter Is Avenged": The Siege and Reduction of Fort Pulaski*. Shippensburg, Pa.: White Mane Publishing, 1995.
Schwarzenbach, Sibyl A. "On Civic Friendship." *Ethics* 107, no. 1 (Oct. 1996): 97–128. Accessed May 21, 2008. http://www.jstor.org.
Scorza, Jason A. "Liberal Citizenship and Civic Friendship." *Political Theory* 32, no. 1 (Feb. 2004): 85–108. Accessed May 21. 2008. http://www.jstor.org.
Seale, William. *The President's House: A History*. Washington, D.C.: Washington White House Historical Association, 1986.
Shelden, Rachel A. *Washington Brotherhood: Politics, Social Life, and the Coming of the Civil War*. Chapel Hill: University of North Carolina Press, 2013.
Sheldon, Addison E. "Land Systems and Land Policies in Nebraska." *Publications of the Nebraska Historical Society* 22 (1996).
Shenk, Joshua Wolf. *Lincoln's Melancholy: How Depression Challenged a President and Fueled His Greatness*. New York: Houghton Mifflin, 2005.
Silbey, Joel H. *The Partisan Imperative: The Dynamics of American Politics before the Civil War*. New York: Oxford University Press, 1985.
Simms, Henry H. *The Life of Robert M. T. Hunter*. Richmond: William Byrd Press, 1935.
Smith, Elbert B. *Magnificent Missourian: The Life of Thomas Hart Benton*. Philadelphia: J. B. Lippincott, 1958.
Smith, Stacy L. "Remaking Slavery in a Free State: Masters and Slaves in Gold Rush California." *Pacific Historical Review* 80, no. 1 (Feb. 2011): 28–63. Accessed Sept. 6, 2016. http:www.jstor.org.
Spencer, Ivor Debenham. *The Victor and the Spoils: A Life of William L. Marcy*. Providence: Brown University Press, 1959.
Stahr, Walter. *Seward: Lincoln's Indispensable Man*. New York: Simon & Schuster, 2012.
Stevens, Walter B. "A Day and Night with 'Old Davy': David Rice Atchison." *Missouri Historical Review* 31, no. 2 (Jan. 1937): 129–39.

Stewart, David O. *Impeached: The Trial of Andrew Jackson and the Fight for Lincoln's Legacy*. New York: Simon and Schuster, 2009.

Stewart, James Brewer. *Holy Warriors: The Abolitionists and American Slavery*. Rev. ed. New York: Hilland Want, 1997.

Swanson, James L. *Manhunt: The Twelve-Day Chase for Lincoln's Killers*. New York: William Morrow, 2006.

Taylor, John M. *William Henry Seward: Lincoln's Right Hand*. New York: Harper Collins, 1991.

Thompson, William Y. *Robert Toombs of Georgia*. Baton Rouge: Louisiana State University Press, 1966.

Tidwell, William. *April '65: Confederate Covert Action in the American Civil War*. Kent, Ohio: Kent State University Press, 1995.

———. *Come Retribution: The Confederate Secret Service and the Assassination of Lincoln*. Jackson: University Press of Mississippi, 1988.

Tindall, George Brown, and David Emory Shi. *America: A Narrative History*. 5th ed., vol. 1. New York: W. W. Norton, 1999.

Townsend, John Wilson. "History of David Rice Atchison of Kentucky: The One Day President of the United States." *Register of Kentucky State Historical Society* 8, no. 23 (May 1910): 39-44.

United States Senate Art and History. Accessed 2009-12. http://www.senate.gov/artandhistory.

Van Deusen, Glyndon G. *William Henry Seward*. New York: Oxford University Press, 1967.

Van Ophem, Marieke. "The Iron Horse: The Impact of Railroads on the 19th Century American Society." From Revolution to Reconstruction. Accessed Jun 4, 2012. http://www.let.rug.nl/usa.

Verbrugge, Lois M. "The Structure of Adult Friendship Choices." *Social Forces* 56, no. 2 (Dec. 1977): 576-97. Accessed May 21. 2008. http://www.jstor.org.

Victor, Orville J. *History of American Conspiracies*. New York: Arno Press and the New York Times, 1969.

Walther, Eric H. *The Shattering of the Union: America in the 1850's*. Lanham: SR Books, 2004.

The Way West: How the West Was Won and Lost. DVD. Produced and directed by Ric Burns, 2006.

White, Laura A. "Was Charles Sumner Shamming, 1856-1859?" *New England Quarterly* 33, no. 3 (Sept. 1960): 291-324. Accessed July 20, 2013. http://www.jstor.org.

White, Richard. *Railroaded: The Transcontinentals and the Making of Modern America*. New York: W. W. Norton, 2011.

White, William S. *Citadel: The Story of the U.S. Senate*. New York: Harper and Brothers, 1957.

White House History. Accessed June 22, 2012. http://www.Whitehousehistory.org.

Wilentz, Sean. *The Rise of American Democracy: Slavery and the Crisis of American Democracy, 1840-1860*, vol. 3. New York: W. W. Norton, 2007.

Williams, Jack Kenny. *Crime and Retribution in Ante-Bellum South Carolina*. Columbia: University of South Carolina Press, 1959.

Wills, Garry. *Henry Adams and the Making of America*. Boston: Houghton Mifflin, 2005.

Wilson, Clyde. Introduction to *The Essential Calhoun: Selections from Writings, Speeches, and Letters*. Edited by Clyde Wilson. New Brunswick: Transaction, 2000.

Wiltse, Charles. *John C. Calhoun: Nullifier, 1829–1839*. Indianapolis: Bobbs-Merrill, 1949.

———. *John C. Calhoun: Sectionalist, 1840–1850*. Indianapolis: Bobbs-Merrill, 1951.

Wishart, David. *An Unspeakable Sadness: The Dispossession of the Nebraska Indians*. Lincoln: University of Nebraska Press, 1994.

Wolfe, Wendy, ed. *The Senate, 1789–1989: Historical Statistics, 1789–1992*, vol. 4. Bicentennial edition. Washington, D.C.: U.S. Government Printing Office, 1993.

Wolff, Gerald W. *The Kansas-Nebraska Bill*. New York: Revisionist Press, 1977.

———. "Party and Section: The Senate and the Kansas-Nebraska Bill." *Civil War History* 18, no. 4 (Dec. 1972): 293–311. Accessed Feb. 22, 2013. http://muse.jhu.edu.

Wood, Gordon S. *The Creation of the American Republic, 1776–1787*. New York: W. W. Norton, 1969.

Woodward, C. Vann, ed. *Mary Chesnut's Civil War*. New Haven: Yale University Press, 1981.

Wunder, John R., and Joann M. Ross, eds. *The Kansas and Nebraska Act of 1854*. Lincoln: University of Nebraska Press, 2008.

Wyatt-Brown, Bertram. *Southern Honor: Ethics and Behavior in the Old South*. Oxford: Oxford University Press, 1982.

Young, James Sterling. *The Washington Community, 1800–1828*. New York: Columbia University Press, 1966.

Young, Robert. *James Murray Mason: Defender of the Old South*. Knoxville: University of Tennessee Press, 1998.

Zasky, Jason. "The Rise and Fall of Gutta Percha." *Failure Magazine*. Accessed July 16, 2013. http://failuremag.com.

INDEX

Abolitionist movement, 4, 14, 20, 25–26, 34, 41, 46–47, 50–51, 56, 111, 114, 116, 120, 128, 130–31, 135–36, 138–42, 145, 147–48, 153, 155, 179, 206n5, 212n11, 213n28, 233n7, 235n44, 242n11

Abolition of slave trade in D.C., 60–61. *See also* Antislavery

Adams, Charles Francis, 241n1, 241n4

Adams, John Quincy, 21, 54, 207n12, 208n24

Adams, Stephen, 76, 133

Address of the Southern Delegates in Congress to their Constituents (Southern Address), 52–53. *See also* Calhoun, John C.

Address to the National Democracy, 182. *See also* Davis, Jefferson

American Civil War, 4, 6–7, 17, 189–90, 194, 197, 204n67, 209n53, 231n69

American Party, 145, 238n1

Antislavery, 5, 7–8, 14, 61, 89, 92, 94, 112, 133–35, 160, 231n68; American Antislavery Society, 206n5; antislavery amendment, 242n11; antislavery petitions, 46, 212n10; California antislavery constitution, 231n70, 232n91

Appeal of the Independent Democrats, 111–16

Armstrong, Robert, 80, 84

Asia, trade interests in, 61, 69–71, 83, 222n15

Atchison, David Rice, 8–9, 11, 15–17, 49–50, 59–60, 83, 99, 111, 113–14, 116–17, 123–24, 133, 172–73, 176, 219n63, 220n78, 220nn87–88; actions in Kansas, 146–50, 154–57, 165–66, 233n11, 233n15, 234n23, 234n28; appointed to U. S. Senate, 41–43, 46; family and early life, 43–45, 62, 64; feud with Thomas Hart Benton, 11, 53–54, 73, 77–78, 119, 147; ideology of, 46, 63, 65, 76, 211n9; life after the Civil War, 194, 196, 242n11; marital status, 62, 211n8; on organizing Nebraska, 75–79, 89, 219n76; photograph of, 105; physical appearance, 8, 46; president of the United States for a day, 194, 242n23; reelections to the U.S. Senate, 51, 119, 142, 145, 147, 234n20; relationship with John C. Calhoun, 52–53, 63, 214n35; relationship with Stephen A. Douglas, 87, 90, 174; on repeal of the Missouri Compromise, 11–12, 85–87, 90–94, 102, 118, 202n14; rhetorical style of, 153, 235n54; role during the Civil War, 189–90; role in the Mormon Wars, 45, 154, 211n7; second in line to the presidency, 74–75, 81, 202n38; slave ownership, 42, 62, 216n13; support of Clayton Amendment, 133–35; support of Texas annexation, 42–43, 63; visit to the White House, 96–98

Badger, George E., 76, 113, 118, 122–23, 131–32, 229n27, 230n42

Bell, John, 38, 83, 87, 92, 98, 137, 142, 183, 223n37, 224n51, 232n92

Benjamin, Judah, 113, 200nn11–12

Benton, Thomas Hart, 11, 37, 41–43, 46, 48, 51–52, 63–64, 210n60, 217n23, 220n87, 232n1, 234n19; campaign against Atchison, 77–78, 86, 119, 134, 145–47, 220n80, 220n83; railroad expansion,

261

72-73, 211n79, 219n64; Senate defeat and election to house, 53-54, 73
Bigler, William, 183, 186
Boggs, Lilburn, 45, 211n7
Booth, John Wilkes, 2, 193, 199n8
Breckinridge, John C., 82, 93-94, 96-97, 183, 194, 222n11, 227n88, 232n1
Bright, Jesse D., 50-51, 65, 82, 86, 88, 93, 146, 224n39, 224n51
Brodhead, Richard, 86, 130-31, 133
Brooks, Preston, 9, 159-60, 162-64, 167, 213n18, 236n66, 236n71, 236n74
Brown, Albert G., 130, 192
Brown, John, 160, 165, 181-82
Buchanan, James, 161, 167, 170, 173-74, 176-77, 184-85, 222n15
Butler, Andrew Pickens, 8, 15-17, 59-60, 65, 74, 76, 81, 85, 94, 111, 118, 120-21, 123-24, 132, 135-36, 143, 146, 150-51, 164, 176, 189, 217n23, 220n78, 220n90, 228n147, 236n57; attacked in Charles Sumner's speech, 157-59, 236n61; death of, 172; defense of Preston Brooks, 160, 162-63, 236n73, 237n75; elected to the Senate, 10, 49; family and early life, 9-10, 48-49, 212n17, 213n18, 213n20, 213n22, 221n2, 236n66; health of, 155-57, 159; Nebraska bill speech, 129-30; photograph of, 108; physical appearance of, 129; relationship with Atchison, 148-49, 233n15; relationship with John C. Calhoun, 26, 43, 52-53, 55-58; slave ownership, 62, 216n12, 238n10
Butler, Pierce Mason, 46, 213n18

Calhoun, John C., 10-11, 19, 30, 37, 70, 111, 113, 161, 167, 171, 183, 185, 205n1, 206n8, 207n13, 208n21, 209n53, 210n73, 212n11, 213n21; constitutionalism of, 26, 89, 143, 164, 169, 186, 195; death of, 58-60, 215n65; Disquisition on Government and the Discourse on the Constitution and the Government of the United States, 51; feud with Andrew Jackson, 23, 26, 207n17; feud with Thomas Hart Benton, 53-54; final days, 51, 54, 55-57; independent Treasury bill, 27, 34, 36; opposition to Oregon and war with Mexico, 50, 63; physical appearance, 19-20; presidential races, 21, 40-41; relationship with the F Street Mess, 13, 15-17, 19, 27-29, 33, 35, 39-44, 48-49, 53, 216n10; secretary of state, 41, 46, 63; secretary of war, 20, 23; senate elections, 26, 47; South Carolina Exposition and Protest and Fort Hill Address, 24-25; Southern Address, 52-53; vice president, 21-22, 24
California, 66, 69, 75, 137, 183; Gold Rush, 68, 71; slaves and proslavery in, 231nn69-70, 232n91; statehood, 60; territorial status and annexation, 50, 52, 54, 58
Campbell, John A, 1-3, 191-93
Cass, Lewis, 24, 51, 91-92, 98, 121, 124, 131, 147, 151-52, 157-58, 213n28, 223n25
Chase, Salmon P., 91, 93, 101, 129, 138, 231n68, 237n100; author and defense of Appeal of the Independent Democrats, 111, 114, 116; opposition and amendments to the Nebraska bill, 117, 120, 123-24, 131-33
Chesnut, Mary Boykin, 8, 190-91
Clay, Clement C., 162, 200n12
Clay, Henry, 21, 24, 26, 54, 91, 117, 206n11, 208n19, 212n13, 215n69, 232n83; on John C. Calhoun's death, 58-59; resolutions on Mexican Cession, 55-56, 60; on Texas annexation, 46-47
Clayton, John M.: amendment to Nebraska bill, 131, 133-35, 229n27; author of Clayton Compromise, 50-52, 214n33
Clinton, DeWitt, 22, 206n8
Cobb, Howell, 53, 213n21
Corcoran, William Walker, 194, 221n95; investment in Lake Superior Properties, 79, 82, 124

Compromise of 1850, 12, 61–62, 65, 84, 88–89, 93, 115–18, 131, 168, 223n28
Confederate Government, 1, 3, 186–87, 190–91, 193–94, 199n3; confederate secret service, 200n11
Congressional nonintervention, 60, 78, 101, 117, 121, 123–24, 137–39, 168. *See also* Popular sovereignty
Constitution of the United States: admission of new states, 177, 239n39; compact theory, 84, 195; Crittenden amendment to 183, 185; Fourteenth Amendment, 196–97; general welfare clause, 25, 125; John C. Calhoun's proposed amending of, 56–57; jurisdiction over territories and states, 89, 95, 121, 124, 127–28, 131; privileges and immunities clause, 126, 140–41, 232n83; Robert M. T. Hunter's proposed changes, 195; southern advantages in 6, 201n23; Thirteenth Amendment, 197; Twenty-Fifth Amendment, 202n38
Continental Divide, 67, 218n39
Crawford, William H., 21–23, 28, 206n9
Crittenden, John, 179. *See also* Crittenden Compromise
Crittenden Compromise, 183–86
Cushing, Caleb, 95, 98, 227n12

Davis, Jefferson, 44, 64, 145, 149, 154, 195, 211n3, 242n9; author of the Address to the National Democracy, 182; capture and imprisonment, 200n12; implicated in Lincoln's assassination, 3, 200n11; member of Crittenden Committee, 184–86; president of the Confederate States, 1–2, 190–93; relationship with Franklin Pierce, 96–98, 227nn87–88; secretary of war, 70, 95, 234n28; U.S. senator, 65, 176, 217n23, 239n31
Dawson, William Crosby, 113, 210n66, 226n66
Declaration of Independence, 9, 31, 97, 120, 129

Democrats, 4, 17, 20, 36, 40, 47, 51, 95, 101, 119, 132, 145, 166, 169, 175, 184, 197, 243n33, 239n37; northern, 46, 92, 141–42, 167, 170, 179–80, 183, 237n100, 239n29; southern, 5–6, 86, 112, 142, 165, 181–83, 232n91; Barnburners, 13–14, 78, 221n91; Hardshell hunkers, 14, 78–79, 221n91; Softshell, 14, 221n91
DeSaussure, William Ford, 146–47
Dixon, Archibald, 91, 113, 117, 120, 131, 226n75; amendment to Nebraska bill, 92–95, 101, 225n53
Dodge, Augustus C., 80, 83, 99, 122, 130, 132–33, 142, 222n12, 230n39; Nebraska bill, 86–88, 101
Dodge, Henry, 134, 222n12, 230n39
Doniphan, Alexander, 45, 147
Douglas, Stephen A., 4–5, 12, 63, 65, 111, 114, 173, 230n45, 234n28, 236n69; author of record Kansas-Nebraska Act, 10–11, 17, 202n41; chairman of Committee on Territories, 13, 52, 60, 62, 70, 80, 85–86, 98, 217n23, 230n44; amendment to substitute bill, 120–23, 224n49; Crittenden Committee, 186; defense of Nebraska bill and substitute, 114–18, 125, 136–40, 228n16, 229n17; expansionism and railroad advocacy, 71–73, 78–79, 220n88; floor leadership on Nebraska bill, 119, 124, 129, 131–32, 134–35; Kansas bill (territorial organization), 150–52, 162, 165; Lake Superior Properties, 79, 82, 124, 196; meeting with Pierce at White House, 96–98, 227n88; Nebraska bill, 74–76, 79; opposes Lecompton Constitution, 174–76, 179–80; photograph of, 109; presidential race, 161, 182–83; response to Charles Sumner, 158–59; role in House vote on Kansas Nebraska, 144–45, 233n4; southern domination of, 14, 112–13, 157; substitute bill, 87–90, 99–101; support of repeal language, 91, 93–94
Dred Scott Decision (1857), 5, 125, 127, 143, 176, 230n31

Eaton, Peggy, affair, 23, 207n17
Everett, Edward, 86, 98, 121–22, 222n20, 223n36, 230n39

Faulkner, Charles James, 166, 171
Federalist Party, 6, 19, 28, 201n21, 201n23, 205n3
Fessenden, William Pitt, 135–36, 231n68
Fillmore, Millard, 54, 61, 84, 215n69
Foot, Solomon, 117, 120, 122, 136
Foote, Henry S., 52, 57, 214n33
Fort Moultrie, 184, 240n50
Fort Pulaski, 3, 196
Fort Sumter, 184, 187, 193, 241n65
Fourteenth Amendment, 196, 197. *See also* Constitution of the United States
Free-Soil, 11, 51, 78, 112, 147, 221n91; in Congress, 13, 41, 43, 63, 79–80, 84–86, 94, 98, 115–16, 132, 140–42, 145, 150, 158, 165, 210n60, 236n60; in Kansas, 148–49, 151–57, 165, 173–74, 176–78, 233n7, 235n30, 235n36, 237n84, 238nn15–17
Friendship, 1, 16–17, 20, 23, 148, 203–4n56, 204n61; F Street Mess's friendship, 15, 17, 59, 76, 220n78; within Congress, 72, 96, 159, 234n24
F Street Mess, 5, 10, 13–14, 16–18, 43, 49, 77, 80–81, 83, 85, 159, 167, 170, 197, 203n55, 204n57, 216n11; control of Nebraska-Kansas bill in Congress, 85, 88, 90–91, 93–96, 98, 111–13, 117, 119, 133, 142, 144–45, 195; decline of power, 143, 172, 176, 181, 189; support of Lecompton Constitution and slave expansion in Kansas, 143, 149–50, 157
Fugitive Slave Act (1850), 55, 60–61, 131, 164

Gadsden (James) Purchase, 79–80, 82, 98, 221n96, 222n15, 226n80
Gag Rule, 46, 205–6n5, 212n10
Geary, John W., 153, 165, 173, 237n84, 238n13
Geyer, Henry S., 54, 76, 214n47, 223n25, 224–25n51
Grant, Ulysses S., 1–3

Great American Desert (Great Plains), 66–69, 73, 218n40
Great Britain: foreign relations with, 83, 88, 98, 161, 181–82, 222n15, 226n80; Mason and Slidell incident, 190, 241n1, 241n4; Oregon Treaty, 47–48, 63; War of 1812, 19, 54, 58, 201n23
Grimes, James. W. 180, 184
Gunston Hall, 9, 32, 209n48
Gwin, William, 91, 121, 136, 224n51, 231n69

Hamilton, James, 25–26, 55, 215n56
Hammond, James Henry, 48, 212n15
Hampton Roads Conference, 1–2, 185, 191–92
Harpers Ferry, 181–82. *See also* Brown, John
Harrison, William Henry, 20, 40, 46, 54, 205n4
Hartford Convention, 201n23, 205n3
Harvie, Lewis E., 30, 171, 182
Holmes, Isaac, E., 47, 149, 210n66
Houston, Sam, 56, 87, 122, 135; opposition to Nebraska-Kansas bill, 123, 137, 140–42, 223n37
Hunter, Robert Mercer Taliaferro: arrest of, 1, 3, 193; author of Tariff of 1857, 171–72, 213n24, 238n9; death of, 197; elected Speaker of the House, 38–39, 53; expelled from the U. S. Senate, 187, 241n64; family and early life, 9, 29–32, 208–9n37, 209nn38–39, 209nn41–42, 209nn44–45; Hampton Roads Conference, 1–2, 191–92; John C. Calhoun's influence on, 19, 27–28, 36, 40–41, 43, 47, 51, 55, 59, 195, 210–11n73; land speculation of and partner in Lake Superior properties, 79–80, 82, 93, 124, 143, 220n90; member of the Confederate Government, 1, 187, 190, 193; Mess affiliations and relations, 8, 15, 17, 62, 76, 78, 81, 111, 189, 155–56, 162; photograph of, 106; physical appearance, 1, 8, 125; postwar losses, 195–96; Poughkeepsie speech, 166–69; presidential ambitions, 71, 142, 160–61,

181–83, 211n74; Secession crisis and Crittenden Committee, 184–86, 240n61, 241n65; slave ownership, 62, 216n12; supports Lecompton constitution and slavery's expansion, 146, 148, 150–51, 163–64, 166–69, 239n32, 240n47; supports Nebraska-Kansas bill and repeal language, 91, 94, 97, 99, 102, 125–29, 134, 215n3, 225n53; in the U.S. Senate, 49–50, 52, 60, 65, 74, 76, 79–80, 84–85, 100, 152, 215n3, 217n23, 222n20m, 238n3

Hyde A., 124, 230n45

Independent Treasury bill, 20, 27, 34–38
Indian Country (Nebraska territory), 65, 68–69, 115, 149, 152, 193, 215n7, 217n25; Bureau of Indian Affairs, 78, 99; Committee on Indian Affairs, 46, 77, 86, 121–22, 137; land titles and concepts of, 12, 46, 61, 65–67, 70, 72, 77, 99, 112, 217n27, 220n87, 227n101; Sam Houston's defense of, 123, 137, 141
Indian Intercourse Act (1834), 65, 68, 74
Indian Removal Act (1830), 68

Jackson, Andrew, 25, 28, 31, 54, 95, 206n8, 206n11; Bank war and Specie Circular, 27, 34, 47, 205n5, 209n43; feud with John C. Calhoun, 23, 207n15, 207n17; Indian policy, 68–69; Nullification Crisis, 24, 26–27, 33; presidential campaign and election in 1828, 19–22, 207n14
Jefferson, Thomas, 9, 28, 31, 66, 97, 158, 163, 201n21, 207n12, 210n64
Jeffersonian ideology, 19, 24, 26–27
Johnson, Andrew, 3, 194, 196, 199–200n10

King, William Rufus, 58, 74, 81, 202n38, 219n73

Lake Superior (syndicate), 11, 79–80, 82, 99, 124, 142
Lee, Robert E., 2, 181, 185, 191, 193, 242n15
Lewis (Meriwether) and Clarke (William), 65–66

Liberty Party, 14, 47, 212n13
Lincoln, Abraham, 3, 56, 64, 190, 199n6, 230n39, 231n68; assassination of, 2, 193–94, 199n8, 199–200n10, 200n12; belief in a slave power conspiracy, 4–7, 170, 181, 201n27; election (1860), 17, 183, 195; Hampton Roads Conference, 1–2, 191–92, 199n3, 242n9; opposes secession and calls for suppression of rebellion, 187, 223n37, 241n1; opposition to Crittenden Compromise, 185–86, 242n11
Linn, Lewis F., 8, 43, 45, 221n6, 230n39
Little Dixie (Missouri), 63–64, 216n17
Louisiana Purchase, 65, 92, 115, 118, 139, 141, 228n16; restriction of slavery north of 36° 30′, 8, 50

Madison, James, 24, 26, 28, 207n12, 239n39
Mallory, Francis, 33, 161, 209n53
Manypenny, George W., 78, 79, 220n87
Marcy, William, 92, 95–96, 98
Marshall, John, 126, 211n9
Mason, George, 9, 31, 209n7
Mason, James Murray, 8, 40, 111, 157, 162, 182, 195–96, 220n90, 236n64; author of Fugitive Slave Act, 60; chairs Select Committee on Harpers Ferry, 181; expelled from Senate, 187; family and early life, 9, 15, 31–33, 209n47, 209nn49–50, 209n53; member of Virginia Chivalry, 84, 171; mess affiliations and relationships, 14, 16–17, 59, 62, 76, 78, 94, 172, 189, 220n78; photograph of, 107; postwar and death of, 194; relationship with John C. Calhoun, 19, 34–35, 41, 43, 49, 56–57, 215n65; secession crisis, 183, 185, 187, 240n61, 241n64; slave ownership, 62, 216n12; Special Commissioner of the Confederate States to the United Kingdom and Ireland, 190, 241nn1–4; supports slavery expansion and Lecompton Constitution in Kansas, 143, 148, 150–52, 158–59, 176, 239n30;

U.S. House of Representatives, 27–28, 33, 35–36; U.S. Senate, 15, 49–50, 52, 54, 60, 65, 74, 81, 83, 85, 101, 118, 122, 130, 133, 138, 143, 217n23; White House meeting with Pierce, 97, 102
Mason and Slidell, 190, 241nn1–2, 241n4
McDuffie, George, 48, 213n21
Mexican-American War, 14, 48, 97, 213n18, 236n70
Mexican Cession, 50, 52, 55, 58, 68, 88–89, 115, 118; Treaty of Guadalupe Hidalgo, 50, 63
Missouri Compromise, 53, 75, 78, 89, 131, 170, 229n17; repeal of, 5, 8, 11, 14, 86, 90–96, 98, 102, 111, 115, 117, 119, 121, 123, 125, 129, 137, 139, 141–42, 145, 161, 168–69, 174, 189, 195, 219n76, 223n28, 226n66, 229n32
Monroe, James, 28, 54, 206n9, 207n12
Monroe Doctrine, 224n41
Mormons, 44–45, 153–54, 211n5

Native Americans. *See* Indian Country
Northwest Ordinance (1787), 127, 150, 168
Nullification, 10, 23–28, 31, 33, 49, 56, 91, 201n23, 225n54
Nullifiers, 20, 25–27, 205n4, 215n56

Oregon Territory, 47–48, 50–51, 56, 63, 68–69, 72, 75, 137, 183
Oregon Trail, 66

Pacific west coast, 65–67, 69–73, 77, 82, 115, 137, 146, 185; railroad to, 85, 90, 99, 112, 120, 224n51, 227n101
Panic of 1837, 27–28, 33–35, 41, 205–6n5
Patent office (U.S.), 8, 86, 94–95, 97, 204n63, 205n3, 226n79
Pettit, John, 122
Phelps, Samuel, 93, 101, 228n107
Phillips, Philip, 91–92, 94–98, 225nn53–54, 227n88; photo, 110
Pickens, Francis, 33, 39, 48, 210nn66–67
Pierce, Franklin, 13–14, 17, 72, 75, 184, 202n38, 217n23, 224n41, 226n80, 227n81, 239n31; actions on Kansas, 149, 165–66, 234n28, 237n84; Annual Message (1853), 83–84, 222n15; consents to repeal language, 97–98; health of, 81, 221n7, 227n87; loses renomination, 160–61; Nebraska-Kansas bill, 92, 95–96, 144–45, 233n2, 233n4; signs Nebraska-Kansas bill, 143
Pike, Zebulon, 66–67
Platte, the, 44, 65, 67, 70, 73–74
Platte Purchase, 44–45, 63, 216n17
Platte River, 66, 217n24
Polk, James K., 46–47, 49, 52, 63, 211n74, 214n37, 242n23
Popular Sovereignty, 44, 60, 71, 78, 89, 91, 94, 111, 115, 118, 138, 168–69, 173–75. *See also* Congressional nonintervention
Pottawatomie Creek. *See* Brown, John
Proslavery, 11–12, 46, 99, 143, 233n11; in Missouri, 43, 51, 54, 63, 75, 145–47; in Kansas, 147–49, 152–54, 156–57, 160, 165–66, 173–74, 176, 180, 189, 234n22, 235n31, 235n36, 238nn15–16, 238n18; in U.S. Senate, 86, 88, 93, 101, 136, 189, 223n25, 224n51, 231n69, 232n91, 240n47

Railroads: construction and legislation, 46, 61, 73, 77, 82–83, 86, 196–97, 205–6n5, 218n51, 221n96, 222n8, 233n2, 234n18; Transcontinental (Pacific) Railroad, 11, 69–72, 74, 79, 84–85, 90, 99, 112, 120, 142, 219n65, 221n93, 224–25n51, 227n101
Readjusters, 197, 243n33
Redfield, Herman J., 98, 113
Reeder, Andrew, 148–49, 156, 234n22, 234n28, 235n31
Republican Party (eighteenth century), 19, 24, 28, 47, 58, 205n3, 206n8, 208n19
Republicanism, 6, 26–27, 32, 169, 237n96
Republican Party (Lincoln): election of 1856, 166–67; election of 1860, 168–69, 180–81, 183; expel southern senators, 187; on Kansas, 160, 176, 202n41, 239n37; majority in U.S.

House of Representatives, 149, 164–65; oppose Crittenden Compromise, 185–86; rhetorical use of slave power conspiracy, 4, 6–8, 10, 189

Richardson, William A., 74, 144, 223n27, 233n4

Richmond Junto, 28, 39–40, 84

Ritchie, Thomas, 28, 40–41, 84, 211n74

Robinson, Charles, 149, 152, 154, 156, 235n52

Rusk, Thomas J., 76, 121, 214n33, 224–25n51

Russell, Lord John, 241n1, 241n4

Sebastian, William K., 86, 121–22, 137, 187

Secession, 1, 17, 24–25, 56, 61, 87, 183–87, 192, 195, 223n37, 240n47, 240n50, 240n61, 241n1; secessionists, 48, 185, 189–90

Seminole Indian War, 23, 213n18

Seward, William, 2, 9, 116, 123, 158, 168, 179, 196, 224–25n51, 228n107, 241n1; Hampton Roads conference, 191–92, 242n11; higher principle theory, 168–69; opposes the Slave Power, 8, 10, 170, 181; opposes Nebraska-Kansas bill, 10, 92, 129, 139–40; Secession crisis, 184, 186–87, 241n65; supports Topeka Constitution, 150–52, 165, 176, 180

Shannon, Wilson, 149–50, 153–54, 234n29, 237n84

Slave Power/Slavocracy, 4–8, 10–12, 14, 17–18, 63–64, 87, 111, 135, 142–43, 147, 149, 157, 159, 166–67, 169–70, 176, 180–84, 186–87, 189, 194–95, 197, 200n18, 201n23, 201n27, 211n74, 222n15, 242n32

Slavery, 5–7, 12, 18, 33, 36, 41, 43, 56–57, 125, 127, 130, 181, 185, 195, 205–6n5, 214n35, 228n16, 232n83; abolition of, 192, 242n11; in Compromise of 1850, 56–57, 60–61, 223n28; in Kansas debate and legislation, 142, 146–50, 152, 173–76, 178–79, 239n26, 239n37; Missouri Compromise restriction of, 8, 10–11, 52–53, 70, 75, 78, 83, 87, 91, 169–70, 189, 201n23, 229n17; in Nebraska debate and legislation, 14–15, 74, 86, 88–95, 101, 112, 114, 121, 123–24, 131–32, 134, 136, 139–40; western expansion of, 47–51, 54–55, 58, 64, 71, 115, 128, 143, 163–63, 168, 182, 216n17

Smith, Joseph, 44–45

South Carolina Exposition and Protest. *See* Nullification

Southern Address, 52–53

South Pass, 7, 70, 82, 219n64

Stanton, Edwin M., 2–3, 194

States' rights: advocates of, 1, 20–21, 26–28, 31, 34–35, 38–39, 46–47, 70, 78, 80, 85, 167, 202n9; ideology of, 32, 36, 84, 164, 211n74

Stephens, Alexander: Southern address committee, 214n33; Nebraska-Kansas bill, 13, 144, 233nn3–4; LeCompton bill, 179–80; Hampton Roads Conference, 1–3, 191–93

Strader v. Graham, 126, 230n49, 230n51

Sumner, Charles, 129, 150, 155, 226nn73–74, 235n56, 236n64; amendments to Nebraska bill, 94–95, 98; author of The Crime against Kansas, 152, 156–59, 172, 235n55, 236nn60–61; caning of (Brooks Sumner Affair), 9, 143, 160, 162, 164, 213n18, 236n69, 236n74; coauthor of Appeal of the Independent Democrats, 111, 114, 116

Sumter, Thomas D., 183, 210n66

Supreme Court (U.S.), 1, 5, 50, 88, 90, 95–96, 122, 126–27, 156, 170, 191, 195, 217n27, 225n54

Taney, Roger B., 5, 125–27, 170, 230n51

Tariffs, 56, 83, 233n2; of 1816, 25, 171; of 1828, 24–26, 208n21; of 1832, 25–26, 208n21; of 1846, 47, 49, 172, 213n24; of 1857, 29, 171–72, 195, 213n24, 238nn8–9; of 1913, 195, 213n24; in nullification crisis and compromise, 26–27, 33, 201n23

Taylor, Zachary, 14, 51–53, 214n37, 224n41, 242n23

Texas: annexation of, 5, 41–43, 46–47, 50, 63, 67, 112, 141, 177, 205–6n5, 212n11; Compromise of 1850, 55, 60, 115, 118; railroad expansion in, 69–70; secession of, 240n59; slavery in, 146, 229n17

Thirteenth Amendment, 197. *See also* Antislavery: antislavery amendment; Constitution of the United States

Toombs, Robert A., 31, 113, 164–65, 176, 182, 184–87, 209n41, 239n31

Transcontinental Railroad. *See* Railroads

Tucker, Beverly, 3, 80, 84–85, 89–90, 200n12

Tucker, Henry St. George, 9, 15, 31, 84

Tyler, John, 41, 46–47, 54, 75

Upshur, Abel, 41

Van Buren, Martin, 4, 20, 24, 26, 39–40, 205n4, 206n8, 207n16; denied democratic nomination in 1844, 5, 46, 201n24, 211n74; early alliance with John C. Calhoun, 20–23; Free-soil nominee (1848), 51, 210n60, 213n28, 221n91; Independent treasury plan, 27, 34–35, 37–38

Virginia and Kentucky Resolutions, 24. *See also* Nullification

Virginia Chivalry, the, 84, 171, 238n3

Waddell, Moses, 10, 48, 213n21

Wade, Benjamin, 93, 120, 129, 184

Walker, Isaac P., 132–33

Walker, Robert J., 47, 49, 82, 213n24

Walker, Robert T., 173–74, 176–77, 238n18, 239n24

Washington City, 2, 20, 206n7, 230n45; housing shortage and Mess arrangements in, 15–16, 64, 78, 112, 204n57, 214n43, 215n9, 216n11; slave trade in, 52, 60–61

Webster, Daniel, 41, 205n4, 215n69; author of The Constitution and Union (Plea for Union), 57, 238n21; relationship with John C. Calhoun, 54–56, 59

Webster, Sidney, 83, 97

Weller, John B., 76, 122, 132, 136, 231nn69–70

Welles, Gideon, 147, 225n54

Whig Party, 13–14, 27–28, 31, 37–40, 49–55, 57, 61, 77, 84–85, 91–93, 101, 145, 147, 164, 205n5, 209n53, 210n62, 212n13, 213n28, 214n47, 219n68, 221n6, 223n25, 223n36, 224–25n51, 228n107, 239n31; formation of, 19–20, 23–24, 205n4, 208n19; opposition to Independent Treasury, 34–36; opposition to Texas annexation, 46–47; Nebraska-Kansas bill and impact on party, 112–13, 118, 120, 123, 130, 132–33, 135, 138, 141–42, 144, 180, 229n27, 229n32, 233nn3–4

White House, 32, 83, 95, 97–99, 101, 111, 113–14, 173–74, 207n17, 214n43

Whitney, Asa, 70–72, 218n55

Wilmot, David, 50

Wise, Henry, 161, 171, 177, 181–82, 184, 238n3, 240n47

Wyandot tribe, 68, 73, 76